Creating Smart Enterprises
Leveraging Cloud, Big Data, Web, Social Media, Mobile and IoT Technologies

Creating Smart Enterprises
Leveraging Cloud, Big Data, Web, Social Media, Mobile and IoT Technologies

By
Vivek Kale

CRC Press
Taylor & Francis Group
Boca Raton London New York

CRC Press is an imprint of the
Taylor & Francis Group, an **informa** business
AN AUERBACH BOOK

CRC Press
Taylor & Francis Group
6000 Broken Sound Parkway NW, Suite 300
Boca Raton, FL 33487-2742

First issued in paperback 2022

© 2018 Vivek Kale
CRC Press is an imprint of Taylor & Francis Group, an Informa business

No claim to original U.S. Government works

ISBN 13: 978-1-03-247653-7 (pbk)
ISBN 13: 978-1-4987-5128-5 (hbk)

DOI: 10.1201/9781315152455

Library of Congress Cataloging-in-Publication Data

Names: Kale, Vivek, author.
Title: Creating smart enterprises : leveraging cloud, big data, web, social media, mobile and IoT technologies / Vivek Kale.
Description: Boca Raton, FL : CRC Press, 2017.
Identifiers: LCCN 2017019839 | ISBN 9781498751285 (hb : alk. paper)
Subjects: LCSH: Technological innovations--Management. | Information technology--Management.
Classification: LCC HD45 .K285 2017 | DDC 658.4/0630285--dc23
LC record available at https://lccn.loc.gov/2017019839

Visit the Taylor & Francis Web site at
http://www.taylorandfrancis.com

and the CRC Press Web site at
http://www.crcpress.com

To

My wife, Girija

who made me a better man,

And whose smile brings light into my days.

Your love and support encouraged

me to chase my dreams,

And any small success I have reached

is as much yours as it is mine.

Contents

List of Figures

List of Tables

Preface

While *smartness* is difficult to define, smartness is perceived as a property of the whole: one that may emerge, like any other emergent property, from coordinated, cooperative, and collaborative behavior of the parts.

A business may be termed *smart*:

by virtue of its behavior in context, and that......
said behavior may be an emergent property of the whole, or ......
it may be vested in the ability of parts within the organization to make *good decisions*, and for ......
other parts to act cooperatively and collaboratively upon those decisions,
so making the whole decisive,
such that smartness may again be perceived as an emergent property of the whole.

Thus, a business may be deemed smart in context by virtue of its organization and configuration, if it adapts to changes and perturbations in its environment such that it can both survive and flourish; this without any apparent discrete focus of *smartness* within the enterprise.

The *smart business* (SB) seeks survival advantage through anticipating changes in situation, environment, and so on, and through perception of opportunities and avoidance of risks. As such, it attempts to "look ahead" to determine the best course of action to take. Making such smart choices depends on the ability to perceive the future, which is not practicable beyond a certain time horizon—the distance ahead being a function of situational and environmental turbulence; the smart business will gather intel to help it identify threats and opportunities and to anticipate trends. SBs can be realized through digital transformation of businesses operations including resources, processes and management.

In this turbulent environment, the goal of the business in the first instance is to survive—not to make a profit. It will prove necessary to make a profit in order to survive, but profitability is a means to survival, not the goal. As with any organism in a hostile, competitive environment, the business needs sustenance. It extracts sustenance from *flowthrough*, that proportion of the flow of energy, materials and information (*emi*) through the network that can be guided to flow through the business. Flowthrough can be processed to create products and services for sale to downstream businesses and markets; flowthrough depends on downstream wants, needs, and ability to pay. Similarly, flowthrough depends upon sufficient and appropriate inflow; a business's sources are as important as its markets.

Changes in flowthrough rate may be "followed" by changes in any or all of *emi*. Ideally, a steady flowthrough enables *emi* stability, which potentially enhances economy, efficiency, and effectiveness. Where flowthrough either dips or rises, there may be a concomitant need for an SB to adjust *emi* inflow/outflow rates to achieve a new point of dynamic balance. Some SBs achieve this adjustment by outsourcing, subcontracting, and so on.

This is the rationale for SBs employing SMACT, that is, social media, mobile computing, analytics, cloud computing and Internet of Things (IoT) technologies for digital transformation.

What Makes This Book Different?

This book proposes that to sustain in an VUCA (volatility, uncertainty, complexity and ambiguity) ecosystem, an enterprise must upgrade as per the IMM (intellignce maturity model) consisting of the following stages: data, communication, information, concept, knowledge, intelligence, wisdom. An enterprise can achieve this progressively by deploying the SMACT (social media, mobile, analytics & big data, cloud computing, and Internet of Things) technologies. This book interprets the 2010s computing phenomena, namely, social networks, mobile computing, analytics and big data, cloud computing, and Internet of things (IoT) from the point of view of business as well as technology. This book unravels the mystery of SMACT environments and applications and their power and potential to transform the operating contexts of business enterprises. It addresses the key differentiator of SMACT environments, namely, that SMACT computing systems combine the power of elastic infrastructure and information management with the ability to analyze and discern recurring patterns in the colossal pools of interactional or conversational, operational and transactions data, to leverage and transform them into success patterns for the enterprise's business.

Here are the characteristic features of this book:

1. It enables information technology (IT) managers and business decision makers to get a clear understanding of what the various components of SMACT computing really mean and what they might do for them.
2. It gives an introduction to the VUCA (volatility, uncertainty, complexity and ambiguity) business ecosystem confronted by businesses today.
3. It describes the challenges of defining the business and IT strategies and the challenges of aligning them, as well as their impact on enterprise governance.
4. It provides a very wide treatment of the various components of SMACT computing, namely, social media, mobile computing, analytics and big data, cloud computing, and (IoT) environments and applications.

5. It introduces the readers to Internet of Things (IoT), with its characteristics and constituting technologies like RFID, wireless networks, sensors, and wireless sensor networks.

In the final analysis, SMACT computing is a realization of the vision of *intelligent infrastructure* that reforms and re-configures automatically to store and/or process incoming data based on the pre-determined context of the requirements. The intelligent infrastructure itself will automatically capture, store, manage, and analyze incoming data, take decisions, and undertake prescribed actions for standard scenarios, while non-standard scenarios would be routed to the DevOperators. An extension of this vision also underlies the future potential of IoT discussed in the last chapter. I wanted to write a book presenting SMACT computing from this novel perspective; the outcome is the book that you are reading now. Thank you!

How Is This Book Organized?

Chapter 1 sets the context for the whole book by introducing the VUCA ecosystem, the intelligence maturity model (IMM) and SMACT. Chapter 2 focuses on the alignment of IT strategy with business because that exercise would help in establishing the specific SMACT technologies that would be significant for the nonfunctional requirements of an operating enterprise. Security and process-orientation are an essential pre-requisites for an successful operating enterprise. Chapter 3 describes the security related aspects of an operating enterprise, namely, identification, authentication, authorization & access control, accountability and audit. Digital transformation invariably entails collective changes in businesses operations, namely, resources, business processes and management systems. Chapter 4 discusses establishing a collaborative enterprise with Business Process Management (BPM) and enterprise BPM methodology. After setting the context in Chapters 1 through 4, SMACT computing is described in Chapters 5 through 11.

Chapter 5 discusses the characteristics of decision-support systems and analytics.

Chapter 6 discusses the nature and characteristics of cloud computing technologies.

Chapter 7 introduces the big data computing technologies.

Chapter 8 discusses now familiar Web-based application environments and technologies.

Chapter 9 focuses on popular social media i.e. sensor networks technologies employed by applications like Facebook and Twitter.

Chapter 10 deals with the burgeoning mobile technologies used by applications like WhatsApp.

Chapter 11 introduces the world of IoT technologies.

In Appendix A of the book, with the reader's indulgence, the author speculates on the reasons why Internet is begetting the revolutionary changes that we are witnessing today by exploring the idea of Internet as Extended Brain. The appendix proposes that the significance of SMACT technologies can be understood in analogy with the significance of the senses for meaningful and intelligence-reflecting functioning of the human brain.

Who Should Read This Book?

All stakeholders of a SMACT computing project can read this book.

This book presents a detailed discussion on various aspects of a SMACT computing solution. The approach adopted in this book will be useful to any professional who must present a case for realizing the SMACT computing solutions or to those who could be involved in a Big Data computing project. It provides a framework that will enable business and technical managers to make the optimal decisions that are necessary for the successful migration to SMACT computing environments and applications within their organizations.

All readers who are involved with any aspect of a SMACT computing project will profit by using this book as a road map to make a more meaningful contribution to the success of their SMACT computing initiative(s).

The book is targeted at the following categories of stakeholders:

- Executives and business and operational managers
- SMACT technologies evaluation and selection team members
- SMACT project technical and project managers and module leaders
- SMACT functional and technical members
- Industry professionals interested in understanding the role of SMACT in business operations
- Students of engineering, management, computer, and technology courses
- General readers interested in the use of SMACT in organizations

Vivek Kale
Mumbai, India

You may want to get a copy of *Enhancing Enterprise Intelligence: Leveraging ERP, CRM, SCM, PLM, BPM, and BI* as a companion volume for this book. While that volume is focused on addressing the *functional* requirements of an enterprise, this book addresses the *non-functional* requirements of an operating enterprise. Together, these two books cover the entire spectrum of strategic solutions that can enhance the smartness and intelligence quotient of the enterprise.

Acknowledgments

I would like to thank all those who have helped me with their clarifications, criticism, and valuable information during the writing of this book.

Thanks again to John Wyzalek for making this book happen and Glenon Butler and his production team for guiding it through to completion.

I have no words to mention the support, sufferings, and sacrifice of my wife Girija and our beloved daughters Tanaya and Atmaja. In spite of my best intention to keep the family unaffected by the book project(s), I generally spend more time thinking about work than I should, even at home. I am indebted to them for their patience and grace.

Vivek Kale
Mumbai, India

Author

Vivek Kale has more than two decades of professional IT experience during which he has handled and consulted on various aspects of enterprise-wide information modeling, enterprise architectures, business process re-design, and, e-business architectures. He has been Group CIO of Essar Group, the steel/oil & gas major of India, as well as Raymond Ltd., the textile & apparel major of India. He is a seasoned practitioner in transforming the business of IT, facilitating business agility, and enhancing IT-enabled Enterprise Intelligence. He is the author of *Guide to Cloud Computing for Business and Technology Managers: From Distributed Computing to Cloudware Applications*, CRC Press (2015), and *Enhancing Enterprise Intelligence: Leveraging ERP, CRM, SCM, PLM, BPM, and BI*, CRC Press (2016).

Other Books by Vivek Kale

Enterprise Performance Intelligence and Decision Patterns (CRC Press, 2018)

Agile Network Businesses: A Collaboration, Coordination, and Competitive Advantage (CRC Press, 2017)

Big Data Computing: A Guide Business and Technology Managers (CRC Press, 2017)

Enhancing Enterprise Intelligence: Leveraging ERP, CRM, SCM, PLM, BPM, and BI (CRC Press, 2016)

Guide to Cloud Computing for Business and Technology Managers: From Distributed Computing to Cloudware Applications (CRC Press, 2015)

Inverting the Paradox of Excellence: How Companies Use Variations for Business Excellence and How Enterprise Variations Are Enabled by SAP (CRC Press, 2015)

Implementing SAP® CRM: The Guide for Business and Technology Managers (CRC Press, 2015)

Chapter 1

VUCA Ecosystem

Agility is the ability to respond to (and ideally benefit from) unexpected change. We must distinguish between agility and flexibility: flexibility is scheduled or planned adaptation to unforeseen yet expected external circumstances, while agility is unplanned and unscheduled adaptation to unforeseen and unexpected external circumstances. The enterprises that can best respond to the fast and frequently changing markets will have better competitive advantages than those that fail to sustain the pace dictated by the process of globalization. And this can be realized through enterprises acquiring better control and efficiency in their ability to manage the changes in their enterprise processes.

1.1 VUCA Ecosystem

VUCA stands for Volatility, Uncertainty, Complexity, and Ambiguity. It describes a situation confronted in the digital economy:

1. Volatility: The term *volatility* is commonly used in statistics and financial theory. Volatility can be defined as a statistical measure, describing the amount of uncertainty about the size of changes. In statistics, it can be quantified by the standard deviation or variance. Real-life examples are increasing price fluctuations on global raw material markets or stock markets. You can see high volatility as significant jumps of values over time, which can be seen as an indicator of increasing pace of the environment.

   Volatility can be understood as an observable output of a complex system that cannot be easily interpreted any more. While complex systems that are in an equilibrium or are oscillating between two or three different equilibria are easy to interpret, a system that runs in so-called deterministic chaos has no obvious pattern to be easily observed.

2. Uncertainty: With increased volatility of the environment, it is increasingly hard to predict the future. While in the past, statistical regression models were able to predict the future, today it is becoming more and more difficult to extrapolate future developments and link them with a probability distribution. Uncertainty can also be described as a lack of clarity to evaluate a situation properly to identify challenges and opportunities.

Uncertainty is a problem that might arise in decision making if there is incomplete information, inadequate understanding of available information or equally attractive options. Across time, there develops an increasing belief in the ability to cope with uncertainty and even to overcome uncertainty through planning and control. Decisions in business are often made based on the assumption that with enough research, collection of information and preparation for decision making, uncertainty can be avoided completely. But this is not the case, and in highly dynamic environments, the speed of change in the context is higher than the speed of learning. In such a situation, it is customary to build up a certain mutually acceptable perception that is used as a reference by all concerned. This helps in reducing the impact of uncertainty to a certain amount, and helps the people to achieve some sense of assurance, security, and stability. But this doesn't mean that it reflects the real-world situation—there is an irreducible gap.

3. Complexity: In an interconnected and networked environment, it becomes more and more difficult to connect cause and effect. The idea of linear causality hits the limits. Complexity can be defined as a situation where interconnectedness of parts and variables is so high that the same external conditions and inputs can lead to very different outputs or reactions of the system. Real-life examples are organizations or even more complex inter-organizational alliance networks where the same inputs can cause very different outputs at different points in time.

From a systems perspective, complexity can be understood as a specific property, defined as the result of the amount of system elements, their relationships, and the dynamics between the elements and the relationships. The more states a system can take, the higher the variety of the system. The variety can be then used as a measure of complexity. In computer science, for example, the algorithmic complexity is measured by the size of the shortest possible computer program that can solve the problem or at least completely describe the problem. Generally speaking, complexity has two aspects:

a. Complex structure is given by the high number of elements that are linked to each other in a non-trivial, non-linear way. In contrast, complicated structures are only characterized by a high amount of system elements, and they are missing these intense internal structures of various relationships and dynamics between the elements.

　　b. Complex behavior is characterized mainly by emergence, which can be described thus: "the action of the whole is more than the sum of the actions of the parts" (Holland). If something contains many interacting objects whose behavior is affected by memory or "feedback," the interaction becomes non-linear.

　　Complexity is also closely linked to organization, decomposability, and nestedness of systems.

4. Ambiguity: Ambiguity is characterized by the fact that causal relationships are completely unclear, and the meaning or interpretation of a situation cannot be definitely resolved according to a rule or process consisting of a finite number of steps. In contrast to vagueness, which characterizes a situation by a lack of clarity, in ambiguity, specific and distinct interpretations are permitted. In real life, business decisions become more and more ambiguous, as there is often more than one possible solution to a problem and there is no analytical process to decide which option should be chosen. If one asks different people for an evaluation of a specific situation and plans for action, one would get different answers that would be equally valid.

Organizations cannot reduce the environment's "degree of VUCA," but a company's capability to deal with VUCA can increase. In times of high dynamics and high interconnectedness, traditional simple mind models and decision-making rules and heuristics are no longer effective. The traditional mechanistic worldview worked well in times when the complex environment stayed in "pockets of order"; it was supported by the human need for simple, rational cause-and-effect mind models to be able to make decisions and to easily deal with the environment. Today, the environment is often in a state at the "edge of chaos" or in a "deterministic state of chaos." In these situations, not only there is a need for different models and approaches in cognition, judgment, and action in management, but performance on all of these aspects can also be enhanced tremendously by *augmenting with technology*.

1.2　Four Industrial Generations

In the earliest stages of industrialization, the focus of the technological revolution was on mechanization and the use of water and steam power. Mechanized production that had previously been organized mainly along craft lines led to larger organizational units and a significantly higher output of goods.

The second industrial revolution was characterized by the assembly line and electrification of factories.

The third industrial revolution brought with it a further automation of production by means of microelectronics and computerization.

The fourth industrial revolution is characterized by the essential digitization of the processes of production and delivery.

1.3 Trends

1.3.1 Social Trends

1. Sharing and Prosuming: The digital transformation blurs the traditional societal categories of production and consumption. This development has enormous consequences for role behavior, expectations, and standards. Increasingly, consumers are becoming producers—and not only producers of digital content. A few years ago, *prosuming* still referred solely to content shared on social networks, generated by users and made available to the general public as, say, on Wikipedia. Today this relationship is increasingly shifting in the direction of digital product design, user experience, or participation in services—up to and including power generation in prosumer networks.

   Companies are increasingly involving customers directly in the design, functionalities, and usability of new products and the development of customer-specific services. This consumer participation is a path taken by carmakers and manufacturers of sporting goods or household appliances in equal measure. So the borders between producers and consumers are growing less clear. Consumers and customers are taking on an extended workbench role. When we consider the future production of articles in daily use or, perhaps, of food on suitably equipped 3D printers, moving from a home office to a home factory is no longer such a major transition, and the Internet of Things will give this trend an additional boost.

2. Digital Inclusion: Just as the meaning of societal categories such as consumers and producers changes, the borders between professional and private life are blurring too. Digital connection has triggered deep-seated societal changes that are perceptible in all areas of life. People are working via the Net on shared projects, maintaining digital friendships across continents and distinguishing less and less between professional and private life. Connecting has become a new form of communicating and living. People are organizing and engaging in networks and setting up vibrant ecosystems in order, for instance, to put their private or professional ideas into practice by means of crowdsourcing or crowdfunding. The central tool in this development is the smartphone. In 2016, around four billion people around the world owned one of this kind of mobile computer. This smart mobile communication device is epicenter of socio-cultural changes. The tool used by digital natives who want to be permanently online, contactable and connected, it is by no means the endpoint of the technological development on which this societal

trend of inclusion is based. Wearable devices and digital implants may well be next steps in this development.

For many working people, the dynamics of everyday working life are moving to the Net. Chats, forums, and Wikis are taking the place of the personal exchange of opinions and experiences at the workplace. The good old telephone conversation is then often the last bastion for keeping up personal (working) relationships. "Always-on" means for communications teams and other employees alike that they can work from a distance—for example from home—which leads to a shift from traditional office hours and workplaces to greater flexibility and independence.

3. More Transparency: In most Western industrial countries, a majority of the population is now registered on social networks and most 14–64-year-olds use the Internet. They do so of their own free will because they see the advantages and do not want to forgo them, even though there are regular warnings about the omnipresent power of algorithms.

Free Internet services and payback or customer cards of any kind also serve specific business models. Furthermore, the user of Internet services is not a customer in the classic meaning of the word. In many cases, the provider's business model is based on collecting personal data and marketing it in a targeted way. Yet that dissuades very few people from divulging their data, from using Facebook, or from posting photos on Instagram. Intentionally or not, that creates a tendentially dangerous transparency that is liable to manipulation and misuse—such as when algorithms are deliberately changed to deliver the results desired or when content is purely and simply falsified.

1.3.2 Organizational Trends

In the field of organization, we see another three basic trends influencing professional communication: the trend toward more connection, a growing demand for creativity, and the quest for identity.

1. Connected Work: Platforms form the basis of nearly all new business models, and the concept of a platform has legal, organizational, and technical aspects. Processes are controlled, business is driven, and communications are distributed via digital platforms. They are also becoming an indispensable collaboration tool in day-to-day work. They simplify closely enmeshed collaboration of teams that are increasingly often engaged in projects across corporate and geographical borders or are jointly taking developments forward.

One of the consequences is that, to provide specific services, companies are less and less dependent on a fixed workforce. The transparency of skills and availabilities of highly qualified specialists brought about by connection leads to "hiring on demand." The employment relationship is changing into an employment deployment. What is more, software increasingly determines work processes. That makes organizations more homogeneous and efficient but, in some areas, perhaps less creative and system driven.

2. Increasing Creativity: With the advent of smart software, learning Artifical Intelligence (AI) systems, and industrial robots, the role of people in production and work processes is changing. The individual's role is changing from that of a provider of job performance to that of a monitor of machines who controls and only intervenes in an emergency. At the same time, new forms of interaction are taking shape between people and machines—up to and including their merger. No one can at present seriously predict what, in the final analysis, that may mean, especially in the production of non-material corporate achievements such as knowledge, transparency, software, or decision making. Kurzweil dealt with this aspect back in 2006. His thesis was that "the exponential increase in technologies like computers, genetics, nanotechnology, robotics and artificial intelligence will lead to a technological singularity in the year 2045, a point where progress is so rapid that it outstrips humans' *ability to comprehend it*". Already, studies are looking into which activities can be taken over by machines in the near future and what effects that will have on global labor markets. One point is clear: there is no simple answer apart, perhaps, from that we currently do not know exactly what shape developments will take.

3. Redefining Identity: The employment relationship is changing into an employment deployment. The result is what counts, no longer just being there. Teams will be set up from case to case, hierarchies will be sidelined, and departments will be discontinued. What is more, services provided in the digital environment will increasingly be delegated to highly specialized "virtual laborers" who will strengthen the company's team from time to time. What that means is simply constant change. Employee management and control will become the major challenge that a "liquid" workforce poses. Compulsory attendance will in any case become an obsolete model, permanent control will no longer be possible, and authoritarian managers will no longer stand a chance. Their place will be taken by openness and transparency, trust, motivation, and recognition along with greater decision-making scope for the individual. Along the lines of the 2001 manifesto for agile software development, the guiding principle will be preferably to try things out and rectify them if need be rather than to die striving for perfection.

Conversely, expectations of the "core competences" of employees and co-workers are also changing. Specific skills are no longer the measure of all things. That measure is now creativity, competency to communicate and to work in a team, and the ability to work as flexibly as possible in changing teams. Other attributes are willingness to change, courage to have an opinion of your own, and an unbending will to assume responsibility.

In the overwhelming majority of cases, the right organization and legal frame-work conditions have yet to be established. This requires concerted action by the workforce, human resources (HR), and the management just as much as it requires new agreements with trade unions and politicians. The agenda includes flexible working time organization, adequate remuneration of performance, and appropriate provision for old age. Especially in view of the growing number of digital working nomads, a collective provision must be made to ensure that binding rules are negotiated that are equally profitable for employees and employers.

Digital nomads are only a challenge when it comes to retaining or creating, in this highly volatile situation, a central resource of every organization that stands apart from individual competences or skills: the ability of employees and managers to identify with the organization, be it a company, an association, or a non-governmental organization (NGO). Only if at least a minimal consensus on vision, mission, values, objectives, and strategy can be established and kept alive are peak performances and excellence to be expected.

1.3.3 Business Model Trends

1. Globalization: The digitally connected individual is the powerful player in globalization. About 2.7 billion people around the world are connected. The enormous success of Google, Amazon, Apple, Facebook, or Twitter is precisely attributable to this development, as is the hitherto inexorable rise of new sharing platforms like Uber or Airbnb.
2. Industries redefined and reframed: New technology-driven companies shake up entire industries and embark on knocking established companies out of the running. In the music industry, Apple is today one of the major providers, Facebook is pestering the banks and Google is proving a problem for the carmakers. That too is a consequence of digitalization, and the Industrial Internet will further step up the pace.

   This is made possible by integrated, open, standardized platform solutions on which the most varied players can meet, share their ideas and know-how, and establish and manage joint value chains. Start-ups in the financial sector, for example, try to make use of the infrastructure of large retail chains in order to set up, at one fell swoop, a "branch network" of cash payment points of which the banks can but dream—a threat to the business model of not only banks but also ATM providers. WhatsApp or Skype use the partly still government-subsidized technical infrastructure of the large telephone companies so as to appear to be able to offer their communications services globally free of charge. Smart "capture" of existing infrastructure can succeed on a global scale and even without major capital expenditure if a convincing customer benefit is combined with digitally enabled user-friendliness.
3. Increasing Supply Chain Integration: In the course of platformization of the economy, value chains are not only better integrated but also redefined in

many places. What is currently under discussion in many manufacturing companies is, for example, the use of 3D printing. It is a technology with highly disruptive potential that in the years ahead will in all probability intervene massively in the traditional value chains of a wide range of manufacturers and industries. The keyword is *co-creation*. Carmakers might in future allow their dealers to 3D print certain plastic and metal parts themselves. It would then be possible to transfer parts of their production not only directly to the *sales* markets in question but also to adjust it to the markets and their specific requirements.

Another example is the development of new services and operator models, with interesting options arising in, for example, the combination and services and leasing or rental models. They could range from coffeemakers via paint shops to turbines. Plant and equipment would remain the property of the manufacturer with payment on the basis of use and availability—such as coffee consumption, the number of car bodies painted, or the number of flight hours logged. This approach may not be fundamentally new, but substantially improved direct access to operating data—in real time if required—offers enormous benefits with regard, say, to the timely delivery of fresh coffee beans or to timely maintenance of machinery. The smart factory of the future will no longer be a group of industrial buildings with intelligent organization and technology; it will break the spatial, organizational, and legal bounds of traditional manufacturing operations.

1.3.4 Technology Trends

1. Increasing connection: Improbable though it may sound, even after more than two decades of the Internet, we are still only at the beginning of comprehensive global interconnection. By 2020, the number of connected devices will increase to 50 billion from 25 billion today. That will mean an increase not only in the connection of computers in production and administration but above all permanent data communication between smart devices and sensors or all kinds, from machines to machines, from machines to people, and from goods and products on their way across the delivery, distribution, and consumption chains, independently of specific devices, increasingly mobile and time independent. This is enabled by new technologies that make this interconnection possible in the first place: software that is capable of understanding and processing data from the widest range of sources, cloud computing that makes it possible to manage this data on an almost unlimited scale, high-powered data transmission networks and mobile devices like smartphones and tablets that provide access to this kind of data anytime, anywhere.
2. Big Data: The market researchers expect globally generated data to increase by 800% in the next 5 years. It will include healthcare, energy, financial, or production data. By 2020, this data mountain will increase to 44 zettabytes—an

inconceivable amount, in that a single zettabyte roughly corresponds to the data capacity of 200 billion DVDs. In addition to machine and sensor data, it will include multi-media content and all kinds of natural verbal communication insofar as it can be recorded by digital systems.

Anyone who can analyze live Twitter or Facebook streams contextually in real time with the aid of AI systems enjoys a clear advantage in certain communication decisions. Anyone who in social media marketing learns from target-group reactions at short intervals and optimizes his campaigns can increase his efficiency dramatically.

3. User-Friendly Technology: What began with the Windows graphic user interface and reached its peak for the time being with smartphone apps that everyone can use is now gaining access to the control of complex technological applications in factories.

For communicators, the relevance of this trend can be seen in the use of numerous technologies in their everyday professional life, such as in analyzing target-group data or using market research and opinion polling systems, using special algorithms to evaluate communication or shopping behavior of individual customers, and, subsequently, automatically initiating individualized communication, cross- and up-selling offerings into the personal digital campaign targeted at these customers.

1.4 From Products to Services to Experiences

By the middle of the last century, products, goods, and property came to increasingly mean an individual's exclusive right to possess, use, and, most importantly, dispose of things as he or she wished. By the 1980s, the production of goods had been eclipsed by the performance of services. These are economic activities that are not products or construction but are transitory, consumed at the time they are produced (and, thus, are unable to be inventoried), and primarily provide intangible value. In a service economy, it is time that is being commodified, not prices, places, or things. This also leads to a transition from *profit and loss* to *market cap* as the base metric of success; what the customer is really purchasing is the access to use rather than ownership of a material good. Since the 1990s, goods have become more information intensive and interactive, are continually upgraded and are essentially evolving into services. Products are rapidly being equated as the cost of doing business rather than as sales items; they are becoming more in the nature of containers or platforms for all sorts of upgrades and value-added services. Giving away products is increasingly being used as a marketing strategy to capture the attention of potential customers. But with the advent of electronic commerce, feedback, and workflow mechanisms, services are being further transformed into multi-faceted relationships between the service providers and customers, and technology is becoming more of a medium of relationships. In the servicized economy, programmable logic controllers (PLCs) and an ever-expanding flow of competitive goods and services, it is the customer attention rather than the resources that is becoming scarce.

> The true significance of a customer's attention can be understood the moment one realizes that time is often used as a proxy for attention. Like time, attention is limited and cannot be inventoried or reused. In the current economy, attention is the real currency of business and, to be successful, enterprises must be adept in getting significant and sustained mindshare of or attention to their prospects or customers. As with any other scarce and valuable resource, markets for attention exist both within and outside the enterprise. For extracting optimum value, the real-time and intelligent enterprises must impart optimal attention to the wealth of operational and management information available within the enterprise. This fact alone should automatically put a bar on overzealous re-engineering and downsizing efforts (although re-engineering and other cost-cutting tactics are necessary, it is essential to ascertain if undertaking such tactics will contribute to the delivery of superior or at least on-par value to the customers).

One major result of this trend toward the importance of experience has been the blurring of lines between the content (the message) and container (the medium) in the market (Figure 1.1). *Convergence* describes the phenomenon in which two or more existing technologies, markets, producers, boundaries, or value chains combine to create a new force that is more powerful and more efficient than the sum of its constituting technologies. The value-chain migration alludes to the development of real-term systems that integrate supply-chain systems and customer-facing systems, resulting in a single and unified integrated process.

This convergence occurs primarily because of three factors:

1. the digitization of information to enable the preparation, processing, storage, and transmission of information regardless of its form (data, graphics, sound, and video or any combination of these)
2. the rapidly declining cost of computing, which has enabled it to become ubiquitous and available with sufficient power
3. the availability of broadband communications, which is critical to convergence because multi-media is both storage intensive and time sensitive

1.5 Technology Advancements

Why is the Internet begetting the revolutionary changes that we are witnessing today? What gives it the power to drive the massive changes that have been

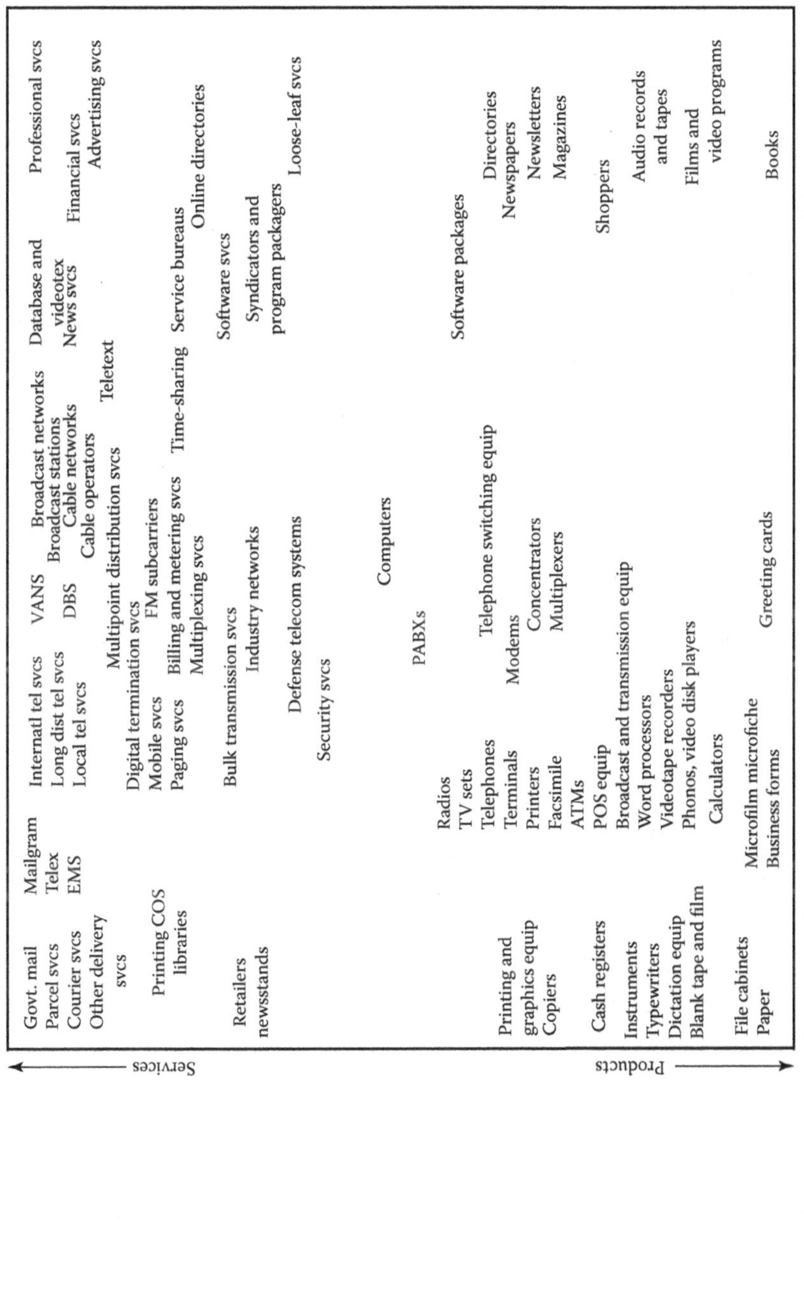

Substance →

Professional svcs
Financial svcs
Advertising svcs

Database and videotex News svcs
Online directories
Software svcs
Syndicators and program packagers
Loose-leaf svcs

Time-sharing   Service bureaus

Broadcast networks
Broadcast stations
Cable networks
Cable operators
Teletext

VANS   DBS
FM subcarriers
Billing and metering svcs
Multiplexing svcs

Internat'l tel svcs
Long dist tel svcs
Local tel svcs
Multipoint distribution svcs
Digital termination svcs
Mobile svcs
Paging svcs
Bulk transmission svcs
Industry networks
Defense telecom systems
Security svcs

Mailgram
Telex
EMS

Govt. mail
Parcel svcs
Courier svcs
Other delivery svcs
Printing COS libraries
Retailers newsstands

← Services

Computers

PABXs

Software packages

Directories
Newspapers
Newsletters
Magazines

Shoppers

Audio records and tapes

Films and video programs

Books

Telephone switching equip
Modems   Concentrators
Multiplexers

Broadcast and transmission equip
Word processors
Videotape recorders
Phonos, video disk players
Calculators

Greeting cards

Radios
TV sets
Telephones
Terminals
Printers
Facsimile
ATMs

POS equip
Instruments
Typewriters
Dictation equip
Blank tape and film

Microfilm microfiche
Business forms

Printing and graphics equip
Copiers

Cash registers

File cabinets
Paper

← Products →

← Form

Figure 1.1 Spectrum of offerings (products/services) versus medium (container or form)/message (content/substance).

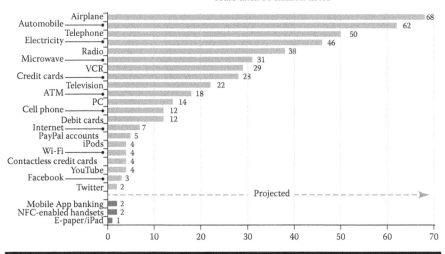

Figure 1.2   Surging contexts of innovations.

witnessed in the last 5 years, while similar changes in the past have taken ages to sweep across the globe? (see Figure 1.2).

The author believes that the fundamental reason is that a medium is always more powerful than a message. It might be that, at certain stages in history, messages (and their messengers) have had a determining effect on the course of history, but these passages have been few and far between. The impact of the medium has always been more powerful and long lasting than any message. Throughout history, the powerful have always recognized this truth and have concentrated on controlling a medium as the most powerful facet of governance, rather than becoming martyrs as revolutionaries with a new message to tell to the world. The print medium has outlasted all ideological and technological revolutions seen in past centuries since the dawn of civilization. In one form or another, this has been a known fact in all fields of human endeavor, but Marshall McLuhan brought this out much more forcefully for the electronic media in the middle of the last century.

Computers were always positioned as messages of the new era, but it is clear that, right from the beginning, the Internet was a medium. Considering that the Internet is not governed or dictated by any specific authority and is one of the most democratic of institutions, one can be absolutely sure that the Internet is destined to herald the next major cultural revolution in human history.

Additionally, underlying all human endeavors lies the quest for immortality, the desire to transcend space and time forever. It might seem that this is only the concern of spiritualists and philosophers or mathematicians, relativists, and other scientists. On the other hand, it might also appear that all commercial endeavors are driven by the pursuit of money, but that could be wrong. At the base of all commercial transactions lie the fundamental concerns of transcending space and time.

All major technological advances, be they discoveries or inventions, that had lasting impact on the future course of human development had to do with one of the following:

1. Sliding space and/or time in a direction that satisfied the basic urge to transcend space and time in practical terms and in a direction that was convenient.
2. Altering space and/or time, that is, expanding or contracting space and/or time to satisfy the basic urge to transcend space and time again in practical terms and in a direction that was convenient. Although such effects are not unknown in physical sciences, here the author is referring to effects that are psychological and experiential in nature.

Figure 1.3 shows a snapshot of the technological advancements witnessed in the last century interpreted in this new light. In the figure, the legend used is as follows:

- Sliding Space:
  +ve = Bringing Near
  −ve = Taking afar
- Sliding Time:
  +ve = Bringing Near
  −ve = Taking afar
- Altering Space:
  +ve = Compressing Space
  −ve = Expanding Space
- Altering Time:
  +ve = Compressing Time
  −ve = Expanding Time

Description	Space				Time			
	Sliding		Altering		Sliding		Altering	
	+ve	−ve	+ve	−ve	+ve	−ve	+ve	−ve
Paper	X	X	X	X	X	X	X	X
Vehicles		X						X
Telephones	X		X		X			
Voice mail	X	X	X		X	X		X
Photographs	X	X	X			X		
Transmitted pictures	X	X	X	X	X	X	X	
Motion pictures		X	X			X	X	
Audio/Video CDs	X	X	X		X			X
Audio/Video CD players	X	X		X		X		X
Deep freezers						X		
Microwaves					X		X	
Credit-card payments	X	X			X			
Telephone charge cards	X				X			
Computers			X	X		X	X	X
Networks	X	X	X	X	X			X
Internet	X	X	X	X	X	X	X	X

Figure 1.3 Technological advances in the last century.

For instance, telephones permit you to converse with a person as if he were close (Sliding Space +ve and Altering Space +ve) and without waiting for a time in the future when you can meet him in person (Sliding Time +ve). It is a simple grid, but it enables us to understand in a powerful way the essential unity behind the technological advances in the last couple of centuries. It also gives rationale for the difference in the degree of impact that these technological inventions have had on human life and thought.

It is evident that Internet's power over the consumer's mind comes from its unprecedented facility to slide and alter both space and time to a degree that is unlikely to be surpassed for quite some time in the future and is matched only by that of printed paper (see Figure 1.4).

1.6 Digital Economy

In the transition from a traditional industrial digital economy, the whole process of value creation is entirely transformed. Information and knowledge play a crucial role both in the traditional and the digital economy. However, in the industrial economy, knowledge generation and application processes are essentially aimed at making production more efficient through cost reductions, while in the digital economy, they are mainly directed to intercepting the customer's preferences and expanding his choice. Information, in the digital economy, is an essential source of value, and every business is an information business. The digital economy offers companies a variety of tools (e.g., Web-based supply-chain management systems, online commerce, interactive customer service) that enable the creation of value not only through the reduction of costs, but also, and above all, by making them more capable of responding to customer needs. In fact, in a world where access to information is permanent, immediate and almost ubiquitous, value creation depends on the ability to locate, select, filter and communicate the information that the consumer perceives as actually useful. (Table 1.1)

The Internet, however, proved to be a destructive force for many companies, completely transforming entire sectors, because the network is not only a tremendous source of access to data and information in a digital format but also constitutes a new channel of distribution and marketing. In fact, the advent of the Internet has challenged the traditional way of doing business, as it has, and still is,

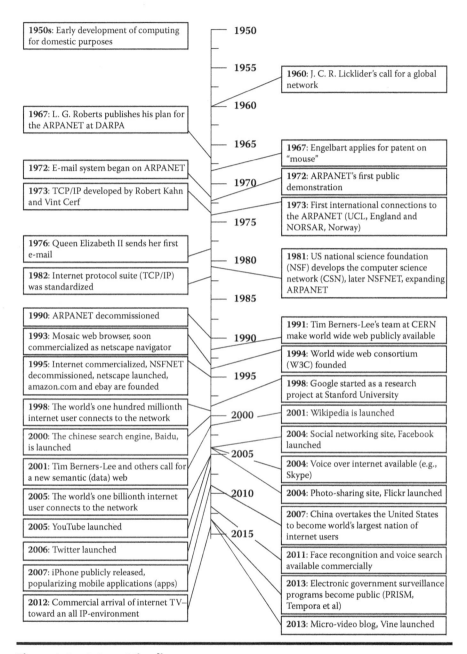

Figure 1.4   Internet timeline.

Table 1.1 Comparison between the Industrial and Digital Economy

	Industrial Economy	*Digital Economy*
Business process orientation	• Guided by offer	• Guided by demand
Economic focus	• Cost minimizing	• Value maximizing
Product policy	• Offer standardization	• Offer personalization
Value chain configuration	• Linear value chain	• Non-linear value network
Key inputs	• Raw materials, intermediate products	• Digital information
Output	• Intermediate or finished products or services	• Products or services with a high information/ knowledge content
The role of information	• A supporting and connecting element during the phases of production	• A source of value

significantly transforming the traditional rules of competition, offer-value propositions, and business models:

1. The market is no longer just a physical place and geographically fragmented, but rather becomes a digital, open, and transparent space.
2. The network has also intensified competition since the easier access to information and the reduction of variable costs stimulates competition on prices and therefore requires the maximization of operational efficiency. In addition, it is easier for potential entrants to access distribution channels and reach new customers.
3. The ability of the network to get the manufacturer and the end user closer and in direct communication has drastically reduced the need for intermediaries in the sale of goods and services. In this sense, the network can undoubtedly be counted among the most significant radical innovations, that is, those innovations that have as a fundamental trait a total discontinuity with previous technologies, whose technical skills they tend to displace (making them in some cases so obsolete to cause their withdrawal from the market), resulting in a drastic transformation of the productive processes of economic activities they touch and producing a different distribution of wealth compared to the situation before their introduction.

The formulation and implementation of an appropriate business model are vital to meet the challenges of the digital economy, which requires a paradigm shift. Companies are called to deal with the Internet and the opportunities of electronic commerce, but, to be able to acquire the benefits, they must be able to identify the disruptive nature of these innovations in order to effectively reconfigure their distribution strategies or the entire business model.

A number of attributes make the Internet and electronic commerce disruptive innovations:

- Open Platform: The Internet represents an open and public network that allows a constant flow of communication and collaboration in real time.
- Network Externalities: Network externalities exist when the value of a given product/ service to any single user becomes greater as the number of users of the same product/service increases.
- Connectivity and Interaction: E-commerce enables the company to establish new relations and ways of interacting with their customers, suppliers, and partners.
- Information Sharing and Exchange: The Internet allows information to reach a large number of people without sacrificing the quality of the information content that it distributes.
- Production and Consumption Convergence: The consumer–user is involved in the early stages of design and production of highly customized goods and services.
- Digital Resources: Information and data in a digital form, duly selected, organized and summarized, become a source of essential value that enables companies to formulate new value propositions.
- Cost Transparency: Users are able to quickly and easily access a vast amount of information regarding prices and characteristics of the products and services offered by the various competitors.
- Industry extension: The value creation made possible by the Internet and new digital technologies allows companies to transcend the boundaries of traditional business.
- Speed and Frequency of Changes: In the digital economy, companies need to continually adapt to changes that are extremely fast and frequent.
- Virtual Capacity: The recent progress in networking and storage technologies has led to the creation of an extensive market place available to users.

1.7 Intelligence Analysis

Management decisions differ depending on the level of responsibility on which they are made and who makes them. A brief overview is helpful here to put this into context:

1. Strategic decisions have significant resource-allocation impact, set the precedents or tone for decisions further down the organization, and have a potentially material effect on the organization's competitiveness within its marketplace. They are made by top managers and affect the business direction of an organization.

   Strategic intelligence is arguably the most vital form of intelligence because it provides a framework within which other forms of intelligence collection and analysis take place. It helps to discern and make sense of important trends, to identify and extract patterns that would otherwise not be visible, and to provide an overall picture of the evolving opportunity and threat environment. Strategic intelligence also provides guidance for tactical and operational assessments, and work done at these levels in turn helps to shape the strategic intelligence focus. As strategic analytic methodologies mature, they will also offer the basis for predictive or anticipatory assessments that can serve to provide warning of potential high impact activities.

   Generic strategic analytical initiatives are:
   - Sector/Competitor Assessments: These assessments focus on emerging or threatening competitors that provide strong potential for impacting the competitive terrain.
   - Pattern or Trend Analyses: These baseline assessments better recognize deviations from current practice, especially those that shape the industry's future.
   - Anti-Pattern or Anomaly Detection: This requires systematic "environmental scanning," as well as the collating of tactical and operational intelligence reports that identify and highlight specific deviations from the norm.
   - Opportunity and Threat (O&T) Assessments: These are used to assess the levels of dependence and vulnerabilities of critical issues, competitive changes that could cause significant impact, and the likelihood of such activities taking place.
   - Impact Assessments: The macro-level view taken in SIA offers a good approach for assessing probable cascade effects of threatening competitive action and activity.

2. Tactical decisions are less pervasive than strategic ones and involve formulating and implementing policies for the organization. They are usually made by mid-level managers and often materially affect functions such as marketing, accounting, production, a business unit, or product, as opposed to the entire organization. Tactical decisions generally have lower resource implications than strategic decisions and are typically semi-structured.

   TIA is a necessary and important complement to work done at the strategic level. It is the natural link between macro and micro-level analysis.

Although SIA provides the framework for TIA, these assessments in turn feed SIA. With a dynamic symbiotic relationship between the two, mutual strength is derived.

Generic tactical analytical initiatives are:

- Cluster and Pattern Analysis: This identifies the use of particular marketplace attack methods, commonalities of targets, and attempts to build profiles of competitors.
- Value Constellation Analysis: This identifies the key stakeholders, important partners, allies, joint venture prospects, outsourcing potential, and agents that a company could utilize.
- Stimulus–Response Analysis: This identifies actions that could be taken by competitors in response to specific events. This analysis could be used both proactively to develop warnings and reactively to design future tactics.

3. Operational decisions support the day-to-day decisions needed to operate the organization and take effect for a few days or weeks. Typically made by a lower-level manager, operational decisions are distinct from tactical and strategic decisions in that they are made frequently and often "on the fly." Operational decisions tend to be highly structured, often with well-defined procedure manuals. OIA is often event-centric and single-case oriented. It provides more immediate but lesser-lasting benefits and typically involves technological assessments of methods used for marketplace battles or investigations of competitive threats.

Generic operational analytical initiatives:

- Competitor analysis helps in planning and executing competitive intelligence efforts at the appropriate time and preventing pre-mature disclosures.
- Vulnerability analysis helps in identification of marketplace vulnerabilities and measures that can rectify, minimize, or eliminate them.

1.7.1 Intelligence Maturity Model (IMM)

Table 1.2 presents Intelligence Maturity Model (IMM) discussed below.

Table 1.2 Intelligence Maturity Model (IMM)

Data	–	Data file
Communication	Metadata	Data tables, mapping, and transformation
Information	Meaning	Databases, indices, and spreadsheets
Intelligence	Analytics	Data warehouses, OLAPs
Knowledge	Context	Knowledge bases
Wisdom	Heuristics	Expert systems

1.7.1.1 Data

Data has experienced a variety of definitions, largely depending on the context of its use. For example, Information Science defines data as unprocessed information, and other domains treat data as a representation of objective facts. Data results from representation of facts, observation or an event. Data is understood as discrete, atomistic, tiny packets that have no inherent structure or necessary relationship between them. It is discrete, it can pile up, it can be captured and retrieved, or it can be recorded and manipulated.

Data are recorded (captured and stored) as symbols and signal readings: symbols include words (text and/or verbal), numbers, diagrams, and images (still &/or video), which are the building blocks of communication; signals include sensor and/or sensory readings of light, sound, smell, taste, and touch. As symbols, "Data" is the storage of intrinsic meaning, a mere representation. The main purpose of data is to record activities or situations, to attempt to capture the true picture or real event.

Data is a measuring unit of cognition that describes transactions between natural, artificial, or semantic systems. In businesses, data can measure performance characteristics of production, distribution, transportation, or service.

1.7.1.2 Communication

Communication is a method of transmission from a generating source to a receiving destination. Communication presumes content, container, and media of communication; thus, communication fidelity is closely connected with architecture, process, protocol and format of the various components.

Characteristics of communication:

- Correct: Is the transmission correct?
- Consistent: Is the transmission consistent?
- Complete: Did the transmission complete without disruption or interruption?
- Clear: Is the transmission accompanied by noise?

1.7.1.3 Information

Information is corpuscular, quantifiable, morselized, commoditized, objective and "out there," transferable, inter-convertible, transparent, autonomous, and measurable. It has shape and can be processed and accessed, generated and created, transmitted, stored, sent, distributed, produced and consumed, searched for, used, compressed, and duplicated. Information can also be of different types with different attributes. It can be sensitive information or qualitative or quantitative information. Modern uses even extend its use to biological cells using and transmitting information, with cancers, for example, seen as spreading misinformation.

Information is a message that contains relevant meaning, implication or input for decision and/or action. Information comes from both current (communication) and historical (processed data or "reconstructed picture") sources. In essence, the purpose of information is to aid in making decisions and/or solving problems or realizing an opportunity.

Characteristics of information:

- Reliability: Can the source of the information be trusted to deliver reliable information?
- Accuracy: Have the data inputs been captured "first hand," or have they been filtered? Is there any reason to think that there might be any deception involved? Is the source able to communicate the data precisely? Is the source truly competent and knowledgeable about the information they provide? Do they have a known vested interest, hidden agenda or other bias that might impact the information's accuracy? Can the source's data be verified by other sources or otherwise triangulated?
- Ease of access: What is the financial opportunity and time cost to access the source? Is this the best use of limited resources, or can equivalent data be gained with lesser expenditure? Does the source speak the right language, or will translation be needed?

It is a comparative unit of cognition that defines a change between the previous and present state of natural, artificial, or semantic systems. Businesses often compare data from two different periods of operations. Accounting systems often compare actual performance with standards.

1.7.1.4 Concept

Existence of concept presumes a language; ontology is defined in terms of concept(s) and relations between the concepts.

It is a perceptive unit of cognition that generates thoughts or ideas that create our intuition and intention—a sense of direction.

1.7.1.5 Knowledge

Knowledge is the cognition or recognition (know-what), capacity to act (know-how), and understanding (know-why) that resides or is contained within the mind or in the brain. The purpose of knowledge is to better our lives. In the context of business, the purpose of knowledge is to create or increase value for the enterprise and all its stakeholders.

Within the field of knowledge management, there exist two quite distinct and widely accepted types of knowledge: tacit and explicit. Tacit knowledge is knowledge that is hard to encode and communicate. It is ephemeral and transitory and "cannot be resolved into information or itemized in the manner characteristic of information." Further, tacit knowledge is personal, context-specific, and hard to formalize. Toward the other end of the scale, explicit knowledge is exactly that kind of knowledge that can be encoded and is transmittable in language, once again via the conduit metaphor. It is explicit knowledge that most current knowledge management practices try to, and indeed are able to, capture, acquire, create, leverage, retain, codify, store, transfer, and share.

Characteristics of knowledge:

■ Assumptions: This is the knowledge that individuals take for granted. Assumptions can come in the form of any of the previously described categories and may refer to things that have occurred in the past or present or can be fairly safely predicted as going to happen in the future. Explicit assumptions are those that are consciously adopted by the analyst, are well understood, and are shared. Implicit assumptions are those that individuals in the analysis process do not consciously elicit, share, or articulate and may not even be aware of. Valuable as they are, as with perceptions and beliefs, assumptions need to be consistently and constantly challenged to reflect changing situations and a shifting competitive landscape.

■ Facts: This is verified information, something known to exist or to have occurred. Facts are unambiguously true statements and are known to be so. Facts come in any form and will be found among virtually any source of data that enters an employee's awareness or the enterprise's communication and information systems. It is surprising how few enterprises subject their collected data and information to fact checking and verification processes. This becomes even more important for strategy decision-making purposes because many of the facts about competitors and competition are time sensitive. What may be accurate today may be dangerously incorrect tomorrow.

■ Perceptions: Perceptions are impressions or opinions that fall short of being facts but are supported to some extent by underlying data or logic. These are often expressed as thoughts or opinions, which are put to test to convert them into facts, pending which have to remain as perceptions for the time being. There is nothing wrong in factoring perceptions into the analysis process, just as long as everybody knows that this is what they are. The error comes when perceptions are mistakenly regarded and treated as facts when they are not. The use of perceptions is perhaps the most exciting element to subject to subsequent analysis, especially when using scenario analysis, war-gaming, what-if analysis, and other such future-oriented techniques.

■ Beliefs: Beliefs are often drawn from a mix of facts and perceptions and commonly describe cause–effect relationships. They can be either explicit or implicit, but they too need to be subjected to verification and justification. Beliefs often color the way individuals understand their world and the way in which they think about the future. Therefore, it becomes critical in the analysis process for beliefs to be aired and made transparent to those individuals who are key parts of the process, whether these individuals are data gatherers, analysts, or decision makers.

■ Projections: Projections are composed of a mixture of assumptions, facts, perceptions and beliefs. They are justified or substantiated judgments about the future. It is again important that analysts be able to powerfully defend or justify their projections as they become a critical part of the knowledge base underlying the decisions made.

■ Synthesis: Having identified the type of knowledge in place, the analyst can proceed with greater confidence toward a high-quality output. Qualified inputs are then subjected to the real heart of analysis—the thinking processes, sifting, synthesis, induction, deduction, abduction, experimentation, mathematical conceptualization, experimentation, research, application of methods, techniques, and a vast array of other activities all designed to generate unique and actionable insights.

Knowledge is a reasoning unit of cognition that creates awareness based on facts, rules, coherent inferences, and well-defined methods. Knowledge provides a point of reference, a standard for analyzing data, information, and concepts.

1.7.1.6 Intelligence

Intelligence requires the ability to sense the environment, to make decisions, and to control action. Higher levels of intelligence may include the ability to recognize objects and events, to present knowledge in a world model, and to reason about the plan for the future. In advanced forms, intelligence provides the capacity to perceive and understand, to choose wisely, and to act successfully under a large variety of circumstances as to survive, prosper, and reproduce in a complex and often hostile environment.

Intelligence is thought or mental processing capacities:

■ Learning: Pattern recognition, memorizing, recalling, correcting mistakes, sense-making
■ Conceptualizing: Modeling, prioritizing, categorizing
■ Analytical thinking: Analyzing, interpretation, understanding, scenario playing, evaluating
■ Critical thinking: Logic, reasoning
■ Creative thinking: Imaging, imagining, supposing, hypothesizing, simulating
■ Quick thinking
■ Performing: Reading, speaking, music, physical activities, etc.
■ Problem solving, decision making, judging
■ Affective thinking: emotion handling

1.7.1.7 Wisdom

Wisdom means more than being cultured and well educated; it implies an ethical obligation to improve society and an attitude of caring. While intelligence is related to action, wisdom is related to options and how to judge what we should do. Therefore, wisdom is making (human) sense of data, communication, information, knowledge, and intelligence, and it is composed of values and vision.

Characteristics of wisdom:

- reasoning ability (has the unique ability to look at a problem or situation and solve it; has good problem-solving ability; has a logical mind)
- expeditious use of information (is experienced; seeks out information, especially details; learns and remembers and gains information from past mistakes or successes)
- sagacity (considers advice; understands people through dealing with a variety of people; feels he or she can always learn from other people; is fair)
- learning from ideas and environment (attaches importance to ideas; looks at different perspectives; learns from other people's mistakes)
- judgment (acts within own physical and intellectual limitations; is sensible; has good judgment at all times; thinks before acting or making decisions)
- perspicacity (can offer solutions that are on the side of right and truth; is able to see through things—read between the lines; has the ability to understand and interpret his or her environment)

Wisdom is a pragmatic unit of cognition that generates volition—a chosen way of acting and communicating. Wisdom is the process of choosing ordered routines, intended to achieve success and eliminate obstacles.

1.8 SMACT Technologies

This book focuses on the extended set of SMACT (social media, mobile technologies, analytics, and cloud computing) technologies.

1. Analytics Technologies: This involves decision making, decision-support systems and analytics.
2. Cloud Technologies: This is a model of technology and Internet-based services in real time or on-demand. According to the National Institute of Standards and Technology (USA), cloud computing is a model that allows access to the ubiquitous network upon request from a shared pool of configurable resources (e.g., networks, servers, storage, applications, and services) that can be rapidly provisioned and released with minimal management effort or interaction with the service provider. The concept involves use anywhere and platform

independent applications through the Internet without being installed on personal computers or organizations. Application providers develop, store, perform maintenance, update, and provide backup and scaling, which allows a reduction of costs through new business models. The concept of cloud computing includes among others the concept of Software as a Service (SaaS), there is no need to purchase software license usage, being paid a value for the resources used and/or by the use of time. The cloud services further include Platform as a Service (PaaS), for example, an application framework; and Infrastructure as a Service (IaaS), which provides technical infrastructure components such as storage, CPU, memory, and network.

3. Big Data Technologies: This is a new phenomenon associated with increased volume of data as a result of the Internet, social networks, and mobile devices. This technology allows data to be captured and interpreted in order to enable companies to have access to details of their operations, so as to make strategic decisions, including intelligence on solutions based on analysis of large volumes of data.

4. Web Technologies: This involves Web 1.0, 2.0, 3.0, Mobile, and Semantic Web.

5. Social Media Technologies: Social media is a new disruptive revolution causing rapid change in the mode of business communication. Businesses must explore and evaluate these media to improve their marketing, sales, customer service, and brand reputation. Smart devices (smartphones, iPads, BlackBerries) are becoming a necessity for sales and field service personnel in many organizations; the bring-your-own-device (BYOD) model is supported by many businesses; and access to internal networks and applications are provided on these devices.

6. Mobile Computing Technologies: Mobile technologies bring new business models for companies and offer opportunities for growth and new working methods. There are innumerable possibilities for using mobile devices as they allow access to information in real time. Examples of these technologies include laptops or notebooks, palmtops or PDAs, smartphones, and GPS (global positioning system) devices. These mobile devices allow you to perform a set of activities that is increasingly important for businesses and for the individual: sending high-definition photos, videos, PowerPoint presentations, and messages; making information updates, making payments, consulting balances and statements, and managing the contact list and calendar; and accessing and sending e-mails quickly and practicing and allowing access to information anywhere, anytime.

7. Internet of Things Technologies: In our business environment, more objects are becoming embedded with sensors and are gaining the ability to communicate. The resulting information networks promise to create new business models, improve business processes and reduce costs and risks. Internet of Things (IoT) is a network of systems, equipment and devices capable of

acquiring and processing information that can be shared using the Internet communication protocol. These technological implications will lead to new business opportunities along with new risks for companies and for society, as they combine the global reach of the Internet with the ability to control the physical world, including machines and plants. The technology will also radically transform work processes due to new interactions between people and machines.

1.9 Summary

After exploring the VUCA (Volatility, Uncertainty, Complexity, and Ambiguity) nature of the business ecosystem, the chapter looked at the characteristics and the significant social, organizational, business and technology trends in the market. It then dealt with the characteristics of the digital economy. It introduced the intelligence maturity model consisting of the following six stages: data, communication, information, knowledge, intelligence and wisdom.

Chapter 2

Aligning Business and IT Strategy

As stated in the preface, continued alignment of IT strategy with business is essential because that helps in establishing and reinforcing the specific SMACT technologies that are significant for addressing the *nonfunctional* requirements of smart enterprises. Strategic management, as the process of business strategy formulation and strategy implementation, is concerned with establishing goals and directions and developing and carrying out plans to achieve those goals. As organizations evolve, so do their strategies and strategic management practices. In recent years, information technology (IT) has become increasingly important in strategic management. IT and IT-enabled systems are now indispensable in supporting business strategies.

The value of information and knowledge has far surpassed that of physical goods. Information resources have become a key differentiator of successful businesses. Companies that manage information well are more likely to maintain a competitive advantage against their peers. Because information has become a major force in driving business activities, every business is in the information business.

In the early days, IT's contribution to the organization was largely information provision, monitoring and control. IT and information systems (IS) are now integrated in almost every aspect of business, from planning to analysis and design, operations management, and strategic decision making. Even for those businesses not in information industries, information plays a vital role in supporting their business functions, from strategizing to routine operations.

IT and IS have experienced dramatic changes in the last few decades. Their major role in business has shifted from tools to support "back-office" operations to an integrated part of business strategies and the maintenance of core competencies. Strategic management, as the process of business strategy formulation and strategy implementation, is concerned with establishing goals and directions and developing and carrying out plans to achieve those goals. As organizations evolve, so do their strategies and strategic management practices.

2.1 Business Strategy

2.1.1 Evolution of Strategy Management

Strategic management is concerned with managerial decisions and actions that determine the long-term prosperity of the organization. An organization must have a clear strategy, and its strategy must be carefully developed and implemented to match its resources and environment in the pursuit of its organizational goals. Two meanings behind the often-used term *strategy* are the ideational content of strategy and the process of formulating this strategy. The former refers to the array of options that one uses to compete and survive, and the latter refers to the planning that leads to the construction of the strategic plan. Thus, IT-enabled strategic management addresses the role IT plays in strategy content options and priorities, strategy formulation processes, and strategy implementation processes. Strategic management focuses on identifying the direction of an organization and on designing and instituting major changes needed to gear the organization toward moving in the established direction. The presentation and approach in this subsection has been adopted from Z. Tang and B. Walters (2009).

Early research in strategic management started in the 1950s, with leading researchers such as Peter Drucker, Alfred Chandler, and Philip Selznick. Drucker pioneered the theory of management by objectives (MBO). He is also one of the first to have recognized the dramatic changes IT brought to management. He predicted in the 1960s the rise of knowledge workers in the information age. Alfred Chandler recognized the importance of a corporate-level strategy that gives a business its structure and direction; as he put it, *structure follows strategy*. Philip Selznick established the ground work of matching a company's internal attributes with external factors.

In the 1970s, theories of strategic management primarily focused on growth, market share, and portfolio analysis. A long-term study aimed at understanding the Profit Impact of Marketing Strategies (PIMS) was carried out from the 1960s to the 1970s. The study concluded that as a result of economies of scale, a company's rate of profit is positively correlated with its market share. As companies pursued larger market share, a number of growth strategies—such as horizontal integration, vertical integration, diversification, franchises, mergers and acquisitions, and joint ventures—were developed. As will be discussed later, those strategies are even more widely used today with the facilitation of information and networking technologies. Another shifting of strategic focus occurring in the 1970s was the move from sales orientation toward customer orientation. Theodore Levitt argued that businesses should start with the customer proposition. Rather than creating a product and then trying to sell it to customers, the right approach is to find out how to create value for customers.

In the 1980s, strategic management theories were largely geared toward gaining competitive advantages. Michael Porter proposed a number of very influential strategic analysis models, such as the Five Forces model of competition, the value chain, and generic competitive strategies. Porter suggested that businesses need to choose either a strategy of cost leadership (with lowest cost), product differentiation, or market focus. Adopting one of Porter's generic strategies helps a company to avoid the so-called stuck-in-the-middle problem. Many of Porter's ideas have been implemented in modern corporate strategic management frameworks.

Strategic IS applications, such as supply-chain management, are based on efficient value chain management and forming strategic alliances to maintain competitive advantages.

R. Lester suggested that companies sustain their strategic positions in the market by following seven best practices: continuously improving products and services, breaking down barriers between functional areas, flattening organizational hierarchies, strengthening relationships with customers and suppliers, effectively using technology, having a global orientation, and enhancing human resource quality. Various information technologies have been used to support those best practices.

G. Hamel and C. K. Prahalad popularized the idea of core competencies. They argued that companies should devote their resources to a few things that they can do better than the competition and relegate non-core business operations to business partners. This laid the foundation for outsourcing, which has grown in popularity since the late 1990s. The wide spread use of network and information technologies has reduced the time and geographic barriers of outsourcing business functions to other companies.

Reengineering, also known as business process redesign, calls for fundamental changes in the way business is carried out. Traditional companies are organized around functional business areas, which often leads to limited communication and cooperation, as well as redundancy due to functional overlap. M. Hammer and J. Champy's book *Reengineering the Corporation* makes a convincing case for restructuring business resources around whole business processes rather than functional tasks. IT and IS have become both an impetus and a facilitator for reengineering projects and efforts.

In the 1990s, researchers increasingly recognized the importance of customer relationship management. Computer and network technologies have played a key role in making customer relationship management efficient and effective. Along the line of improving value to the customers, mass customization provides competitive advantages. Reaching and custom serving individual customers are only feasible with the proliferation of information and communication technologies.

Peter Senge, in his book *The Fifth Discipline*, popularized the concept of the learning organization. The rationale in creating a learning organization is that the business environment has become more dynamic and complex. Companies must have the ability to learn continuously and adapt to the changing environment. People in a learning organization need to continuously expand their capacity to become more productive or to maintain their level of competency.

Recently, many researchers have recognized that organizations are complex adaptive systems in which multiple agents set their own goals, share information, collaborate, and interact with one another (V. Kale, 2017).

2.1.2 Sustaining Competitive Advantage

Competitive advantage is an advantage that a firm has over its competitors, allowing it to generate greater sales or margins and/or retains more customers than its competition. There can be many types of competitive advantages, including the firm's cost structure, product offerings, distribution network and customer support and information systems. Different organizations evolve and adopt different strategies to seek competitive advantage, and different strategies in turn result in different competitive advantages. Competitive advantages give a company an edge over its rivals and an ability to generate greater value for the firm and its shareholders. The more sustainable the competitive advantage, the more difficult it is for competitors to neutralize the advantage.

Competitive advantage can be defined as *a product or service that an organization's customers value more highly than similar offerings from its competitors*. Competitive advantages are typically temporary as competitors often seek ways to duplicate the competitive advantage. In order to stay ahead of competition, organizations have to continually renew or develop new competitive advantages.

Competitive advantage is the favorable position an organization seeks in order to be more profitable than its competitors. It involves communicating a greater perceived value to a target market than its competitors can provide. This can be achieved through many avenues, including offering a better quality product or service, lowering prices, and increasing marketing efforts. Sustainable competitive advantage refers to maintaining a favorable position over the long term, which can help boost a company's image in the marketplace, its valuation, and its future earning potential. Porter maintains that achieving competitive advantage requires a firm to make a choice about the type and scope of its competitive advantage.

There are two main types of competitive advantages:

■ Comparative advantage, or cost advantage, is a firm's ability to produce a good or service at a lower cost than its competitors, which gives the firm the ability sell its goods or services at a lower price than its competition or to generate a larger margin on sales.

■ Differential advantage is created when a firm's products or services differ from its competitors and are seen as better than a competitor's products by customers.

Organizations can analyze, identify and develop competitive advantages using tools such as Porter's Five Forces, three generic strategies, and value chains.

2.1.2.1 Competitive Priorities

Competitive priorities represent a critical dimension that a process or value chain must focus on to satisfy both the current and future customers. There are four basic competitive priorities:

1. *Cost*: In most business environments, cost is the important competitive priority as lowering price will facilitate gaining customers and increasing market share. To reduce cost, operations strategy should focus on achieving efficiency by redesigning the product, reengineering the processes, addressing supply chain issues, and exploring global opportunities.
2. *Quality*: Competing on the basis of quality implies that the company wants to sell products and services to a niche market. For example, a small private airline has a fleet of luxury planes to serve corporate CEOs. If a company uses quality as a competitive priority, then it should focus on two aspects of quality:
   - *Top quality* is those characteristics of a product and or service that create an impression of superiority. This may need superior product with greater tolerances, demanding requirements, high aesthetics, and personal attention.
   - *Consistent quality* is producing products and or services that meet customer requirements and expectations on continual basis. For example, a luxury private airline will be always punctual in picking up the clients, flying the plane, and arriving at the destination.
3. *Time*: For many firms, time is a competitive priority. Especially as the product life cycle is becoming short, it is imperative to bring out products and services ahead of your competition. There are three approaches to time-based competition:
   - *Delivery speed* is how quick a customer's order can be filled. The time between the receipt of a customer's order and filling it is called *lead time*. To compete on delivery speed, one must try to design the order fulfillment process so that the lead time can be reduced. Sometimes companies may keep inventory or cushion or back-up capacities to compete on delivery speed.
   - *On-time delivery* is meeting the promised schedule. This could be important for an airline. Also it is important for customers who are working on just-in-time inventory basis.

- *Development speed* is important for those companies where it is important to bring in new products or new versions of products before the competition. For example, Intel and AMD use this competitive priority. Whoever can introduce the newest computer chip in the market gains market share.
4. *Flexibility*: Competitive priority based on flexibility allows a company to react to changing customer needs quickly and efficiently. A company may compete based on flexibility using one or more of the following strategies:
   - *Customization* is catering to individual customers' needs. For example, a custom home builder builds different houses for different customers. Customization generally implies that the products and/or services are produced in low volume and have a higher degree of complexity. This requires that the organization has people with higher skills and who should be able to work closely with customers.
   - *Variety* is producing products and or services with wide array of choices. Variety is different from customization, in the sense that customization is unique to each customer, while variety could entail different features in the product but the product is not unique.
   - *Volume flexibility* is the ability to produce in smaller or larger volumes within the confines of production parameters. The companies that use volume flexibility as a competitive priority must design their processes so that set-up cost is minimal.

2.1.2.2 Porter's Five Forces Model

M. Porter developed a model for describing competitive advantage for organizations. As per the model, there are two competitive threats to any organization. The first one is threats from external sources, such as competition from macro environment (government policy changes, competitors with products and services that offer similar value for money to the customers). The second threat constitutes threats from buyers' and suppliers' bargaining power and easy adoption of products and services (easy entry barrier).

Michael Porter's Five Forces Model is a useful tool to assist in assessing the competition in an industry and determining the relative attractiveness of that industry. In order to do an industry analysis, a firm must analyze five competitive forces:

1. *Rivalry of competitors within its industry*: Rivalries exist in the form of price wars, features made available in rival products and services, and time taken to introduce new competitive products in the market. These conditions become prevalent because of rivalry among existing players and are compounded by too many players without much product differentiation, existing monopoly,

operating in a niche market, lack of core capabilities to expand in other sectors, and high cost of exit. When Common Rail Diesel Injection (CRDI) was introduced for diesel vehicles in India, Hyundai took the market lead as it took quite some time for its competitors to introduce a similar vehicle.

2. *Threat of new entrants into an industry and its markets*: Any sunrise industry witnesses a plethora of companies offering similar products and services till the markets gets flooded with "me too" products.

   The conditions acting as deterrent for a new entrant are
   a. limited access to raw materials for new entrants
   b. high brand loyalty with existing suppliers
   c. long-serving contracts for existing suppliers, which make it legally difficult for customers to switch to others
   d. intellectual property rights owned by existing players for existing products
   e. high investment cost

3. *Threat posed by substitute products that might capture market share*: The established product, for example, has a direct threat from the substitutes and its market potential reduces drastically. In the automobile industry, when engine blocks made out of cast iron were substituted by aluminum alloy–based engines, many ancillary industries dealing in making cast iron faced closure. The travel industry lost some of its market potential with the development of videoconferencing, which could reduce the geographical distance through technology. Sometimes the substitutes come in different forms and are difficult to recognize. Such substitutes can threaten the market potential of existing established products. To counter the threat of substitutes, existing products need to create Unique Selling Propositions (USPs) and provide features which will offer value to the customers compared to substitutes

   Goods manufactured by India and China have been produced at costs much lower than that of developed countries and have substantially eroded market share of existing players in almost all sectors (pharmaceutical, construction, household, electronics, and automobiles, to name a few).

4. *Bargaining power of customers*: With more information available on products and services, customers can pick and choose their service provider after making a thorough comparison of available information. Also, buyers are better placed compared to suppliers or vendors when the buyers can buy in large volume and have several options to either substitute the product or vendor (Porter 1979). When the products are not critical for a customer's business model, some of the buyers also can integrate backward to manufacture products themselves and as a result can be better placed to negotiate with present manufacturers. Car manufacturers such as Maruti Suzuki have started

manufacturing floor mats and other accessories, which were earlier supplied by other manufacturers, often at a higher cost. As a result, Maruti Suzuki is better placed to negotiate with these manufacturers on price and quality.

5. *Bargaining power of suppliers*: The word *suppliers* indicates all the sources of inputs that are required to produce the company's product or to deliver a service. The supplier power can get higher when the supplier market is monopolistic in nature. This happens when one or very few suppliers or the customers have limited bargaining power because of inequality in supply-and-demand conditions. Also, suppliers' bargaining power can be higher when the costs of changing to a new supplier are high or when the suppliers have a cartel and exercise monopoly in pricing decisions.

2.1.2.3 Porter's Framework of Generic Strategies

To survive and succeed, a business must develop and implement strategies to effectively counter the above five competitive forces. The most widely known strategy framework is the three generic strategies introduced by M. Porter. Subsequently, Porter added a further aspect to his model: whether the strategic target is industrywide or focused on a particular segment.

The three generic competitive strategies are

1. *Cost leadership* strategy, which dictates that the firm construct efficient and appropriately scaled facilities, pursue cost reduction based on the experience curve and tightly control direct costs and overheads. Even though lower cost relative to competitors is the major strategic target, a watchful eye must be placed on quality, service, and customer satisfaction. Achieving overall cost leadership yields above-average returns due to the lower costs, while competitors have competed away their profits.

2. *Differentiation* strategy dictates that the firm creates a product offering that is perceived industrywide as being unique. The differentiation can take many forms: design, brand, technology, features, customer service, dealer network, and many more. The firm differentiates itself along several dimensions. While costs are not allowed to be ignored, they are not the primary strategic target. If differentiation is achieved, above-average returns can be yielded due to the defensible position it creates. Differentiation has proven to be a viable strategy resulting in brand loyalty and lower sensitivity to price:
   - margins that avoid the urge for a low-cost position
   - decreased buyer power due to a lack of comparable alternatives
   - entry barriers for competitors

3. *Focus* strategy dictates that the firm caters to a particular segment only (e.g., one particular buyer group, geographic market). It bases its above-average returns on serving a particular target very well, that is, more efficiently than competitors competing more broadly. A focus strategy either achieves

differentiation by better meeting the needs and wants of the particular target it focuses on, or it manages to maintain lower costs in serving this target, or both. The differentiation or lower cost position is not achieved for the entire market but only for the narrow market target.

Although initially, cost leadership and differentiation were regarded as being incompatible, subsequently hybrid competitive strategies combining the above strategies were explored. While the generic hybrid strategies (high relative differentiation/high relative cost position, and low relative differentiation/low relative cost position) were only ascribed an average competitive position, the combination of high relative differentiation position and a low relative cost position was considered powerful. The strategy resulting from such a hybrid combination of differentiation (customization) and cost leadership (standardization) is called *mass customization*.

The above strategies can be expanded to an extended set of five generic strategies enabled by IT:

1. Cost Leadership: Organizations can use information systems to fundamentally shift the cost of doing business or reduce the costs of business processes or/and lower the costs of engaging customers or suppliers, that is, using online business-to-consumer (B2C) and business-to-business (B2B) models and e-procurement systems to reduce operating costs.

2. Differentiation: Organizations can use information systems to develop differentiated features or/and to reduce competitors' differentiation advantages, that is, using online live chatting systems and social networks to better understand and serve customers; using technology to create infomediaries to offer value-added service and improve customers' stickiness to the website/business; applying advanced and established measures for online operations to offline practices (i.e., more accurate and systematic ways of measuring efficiency and effectiveness of advertising).

3. Innovation: Organizations can use information systems to identify and create (or assist in creating) new products and services or/and to develop new/niche markets or/and to radically change business processes via automation (i.e., using digital modeling and simulation of product design to reduce the time and cost to the market). They also can work on new initiatives of establishing pure online businesses/operations. Everyone is connected via personal computers, laptops, and other mobile devices through cabled Internet or wireless networks or mobile networks; there are plenty of opportunities to co-create with customers, external partners, and internal people. The Internet and telecommunications networks provide better capabilities and opportunities for innovation. There are a large number of component parts on the networks that are very expensive or extremely disparate before the establishment of the networks, and organizations could combine or recombine components/parts on the networks to create new innovations.

4. Growth (Including Mergers and Acquisitions): Organizations can use information systems to expand domestic and international operations or/and to diversify and integrate into other products and services, that is, establishing global intranet and global operation platform; and establishing an omni-channel strategy to gain growth (omni-channel strategy looks at leveraging advantages of both online (or digital) and offline (or non-digital) channels).

5. Strategic Alliance: Organizations can use information systems to create and enhance relations with partners via applications, such as developing virtual organizations and inter-organizational information systems.

Supplementary strategies enabled by information systems (IS) are

1. raising barriers to entry through improving operations or/and optimizing/flattening organizational structure by increasing the amount or the complexity of the technology (for example Google's search engine and P&G's digitization strategy to make it the world's most technologically enabled firm)

2. building switching costs via extranets and proprietary software applications (for example Amazon's user-friendly and useful B2C website)

3. locking in customers or suppliers by enhancing relations and building valuable new relationships via customer/partner relationship management systems/applications (i.e., providing a bank's customers with multiple touch points via telephones, Internet, fax machines, videos, mobile devices, ATMs, branches, the bank's agents)

2.1.2.4 Porter's Value Chain

The value-chain approach views an organization as a chain, or series, of processes, and it classifies an organization's activities into two categories: primary activities (i.e., inbound logistics, operations, sales and marketing, customer service, outbound logistics) and secondary/support activities (i.e., administration, human resources, technology, procurement). The value chain helps an organization to determine the value of its business processes for its customers. The model highlights specific activities in the business where competitive strategies can be best applied.

Value chain is an important concept and tool that can help a business identify competitive advantage and opportunities for strategic use of information systems. By creating/adding value and thus creating competitive advantages, information systems can contribute to each part of an organization's value chain and extended value chain (including interactions/ties with external partners and strategic alliances):

■ By leveraging on the Internet technologies; organizations could also create a value web or a hub structure, both of which could improve the efficiency and the effectiveness of value chain and supply chain.

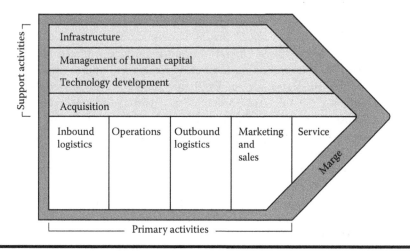

Figure 2.1 Porter's value chain.

- By digitally connecting customers, suppliers, and partners and by reducing the information gaps/errors along the chain (especially demand and supply).
- By bettering communication, cooperation, and collaboration.

Figure 2.1 shows Porter's value chain.

2.1.2.4.1 Core Activities

Core activities include inbound logistics (receiving), operations and manufacturing, outbound logistics (shipping), marketing and sales, and customer service. These activities may differ widely depending on the unique requirements of the industry in which a company operates, although the basic concepts hold in most organizations.

a. Inbound Logistics Activities: Inbound logistics involves the business activities associated with receiving and stocking raw materials, parts, and products. For example, inbound logistics at Amazon.com involves not only the receipt of books, e-book readers, and various other products for sale, but also the receipt of packaging materials and shipping labels. Shippers deliver these products to Amazon.com, where employees unwrap the packages and stock the products in the company's warehouse or directly route the products to operations in order to fill open orders. Amazon.com can automatically update inventory levels at the point of delivery, allowing purchasing managers access to up-to-date information related to inventory levels and reorder points. Inbound logistics activities are a crucial part of the procure-to-pay business process, as these activities enable the company to efficiently and effectively fill customer orders.

b. Operations and Manufacturing Activities: Once the components have been stocked in inventory, operations and manufacturing activities transform the inputs into outputs. Operations and manufacturing can involve such activities as order processing (e.g., at Amazon.com) and/or manufacturing or assembly processes (e.g., at Dell) that transform raw materials and/ or component parts into end products (i.e., the make-to-stock and make-to-order business processes). Companies such as Dell utilize Web-based information systems to allow customers to enter orders online. This information is used to coordinate the manufacturing of a customized personal computer in which the component parts are gathered and assembled to create the end product. During this process, inventory levels from inbound logistics are verified; if the appropriate inventory exists, workers pick the components from existing supplies and build the product to the customer's specifications. When components are picked, items are deducted from inventory; once the product is assembled, inventory levels for the final product are updated.

c. Outbound Logistics Activities: The activities associated with outbound logistics mirror those of inbound logistics. Instead of involving the receipt of raw materials, parts, and products, outbound logistics focuses on the distribution of end products within the order-to-cash business process. For example, outbound logistics at Amazon.com involves the shipping of books that customers have ordered. Orders that have been processed by operations are forwarded to outbound logistics, which picks the products from inventory and coordinates shipment to the customer. At that point, items are packaged and deducted from the company's inventory, and an invoice is created that will be sent to the customer. Amazon.com can automatically update sales information at the point of distribution, allowing managers to view inventory and revenue information in real time.

d. Marketing and Sales Activities: Marketing and sales activities are associated primarily with the pre-sales (i.e., before the sale) activities of the company. These activities include the creation of marketing literature, communication with potential and existing customers, and pricing of goods and services. Most companies support the business activity of marketing and sales by creating e-brochures, building pages on Facebook, or communicating on other social media such as Twitter. Many companies, especially those focused on selling products or services to the end consumer (e.g., passenger airlines such as United or online retailers such as Amazon.com), use information systems to update pricing information and/or schedules. This information is entered directly into the pricing and scheduling systems, allowing the information to become immediately accessible throughout the organization and to end consumers through the organization's website.

e. Customer Service Activities: Whereas marketing and sales focus on pre-sales activities, customer service focuses on post-sales (i.e., after the sale) activities.

Customers may have questions and need help from a customer service representative. For most companies, such as Amazon.com, utilizing information systems to provide customer service is essential, especially given the vast number of products offered. These applications allow customers to search for and download information related to the products that they have purchased or the purchase itself. For example, on Amazon.com, customers can view their order status or can view and print invoices of current and past orders. Similarly, customers can find additional information and support about the Amazon Kindle or other digital products. Rather than calling a customer service representative, customers can easily find the needed information through a self-service customer support application. Information systems also enable customer service representatives to quickly locate information about products or services offered.

2.1.2.4.2 Support Activities

Support activities are business activities that enable the primary activities to take place. Support activities include administrative activities, infrastructure, human resources, technology development, and procurement.

a. Administrative Activities: Administrative activities focus on the processes and decision making that orchestrate the day-to-day operations of an organization, particularly those processes that span organizational functions and levels. Administration includes systems and processes from virtually all functional areas—accounting, finance, marketing, operations, and so on—at all levels of an organization.

b. Infrastructure Activities: Infrastructure refers to the hardware and software that must be implemented to provide the necessary components that facilitate both primary and support activities. For example, an order entry application requires that employees who enter orders have a computer and the necessary software to accomplish their business objectives. In turn, the computer must be connected via the network to a database containing the order information so that the order can be saved and recalled later for processing.

c. Human Resource Activities: Human resource activities encompass all business activities associated with employee management, such as hiring, interview scheduling, payroll, and benefits management. Human resource activities are classified as support activities since the primary activities cannot be accomplished without the employees to perform them. In other words, all the primary activities rely on human resource–related business activities.

d. Technology Development Activities: Technology development includes the design and development of applications that support the primary business activities so as to improve products and/or services. If you are planning on pursuing a career in the field of management information systems (MIS), you will frequently participate in activities related to the development or acquisition of new applications and systems. Technology development can involve a wide array of responsibilities, such as the selection of packaged software or the design and development of custom software to meet a particular business need. Many companies are leveraging the technology development business activity to build Internet, intranet, extranet, or mobile applications to support a wide variety of primary business activities.

e. Procurement Activities: Procurement refers to the purchasing of goods and services that are required as inputs to the primary activities. Procurement receives, approves, and processes requests for goods and services from the primary activities and coordinates the purchase of those items. Allowing each functional area to send out purchase orders can create problems for companies, such as maintaining relationships with more suppliers than necessary and not taking advantage of volume discounts. The procurement business activity can leverage information systems by accumulating purchase orders from the different functional areas within the organization and combining multiple purchase orders containing the same item into a single purchase order. This facilitates negotiating volume discounts and allows the primary activities to concentrate on running the business rather than adding to their workload.

2.1.2.4.3 Service Activities

Originally, the value-chain framework was developed for analyzing the value-adding activities of manufacturing industries, but it can also be used to understand service-based industries. Many of the processes within service industries are similar to processes performed in manufacturing industries (e.g., customer service, sales, and support). However, whereas manufacturing industries deal with physical products, service industries deal primarily with information-based products. As a result, activities such as inbound logistics and outbound logistics are often less important in the service sector. Likewise, in the manufacturing sector, operations include the physical handling of goods when transforming them from raw materials or components to finished products; in contrast, operations in the service sector typically encompass the manipulation of data and information. For example, in the service sector, a finished product equates to a closed file such as a bank loan that has been issued, an insurance claim that has been filed, or an investment that has been made. As a result, optimizing the value-adding activities in the services sector does typically not include eliminating physical bottlenecks or improving inventory management but enhancing the flow of information.

2.2 Information Technology and Information Systems (IT/IS)

Strategic management and IT/IS have progressed in their separate paths, but there are many instances where their paths have converged. The motivation of

IS has shifted from efficiency to effectiveness and, in the Internet era, to value creation. On one hand, IT is playing a more active and important role in strategic management. On the other hand, strategic management concerns have influenced the development of IS. In many cases, the theories and principles of strategic management led the way for IS development. IT and IS, in turn, have made it more feasible for those theories and principles to be practiced in businesses. The presentation and approach in the next couple of subsections is adapted from Z. Tang and B. Walters (2009).

2.2.1 Evolution of IT

The short history of computer IT development can be divided into three eras:

■ The mainframe era from the 1950s to the 1970s.
■ The microcomputer era from the 1980s to the early 1990s.
■ The Internet era from the 1990s to the present.

The mainframe era was characterized by centralized computing, where all computing needs were serviced by powerful computers at a computer center. The proliferation of microcomputers led to decentralized computing. Computing resources become readily accessible to more users. This is a period that witnessed improved user performance and decision-making quality. When computer networks became pervasive in the Internet era, decentralized computing evolved to distributed computing, where computing resources are located in multiple sites, as in decentralized systems, but all of the computing resources are connected through computer networks. People in the Internet era are far more empowered than in previous eras, because they have access not only to technology tools as before but also to shared knowledge from others. The value of a network increases with the square of the number of users connected to the network. Assuming bilateral interaction, the wide accessibility of the Internet has created numerous opportunities for businesses and has brought fundamental changes to the way businesses operate.

One of the milestones in the computer industry was the arrival of the IBM System/360 in 1964 running the same operating systems and using the same peripherals. Thus, companies could start with a lower configuration model and with increasing requirements, expand capacity with more powerful models without the need to replace system software and peripheral components. Easy adoption through inter-changeability of hardware and software prompted significant growth of computer system usage in businesses in the 1960s and 1970s (with later models such as the System/370). IBM first started unbundling software from hardware by selling software separate from its computer in 1969. That set the stage for the launch of an independent software industry. The fast growth of packaged software applications, in turn, spurred the growth of computer hardware.

The next major event in the computer industry was the birth of personal computers (PCs) in the mid-1970s. Intel introduced the first semi-conductor microchip (the Intel 4004) in 1971. However,

PCs were not widespread until the early 1980s, when IBM launched its standardized PC (known as the IBM PC). The IBM PC became "Machine of the Year," taking the place of traditional "Man of the Year" on the cover of *Time Magazine* in 1983. Other computer vendors jumped on the IBM PC bandwagon by producing IBM-compatible PCs. During the decade of the 1980s, the number of PCs grew more than 100-fold to over 100 million.

Low-cost computing changed organizational computing architecture from centralized computing to distributed computing systems in the 1980s. Once scarce and expensive, computer systems are now abundant and inexpensive because of the availability of desktop computers, laptop computers, and even handheld computing devices enabled by the relentless progress dictated by Moore's Law. The continued growth of the PC industry is driven by the well-known Moore's Law, which stipulates that the number of transistors per silicon chip doubles roughly every 18 months; hence, the corresponding performance of the central processing unit—the brain of micro-computers. Moore's Law has remained valid for the last six decades. The power of exponential growth resulted in dramatic cost and performance improvement of computer hardware.

In the history of IT, the 1990s is perhaps best known as the decade of Internet booming. The Internet started as the US Department of Defense's ARPAnet, with the aim of creating a distributed computer network that could withstand a nuclear attack. In the 1970s and 1980s, the Internet was used mainly by academics and scientists and was not accessible largely to the general public because its use, although open, required substantial learning of specific application protocols. Two major events led to the explosive growth of the Internet:

1. The first was the development of the World Wide Web (WWW or the Web) by Tim Berners-Lee, a researcher at the CERN in Switzerland in 1990. The Web made it possible to link information resources all over the world on the Internet. Users could retrieve information without knowing the location of the information by simply following the hyperlinks (or links).
2. The second was the arrival of graphic browsers. Initial access to the WWW was text-based; hence, its richness in content and its usability were limited. The WWW took off after 1993 when the first graphic Web browser, Mosaic, was released by the National Center for Supercomputing Applications (NCSA) at the University of Illinois at Urbana Champaign. The ensuing Internet growth was unprecedented in the history of technology development. Internet users grew from a few thousand to more than 300 million during the 1990s. As of June 2016, there were more than 3.6 billion Internet users worldwide (www.internetworldstats.com/stats.htm). The Internet provides a low-cost way of connecting virtually everyone in modern society to an open and shared common network.

Since the late 1990s, mobile computing based on wireless network technologies has gained much momentum. Intelligent appliances, such as cellular phones, personal digital assistants, and other handheld computing devices, have become a significant part of the IS infrastructure. IDC predicts that the number of devices connected to the Internet will surpass 20 billion by 2020. The total number of networked devices may approach 6 billion by 2012. Ubiquitous computing that allows *anytime, anyplace* access to information resources will bring dramatic changes to the business environment.

The next major development of the Web may be network intelligence through Web Services. The non-profit Internet governing organization W3C defines Web services as the programmatic interfaces for application–application communication on the Web. Web Services create a promising infrastructure to support loosely coupled, distributed and heterogeneous applications on the Internet. Applications based on Web Services can be described, published, located, and invoked over the Internet to create new products and services based on open Internet protocols such as HTTP, XML, and Simple Object Access Protocol (SOAP). The significance of Web Services is that system-to-system communications can be automated; hence, building business alliances and virtual organizations becomes much easier than with current Internet technology (V. Kale, 2017).

2.2.2 Evolution of IS

The role of business IS has evolved and expanded over the last six decades. Early systems in the 1950s and 1960s were used primarily for dealing with business transactions with associated data collection, processing, and storage. Management information systems (MIS) were developed in the 1960s to provide information for managerial support. Typical MIS are report based, with little or no decision-making support capabilities. Decision support systems (DSS) first appeared in the 1970s they offered various analytical tools, models, and flexible user interfaces for decision support at solving difficult problems, such as planning, forecasting, and scheduling. Executive support systems (ESS) are specialized DSS designed to support top-level management in strategic decision making.

A strategic information system include any type of IS that plays a key role in supporting business strategies. McFarlan's strategic grid defines four categories of IT impact: support, factory, turnaround and strategic. When the IT has a significant impact on business core strategy, core operations or both, the corresponding IS are considered strategic information systems.

The 1990s saw an increased emphasis on strategic information systems as a result of the changing competitive environment. IT and IS were developed to support business strategic initiatives. The commercialization of the Internet in the mid-1990s created an explosive growth in the Internet and Internet-based business applications. Using the Internet standards, corporations were converting their old incompatible internal networks to intranets; similarly extranets were built to link companies with their customers, suppliers, and other business partners.

IT and IS have made it possible to access vast amounts of information easily and quickly. Systems such as enterprise resource planning (ERP) give managers the ability to monitor the operation of the entire organization in real time. Executive information portals have allowed senior managers to take a much more comprehensive view of strategic management than ever before. Tools such as the balanced scorecard give a holistic view of business performance by integrating factors in multiple business functions.

In the last few years, business process management (BPM) software has been designed with the intent of closing gaps in the existing ERP deployments. As companies are increasingly faced with problems associated with incompatible functional systems from different vendors, enterprise application integration (EAI) has become an important area. BPM systems have been deployed to lower the cost and complexity of application and data integration. Another recent development is Web services enabled by standards-based protocols (such as XML, SOAP, UDDI, and WSDL). The wide acceptance of Internet protocols also led to the emergence of service-oriented architectures (SOA). SOA focus on building robust and flexible systems that provide services as required in a dynamic business process environment. Instead of being programmed in advance, services are generated, brokered, and delivered on the fly.

2.2.3 IS/IT Governance

Enterprise governance of IT/IS addresses the definition and implementation of processes, structures and relational mechanism that enable both business and IT/IS people to execute their responsibilities in support of business/IT IS alignment and the creation of value from IT/IS-enabled business investments. Enterprise governance of IT is an important enabler for business/IT IS alignment. Business/IT alignment is a complex construct, with important models developed by Henderson and Venkatraman. These models stress the importance of balancing business and IT/IS strategic and operational issues to obtain alignment. For practitioners in the field, the business/IT IS alignment concept can be translated into a cascade of business goals and IT/IS goals.

Achieving a high degree of business/IT alignment in turn will enable the achievement of business value from IT, which, by itself, will not generate value for the business. Value will only be realized when both IT and the business are involved (aligned). For practitioners, both Control Objectives for Information Technology (COBIT) and Val IT are important international best practice frameworks to realize and implement enterprise governance of IT as enablers for business/IT alignment and value creation from IT.

2.2.3.1 Alignment IT/IS with Business Strategy

IT/IS in business has evolved and has become increasingly integrated with business organizations. Strategic management now encompasses corporate strategy, functional business strategy, information strategy, and IT/IS strategy. For most businesses, their strategies form a multi-level hierarchy. At the very top is corporate strategy, which sets the direction for corporate-level decision making. Below corporate strategy, there are functional strategies, business unit strategies, and operational strategies. Building a comprehensive strategic IT/IS plan that aligns with the business strategy is essential to ensuring the success of the organization.

Henderson and Venkatraman (1993) introduced "business-IT alignment," in short "alignment," intended to support the integration of IT into business strategy. They distinguish in their classic "Strategic Alignment Model" between the business domain (consisting of "business strategy" and "business processes") and the technology domain (consisting of "IT strategy" and "IT processes," including systems development and maintenance) in an organization.

Figure 2.2 shows the schematic of the strategic alignment model.

Henderson and Venkatraman described four types of alignment:

1. Strategic Execution: Business strategy drives organizational infrastructure and processes, ultimately influencing IS infrastructure and processes.
2. Technology Transformation: Business strategy drives IT strategy, ultimately influencing IT processes.
3. Competitive Potential: Information strategy influences business strategy, ultimately influencing organizational infrastructure and processes.
4. Service Level: Information strategy influences IT infrastructure and processes.

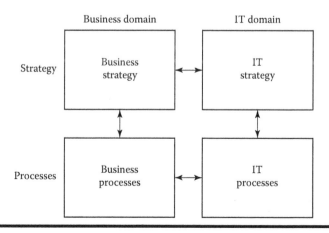

Figure 2.2 Strategic alignment model.

IT/IS alignment with business strategy is vital to achieve expected results. IT/IS alignment with business strategy can improve business performance. Measuring the degree of IT alignment has been difficult for many businesses. An IT/IS and business strategy alignment maturity model on the lines of the five-level Capacity Maturity Model (CMM) for software engineering can be proposed:

- At the base level, called *Non-existent*, there is IT alignment with business strategy. IT plays only a supportive role for operations.
- At the *Ad hoc* level, the need for IT alignment is recognized, but a systematic approach is lacking. IT supports business goals on a case-by-case basis. There is no attempt to measure the success of IT alignment.
- At the *Repeatable* level, IT alignment is considered at the enterprise level. However, it is only implemented in some business units. Limited measures of IT alignment exist.

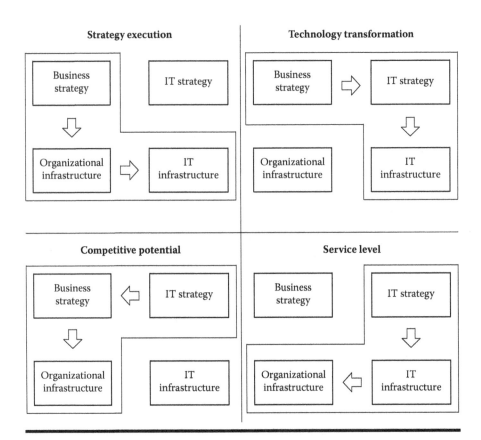

Figure 2.3 Perspectives on strategic alignment.

- At the *Defined process* level, IT alignment is systematically implemented throughout the enterprise, with appropriate policies and procedures to monitor and measure the benefits of the IT alignment.
- At the *Optimized* level, IT strategy is seamlessly aligned with business strategy at all managerial levels and in all business units. IT alignment processes have been extended to external best practices with other organizations. Measures of IT alignment and feedback mechanisms exist to ensure that IT alignment stays at this level.

Obviously, IT alignment is one of the key issues in strategic management. However, IT alignment is more than simply formulating IT strategy to fit the business strategy. Business strategy is future oriented and is subject to external forces and environmental uncertainty. IT alignment should build adaptability into IT strategy. Furthermore, for some technology companies, IT may be the driver of corporate strategy. Strategic management is concerned with the long-term survival and prosperity of organizations. As the environment changes, organizations must also adapt to maintain their viability. Organizations evolve, and so do strategies. Thus, strategic management is also a learning process. There are four basic learning behaviors in strategy formulation: natural selection, imitation, reinforcement, and best reply. In each of the four learning processes, IT and IS are becoming indispensable:

- *Natural selection* stipulates that organizations that use high-payoff strategies have competitive advantages over those using low-payoff strategies. As a result, high-payoff strategies have a better chance of being continued by surviving organizations. Determining the payoff of strategies, thus, is very important in this kind of strategic learning behavior.
- *Imitation* describes how organizations mimic the practices of successful peers in their industry. This is the cause of herding behavior in which the outcome is not clear, but organizations jump on the bandwagon, simply following what many of their peers are doing. A classic example was the dot.com bubble during the late 1990s.
- *Reinforcement* is concerned with how organizations monitor their own behaviors and favor the strategies that resulted in high payoffs in the past. In contrast to natural selection, reinforcement learning is based on one's own experience rather than others' experience.
- *Best reply* is the behavior whereby organizations formulate their strategies based on what they expect their competitors will do. Many of the popular competitive strategies, such as low-cost leadership and differentiation, fall into this category.

2.2.3.2 Aligning Business Goals and IT Goals

Figure 2.4 shows how concrete business goals can drive IT/IS goals and vice-versa. The top 10 generic business goals are listed below:

1. Improve customer orientation and service
2. Comply with external laws and regulations
3. Establish service continuity and availability
4. Manage (IT-related) business risks
5. Offer competitive products and services
6. Improve and maintain business process functionality
7. Provide a good return on investment of (IT-enabled) business investments
8. Acquire, develop, and maintain skilled and motivated people
9. Create agility in responding to changing business requirements
10. Obtain reliable and useful information for strategic decision making

The top 10 IT/IS goals are listed below:

1. Align the IT/IS strategy to the business strategy
2. Maintain the security (confidentiality, integrity, and availability) of information and processing infrastructure
3. Make sure that IT/IS services are reliable and secure
4. Provide service offerings and service levels in line with business requirements
5. Provide IT/IS compliance with laws and regulations
6. Translate business functional and control requirements in effective and efficient automated solutions
7. Deliver projects on time and on budget, meeting quality standards
8. Drive commitment and support of executive management

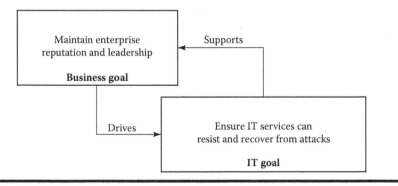

Figure 2.4   Business goals driving IT goals.

9. Improve IT/IS cost-efficiency
10. Account for and protect all IT/IS assets

Table 2.1 presents the final list of business and IT goals, categorized by their corresponding balanced scorecard (BSC) perspectives.

2.2.3.3 Aligning Business with IT/IS and Business Value from IT

The notion of IT/IS alignment with business is fundamentally important to an organization's success because the strategic alignment of business strategy and IT/IS strategies improves business performance—the relative direct impact of strategic alignment on business performance is higher compared to the direct impact of business strategy or IT strategy on business performance (Figure 2.5).

The value that IT/IS adds to the business is a function of the degree to which the IT/IS organization is aligned with the business and meets the expectations of the business. Best practices frameworks like COBIT and Val IT provide a comprehensive model to demonstrate how applying governance practices can enable the achievement of IT goals, which, in turn, enable the achievement of business goals and consequently business benefits.

2.2.3.4 Governance Frameworks

IT governance can be regarded as a business activity undertaken at high-level management that

- Ensures alignment of IT strategies with those of the business
- Ensures the responsible use of IT
- Clearly defines roles and accountabilities
- Continually monitors IT assets and projects to ensure they are performing effectively in support of the organization

IT Governance is the organizational capacity exercised by the board, executive management, and IT management to control the formulation and implementation of IT strategy and in this way ensure the fusion of business and IT. Good IT governance is the effective combination of three components:

1. What decisions have to be made (leadership): IT governance leadership relates to the setting of long-term strategies for IT and ensuring that goal alignment exists with those set by the organization that require frequent dialogue between the board of directors and the managers in the IT department.
2. Who makes them (accountability): The accountability in IT governance is the assigning of decision rights and creation of an accountability framework

Table 2.1 Business goals and the corresponding IS/IT goals

Business Goals	IT Goals
Financial perspective • Manage (IT related) business risks • Provide a good return on investment of (IT enabled) business investments • Improve financial transparency • Comply with external laws and regulations	**Corporate contribution** • Offer transparency and understanding of IT cost, benefits and risks • Provide IT compliance with laws and regulations • Account for and protect all IT assets • Drive commitment and support of executive management • Improve IT's cost-efficiency • Align the IT strategy to the business strategy
Customer perspective • Improve customer orientation and service • Establish service continuity and availability • Offer competitive products and services • Achieve cost optimization of service delivery • Create agility in responding to changing business requirements • Obtain reliable and useful information for strategic decision making	**User orientation** • Make sure that IT services are reliable and secure • Provide service offerings and service levels in line with business requirements • Translate business functional and control requirements in effective and efficient automated solutions • Accomplish proper use of applications, information and technology solutions
Internal perspective • Improve and maintain business process functionality • Improve and maintain operational and staff productivity • Enable and Manage business change • Comply with internal policies • Optimize business process costs	**Operational excellence** • Maintain the security (confidentiality, integrity and availability) of information and processing infrastructure • Deliver projects on time and on budget meeting quality standards • Optimize the IT infrastructure, resources and capabilities • Provide IT agility (in responding to changing business needs) • Seamlessly integrate applications and technology solutions into business processes
Learning and growth perspective • Acquire, develop and maintain skilled and motivated people • Identify, enable and manage product and business innovation	**Future orientation** • Acquire, develop and maintain IT skills that respond to the IT strategy • Acquire knowledge and expertise in emerging technologies for business innovation and optimization • Ensure that IT demonstrates continuous improvement and readiness for future change

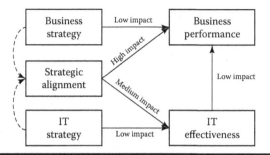

Figure 2.5   Business IT/IS alignment and business performance.

that encourages desirable behavior in the use of the organization's IT, which includes definitions of organizational rules and regulations, who sets them, and how compliance is monitored.

3. How they are enacted (oversight): IT governance is concerned with the appraisal and critical review of major IT projects, technology architecture decisions, and the measurement metrics that quantify the performance of IT as well as encompassing the management of technology-related business risks and determination of the financial value returned by enterprises' IT.

There are a number of practical governance frameworks that can assist business organizations in the delivery of an effective governance structure that in part incorporates IT governance. The two primary IT governance frameworks are the American-based Control Objectives for Information Technology (COBIT) and the English-based Information Technology Infrastructure Library (ITIL). Both COBIT and ITIL are utilized extensively in the implementation of an IT governance framework within organizations, but their individual focus remains broadly different. ITIL is based upon the principles of service management and takes a bottom-up approach, while in comparison the COBIT focus is primarily a top-down, high-level focus on audit and control. As a result, these two frameworks tend to complement each other, with COBIT providing managerial processes and objectives that are applicable from the board-level perspective, and the ITIL delivering operational best practice that can be applied from the help-desk level upwards in the implementation of IT governance within an organization. Generally, COBIT is utilized where there is a need for auditing functions, while ITIL is better suited to operational process improvement.

COBIT consists of several documents including an Executive Summary, Framework, Control Objectives, Audit Guidelines, Implementation Tool Set, and Management Guidelines. The main document is the framework, which consists of 34 high-level IT processes that come under 4 different control domains:

■ Planning and organization controls
■ Acquisition and implementation controls

■ Delivery and support controls
■ Monitoring controls

Each of these 34 organizational processes has a number of control objectives, with critical success factors that are required to successfully implement the process that incorporate specific numerical metrics that gauge improvements in quality and a maturity model to define the extent of business process automation. Altogether, these 34 processes can be further broken down into 318 specific control objectives for implementing the framework, including Key Goal Indicator and Key Performance Indicator measures as part of the continuous improvement cycle existing within the COBIT framework.

ITIL is a collection of best practices with an IT operational focus. The ITIL framework consists of a series of eight books, each of which details a different aspect of the information framework required for implementation:

■ *Planning to Implement Service Management*
■ *The Business Perspective*
■ *Software Asset Management*
■ *Service Support*
■ *Service Delivery*
■ *Security Management*

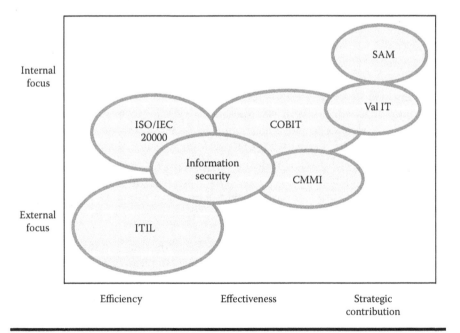

Figure 2.6   Classification of frameworks.

■ *ICT Infrastructure Management*
■ *Application Management*

Figure 2.6 shows a high-level view of the classification of different frameworks within the categories:

1. *focus* (external alignment of business with IT/IS and internal IT perspective)
2. *efficiency, effectiveness, and strategic contribution*

2.3 Summary

IT alignment is one of the key issues in strategic management. However, IT alignment is more than simply formulating IT strategy to fit the business strategy. Business strategy is future oriented and subject to external forces and environmental uncertainty. IT alignment should build adaptability into IT strategy. Furthermore, for some technology companies, IT may be the driver of corporate strategy.

Chapter 3

Enterprise Security

As stated in the preface, enterprise security is an essential pre-requisite for smart enterprises. The goal of enterprise security is to protect an organization's information assets and infrastructure from accidental or malicious disclosure, modification, misuse and erasure. While people—especially the trusted people inside the organization—are the most important factor in information integrity and protection, the technology of security also plays a vital role. Technical controls protect information assets and infrastructure primarily from people outside the organization—those who are not trusted. Security technology plays an important role for insiders, too, through access controls and audit capabilities. These help to reinforce accountability and also provide valuable information during investigations.

This chapter discusses the concepts, mechanisms and technologies used to protect information assets and infrastructure. The topics discussed are

- Confidentiality: Obscuring information from prying eyes
- Integrity: Assurance of the accuracy of information
- Availability: Assurance that information is accessible when needed
- Authentication: Identifying people who are allowed to access information
- Authorization: Controlling what information and functions a person is allowed to access
- Access control: Managing access to information and infrastructure
- Acccountability: Hold users accountable for what they do with the access to information
- Audit: Recording events for possible subsequent problem solving, fact finding, or investigation

3.1 Concept of Security

3.1.1 The Triad of Confidentiality, Integrity, and Availability

3.1.1.1 Confidentiality

Confidentiality is a concept similar to, but not the same as, privacy. Confidentiality is a necessary component of privacy and refers to our ability to protect our data from those who are not authorized to view it. Confidentiality is a concept that may be implemented at many levels of a process.

As an example, if we consider the case of a person withdrawing money from an ATM, the person in question will likely seek to maintain the confidentiality of the personal identification number (PIN) that allows him, in combination with his ATM card, to draw funds from the ATM. Additionally, the owner of the ATM will hopefully maintain the confidentiality of the account number, balance and any other information needed to communicate to the bank from which the funds are being drawn. The bank will maintain the confidentiality of the transaction with the ATM and the balance change in the account after the funds have been withdrawn. If at any point in the transaction, confidentiality is compromised, the results could be bad for the individual, the owner of the ATM and the bank, potentially resulting in what is known in the information security field as a *breach*.

Confidentiality can be compromised by the loss of a laptop containing data, a person looking over our shoulder while we type a password, an e-mail attachment being sent to the wrong person, an attacker penetrating our systems or similar issues.

3.1.1.2 Integrity

Integrity refers to the ability to prevent our data from being changed in an unauthorized or undesirable manner. This could mean the unauthorized change or deletion of our data or portions of our data, or it could mean an authorized, but undesirable, change or deletion of our data. To maintain integrity, we not only need to have the means to prevent unauthorized changes to our data but also the ability to reverse authorized changes that need to be undone.

We can see a good example of mechanisms that allow us to control integrity in the file systems of many modern operating systems such as Windows and Linux. For purposes of preventing unauthorized changes, such systems often implement permissions that restrict what actions an unauthorized user can perform on a given file. Additionally, some such systems, and many applications, such as databases, can allow us to undo or roll back changes that are undesirable.

Integrity is particularly important when we are discussing the data that provides the foundation for other decisions. If an attacker were to alter the data that contained the results of medical tests, we might see the wrong treatment prescribed, potentially resulting in the death of the patient.

3.1.1.3 Availability

The final leg of the confidentiality, integrity, and availability (CIA) triad is availability. Availability refers to the ability to access our data when we need it. Loss of availability can refer to a wide variety of breaks anywhere in the chain that allows us access to our data. Such issues can result from power loss, operating system or application problems, network attacks, compromise of a system or other problems. When such issues are caused by an outside party, such as an attacker, they are commonly referred to as a *denial of service* (DoS) attack.

3.1.2 Types of Attacks

3.1.2.1 Interception

Interception attacks allow unauthorized users to access our data, applications, or environments, and are primarily an attack against confidentiality. Interception might take the form of unauthorized file viewing or copying, eavesdropping on phone conversations or reading e-mail and can be conducted against data at rest or in motion. Properly executed, interception attacks can be very difficult to detect.

3.1.2.2 Interruption

Interruption attacks cause our assets to become unusable, or unavailable for our use, on a temporary or permanent basis. Interruption attacks often affect availability but can be an attack on integrity as well. In the case of a DoS attack on a mail server, we would classify this as an availability attack. In the case of an attacker manipulating the processes on which a database runs in order to prevent access to the data it contains, we might consider this an integrity attack, due to the possible loss or corruption of data; or we might consider it a combination of the two. We might also consider such a database attack to be a modification attack rather than an interruption attack.

3.1.2.3 Modification

Modification attacks involve tampering with our asset. Such attacks might primarily be considered an integrity attack but could also represent an availability attack. If we access a file in an unauthorized manner and alter the data it contains, we have affected the integrity of the data contained in the file. However, if we consider the case where the file in question is a configuration file that manages how a particular service behaves, perhaps one that is acting as a Web server, we might affect the availability of that service by changing the contents of the file. If we continue with this concept and say the configuration we altered in the file for our Web server is one that alters how the server deals with encrypted connections, we could even make this a confidentiality attack.

3.1.2.4 Fabrication

Fabrication attacks involve generating data, processes, communications, or other similar activities with a system. Fabrication attacks primarily affect integrity but could be considered an availability attack as well. If we generate spurious information in a database, this would be considered to be a fabrication attack. We could also generate e-mail, which is commonly used as a method for propagating malware, such as we might find being used to spread a worm. In the sense of an availability attack, if we generate enough additional processes, network traffic, e-mail, Web traffic, or nearly anything else that consumes resources, we can potentially render the service that handles such traffic unavailable to legitimate users of the system.

3.1.3 Threats, Vulnerabilities, and Risk

3.1.3.1 Threats

When we spoke of the types of attacks we might encounter in the "Attacks" section earlier in this chapter, we discussed some of the things that have the potential to cause harm to our assets. Ultimately, this is what a threat is—something that has the potential to cause us harm. Threats tend to be specific to certain environments, particularly in the world of information security. For example, although a virus might be problematic on a Windows operating system, the same virus will be unlikely to have any effect on a Linux operating system.

3.1.3.2 Vulnerabilities

Vulnerabilities are weaknesses that can be used to harm us. In essence, they are holes that can be exploited by threats in order to cause us harm. A vulnerability might be a specific operating system or application that we are running, a physical location where we have chosen to place our office building, a data center that is populated over the capacity of its air-conditioning system, a lack of backup generators, or other factors.

3.1.3.3 Risk

Risk is the likelihood that something bad will happen. In order for us to have a risk in a particular environment, we need to have both a threat and a vulnerability that the specific threat can exploit. For example, if we have a structure that is made from wood and we set it on fire, we have both a threat (the fire) and a vulnerability that matches it (the wood structure). In this case, we most definitely have a risk.

Likewise, if we have the same threat of fire but our structure is made of concrete, we no longer have a credible risk, because our threat does not have a vulnerability to exploit. We can argue that a sufficiently hot flame could damage the concrete, but this is a much less likely event.

We will often have similar discussions regarding potential risk in computing environments and potential, but unlikely, attacks that could happen. In such cases, the best strategy is to spend our time mitigating the most likely attacks. If we sink our resources into trying to plan for every possible attack, however unlikely, we will spread ourselves thin and will be lacking in protection where we actually need it the most.

3.1.4 Controls

In order to help us mitigate risk, we can put measures in place to help ensure that a given type of threat is accounted for. These measures are referred to as *controls*. Controls are divided into three categories: physical, logical, and administrative.

3.1.4.1 Physical

Physical controls are those controls that protect the physical environment in which our systems sit or where our data is stored. Such controls also control access in and out of such environments. Physical controls logically include items such as fences, gates, locks, bollards, guards, and cameras, but they also include systems that maintain the physical environment, such as heating and air-conditioning systems, fire suppression systems, and backup power generators. Although at first glance, physical controls may not seem like they would be integral to information security, they are actually one of the more critical controls with which we need to be concerned. If we are not able to physically protect our systems and data, any other controls that we can put in place become irrelevant. If an attacker is able to physically access our systems, he can, at the very least, steal or destroy the system, rendering it unavailable for our use in the best case. In the worst case, he will have access directly to our applications and data and will be able to steal our information and resources or subvert them for his own use.

3.1.4.2 Logical

Logical controls, sometimes called *technical controls*, are those that protect the systems, networks, and environments that process, transmit, and store our data. Logical controls can include items such as passwords, encryption, logical access controls, firewalls, and intrusion detection systems. Logical controls enable us, in a logical sense, to prevent unauthorized activities from taking place. If our logical controls are implemented properly and are successful, an attacker or unauthorized user cannot access our applications and data without subverting the controls that we have in place.

3.1.4.3 Administrative

Administrative controls are based on rules, laws, policies, procedures, guidelines, and other items that are "paper" in nature. In essence, administrative controls set out the rules for how we expect the users of our environment to behave. Depending on the environment and control in question, administrative controls can represent differing levels of authority. We may have a simple rule such as "turn the coffee pot off at the end of the day," aimed at ensuring that we do not cause a physical security problem by burning our building down at night. We may also have a more stringent administrative control, such as one that requires us to change our password every 90 days.

3.1.5 Defense in Depth

Defense in depth is a strategy common to both military maneuvers and information security. In both senses, the basic concept of defense in depth is to formulate a multi-layered defense that will allow us to still mount a successful defense should one or more of our defensive measures fail. In Figures 3.1 and 3.2, we can see an example of the layers we might want to put in place to defend our assets from a logical perspective; we would at the very least want defenses at the external network, internal network, host, application, and data levels. Given well-implemented defenses at each layer, we will make it very difficult to successfully penetrate deeply into our network and attack our assets directly.

One important concept to note when planning a defensive strategy using *defense in depth* is that it is not a magic bullet. No matter how many layers we put in place or how many defensive measures we place at each layer, we will not be able to keep every attacker out for an indefinite period of time, nor is this the ultimate goal of defense in depth in an information security setting. The goal is to place enough defensive measures between our truly important assets and the attacker so that we will both notice that an attack is in progress and also buy ourselves enough time to take more active measures to prevent the attack from succeeding.

 The idea behind defence in depth is not to keep an attacker out permanently but to delay him long enough to alert us to the attack and to allow us to mount a more active defence.

3.2 Identification

We can identify ourselves by our full names, shortened versions of our names, nicknames, account numbers, usernames, ID cards, fingerprints, DNA samples, and an enormous variety of other methods. Other than a few exceptions, such methods of identification are not unique, and even some of the supposedly unique methods of identification, such as the fingerprint, can be duplicated in many cases.

One very common example of an identification and authentication transaction can be found in the use of payment cards that require a personal identification

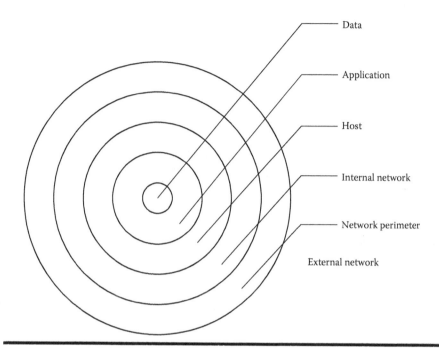

Figure 3.1   Defense in depth.

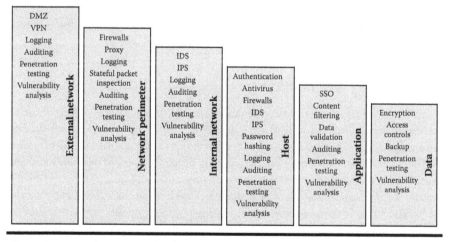

Figure 3.2   Defenses in each layer.

number (PIN). When we swipe the magnetic strip on the card, we are asserting that we are the person indicated on the card. At this point, we have given our identification but nothing more. When we are prompted to enter the PIN associated with the card, we are completing the authentication portion of the transaction, hopefully meeting with success.

Identification, as we mentioned in the preceding section, is simply an assertion of who we are. This may include

- Who we claim to be as a person
- Who a system claims to be over the network
- Who the originating party of an e-mail claims to be
- Similar transactions

Who we claim to be can, in many cases, be an item of information that is subject to change. For instance, our names can change, as in the case of women who change their last name upon getting married, people who legally change their name to an entirely different name, or even people who simply elect to use a different name. In addition, we can generally change logical forms of identification very easily, as in the case of account numbers, usernames, and the like. Even physical identifiers, such as height, weight, skin color, and eye color, can be changed. One of the most crucial factors to realize when we are working with identification is that an unsubstantiated claim of identity is not reliable information on its own.

 It is important to note that the process of identification does not extend beyond this claim and does not involve any sort of verification or validation of the identity that we claim. That part of the process is referred to as authentication and is a separate transaction.

3.2.1 Identity Verification

Identity verification is a step beyond identification, but it is still a step short of authentication, which we will discuss in the next section. When we are asked to show a driver's license, social security card, birth certificate, or other similar form of identification, this is generally for the purpose of identity verification, not authentication. We can take the example a bit further and validate the form of identification—say, a passport—against a database holding an additional copy of the information that it contains and matching the photograph and physical specifications with the person standing in front of us. This may get us a bit closer, but we are still not at the level of surety we gain from authentication.

Identity verification is used not only in our personal interactions but also in computer systems. In many cases, such as when we send an e-mail, the identity we provide is taken to be true, without any additional steps taken to authenticate us. Such gaps in security contribute to the enormous amount of spam traffic that we see.

3.2.2 Identity Falsification

Some of the identification methods that we use in daily life are particularly fragile and depend largely on the honesty and diligence of those involved in the transaction. Many such exchanges that involve the showing of identification cards, such as the purchase of items restricted to those above a certain age, are based on the theory that the identification card being displayed is genuine and accurate. We also depend on the person or system performing the verification being competent and capable of not only performing the act of verification but also being able to detect false or fraudulent activity.

The methods of identification are subject to change, including falsification. Certain primary means of identification, such as birth certificates, once falsified, can also provide a means to gain additional forms of identification, such as social security cards or driver's licenses, that can help in further strengthening the false identity. Identity theft, based on falsified information, is quite common and easy to execute. Given a minimal amount of information—usually a name, address, and social security number—it is possible to impersonate someone to a sufficient degree to be able to act as that person in many cases. Victims of identity theft may find that using their stolen identity the acquisition of lines of credit, credit cards, vehicle loans, home mortgages, and other transactions have taken place.

Such crimes occur only due to the lack of authentication requirements for many of the activities in which we engage every day. Merely qualifying through a verification is not a very difficult obstacle, and it can easily be circumvented using falsified forms of identification. To rectify this situation, we need to couple the process identification with that of in authentication order to ascertain that they are actually the people whom they claim to be.

3.3 Authentication

Authentication is, in an information security sense, the set of methods we use to establish a claim of identity as being true. It is important to note that authentication only establishes whether the claim of identity that has been made is correct. Authentication does not infer or imply anything about what the party being authenticated is allowed to do; this is a separate task known as authorization.

When we are attempting to authenticate a claim of identity, there are several methods we can use, with each category referred to as a *factor*; the more factors we use, the more positive our results will be. The factors are

1. Something you know: Something you know is a very common authentication factor. This can include passwords, PINs, passphrases, or most any item of information that a person can remember. We can see a very common implementation of this in the passwords we use to log in to our accounts on

computers. This is somewhat of a weak factor because if the information the factor depends on is exposed, this can nullify the uniqueness of our authentication method.

Passwords are familiar to the vast majority of us who use computers regularly. In combination with a username, a password will generally allow us access to a computer system, an application, a phone, or similar devices. Passwords, although only a single factor of authentication, can, when constructed and implemented properly, represent a relatively high level of security.

2. Something you have: Something you have is a factor generally based on the physical possession of an item or a device, although this factor can extend into some logical concepts as well. We can see such factors in general use in the form of ATM cards, state or federally issued identity cards, or software-based security tokens. This factor can vary in strength depending on the implementation. In the case of a security token, we would actually need to steal a specific device in order to falsify the authentication method. In the case of access to an e-mail address being used as this type of factor, we have a measure of considerably less strength. Some institutions, such as banks, have begun to use access to logical devices such as cell phones or e-mail accounts as methods of authentication as well.

A hardware token is a small device, typically in the general form factor of a credit card or keychain fob. The simplest hardware tokens look identical to a USB flash drive and contain a small amount of storage holding a certificate or unique identifier, and they are often called *dongles*. More complex hardware tokens incorporate LCD displays, keypads for entering passwords, biometric readers, wireless devices, and additional features to enhance security. Many hardware tokens contain an internal clock that, in combination with the device's unique identifier, an input PIN or password, and potentially other factors, is used to generate a code, usually output to a display on the token. This code changes on a regular basis, often every 30 s. The infrastructure used to keep track of such tokens can predict, for a given device, what the proper output will be at any given time and can use this to authenticate the user.

3. Something you are: Something you are is a factor based on the relatively unique physical attributes of an individual, often referred to as *biometrics*. This factor can be based on simple attributes such as height, weight, hair color, or eye color, but these do not tend to be unique enough to make very secure identifiers. More commonly used are more complex identifiers such as fingerprints, iris or retina patterns, or facial characteristics. When we complete an authentication transaction with a biometric identifier, we are essentially asking the user to provide evidence that he or she is who he or she claims to be; this is, by definition, verification and not authentication. This factor is a bit stronger, as forging or stealing a copy of a physical identifier is a somewhat more difficult, although not impossible, task. Although some biometric identifiers may be more difficult to falsify than others, this is only

due to limitations in today's technology. At some point in the future, we will need to develop more robust biometric characteristics to measure or stop using biometrics as an authentication mechanism.

We can use biometric systems in two different manners. We can use them to verify the claim of identity that someone has put forth, as we discussed earlier; or we can reverse the process and use biometrics as a method of identification. This process is commonly used by law enforcement agencies to identify the owner of fingerprints that have been left on various objects, and it can be a very time-consuming effort, considering the sheer size of the fingerprint libraries held by such organizations.

Biometric factors are defined by seven characteristics:

a. *Universality* stipulates that we should be able to find our chosen biometric characteristic in the majority of people we expect to enroll in the system.

b. *Uniqueness* is a measure of how unique a particular characteristic is among individuals. We can select characteristics with a higher degree of uniqueness, such as DNA or iris patterns, but there is always a possibility of duplication, whether intentional or otherwise.

c. *Permanence tests* show how well a particular characteristic resists change over time and with advancing age. We can use factors such as fingerprints that, although they can be altered, are unlikely to be altered without deliberate action.

d. *Collectability* measures how easy it is to acquire a characteristic with which we can later authenticate a user. Most commonly used biometrics, such as fingerprints, are relatively easy to acquire, and this is one reason they are in common use.

e. *Acceptability* is a measure of how acceptable the particular characteristic is to the users of the system. In general, systems that are slow, difficult to use, or awkward to use are less likely to be acceptable to the user.

f. *Circumvention* describes the ease with which a system can be tricked by a falsified biometric identifier. The classic example of a circumvention attack against the fingerprint as a biometric identifier is found in the "gummy finger." In this type of attack, a fingerprint is lifted from a surface, potentially in a covert fashion, and is used to create a mold with which the attacker can cast a positive image of the fingerprint in gelatin.

g. *Performance* is a set of metrics that judge how well a given system functions. Such factors include speed, accuracy, and error rate.

4. Something you do: Something you do, sometimes considered a variation of something you are, is a factor based on the actions or behaviors of an individual, including the individual's hand gestures, measurement of multiple factors in his or her handwriting, the time delay between keystrokes as he or she types a passphrase, or similar factors. These factors present a very strong method of authentication and are very difficult to falsify. They do, however, have the potential to incorrectly reject legitimate users at a higher rate than

some of the other factors, resulting in denials for some users that should have actually got authenticated successfully.

5. Where you are: Where you are is a geographically based authentication factor. This factor operates differently than the other factors, as its method of authentication depends on the person being authenticated as being physically present at a particular location or locations. This factor, although potentially of less utility than some of the other factors, is very difficult to counter without entirely subverting the system performing the authentication. A fairly accurate implementation can be achieved co-jointly with a location-aware mobile application. We can see a somewhat loose implementation of this factor in the act of drawing funds from an ATM. Although this is certainly not a design decision due to security reasons, it is true that this can only be done in particular geographic locations.

3.3.1 Mutual Authentication

Mutual authentication refers to an authentication mechanism in which both parties authenticate each other. In the standard authentication process, which is one-way authentication only, the client authenticates to the server to prove that it is the party that should be accessing the resources the server provides. In mutual authentication, not only does the client authenticate to the server, but the server authenticates to the client as well. Mutual authentication is often implemented through the use of digital certificates, that is, both the client and the server would have a certificate to authenticate the other.

3.3.2 Multi-Factor Authentication

Multi-factor authentication uses one or more of the factors we discussed in the preceding section. We can see a common example of multi-factor authentication in using an ATM. In this case, we have something we know, our PIN; and something we have, our ATM card. Our ATM card does double duty as both a factor for authentication and a form of identification. We can see a similar example in writing checks that draw on a bank account—in this case, something we have, the checks themselves; and something we do, applying our signature to them.

3.4 Authorization

Once we have authenticated the user in question, authorization enables us to determine exactly what they are allowed to do. Authorization allows us to specify where the party should be allowed or denied access.

The principle of least privilege dictates that we should only allow the bare minimum of access to a user—this might be a person, user account, or process—to allow it to perform the functionality needed of it. For example, someone working in a sales department should not need access to data in our internal human resources system in order to do their job. Violation of the principle of least privilege is the heart of many of the security problems we face today. If we have a service running a Web server, for instance, this service only needs sufficient permission to access the files and scripts that directly pertain to the Web content it is serving and nothing more. If we allow the Web service to access additional files in the file system, an attacker could potentially read or alter these files to gain unauthorized access to more sensitive information than we would normally make public, thus giving the attacker an inroad to attack deeper into the system.

We can take away some of the more easily accessed tools that attackers can use against us by carefully following the principle of least privilege when configuring systems, allocating permissions for accounts, and planning out our security.

3.5 Access Control

Authorization is implemented through the use of access controls, more specifically through the use of access control lists and capabilities, although the latter are often not completely implemented in most of the common operating systems in use today.

Access control enables us to manage this access at a very granular level. Access controls can be constructed in a variety of manners. We can base access controls on physical attributes, sets of rules, lists of individuals or systems, or more complex factors. The particular type of access control often depends on the environment in which it is to be used. We can find simpler access controls implemented in many applications and operating systems, while more complex multi-level configurations might be implemented in military or government environments. In such cases, the importance of what we are controlling access to may dictate that we track what our users have access to across a number of levels of sensitivity.

Access control issues or situations can be categorized among these four actions:

1. *Allowing access* lets us give a particular party, or parties, access to a given resource. For example, we might want to give a particular user access to a file, or we may want to give an entire group of people access to all the files in a given directory.
2. *Limiting access* refers to allowing some access to our resource but only up to a certain point. This is very important when we are using applications that may be exposed to attack-prone environments, as we see with Web browsers used on the Internet. In such cases, we might see the application being run in a sandbox in order to limit what can be done outside the context of the application. In a physical sense, we can see the concept of access control limitations

in the different levels of keying that we might see in the locks in a building. We may have a master key that can open any door in the building, an intermediate key that can open only doors on a particular floor, and a low-level key that can open only one particular door.

3. *Denying access* is the diametric opposite of granting access. When we deny access, we are preventing access by a given party to the resource in question. We might be denying access to a particular person attempting to log on to a machine based on the time of day, or we might deny unauthorized individuals from entering the lobby of our building beyond business hours. Many access control systems are set to deny by default, with the authorized users only being permitted access.

4. *Revocation of access* is a very important idea in access control. It is vital that, once we have given a party access to a resource, we be able to take that access away again. If we were, for instance, to fire an employee, we would want to revoke any accesses that they might have. We would want to remove access to their e-mail account, disallow them from connecting to our virtual private network (VPN), deactivate their badge so that they can no longer enter the facility, and revoke other accesses that they might have. Particularly when we are working with computer-oriented resources in some fashion, it may be vital to be able to revoke access to a given resource very quickly.

When we look to implement access controls, there are two main methods that we might use:

1. Access control lists (ACLs), often referred to as "ackles," are a very common choice for access control implementation. ACLs are usually used to control access in the file systems on which our operating systems run and to control the flow of traffic in the networks to which our systems are attached. When ACLs are constructed, they are typically built specifically to a certain resource, and they contain the identifiers of the party allowed to access the resource in question and what the party is allowed to do in relation to the resource:

   – Files access ACLs: When we look at the ACLs in most file systems, we commonly see three permissions in use: read, write, and execute, respectively allowing us to access the contents of a file or directory, write to a file or directory, and, presuming that a file contains either a program or a script capable of running on the system in question, execute the contents of the file. By using such sets of file permissions, we can, in a simple fashion, control access to the operating systems and applications that utilize our file system.

   In the case of file systems, a file or directory may also have multiple ACLs attached to it. In UNIX-like operating systems, for instance, we can see separate access lists for a given file in the form of user, group, and other ACLs. We can give an individual user read, write, and execute permissions; a group of users different read, write, and execute permissions; and, to anyone that is not an individual or group that we have already covered, a different set of read, write, and execute permissions. These three sets of permissions will display as rwxrwxrwx, with the first rwx set representing the user, the second the group, and the third other.

– Network ACLs: In the case of network ACLs, we typically see access controlled by the identifiers we use for network transactions, such as Internet Protocol (IP) addresses, Media Access Control (MAC) addresses, and ports. We can see such ACLs at work in network infrastructure such as routers, switches, and firewall devices, as well as in software firewalls, Facebook, Google, e-mail, or other forms of software. Permissions in network ACLs tend to be binary in nature, generally consisting of *allow* and *deny*. When we set up the ACL, we use our chosen identifier or identifiers to dictate which traffic we are referring to and simply state whether the traffic is to be allowed or not. One of the simplest forms of network-oriented ACLs that we might see in place is MAC address filtering. MAC addresses are, in theory, unique identifiers attached to each network interface in a given system. Each network interface has a hardcoded MAC address issued when it is created.

We can also choose to use IP addresses as the basis for filtering in our ACL. We can implement such filtering based on individual addresses or on an entire range of IP addresses. Similar to the issue with using MAC addresses for ACLs, IP addresses can be falsified and are not unique to a particular network interface. Additionally, IP addresses issued by Internet service providers (ISPs) are subject to frequent change, making IP addresses as the sole basis for filtering a shaky prospect, at best.

We can also filter by the port being used to communicate over the network. Many common services and applications use specific ports to communicate over networks. For instance, FTP uses ports 20 and 21 to transfer files, Internet Message Access Protocol (IMAP) uses port 143 for managing e-mail, Secure Shell (SSH) uses port 22 to manage remote connections to systems, and many more—65,535 ports in all. We can control the use of many applications over the network by allowing or denying traffic originating from or sent to any ports that we care to manage. Like MAC and IP addresses, the specific ports that are used for applications are a convention, not an absolute rule.

 Using single attributes to construct ACLs is likely to present a variety of issues, including the attribute not being guaranteed to be unique, such as an IP address; or being easy to alter, such as a MAC address. When we use several attributes in combination, we begin to arrive at a more secure technique. A very commonly used combination is that of IP address and port, typically referred to as a socket.

2. Capability-based security can provide us with an alternate solution to access control that uses a different structure than what we see in ACLs. Where ACLs define the permissions based on a given resource, an identity, and a set of permissions, all generally held in a file of some sort, capabilities are oriented around the use of a token that controls our access. We can think of a token in a capability as being analogous to the badge we might use to open the door in a building. The right to access a resource is based entirely on possession of the token and not who possesses it. If we were to give our badge to someone else, he would be able to use it to access the building with whatever set of permissions we have.

   Similarly, the badge can have differing levels of access. Where one person might be able to access the building only during business hours on weekdays, another person may have permission to enter the building at any time of day on any day of the week.

3.5.1 Access Control Models

The specifics of access control are defined through the various models that are used when putting together such systems. We often see the use of the simpler access control models such as discretionary access control, mandatory access control, role-based access control, and attribute-based access control. In environments that handle more sensitive data, such as those involved in the government, military, medical, or legal industry, we may see the use of multi-level access control models, including Biba and Bell–LaPadula.

Access controls are the means by which we implement authorization and deny or allow access to parties, based on what resources we have determined they should be allowed access to. There are different models of access controls:

1. *Mandatory Access Control*: Mandatory access control (MAAC) is a model of access control in which the owner of the resource does not get to decide who gets to access it, but instead access is decided by a group or individual who has the authority to set access on resources. We can often find MAAC implemented in government organizations, where access to a given resource is largely dictated by
   - The sensitivity label applied to it (*secret*, *top secret*, etc.)
   - The level of sensitive information the individual is allowed to access (perhaps only *secret*)
   - Whether the individual actually has a need to access the resource
2. *Discretionary Access Control*: Discretionary access control (DAC) is a model of access control based on access being determined by the owner of the resource

in question. The owner of the resource can decide who does and does not have access and exactly what access they are allowed to have.

3. *Role-Based Access Control*: Role-based access control (RBAC) is a model of access control that functions on access controls set by an authority responsible for doing so, rather than by the owner of the resource. The difference between RBAC and MAC is that access control in RBAC is based on the role the individual being granted access is performing. For example, if we have an employee whose only role is to enter data into a particular application, through RBAC, we would only allow the employee access to that application, regardless of the sensitivity or lack of sensitivity of any other resource he might potentially access. If we have an employee with a more complex role—customer service for an online retail application, perhaps—the employee's role might require him to have access to information about customers' payment status and information, shipping status, previous orders, and returns in order to be able to assist said customers. In this case, RBAC would grant him considerably more access.

4. *Attribute-Based Access Control*: Attribute-based access control (ABAC) is based on attributes of a particular person, of a resource, or of an environment. For instance, CAPTCHA (Completely Automated Public Turing Test to Tell Humans and Computers Apart) are used to control access based on whether the party on the other end can pass a test that is, in theory, too difficult for a machine to complete, thus proving the party to be human.

    Resource attributes are those that relate to a particular resource, such as an operating system or application. We often see this occur when we encounter software that only runs on a particular operating system, or Web sites that only work with certain browsers. We might apply this type of access control as a security measure by requiring specific software to be used or particular protocols for communication.

    Environmental attributes can be used to enable access controls that operate based on environmental conditions. We commonly use the time attribute to control access, in both a physical and a logical sense, based on elapsed time that is length of time passed or time of day. Access controls on buildings are often configured to only allow access during certain hours of the day, such as during business hours on a particular day. We also see time limits set on VPN connections, forcing the user to reconnect every 24 h. This is often done to prevent users from keeping such a connection running after their authorization for using it has been removed. We can often find ABAC implemented on infrastructure systems such as those in network or telecommunications environments.

5. *Multi-Level Access Control*: Multi-level access control (MLAC) models are used where the simpler access control models that we just discussed are considered to not be robust enough to protect the information to which we are controlling access. Such access controls are used extensively by military and

government organizations or those that often handle data of a very sensitive nature. We might see multi-level security models used to protect a variety of data in industries like the financial, medical, and legal industries.

The Biba model of access control is primarily concerned with protecting the integrity of data, even at the expense of confidentiality. Biba has two security rules:

1. The Simple Integrity Axiom: The level of access granted to an individual must be no lower than the classification of the resource.
2. The Integrity Axiom: Anyone accessing a resource can only write its contents to one classified at the same level or lower.

We can summarize these rules as "no read down" and "no write up," respectively. In this case, we are protecting integrity by ensuring that our resource can only be written to by those with a high level of access and that those with a high level of access do not access a resource with a lower classification.

In contrast, the Bell–LaPadula model of access is primarily concerned with protecting the confidentiality of data, even at the expense of integrity. Bell–LaPadula has two security rules:

1. The Simple Security Property: The level of access granted to an individual must be at least as high as the classification of the resource in order for the individual to be able to access it.
2. The Property: Anyone accessing a resource can only write its contents to one classified at the same level or higher.

These properties are generally summarized as "no read up" and "no write down," respectively. In short, this means that when we are handling classified information, we cannot read any higher than our clearance level, and we cannot write classified data down to any lower level.

Access control concepts in general largely apply to both logical and physical areas, but we do see some specialized applications when looking specifically at physical access control. Here we have several sets of access controls that apply to ensuring that people and vehicles are restricted from exiting or entering areas where they are not authorized to be. We can see examples of such controls in our daily lives at office buildings, parking areas, and high-security facilities in general.

3.6 Accountability

Upon implementing monitoring and logging on our systems and networks, this information to maintain can be used to adopt a higher security posture than we would be able to otherwise. Specifically, the tools that allow us accountability also enable non-repudiation, deter those that would misuse our resources, help us in detecting and preventing intrusions, and assist us in preparing materials for legal proceedings.

3.6.1 Non-repudiation

Non-repudiation refers to a situation in which sufficient evidence exists to prevent an individual from successfully denying that he or she has made a statement or taken an action. In information security settings, this can be accomplished in a variety of ways. We may be able to produce proof of the activity directly from system or network logs or to recover such proof through the use of digital forensic examination of the system or devices involved. We may also be able to establish non-repudiation through the use of encryption technologies, more specifically through the use of hash functions that can be used to digitally sign a communication or a file.

An example of this might be a system that digitally signs every e-mail that is sent from it, thus rendering useless any denial that might take place regarding the sending of the message in question.

3.6.2 Deterrence

Accountability can also prove to be a great deterrent against misbehavior in our environments. If those we monitor are aware of this fact, and it has been communicated to them that there will be penalties for acting against the rules, these individuals may think twice before straying outside the lines.

For example, if, as part of our monitoring activities, we keep track of the badge access times for when our employees pass in and out of our facility, we can validate this activity against the times they have submitted on their time card for each week in order to prevent our employees from falsifying their time card and defrauding the company for additional and undeserved pay. Such methods are often used in areas with large numbers of employees working specific shifts, such as those that run technical support help desks.

3.6.3 Intrusion Detection and Prevention

One of the motivations behind logging and monitoring in our environments is to detect and prevent intrusions in both the logical and physical sense. If we implement alerts based on unusual activities in our environments and check the information we have logged on a regular basis, we stand a much better chance of detecting attacks that are in progress and preventing those for which we can see the precursors.

Particularly in the logical realm, where attacks can take place in fractions of a second, we would also be wise to implement automated tools to carry out such tasks.

We can divide such systems into two major categories: intrusion detection systems (IDSes) and intrusion prevention systems (IPSes). An IDS performs strictly as a monitoring and alert tool, only notifying us that an attack or undesirable activity is taking place. An IPS, often working from information sent by the IDS, can actually take action based on what is happening in the environment. In response to an attack over the network, an IPS might refuse traffic from the source of the attack.

3.6.4 Admissibility of Records

When we seek to introduce records in legal settings, it is often much easier to do so and have them accepted when they are produced from a regulated and consistent tracking system. For instance, if we seek to submit digital forensic evidence that we have gathered for use in a court case, the evidence will likely not be admissible to the court unless we can provide a solid and documented chain of custody for said evidence. We need to be able to show where the evidence was at all times, how exactly it passed from one person to another, how it was protected while it was stored, and so forth.

Our accountability methods for evidence collection, if properly followed, will hopefully let us display this unbroken chain of custody. If we cannot demonstrate this, our evidence will likely only be taken as hearsay at best, considerably weakening our case and perhaps placing us on the losing side in court.

3.7 Audit

One of the primary ways we can ensure accountability through technical means is by ensuring that we have accurate records of who did what and when they did it. Auditing provides us with the data with which we can implement accountability, because if we do not have the ability to assess our activities over a period of time, we do not have the ability to facilitate accountability on a large scale. Particularly in larger organizations, our capacity to audit directly equates to our ability to hold anyone accountable for anything.

We may also be bound by contractual or regulatory requirements that compel us to be subject to audit on some sort of reoccurring basis. In many cases, such audits are carried out by unrelated and independent third parties certified and authorized to perform such a task. Good examples of such audits are those mandated by SOX, which exist in order to ensure that companies are honestly reporting their financial results.

Audit could target data related to various items:

1. Passwords are a commonly audited item, as we should be setting out policy to dictate how they are constructed and used. If we do not take care to construct passwords in a secure manner, they can be easily cracked by an

attacker. We should also be concerned with the frequency with which pass-words are changed. If we do happen to have a password fall into the hands of someone who should not have it, we want to change the password at a relatively frequent interval in order to ensure that this person does not have permanent access. In many cases, checking password strength and managing password changes are accomplished in an automated fashion by functions within an operating system or by utilities designed to do so, and these need to be audited as well to ensure that they are in place and configured properly.

2. Software licensing is another common audit topic. Particularly on systems owned by the organization for which we work, ensuring that all of our soft-ware is appropriately licensed is an important task.

3. Internet usage is a very commonly audited item in organizations, often largely focused on our activities on the Web, although it may include instant messag-ing, e-mail, file transfers, or other transactions. In many cases, organizations have configured proxy servers so that all such traffic is funneled through just a few gateways in order to enable logging, scanning, and potentially filtering such traffic. Such tools can give us the ability to examine how exactly such resources are being utilized and to take action if they are being misused.

Audit involves various functions:

3.7.1 Logging

Logging gives us a history of the activities that have taken place in the environ-ment being logged. We typically generate logs in an automated fashion in operat-ing systems and keep track of the activities that take place on most computing, networking, and telecommunications equipment, as well as most any device that can be remotely considered to incorporate or be connected to a computer. Logging is a reactive tool, in that it allows us to view the record of what happened after it has taken place. In order to immediately react to something taking place, we would need to use a tool more along the lines of an IDS/IPS.

Logging mechanisms are often configurable and can be set up to log anything from solely critical events, which is typical, to every action carried out by the system or software, which is typically only done for troubleshooting purposes when we see a problem. We will often find events such as software errors, hardware failures, users logging in or out, resource access, and tasks requiring increased privileges in most logs, depending on the logging settings and the system in question.

Logs are generally only available to the administrators of the system for review and are usually not modifiable by the users of the system, perhaps with the excep-tion of writing to them. Usually, it may be necessary to analyze the contents of logs in relation to a particular incident or situation. These types of activities often fall to security personnel in the case of investigations, incidents, and compliance checks. In these cases, this can be a difficult task if the period of time in question is greater than a few days. Even searching the contents of a relatively simple log, such as that generated by a Web proxy server, can mean sifting through enormous amounts of data from one or more servers. In such cases, custom scripts or even a tool such as grep can be invaluable to accomplish such tasks in a reasonable amount of time.

3.7.2 Monitoring

Monitoring is a subset of auditing and tends to focus on observing information about the environment being monitored in order to discover undesirable conditions such as failures, resource shortages, security issues, and trends that might signal the arrival of such conditions. Monitoring is largely a reactive activity, with actions taken based on gathered data, typically from logs generated by various devices. Even in the case of trend analysis, the objective is ultimately to forestall worse conditions in future than those we see at present.

When conducting monitoring, we are typically watching specific items of data we have collected, such as resource usage on computers, network latency, particular types of attacks occurring repeatedly against servers with network interfaces that are exposed to the Internet, traffic passing through our physical access controls at unusual times of day, and so forth. In reaction to such activity occurring at levels above what we normally expect, called *the clipping level*, our monitoring system might be configured to send an alert to a system administrator or physical security personnel, or it might trigger more direct action to mitigate the issue, such as dropping traffic from a particular IP address, switching to a backup system for a critical server, summoning law enforcement officials, or other similar tasks.

3.7.3 Assessments

The audits may directly perform a determination of whether everything is as it should be and is compliant with the relevant laws, regulations, or policies by examining the environments for vulnerabilities. There are two main approaches to achieve this:

1. *Vulnerability assessments* generally involve using vulnerability scanning tools, such as Nessus, that generally work by scanning the target systems to discover which ports are open on them and then interrogating each open port to find out exactly which service is listening on the port in question. Given this information, the vulnerability assessment tool can then consult its database of vulnerability information to determine whether any vulnerabilities may be present. Although the databases of such tools do tend to be rather thorough, newer attacks may go undetected.
2. *Penetration testing* mimics, as closely as possible, the techniques an actual attacker would use. We may attempt to gather additional information on

the target environment from users or other systems in the vicinity, exploit security flaws in Web-based applications or Web-connected databases, conduct attacks through unpatched vulnerabilities in applications or operating systems, or similar methods. The ultimate goal in performing assessments of either type is to find and fix vulnerabilities before any attackers do. If we can do so successfully and on a reoccurring basis, we will considerably increase our security posture and stand a much better chance of resisting attacks.

3.8 Summary

This chapter introduced the primary concepts in information security, namely, confidentiality, integrity, and availability, commonly known as the *confidentiality, integrity,* and *availability* (CIA) *triad. Defense in depth* entails putting in place multiple layers of defense, each giving an additional layer of protection. The *identification* and *authentication* is introduced as the first line of defense protecting an organization's information assets and infrastructure. *Authorization* provides the segregation of duties control that is necessary for many organization functions. *Access control* refers to mechanisms used to limit access to networks and systems. Once granted access, the users need to be accountable for what they do with the resources or information. *Auditing* is the process we go through to ensure that our environment is compliant with the laws, regulations, and policies that bind it.

Chapter 4

Process-Driven Organization

As stated in the preface, smart businesses are realized through digital transformation of businesses operations including resources, processes and management systems. Digital transformation invariably entails collective changes in businesses operations, namely, resources, business processes and management. This chapter focuses on enabling process changes. The advantages of a functional organization are that it is easier to adhere to standards because different groups specialize in a function or task, it expedites function-specific or vertical information flow, it achieves scale economies because each functional group is dedicated to just that function, and there is clarity in roles. On the other hand, a functional organization is typically much slower to respond to an external need because it has to co-ordinate action or response across multiple functions, lacks flexibility at a process level, and does not provide adequate visibility or information flow across a business process that spans multiple functions. A functional organization has been found to lead to significant coordination and control issues and to be unresponsive to customer or market needs.

A process-centric organization, in contrast, revolves around end-to-end business processes. While a function-centric organization has enabled enterprises to increase scale in the post–Industrial Revolution era, dramatic increases in scale, along with specialization, have led to organizational silos and have made them less responsive to the market, changes in customer expectations fueled by the Internet, and mobile communications. This weakness of the function-centric organization has become more apparent in today's highly dynamic world, in which it is a critical competitive necessity for businesses to adapt and innovate their processes end to end.

Information technology can fulfill its role as a strategic differentiator only if it can provide enterprises with a mechanism to provide sustainable competitive advantage—the ability to change business processes in sync with changes in the business environment and that too at optimum costs. This is achievable on the foundation of Service-Oriented Architecture (SOA) that exposes the fundamental business capabilities as flexible, reusable services; SOA along with the constituting services is the foundation of modern Business Process Management Systems (BPMS). The services support a layer of agile and flexible business processes that can be easily changed to provide new products and services to keep ahead of the competition. The most important value of SOA is that it provides an opportunity for information technology (IT) and the business to communicate and interact with each other at a highly efficient and equally understood level. That common, equally understood language is the language of business process or enterprise processes in Business Process Model and Notation (BPMN).

4.1 Process-Oriented Enterprise

Enterprise systems (ES) enable an organization to truly function as an integrated enterprise, with integration across all functions or segments of the traditional value chain—sales order, production, inventory, purchasing, finance and accounting, personnel and administration, and so on. They do this by modeling primarily the business processes as the basic business entities of the enterprise rather than by modeling data handled by the enterprise (as done by the traditional IT systems). However, every ES might not be completely successful in doing this. In a break with the legacy enterprise-wide solutions, modern ES treats business processes as more fundamental than data items.

Collaborations or relationships manifest themselves through the various organizational and inter-organizational processes. A process may be generally defined as the set of resources and activities necessary and sufficient to convert some form of input into some form of output. Processes are internal, external, or a combination of both; they cross functional boundaries; they have starting and ending points; and they exist at all levels within the enterprise.

The significance of a process to the success of the enterprise's business is dependent on the value, with reference to the customer, of the collaboration that it addresses and represents. In other words, the nature and extent of the value addition by a process to a product or services delivered to a customer is the best index of the contribution of that process to the company's overall customer satisfaction or customer collaboration. Customer knowledge by itself is not adequate; it is only when the enterprise has effective processes for sharing this information and integrating the activities of frontline workers and has the ability to coordinate the assignment and tracking of work that the enterprise can become effective.

Thus, this approach not only recognizes inherently the significance of various process-related techniques and methodologies such as process innovation (PI), business process improvement (BPI), business process redesign (BPRD), business process re-engineering (BPR), and business process management (BPM) but also treats them as fundamental, continuous, and integral functions of the management of a company itself. A collaborative enterprise enabled by the implementation of an ES is inherently amenable to business process involvement, which is also the essence of any total quality management (TQM)-oriented effort undertaken within an enterprise.

4.1.1 Value-Add Driven Enterprise

Business processes can be seen as the very basis of the value addition within an enterprise that was traditionally attributed to various functions or divisions in an enterprise. As organizational and environmental conditions become more complex, global, and competitive, processes provide a framework for dealing effectively with the issues of performance improvement, capability development, and adaptation to the changing environment.

Along a value stream (i.e., a business process), analysis of the absence or creation of added value or (worse) destruction of value critically determines the necessity and effectiveness of a process step. The understanding of value-adding and non-value-adding processes (or process steps) is a significant factor in the analysis, design, benchmarking, and optimization of business processes leading to BPM in the companies. BPM provides an environment for analyzing and optimizing business processes.

Values are characterized by both value determinants such as

■ Time (cycle time, etc.)
■ Flexibility (options, customization, composition, etc.)
■ Responsiveness (lead time, number of hand-offs, etc.)
■ Quality (rework, rejects, yield, etc.)
■ Price (discounts, rebates, coupons, incentives, etc.)

We must hasten to add that we are not disregarding cost (materials, labor, overhead, etc.) as a value determinant. However, the effect of cost is truly a result of a host of value determinants such as time, flexibility, and responsiveness.

The nature and extent of a value addition to a product or service is the best measure of that addition's contribution to the company's overall goal for competitiveness. Such value expectations are dependent on the following:

■ The customer's experience of similar product(s) and/or service(s)
■ The value delivered by the competitors
■ The capabilities and limitations of locking into the base technological platform

However, value as originally defined by Michael Porter in the context of introducing the concept of the value chain means more in the nature of the cost at various stages. Rather than a value chain, it is more of a cost chain! Porter's value chain is also a structure-oriented and hence a static concept. Here, we mean value as the satisfaction of not only external but also internal customers' requirements, as defined and continuously redefined, as the least total cost of acquisition, ownership, and use.

Consequently, in this formulation, one can understand the company's competitive gap in the market in terms of such process-based, customer-expected levels of value and the value delivered by the company's process for the concerned products or services. Customer responsiveness focuses on costs in terms of the yield. Therefore, we can perform market segmentation for a particular product or services in terms of the most significant customer values and the corresponding value determinants or what we term *critical value determinants* (CVDs).

Strategic planning exercises can then be understood readily in terms of devising strategies for improving on these process-based CVDs based on the competitive benchmarking of these collaborative values and processes between the enterprise and customers. These strategies and the tactics resulting from analysis, design, and optimization of the process will in turn focus on the restrategizing of all relevant business process at all levels. This can result in the modification or deletion of the process or the creation of a new one.

4.2 Concept of Business Process Management (BPM)

Business Process Management (BPM) addresses the following two important issues for an enterprise:

1. The strategic long-term positioning of the business with respect to the current and envisaged customers, which will ensure that the enterprise would be competitively and financially successful, locally and globally
2. The enterprise's capability/capacity, which is the totality of all the internal processes that dynamically realize this positioning of the business

Traditionally, positioning has been considered as an independent set of functional tasks split within the marketing, finance, and strategic planning functions. Similarly, capability/capacity has usually been considered the preserve of the individual operational departments that may have mutually conflicting priorities and measures of performances.

The problem for many enterprises lies in the fact that there is a fundamental flaw in the organizational structure—organizational structures are hierarchical, while the transactions and workflows that deliver the solutions (i.e., products and services) to the customers are horizontal. Quite simply, the structure determines who the customer really is. The traditional management structures condition managers to put functional needs above those of the multifunctional processes to which their functions contribute. This results in

- Various departments competing for resources
- Collective failure in meeting or exceeding the customers' expectations
- Inability to coordinate and collaborate on multifunctional customer-centric processes that would truly provide the competitive differentiation in future markets

The traditional mass marketing type of organization works well for researching market opportunities, planning the offering, and scheduling all of the steps required to produce and distribute the offering to the marketplace (where it is selected or rejected by the customer). It takes a very different kind of organization, namely the customized marketing-type organization, to build long-term relationships with customers so that they call such organizations first when they have a need because they trust that such enterprises will be able to respond with an effective solution. This is customer-responsive management, which we will discuss in the section that follows.

BPM is the process that manages and optimizes the inextricable linkages between the positioning and the capability/capacity of an enterprise. A company cannot position the enterprise to meet a customer need that it cannot fulfill without an unprofitable level of resources, nor can it allocate enhanced resources to provide a cost-effective service that no customer wants!

Positioning leads to higher levels of revenue through increasing the size of the market, retaining first-time customers, increasing the size of the wallet share, and so on. Positioning has to do with factors such as

- Understanding customer needs
- Understanding competitor initiatives
- Determining the businesses' financial needs
- Conforming with legal and regulatory requirements
- Conforming with environmental constraints

The capability/capacity has to be aligned with the positioning or else it has to be changed to deliver the positioning. Capability/capacity has to do with internal factors such as

- Key business processes
- Procedures and systems
- Competencies, skills, training, and education

The key is to have a perceived differentiation of being better than the competition in whatever terms the customers choose to evaluate or measure and to deliver this at the lowest unit cost.

In practice, BPM has developed a focus on changing capability/capacity in the short term to address current issues. This short-term change in capability/capacity is usually driven by the need to

■ Reduce the cycle time to process customer orders
■ Improve quotation times
■ Lower variable overhead costs
■ Increase product range to meet an immediate competitor threat
■ Rebalance resources to meet current market needs
■ Reduce work-in-progress stocks
■ Meet changed legislation requirements
■ Introduce short-term measures to increase market share (e.g., increased credit limit from customers hit by recessionary trends)

4.2.1 Business Process

A business process is typically a coordinated and logically sequenced set of work activities and associated resources that produce something of value to a customer. A business process can be simply defined as a collection of activities that create value by transforming inputs into more valuable outputs. These activities consist of a series of steps performed by actors to produce a product or service for the customer. Each process has an identified customer; it is initiated by a process trigger or a business event (usually a request for product or service arriving from the process customer); and it produces a process outcome (the product or a service requested by the customer) as its deliverable to the process customer.

A business process is a set of logically related tasks performed to achieve a well-defined business outcome. A (business) process view implies a horizontal view of a business organization and looks at processes as sets of interdependent activities designed and structured to produce a specific output for a customer or a market. A business process defines the results to be achieved, the context of the activities, the relationships between the activities, and the interactions with other processes and resources. A business process may receive events that alter the state of the process and the sequence of activities. A business process may produce events for input to other applications or processes. It may also invoke applications to perform computational functions, and it may post assignments to human work lists to request actions by human actors. Business processes can be measured, and different performance measures apply, like cost, quality, time, and customer satisfaction.

 There is a substantial difference between the concept of Business Process Management (BPM) and Business Process Management

Systems (BPM Systems). BPM is a concept of much broader scope than the BPM Systems that implement a subset of the tenets of BPM.

4.3 Business Process Management (BPM)

Business Process Management (BPM) refers to activities performed by enterprises to design (capture processes and document their design in terms of process maps), model (define business processes in a computer language), execute (develop software that enables the process), monitor (track individual processes for performance measurement), and optimize (retrieve process performance for improvement) operational business processes by using a combination of models, methods, techniques, and tools. BPM approaches based on IT enable support or automate business processes, in whole or in part, by providing computer-based systems support. These technology-based systems help coordinate and streamline business transactions, reduce operational costs, and promote real-time visibility in business performance.

BPM can be defined as *managing the achievement of an organization's objectives through the improvement, management, and control of essential business processes.* BPM is focused on improving corporate performance by managing a company's business processes.

BPM is a commitment to expressing, understanding, representing, and managing a business (or the portion of business to which it is applied) in terms of a collection of business processes that are responsive to a business environment of internal or external events. The term *management of business processes* includes process analysis, process definition and redefinition, resource allocation, scheduling, measurement of process quality and efficiency, and process optimization. Process optimization includes collection and analysis of both real-time measures (monitoring) and strategic measures (performance management) and their correlation as the basis for process improvement and innovation. A BPM solution is a graphical productivity tool for modeling, integrating, monitoring, and optimizing process flows of all sizes, crossing any application, company boundary, or human interaction. BPM codifies value-driven processes and institutionalizes their execution within the enterprise. This implies that BPM tools can help analyze, define, and enforce process standardization. BPM provides a modeling tool to visually construct, analyze, and execute cross-functional business processes.

Scenarios suitable for considering application of BPM within various areas are as follows:

1. Management
   – Lack of reliable or conflicting management information—process management and performance management

- The need to provide managers with more control over their processes
- The need for the introduction of a sustainable performance environment
- The need to create a culture of high performance
- The need to gain the maximum return on investment (RoI) from the existing legacy systems
- Budget cuts

2. Customers/suppliers/partners
   - An unexpected increase in number of customers, suppliers, or partners
   - Long lead times to meet customer/ supplier/ partner requests
   - Dissatisfaction with service, which could be due to:
     • High churn rates of staff
     • Inability of staff to answer questions adequately within the required time frames (responsiveness)
   - An organizational desire to focus upon customer intimacy
   - Customer segmentation or tiered service requirements
   - The introduction and strict enforcement of service levels
   - Major customers, suppliers, and/or partners requiring a unique (different) process
   - The need for a true end-to-end perspective to provide visibility or integration

3. Product and services
   - An unacceptably long lead time to market (lack of business agility)
   - Product-specific services like quality, compliance, and so on
   - New products or services comprise existing product/service elements
   - Products or services are complex

4. Organization
   - The need to provide the business with more control of its own processes
   - Organization objectives or goals are not being met—introduction of process management, linked to organizational strategy, performance measurement, and management of people
   - Compliance or regulation—for example, organizations currently have to comply with pollution, environment, and forest cover violation norms, hence process projects have been initiated—this process project has provided the platform to launch process improvement or bpm projects
   - The need for business agility to enable the enterprise to respond to opportunities as they arise
   - High growth—difficulty coping with high growth or proactively planning for high growth
   - Change in strategy—deciding to change direction or pace of operational excellence, product leadership, or customer intimacy
   - Reorganization or restructuring—changing roles and responsibilities

- Mergers and acquisition scenarios—these cause the organization to "acquire" additional complexity or necessitate rationalization of processes. The need to retire acquired legacy systems could also contribute. BPM projects enable a process layer to be "placed" across these legacy systems, providing time to consider appropriate conversion strategies.

 Existing functioning processes also are prone to progressive degradation, loss of efficiencies because of altered circumstances, changes in products or services, and so on. Business Processes may become candidates for BPM because of:

- The need for provision of visibility of processes from an end-to-end perspective
- Lack of communications and understanding of the end-to-end process by the parties performing parts of the process
- Unclear roles and responsibilities from a process perspective
- Lack of process standardization
- Poor quality and a substantial volume of rework
- Lack of clear process goals or objectives
- Too many hand-offs or gaps in a process, or no clear process at all
- Processes change too often or not at all

4.4 Enterprise BPM Methodology

In this section, we look at the full life cycle of an enterprise's BPM methodology.

 Outsourcing is distancing the company from non-core but critical functions; as against this reengineering, that is associated with BPM, is exclusively about the core.

We present an overview of the seven steps in a BPM methodology. These steps are as follows:

1. Develop the context for undertaking the BPM and in particular reengineer the enterprise's business processes. Then identify the reason behind redesigning the process to represent the value perceived by the customer.
2. Select the business processes for the design effort.
3. Map the selected processes.
4. Analyze the process maps to discover opportunities for design.

5. Design the selected processes for increased performance.
6. Implement the designed processes.
7. Measure the implementation of the designed processes.

The eight steps of the enterprise BPR methodology are shown in Figure 4.1

The BPR effort within an enterprise is not a one-time exercise but an ongoing one. One could also have multiple BPR projects in operation simultaneously in different areas within the enterprise. The BPR effort involves business visioning, identifying the value gaps, and, hence, selecting the corresponding business processes for the BPR effort. The reengineering of the business processes might open newer opportunities and challenges, which in turn triggers another cycle of business visioning followed by BPR of the business processes concerned. Figure 4.2 shows the iteration across the alternating activities without end.

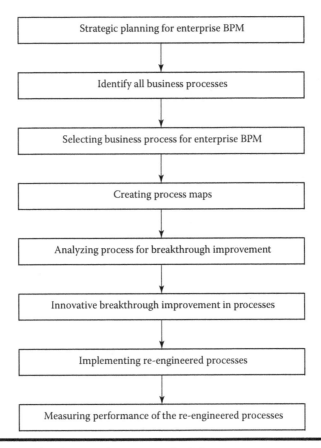

Figure 4.1   A cycle of enterprise BPR methodology.

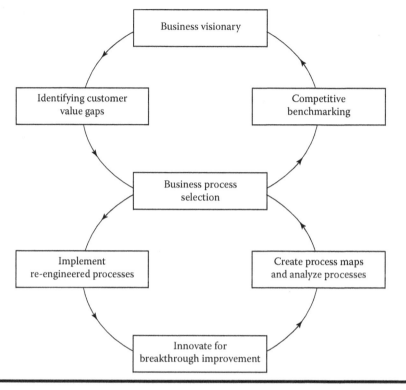

Figure 4.2 The alternate activities of business visioning and BPM.

4.4.1 Strategic Planning for Enterprise BPM

All markets are fluid to some degree, and these dynamic forces and shifting customer values necessitate changes in a company's strategic plans. The significance of a process to the success of a company's business is dependent on the nature and extent of the value addition to a product or service. Consequently, as stated earlier, one can understand the competitive value gap in terms of the customer-expected level of value and the value delivered by the enterprise for the concerned product or service.

The competitive gap can be defined as the gap between the customer's minimum acceptance value (MAV) and the customer value delivered by the enterprise. Companies that consistently surpass MAVs are destined to thrive, those that only meet the MAVs will survive, and those that fall short of the MAVs may fail.

CVDs are those business imperatives that must happen if the enterprise wants to close the competitive gap, and they are similar to the critical success factors (CSF) at the enterprise level. CVDs are in terms of factors like

- Time (lead time, cycle time, etc.)
- Flexibility (customization, options, composition, resource network interfaces, etc.)
- Responsiveness (lead time, duration, number of hand-offs, priority, number of queues, etc.)
- Quality of work (rework, rejects, yield, etc.)

Market segmentation is performed based on the customer value and the corresponding CVDs. Such a market segmentation helps in suggesting corrective strategic and tactical actions that may be required, such as in devising a process-oriented strategic business plan. The strategic plan can in turn help identify the major processes that support these critical value determinants that must be innovatively improved and reengineered.

4.4.1.1 Identifying the Business Processes in the Company

All business processes in an enterprise are identified and recorded. A process can be defined as a set of resources and activities necessary and sufficient to convert some form of input into some form of output. Processes can be internal or external or a combination of both. They cross functional boundaries, they have starting and ending points, and they exist at all levels within the enterprise, including section, department, division, and enterprise levels. In fact, processes exist across enterprise boundaries as well. Processes evolve and degrade in terms of their efficiency and effectiveness.

A process itself can consist of various sub-steps. The sub-steps in a process could be

- Value-added steps
- Non-value-added steps
- Legal and regulatory steps (which are treated as value-added steps)

4.4.2 Selecting Business Processes for BPM

Selecting the right processes for an innovative process reengineering effort is critical. The processes should be selected for their high visibility, relative ease of accomplishing goals, and, at the same time, their potential for great impact on the value determinants.

Customers will take their business to the company that can deliver the most value for their money. Hence, the MAVs have to be charted in detail. MAV is dependent upon several factors, such as

- The customer's prior general and particular experience base with an industry, product, and/or service

- What competition is doing in the concerned industry, product, or service
- What effect technological limitations have on setting the upper limit

As mentioned earlier, MAVs can be characterized in terms of the CVDs; only four to six value determinants may be necessary to profile a market segment. CVDs can be defined by obtaining data through

1. The customer value survey
2. Leaders in non-competing areas
3. The best-in-class performance levels
4. Internal customers

A detailed customer value analysis analyzes the value gaps and helps in further refining the goals of the process reengineering exercise. The value gaps are as follows:

- Gaps that result from different value perceptions in different customer groups
- Gaps between what the company provides and what the customer has established as the minimum performance level
- Gaps between what the company provides and what the competition provides
- Gaps between what the enterprise perceives as the MAV for the identified customer groups and what the customer says are the corresponding MAVs

It must be noted that analyzing the value gaps is not a one-time exercise; neither is it confined to the duration of a cycle of the breakthrough improvement exercise. Like the BPM exercise itself, it is an activity that must be done on an ongoing basis.

As a goal for the improvement effort, a clear, competitive advantage can be gained if best-in-class performance levels can be achieved in some key customer value areas and at least some MAVs can be achieved in all others.

4.4.3 Creating Process Maps

A process map documents the flow of one unit of work (the unit may be one item, one batch, or a particular service that is the smallest unit possible to follow separately) or what actually happens to the work going through the process. A process map is developed at several process levels, starting at the highest level of the enterprise. It documents both value-added and non-value-added steps. A process map could either be sequential or concurrent in nature.

Process could be mapped in two forms:

- Workflow chart form
- Work breakdown structure form

Process workflows fall into three categories: continuous workflows, balanced workflows, and synchronized workflows.

Workflow becomes non-synchronized because of

1. Steps or tasks produced at different rates, that is, an imbalanced workflow
2. Physical separation of operations causing work to move in batches, that is, a non-continuous workflow
3. Working in batches, causing intermittent flow
4. Long setup or change-over times resulting in batched work along with its problems
5. Variations in process inputs in terms of quality availability on time

All these add time and costs to the process and reduce flexibility and responsiveness.

Using the value-added workflow analysis of the process map, we can

1. Identify and measure significant reengineering opportunities
2. Establish a baseline of performance against which to measure improvement
3. Determine which tools may be most useful in the reengineering effort

Evidently, the major goal in reengineering the process is to eliminate non-value-added steps and wait times within processes. A good rule of thumb is to remove 60%–80% of the non-value-added steps, resulting in the total number of remaining steps to be no more than one to three times the number of value-added steps. Even this would be a credible goal for the first iteration of the BPR effort.

4.4.4 Analyzing Processes for Breakthrough Improvements

An enterprise's competitive strength lies in eliminating as many costly non-value-added steps and wait times as possible. The key to eliminating any non-value-added steps is to understand what causes them and then eliminate the cause.

For breakthrough improvements, the process maps are analyzed for

- Enterprise complexity: commonly organizational issues are a major deterrent to efficiency of the processes.
- Number of hand-offs: this involves especially those other than those associated with resource network interfaces.
- Work movement: Workflow charts are utilized to highlight move distances, that is, work movements.
- Process problems: several factors may have a severe effect on the continuity, balance, or synchronicity of the workflow. Examples are loops of non-value-added steps designed to address rework, errors, scraps, and so on. These may be on account of

- Long changeover times
- Process input/ output imbalances
- Process variabilities
- Process yields

■ These problems need to be identified, measured, analyzed, and resolved through innovative problem-solving methodology.

4.4.5 Innovative Breakthrough Improvement in Processes

The steps involved in innovative problem-solving methods are as follows:

1. Define a problem.
2. Find alternate solutions.
3. Evaluate the solutions.
4. Implement the best solution.
5. Measure and monitor the success.

The responsive process consists of the following components:

■ Diagnosing customer need
■ Developing customized solutions specific to organizational interfaces
■ Dynamically assigning work to the appropriate delivery unit
■ Tracking performance as each task is completed

Business problems fall into three basic categories:

■ System problems (methods, procedures, etc.)
■ Technical problems (engineering, operational, etc.)
■ People problems (skills, training, hiring, etc.): these problems arise because "if you change what a person does, you change what he or she is."

4.4.6 Implementing Designed Processes

This involves the following:

■ Reengineered vision and policies
■ Reengineered strategies and tactics
■ Reengineered systems and procedures
■ Reengineered communication environment
■ Reengineered organization architecture
■ Reengineered training environment

4.4.7 Measuring the Performance of Designed Processes

Measuring the performance of any process is very important, because lack of measurement would make it impossible to distinguish such a breakthrough effort from an incremental improvement effort of a Total Quality Management (TQM) program.

Measurements are essential because they are:

- Useful as baselines or benchmarks
- A motivation for further breakthrough improvements, which are important for future competitiveness

The measures for innovative process reengineering should be:

- Visible
- Meaningful
- Small in number
- Applied consistently and regularly
- Quantitative
- Involve the personnel closest to the process

Table 4.1 enlists tools and techniques for continuous improvement, and Table 4.2 lists some of the advanced techniques.

4.5 Business Process Reengineering (BPR)

Although BPR has its roots in information technology (IT) management, it is basically a business initiative that has major impact on the satisfaction of both the internal and external customer. Michael Hammer, who triggered the BPR revolution in 1990, considers BPR as a "radical change" for which IT is the key enabler. BPR can be broadly defined as *the rethinking and change of business processes to achieve dramatic improvements in the measures of performances such as cost, quality, service, and speed.*

Some of the principals advocated by Hammer are as follows:

- Organize around outputs, not tasks.
- Put the decisions and control, and hence all relevant information, into the hands of the performer.
- Have those who use the outputs of a process perform the process, including the creation and processing of the relevant information.
- The location of user, data, and process information should be immaterial; it should function as if all were in a centralized place.

Table 4.1 Tools, Techniques and Benefits for Continuous Improvement

Tools or Technique	Use
External customer survey	To understand the needs of the external customers
Internal customer survey	To understand the perceptions of internal Services
Staff survey	To obtain employee feedback on work environment
Brainstorming	To generate ideas for improvements
Cause and effect diagrams	To prompt ideas during brainstorming
Benchmarking	To compare similar processes to find the best practice
Service Performance	To quantify the importance/performance of services
Activity data	To underhand the allocation of time in processes
Activity categories	To obtain the level of core/support/divisionary activities
Activity drivers	To relate volumes of activity causes
High-low diagram	To group objects using two variables
Force-field analysis	To show the forces acting for/against a variable
Histogram	To show frequency of a variable in a range
Scatter diagram	To view the correlation between two variables
Affinity analysis	To measure the strength of functional relationships
Bar chard	To plot the frequency of an event
Run chart	To show how a variable changes over time
Pie chart	To show frequency of a variable in a range

As will become evident when perusing the above points, the implementation of enterprise systems (ES), especially BPM, possesses most of the characteristics mentioned above.

The most important outcome of BPR has been viewing business activities as more than a collection of individual or even functional tasks; it has engendered the process-oriented view of business. However, BPR is different from quality management efforts like TQM, ISO 9000, and so on, which refer to programs and

Table 4.2 Advanced Techniques for Continuous Improvement

Tools or Technique	Use
Statistical process Control (SPC)	SPC is a means to understand if a process is producing and is likely to produce an output that meets the spoliations within limits.
Failure mode and effects analysis (FMEA)	FMEA is a means to understand the nature of potential failure of component and the effect this will have on the complete systems.
Quality function deployment (QFD)	QFD is a structured process to build.
Taguchi methods	The design of experiments to create robust processes/ products where final quality is subject to many variables.

initiatives that emphasize bottom-up incremental improvements in existing work processes and outputs on a continuous basis. In contrast, BPR usually refers to top-down dramatic improvements through redesigned or completely new processes on a discrete basis. In the continuum of methodologies ranging from ISO 9000, TQM, ABM, and so on on one end and BPR on the other, ES, especially BPM, implementation definitely lies on the BPR side of the spectrum when it comes to corporate change management efforts.

BPR is based on the principle that there is an inextricable link between positioning *and* capability/capacity. A company cannot position the enterprise to meet a customer need that it cannot fulfill without an unprofitable level of resources, nor can it allocate enhanced resources to provide a cost-effective service that no customer wants!

BPR in practice has developed a focus on changing capability/capacity in the short term to address current issues. This short-term change in capability/capacity is usually driven by the need to:

■ Reduce the cycle time to process customer orders
■ Improve quotation times
■ Lower variable overhead costs
■ Increase product range to meet an immediate competitor threat
■ Rebalance resources to meet current market needs
■ Reduce work-in-progress stocks
■ Meet changed legislation requirements
■ Introduce short-term measures to increase market share (e.g., increased credit limit from customers hit by recessionary trends)
■ And so on

Outsourcing is distancing the company from non-core but critical functions; as against this, re-engineering is exclusively about the core.

An overview of a seven-step methodology is as follows:

1. Develop the context for undertaking the BPR and, in particular, reengineer the enterprise's business processes. Then identify the reason behind redesigning the process to represent the value perceived by the customer.
2. Select the business processes for the reengineering effort.
3. Map the selected processes.
4. Analyze the process maps to discover opportunities for reengineering.
5. Redesign the selected processes for increased performance.
6. Implement the reengineered processes.
7. Measure the implementation of the reengineered processes.

The BPR effort within an enterprise is not a one-time exercise but an ongoing one. One could also have multiple BPR projects in operation simultaneously in different areas within the enterprise. The BPR effort involves business visioning, identifying the value gaps, and, hence, selecting the corresponding business processes for the BPR effort. The reengineering of the business processes might open newer opportunities and challenges, which in turn triggers another cycle of business visioning followed by BPR of the concerned business processes.

The competitive gap can be defined as the gap between the customer's minimum acceptance value (MAV) and the customer value delivered by the enterprise. Companies that consistently surpass MAVs are destined to thrive, those that only meet the MAVs will survive, and those that fall short of the MAVs may fail. Customers will take their business to the company that can deliver the most value for their money. Hence, the MAVs have to be charted in detail. MAV is dependent on several factors, such as

- The customer's prior general and particular experience base with an industry, product, and/or service
- What competition is doing in the concerned industry, product, or service
- What effect technological limitations have on setting the upper limit

As mentioned earlier, MAVs can be characterized in terms of the CVDs; only four to six value determinants may be necessary to profile a market segment. CVDs can be defined by obtaining data through

1. The customer value survey
2. Leaders in noncompeting areas

3. The best-in-class performance levels
4. Internal customers

A detailed customer value analysis analyzes the value gaps and helps in further refining the goals of the process reengineering exercise. The value gaps are as follows:

■ Gaps that result from different value perceptions in different customer groups
■ Gaps between what the company provides and what the customer has established as the minimum performance level
■ Gaps between what the company provides and what the competition provides
■ Gaps between what the organization perceives as the MAV for the identified customer groups and what the customer says are the corresponding MAVs

It must be noted that analyzing the value gaps is not a one-time exercise; neither is it confined to the duration of a cycle of the breakthrough improvement exercise. Like the BPR exercise itself, it is an activity that must be done on an ongoing basis. Above all, selecting the right processes for an innovative process reengineering effort is critical. The processes should be selected for their high visibility, relative ease of accomplishing goals, and at the same time, their potential for great impact on the value determinants.

4.6 Management by Collaboration (MBC)

The business environment has been witnessing tremendous and rapid changes since the 1990s. There is an increasing emphasis on being customer focused and on leveraging and strengthening the company's core competencies. This has forced enterprises to learn and develop abilities to change and respond rapidly to the competitive dynamics of the global market.

Companies have learned to effectively reengineer themselves into flatter organizations, with closer integration across the traditional functional boundaries of the enterprise. There is increasing focus on employee empowerment and cross-functional teams. In this book, we are proposing that what we are witnessing is a fundamental transformation in the manner that businesses have been operating for the last century.

This change, which is primarily driven by the information revolution of the past few decades, is characterized by the dominant tendency to integrate across transaction boundaries, both internally and externally. The dominant theme of this new system of management, which has significant implications for organizational development, is *collaboration*. We will refer to this emerging and maturing constellation of concepts and practices as Management by Collaboration (MBC). ES, especially BPM, are major instruments for realizing MBC-driven enterprises.

MBC is an approach to management primarily focused on relationships; relationships by their very nature are not static and are constantly in evolution. As organizational and environmental conditions become more complex, globalized, and, therefore, competitive, MBC provides a framework for dealing effectively with the issues of performance improvement, capability development, and adaptation to the changing environment. MBC, as embodied by ES packages such as BPM, has had a major impact on the strategy, structure, and culture of the customer-centric enterprise.

The beauty and essence of MBC are that it incorporates in its very fabric the basic urge of humans for a purpose in life; for mutually beneficial relationships; for mutual commitment; and for being helpful to other beings, that is, for collaborating. These relationships could be at the level of individual, division, enterprise, or even between enterprises. Every relationship has a purpose, and manifests itself through various processes as embodied mainly in the form of teams; thus, the relationships are geared toward attainment of these purposes through the concerned processes optimally.

Because of the enhanced role played by the individual members of an enterprise in any relationship or process, MBC not only promotes their motivation and competence but also develops the competitiveness and capability of the enterprises as a whole. MBC emphasizes the roles of both the top management and the individual member. Thus, the MBC approach covers the whole organization through the means of basic binding concepts such as relationships, processes, and teams. MBC addresses readily all issues of management, including organization development. The issues range from organizational design and structure, role definition and job design, output quality and productivity, interaction and communication channels, and company culture to employee issues such as attitudes, perception, values, and motivation.

The basic idea of collaboration has been gaining tremendous ground with the increasing importance of business processes and dynamically constituted teams in the operations of companies. The traditional bureaucratic structures, which are highly formalized, centralized, and functionally specialized, have proven too slow, too expensive, and too unresponsive to be competitive. These structures are based on the basic assumption that all the individual activities and task elements in a job are independent and separable. Organizations were structured hierarchically in a "command-and-control" structure, and it was taken as an accepted fact that the output of the enterprise as a whole could be maximized by maximizing the output of each constituent organizational unit.

On the other hand, by their very nature, teams are flexible, adaptable, dynamic, and collaborative. They encourage flexibility, innovation, entrepreneurship, and responsiveness. For the last few decades, even in traditionally bureaucratic-oriented manufacturing companies, teams have manifested themselves and flourished successfully in various forms as super-teams, self-directed work teams (SDWT), quality circles, and so on. The dynamic changes in the market and global competition being confronted by companies necessarily lead to flatter and more flexible organizations with a dominance of more dynamic structures like teams.

People in teams, representing different functional units, are motivated to work within constraints of time and resources to achieve a defined goal. The goals might range from incremental improvements in responsiveness, efficiency, quality, and productivity to quantum leaps in new-product development. Even in traditional businesses, the number and variety of teams instituted for various functions, projects, tasks, and activities has been on the increase.

Increasingly, companies are populated with worker-teams that have special skills, operate semi-autonomously, and are answerable directly to peers and to the end customers. Members must not only have higher level of skills than before, but must also be more flexible and capable of doing more jobs. The empowered workforce with considerably enhanced managerial responsibilities (pertaining to information, resources, authority, and accountability) has resulted in an increase in worker commitment and flexibility. Whereas workers have witnessed gains in the quality of their work life, corporations have obtained returns in terms of increased interactivity, responsiveness, quality, productivity, and cost improvements.

Consequently, in the past few years, a new type of non-hierarchical network organization with distributed intelligence and decentralized decision-making powers has been evolving. This entails a demand for constant and frequent communication and feedback among the various teams or functional groups. ES packages such as BPM essentially provide such an enabling environment through modules like BI, Product Lifecycle Management (PLM), and so on.

4.7 Collaboration Technologies

Communication is the vehicle for creating synergy and for keeping a team together and moving it forward. However, communicating with one's team members can become problematic when those team members are geographically dispersed throughout the globe, reside in different time zones, possess different levels of technological proficiency, and come from different cultural backgrounds. Thus, one of the key challenges facing virtual teams is how to effectively communicate with one another across distance.

The reasons for difficulties in communicating and exchanging information virtually are:

1. Differing speed: Rate or speed at which communication flows can result in information overload at the receiving end. As virtual team members attempt to deal with information overload, they may block out potentially important communication exchanges.

    Table 4.3 shows the typical download requirements of applications.
2. Differing time: Time refers to *when* people work. Virtual team members may be assigned different hours, different shifts, and different days to work. They may also work at the same moment but in a different time zone.

Table 4.3   Typical Download Requirements for Applications

Application	Download speed	Delay requirements	Other
Voice over IP (VoIP)	64 kbps	200 ms	Protection
Videoconferencing	2 Mbps	200 ms	Protection
File sharing	3 Mbps	1 s	–
Standard-definition television (SDTV)	4.5 Mbps/channel	10 s	Multicasting
Real-time video	10 Mbps	200 ms	Content distribution
Video 011 demand (VoD)	20 Mbps	10 s	Low packet loss
High-definition television (HDTV)	20 Mbps/channel	10 s	Multicasting
Network-hosted software	25 Mbps	200 ms	Data security

3. Differing space: Space refers to *where* people work. Virtual team workers may work in close proximity to one another or be quite remote. They may share the same office or a different one on the same floor or another floor in a given building. Or they may also be located in different buildings, in different cities, and even in different countries.

4. Differing information richness: Information richness refers to the potential information carrying capacity of data.

More specifically, communication channels differ in their ability to handle multiple cues simultaneously, facilitate rapid feedback, and be personal. Rich communication methods are highly interactive and rely on a great deal of information, thereby reducing confusion and misunderstanding. Face-to-face communication is the richest channel because it provides for the maximum amount of information to be transmitted during a communication exchange. Multiple cues (such as words, posture, facial expression, gestures, and intonations) and immediate feedback (both verbal and non-verbal) can be shared. Lean or less rich communication methods are static or one-way and convey much less information.

Moderately rich forms of communication include videoconferencing, audioconferencing, and telephone conversations. Computer-mediated communication is a lean channel, because no non-verbal cues are present. Written letters and memos are the leanest forms of communication.

5. Differing social presence: Social presence refers to the degree to which a specific type of technology facilitates warmth, sensitivity, and a personal connection with others. Face-to-face meetings have a high level of social presence, allowing for facial expressions, touch, posture, and other non-verbal cues to be communicated along with the verbal message. E-mail and other forms of written communication have far less social presence. E-mail is more of a one-way communication answered by another one-way communication rather than a two-way personal dialogue exchange. Despite the fact that we can add emotions in our written messages by way of a variety of emoticons (i.e., sad or happy face icons), it is still much harder for a virtual team member to feel a high level of involvement or sense of interpersonal dialogue in this medium.

   Whether communications are synchronous or asynchronous also adds to the degree of social presence experienced. Synchronous communication tools, such as face-to-face, audioconferences, and videoconferences, have more social presence than asynchronous communication tools such as e-mail or voice mail.

6. Differing cultures: Culture refers to *how* people work together—the ways in which they deal with each other. Elements of culture include languages, races, nationalities, professions, and education, as well as religious, political, social, and economic factors. In a way, even gender can influence culture.

Figure 4.3 shows space and time dimensions of collaboration

		Time	
		Same "Synchronous"	Different "Asynchronous"
Space	Same "Co-located"	Face-to-Face, Voting, Presentation Support, etc.	E-mail, Voicemail, Document Repositories, etc.
	Different "Virtual"	Video/audio-conferencing, Chat, Instant messaging, etc.	E-mail, Threaded Discussions, Document Repositories, etc.

Figure 4.3 Collaboration in space and time dimensions.

The various possible interactions are

- Same Time (synchronous) and Same Place (collocated): this characterizes face-to-face interaction, and it can happen using meeting rooms, shared tables, and whiteboards.
- Different Time (asynchronous) and Same Place (collocated): this represents continuous work on the same task, and it can occur in meeting rooms and by using large displays and whiteboards or through shared workstations.
- Same Time (synchronous) and Different Place (remote): this represents remote interaction, and it is supported by technologies such as electronic meeting systems, video-conferencing systems, and instant messaging software applications like chat programs.
- Different time (asynchronous) and Different Place (remote): this is accomplished by continuous communication and coordination, and it uses systems like e-mail, voice mail, fax machines, electronic meeting systems, blogs, workflow management systems and shared database systems.

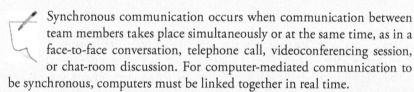 Synchronous communication occurs when communication between team members takes place simultaneously or at the same time, as in a face-to-face conversation, telephone call, videoconferencing session, or chat-room discussion. For computer-mediated communication to be synchronous, computers must be linked together in real time.

Asynchronous communication occurs when communication between team members is not simultaneous and does not occur at the same time. Common asynchronous forms of communications are e-mail, shared database systems, and bulletin boards (an electronic notice board where users post notices).

4.7.1 Synchronous Communication Tools

The most obvious and yet least-used method for communicating is the face-to-face meeting or discussion. When it is not feasible to hold a meeting face to face, holding team meetings via a computer network is a workable option. And if these computer meetings are synchronous and have the capability to include text, audio, and video links, they can come quite close to possessing the levels of information richness and social presence that exist in face-to-face interactions. In these synchronous meetings, team members can transfer and send one another text and data files. A variety of tools may be incorporated into a synchronous computer meeting.

Internet Relay Chat (IRC) technology is basically an online equivalent of a conversation in real time. For creative work, setting up separate, dedicated chat rooms to discuss different ideas, topics, or projects may be useful. Instant messaging (IM) is similar to a chat room except it is between two people (not an entire team) and one does not have to enter the chat room to converse—the IM chat box pops up on the screen, allowing team members to talk through text in a live, synchronous conversation.

Electronic chat rooms may be combined with interactive whiteboards that display shared documents and allow users to sketch thoughts or ideas. Desktop video systems are useful in allowing team members to transmit and share either still visual images or full motion video. In addition, desktop audio links allow for real-time, parallel voice discussion about the shared work. Synchronous computer meetings require that all team members have computer, video, and audio capabilities and specialized groupware software.

4.7.2 Asynchronous Communication Tools

There are a variety of groupware software tools that allow virtual team members to work on projects asynchronously through shared database systems or shared files. Shared database systems allow team members to transform textual documents and e-mail messages into databases and to create fields that can be searched and indexed. Information is frequently distributed on servers, and individual team members have the ability to search the database and transfer information to their personalized databases and tailor it for their own use. More sophisticated systems have the capability to store a variety of data, including multi-media information.

Bulletin-board tools provide shared space for the posting of messages and ideas and for asynchronous discussions about questions or issues that do not require immediate answers. Discussions can be structured as linear or threaded. In a linear discussion, responses are added to the end of a linear chain of messages. In threaded discussions, a response can be attached directly to any message, so a discussion can potentially branch out infinitely. In general, threaded discussions seem better for question-and-answer applications (e.g., technical support), while linear structures are more useful for extended conversation on deeper issues. Bulletin boards allow participants to become involved at their own convenience rather than having to match the schedule of others.

E-mail is the most common and best understood form of information technology used for work from a distance. E-mail is a destination address where an individual can be reached virtually, regardless of geographic address. E-mail is best suited for one-to-one communication and sometimes group messaging or copying others. E-mail can also be merged with other collaborative technologies (e.g., audio and video links) to provide higher levels of information richness and social presence.

Group calendars and scheduling tools assist team members in creating and manipulating information on their individual calendars and in scheduling and coordinating team meetings and requests for resources or information that are shared among team members. Each team member's calendar and schedule can be accessible anytime from any Web browser, which reduces scheduling conflicts.

4.8 Collaborative Systems and Tools

Traditional forms of communication, such as telephones, mail, and even face-to-face meetings, are slowly being replaced by computer-based systems where different kinds of socialization are enhanced through media sharing, reflection on past experiences, and a bundle of additional services, supporting socialization among people. Based on the previous facts, organizations are trying to integrate social collaboration capabilities into their strategies, operations, and processes. Whether it is with customers, partners, or employees, these organizations use social collaboration tools to improve efficiency, solve problems, create opportunities, boost productivity, and drive innovation that makes them more competitive and successful.

4.8.1 Skype

This application is a free voice over Internet Protocol (VOIP) service and instant messaging developed by the company recently acquired by the software giant Microsoft. Skype can be used to meet the following goals:

■ Calling and videoconferencing over the Internet
■ Training team members on using software using screen-sharing ability with others
■ Making cheap calls on landlines and mobile devices
■ Instant text messaging from computer to computer;
■ Conducting meetings and conferences

4.8.2 Dropbox

Dropbox is a file hosting service that offers many capabilities such as cloud storage and file synchronization. It allows users to share contents through folders, which they can create on their computers. Dropbox synchronizes those folders in order to show the same folder (with the same contents) despite the media or the device that is used to view them. This product can be used to meet the following goals:

■ Storing and backing up any kind of file
■ Immediate synchronization and sharing of files across computers and among users who are located in different geographical locations
■ Sending and sharing files that are too large to e-mail.

4.8.3 Google Drive and Google Docs

Google Drive is a file storage and synchronization service provided by Google, and it provides users with features related to cloud storage, file sharing, and documents editing in a collaborative manner. In this service, the files shared publicly on Google Drive can be searched with web search engines. Google Docs is a freeware Web-based office suite offered by Google within its Google Drive service. It allows users to create and edit documents, spreadsheets, and presentations online while collaborating with other users live. With Google Docs, users and companies can do the following:

- Create, collaborate on, share, and edit documents online
- Collaborate in real time, which means that the users can see the changes instantly
- Manage different revisions of a document
- Create online forms for conducting community surveys

4.8.4 Microsoft SkyDrive

SkyDrive is a file hosting service from Microsoft that allows users to upload and sync files to cloud storage and then access them from a Web browser or their local device. It allows users to keep the files private, share them with contacts, or make the files public, which means that users do not require a Microsoft account to access them. The features of the Microsoft SkyDrive service include that

- It allows users to upload, create, edit, and share Microsoft Office documents directly within a Web browser.
- It provides the ability to integrate with Microsoft Office and Outlook.
- Users can share the documents on social networks.
- It supports geo-location data for photos uploaded onto the service.

4.8.5 Microsoft OneNote

OneNote is a software from Microsoft that enables free-form information gathering and provides capabilities for multi-user teamwork. It can accept entries such as users' handwritten or typed notes, sketches, and audio explanations. Notes can be shared with other OneNote users over the Internet or a network, and it is available for different operating systems. Also, Microsoft offers a Web-based version of OneNote as part of the SkyDrive or Office Web Apps, providing users with the ability to modify notes via a Web browser. This software allows companies and users to

- Create notes, outlines, clippings of websites, and collections of images
- Share and collaborate the created notes
- Access the notes from mobiles, Web, or desktop devices
- Outline collaborative presentations

- Maintain a shared repository for research and project notes
- Maintain a digital field journal

4.9 Summary

BPMs enable the reconciled, that is, collaborative, working of different cross-company stakeholders of any business process, activity, or decision in compliance with its strategy, policy, and procedures. After introducing the concept of BPM, the chapter described the BPM methodology in detail. The chapter looked at Management by Collaboration (MBC) as a unifying framework in the context of the customer-centric and customer-responsive enterprise.

Chapter 5

Analytics

This chapter introduces the nature, type, and scope of decisions. It discusses the decision-making process and the techniques used for making decisions. Five broad categories of decision-support systems (DSSs) are explained, including data-driven, model-driven, communications-driven, document-driven, and knowledge-driven DSSs. The latter half of the chapter presents a generic DSS architecture to enable discussion of text, hypertext, database, spreadsheet, rule-oriented DSSs, and compound DSSs.

An inevitable consequence of organizations using the pyramid-shaped hierarchy is that there is a decision-making bottleneck at the top of the organization. The people at the top are overwhelmed by the sheer volume of decisions they have to make; they are too far away from the scene of the action to really understand what is happening; and, by the time decisions are made, the actions are usually too little and too late. Consequently, companies suffer by staggering from one bad decision to another. No small group of executives, regardless of their smarts, hard work, or sophisticated computer systems, can make all those decisions in a timely or competent manner. Given the pace of change, companies need something more agile and responsive.

The centralized command and control methods that worked for hierarchies will not work for service delivery networks. Instead of a small group of executives telling everybody else what to do, people need to get the authority to figure out for themselves what to do. The need to be responsive to evolving customer needs and desires creates operational structures and systems where business analysis and decision making are pushed out to operating units that are closest to the scene of the action—which, however, lack the expertise and resources to access, process, evaluate, and decide on the course of action. This engenders the significance of analysis systems that are essential for enabling decisive action as close to the customer as possible. Closed-loop decision making resulting from combination of ongoing performance management with ongoing business analysis can lead to an effective responsive enterprise; hence, the need for intelligent business analysis.

5.1 Decisions

A decision is a choice from multiple alternatives, usually made with a fair degree of rationality. In an enterprise, these decisions may concern the development of a strategic plan and imply therefore substantial investment choices, the definition of marketing initiatives and related sales predictions, and the design of a production plan that allows the available human and technological resources to be employed in an effective and efficient way.

The decision-making process is part of a broader subject usually referred to as *problem solving*, which refers to the process through which individuals try to bridge the gap between the current operating conditions of a system (as is) and the supposedly better conditions to be achieved in the future (to be). In general, the transition of a system toward the desired state implies overcoming certain obstacles and is not easy to attain. This forces decision makers to devise a set of alternative feasible options to achieve the desired goal, and then to choose a decision based on a comparison between the advantages and disadvantages of each option. Hence, the decision selected must be put into practice and then verified to determine if it has enabled the planned objectives to be achieved. When this fails to happen, the problem is reconsidered, according to a recursive logic.

5.1.1 Types of Decisions

Organizational decision problems are of various types, from daily operational decisions to long-term strategy business decisions and from internal single decisions to multi-level decisions or multi-organizational decisions. Decision makers can be at various levels according to their decision problems, such as a product distributor, a supermarket manager, or a head of department. Organizational decision making seeks to find the optimal or most satisfactory solution for a decision problem such as selecting the best from a set of product prototypes, making an optimized resource plan, choosing the most suitable supplier, and determining a product's price. Different decision-making tasks may have different features and therefore are modeled in different forms or presented by different methods and solved by different decision-support techniques.

A classical classification is based on a given problem's degree of complexity:

1. Structured: A structured decision problem can be described by classic mathematical models, such as linear programming or statistics methods. A typical structured decision example is to select a supplier who has the lowest price

of all the suppliers with the same quality/type of products or determines a product plan that will bring the highest profit of all the possible product plans in a factory. The procedure for obtaining an optimal solution is known by standard solution methods. For example, goal programming can be used to solve a linear programming model when the decision maker provides a goal for their decision objective.

2. Semi-structured: Semi-structured decision problems fall between structured and unstructured problems, having both structured and unstructured features and reflecting most real-world situations. Solving semi-structured decision problems involves a combination of both standard optimization solution procedures and human judgment, and it also needs the support of related intelligent information processing techniques and inference approaches.

3. Unstructured: An unstructured decision problem is fuzzy, uncertain, and vague, one for which there is no standard solution method for obtaining an optimal solution or where such an optimal solution does not exist. Human intuition is often the basis for decision making in an unstructured problem. Typical unstructured problems include planning new services to customers, hiring an executive for a big company, choosing a set of development projects for a long period, or making a set of policies for a social issue.

Multi-level decision making (MLDM) problems appear in many situations that require compromise between the objectives of two or more interacting entities and these entities are arranged within a hierarchical structure with independent and perhaps conflicting objectives.

Computer-based decision-support techniques can be more useful in structured and semi-structured decision problems than unstructured decision problems. In an unstructured decision problem, only part of the problem can be assisted by computerized decision-support techniques. For semi-structured decision problems, a computerized decision-support technique can improve the quality of the information on which a decision is based, therefore increasing the decision maker's situation awareness to reach a better decision and improve decision efficiency.

5.1.2 Scope of Decisions

The characteristics of the intelligence required in a decision-making process will change depending on the scope of the decisions to be supported (Figure 5.1):

1. Strategic decisions: Decisions are strategic when they affect the entire organization or at least a substantial part of it for a long period of time. Strategic decisions strongly influence the general objectives and policies of an enterprise. As

Enterprise intelligence characteristics	Scope of decisions		
Accuracy	High	←——→	Low
Level of detail	Detailed	←——→	Aggregate
Time horizon	Present	←——→	Future
Frequency of use	High	←——→	Low
Source	Internal	←——→	External
Scope of information	Quantitative	←——→	Qualitative
Nature of information	Narrow	←——→	Wide
Age of information	Present	←——→	Past

Figure 5.1   Characteristics of enterprise intelligence in terms of the scope of the decisions.

a consequence, strategic decisions are taken at a higher organizational level, usually by the company's top management.

2. Managerial decisions: Tactical decisions affect only parts of an enterprise and are usually restricted to a single department. The time span is limited to a medium-term horizon, typically up to a year. Tactical decisions place themselves within the context determined by strategic decisions. In a company hierarchy, tactical decisions are made by middle managers, such as the heads of the company departments.

3. Operational decisions: Operational decisions refer to specific activities carried out within an organization and have a modest impact on the future. Operational decisions are framed within the elements and conditions determined by strategic and tactical decisions. Therefore, they are usually made at a lower organizational level by knowledge workers responsible for a single activity or task, such as sub-department heads, workshop foremen, or back-office heads.

5.2 Decision-Making Process

The nature of a decision process depends on many factors, like the characteristics of the organization within which the system is placed: the subjective attitudes of the decision makers, the availability of appropriate problem-solving methodologies, and the availability of effective decision-support tools.

The decision-making process is characterized by various factors:

- The decisions made within a public or private enterprise or organization are often interconnected and determine broad effects. Each decision has consequences for many individuals and several parts of the organization.
- Decisions are often devised by a group of individuals instead of a single decision maker.
- The number of alternative actions may be very high and sometimes unlimited.
- The effects of a given decision usually appear later, not immediately.
- Experiments carried out in a real-world system, according to a trial-and-error scheme, are too costly and risky to be of practical use for decision making.
- The dynamics in which an enterprise operates is strongly affected by the pressure of a competitive environment, implying that knowledge workers need to address situations and make decisions quickly and in a timely fashion.
- During the decision-making process, knowledge workers are asked to access data and information and work on them based on a conceptual and analytical framework.
- Feedback plays an important role in providing information and knowledge for future decision-making processes within a given organization.
- In most instances, the decision-making process has multiple goals, with different performance indicators, that might also be in conflict with one another.
- Many decisions are made in a fuzzy context and entail risk factors. The level of propensity or aversion to risk varies significantly among different individuals.

Decision-making processes consist of the following steps:

1. Intelligence: In the intelligence phase, the task of the decision maker is to identify, circumscribe, and explicitly define the problem that emerges in the system under study. The analysis of the context and all the available information may allow decision makers to quickly grasp the signals and symptoms pointing to a corrective action to improve the system performance. For example, during the execution of a project, the intelligence phase may consist of a comparison between the current progress of the activities and the original development plan. In general, it is important not to confuse the problem with the symptoms. For example, suppose that an e-commerce bookseller receives a complaint concerning late delivery of a book order placed online. Such inconvenience may be interpreted as the problem and be tackled by arranging a second delivery by priority shipping to circumvent the dissatisfaction of the customer.
2. Design: In the design phase, actions aimed at solving the identified problem should be developed and planned. At this level, the experience and creativity

of the decision makers play a critical role, as they are asked to devise viable solutions that ultimately allow the intended purpose to be achieved. Where the number of available actions is small, decision makers can make an explicit enumeration of the alternatives to identify the best solution. If, on the other hand, the number of alternatives is very large or even unlimited, their identification occurs in an implicit way, usually through a description of the rules that feasible actions should satisfy. For example, these rules may directly translate into the constraints of an optimization model.

3. Choice: Once the alternative actions have been identified, it is necessary to evaluate them on the basis of the performance criteria deemed significant. Mathematical models and the corresponding solution methods usually play a valuable role during the choice phase. For example, optimization models and methods allow the best solution to be found in very complex situations involving countless or even infinite feasible solutions. On the other hand, decision trees can be used to handle decision-making processes influenced by stochastic events.

4. Implementation: When the best alternative has been selected by the decision maker, it is transformed into action by means of an implementation plan. This involves assigning responsibilities and roles to all those involved into the action plan.

5. Control: Once the action has been implemented, it is finally necessary to verify and check that the original expectations have been satisfied and the effects of the action match the original intentions. In particular, the differences between the values of the performance indicators identified in the choice phase and the values actually observed at the end of the implementation plan should be measured. In an adequately planned DSS, the results of these evaluations translate into experience and information, which are then transferred into the data warehouse to be used during subsequent decision-making processes.

5.3 Decision-Making Techniques

Decision techniques involved in modeling and executing the decision-making process:

5.3.1 Mathematical Programming

Mathematical programming, or optimization, refers to the study of decision-making problems in which one seeks to minimize or maximize a function by systematically choosing the values of variables from an allowed set (a feasible set). A mathematical programming model includes three sets of elements: decision variables, objective functions, and constraints (constraint conditions), where uncontrollable variables or parameters are within the objective functions and the constraints. Many real-world decision problems can be modeled by mathematical programming models.

Different types of mathematical programming models:

- Linear programming
- Multi-objective programming
- Bi-level/multi-level programming

Linear programming is an important type of mathematical optimization in which there is only one objective function, and the objective function and constraints are expressions of linear relationships among decision variables. Linear programming is heavily used in various management activities, either to maximize the profit or minimize the cost of an organization.

5.3.2 Multi-Criteria Decision Making

When we need to select the best option from a list of alternatives based on multiple criteria for a decision problem, it is often necessary to analyze each alternative in the light of its determination of each of these criteria. Multi-criteria decision making (MCDM), also called multi-attribute decision making (MADM), refers to making preferred decisions (e.g., evaluation, prioritization, and selection) in the presence of multiple and conflicting criteria over the alternatives available. An MCDM utility model combines all the criteria of a given alternative simultaneously through the use of a specific utility formula or utility function. Problems for MCDM may range from those in our daily life, such as the selection of a restaurant, to those affecting entire nations

The taxonomy of strategies and corresponding criteria for decision making can be classified into four categories known as *intuitive, empirical, heuristic,* and *rational* as shown in Table 5.1; 4.1.3.2–Risks, 4.1.3.3–Uncertainty, 4.1.3.3–Pessimist—Optimist, and 4.1.3.3.3–Regretist.

5.3.3 Case-Based Reasoning

Many decision problems cannot be modeled by mathematical programming models. Managers often produce a solution for a given problem based on their previous experience and knowledge. Case-based reasoning (CBR) provides an effective methodology for DSS in solving a new problem based on the solutions of similar past problems. The technique of CBR provides a powerful learning ability that uses past experiences as a basis for dealing with new similar problems. A CBR system can, therefore, facilitate the knowledge acquisition process by eliminating the time required to elicit solutions from experts. In dynamically changing situations where the problem cannot be modeled by mathematical models and solutions are not easy to generate, CBR is the preferred method of reasoning.

Table 5.1 Taxonomy of Strategies and Corresponding Criteria for Decision Making

No.	Category	Strategy	Criterion (C)
1	**Intuitive**		
1.1		Arbitrary	Based on the easiest or most familiar choice
1.2		Preference	Based on propensity, hobby, tendency, expectation
1.3		Common sense	Based on axioms and judgment
2	**Empirical**		
2.1		Trial and error	Based on exhaustive trial
2.2		Experiment	Based on experiment results
2.3		Experience	Based on existing knowledge
2.4		Consultant	Based on professional consultation
2.5		Estimation	Based on tough evaluation
3	**Heuristic**		
3.1		Principles	Based on scientific theories
3.2		Ethics	Based on philosophical judgment and belief
3.3		Representative	Based on common rules of thumb
3.4		Availability	Based on limited information or local maximum
3.5		Anchoring	Based on presumption or bias and their justification
4	**Rational**		
4.1	Static		
4 1.1		Minimum cost	Based on minimizing energy, time, money

(*Continued*)

Table 5.1 (Continued)   Taxonomy of Strategies and Corresponding Criteria for Decision Making

No.	Category	Strategy	Criterion (C)
4.1.2		Maximum benefit	Based on maximizing gain of usability, functionality, reliability, quality, dependability
4.1.3		Maximum utility	Based on cost-benefit ratio
4.1.3.1		• Certainty	Based on maximum probability, statistic data
4.1.3.2		• Risks	Based on minimum loss or regret
		• Uncertainty	
4.1.3.3		• Pessimist	Based on maximum
4.1.3.4		• Optimist	Based on maximum
4.1.3.5		• Regretist	Based on maximum of regrets
4.2	Dynamic		
4.2.1		Interactive events	Based on automata
4.2.2		Games	Based on conflict
4.2.2.1		• Zero sum	Based on $\sum (gain + loss) = 0$
4.2.2.2		• Non-zero sum	Based on $\sum (gain + loss) \neq 0$
4.2.3		Decision gilds	Based on a series of choices in a decision grid

5.3.4 Data Warehouse and Data Mining

Data warehouse is a repository of an organization's electronically stored data. A data warehouse system involves not only data storage but also the techniques to retrieve and analyze data; to extract, transform, and load data; and to manage the data dictionary. In particular, the data warehouse includes business intelligence tools to implement the above functions to better support business decision making.

Data mining is the process of extracting hidden and undiscovered patterns from data and is commonly used in a wide range of profiling practices and knowledge discovery projects. Rules and patterns are discovered from data with the aim of leading to a set of options or decisions. In most data-mining applications, a data file of query results is created from a data warehouse and then analyzed by a specialist using artificial intelligence or statistical tools.

5.3.5 Decision Tree

A decision tree is a graphic description of a set of decision rules and their possible consequences. It can be used to create a plan to reach a goal of decision. A decision tree, as a special form of tree structure, is a predictive model to map observations about an item with conclusions about the item's target value. Each interior node corresponds to a variable, and an arc to a child node represents a possible value or splitting condition of that variable. The decision-tree approach, as a decision-support tool, models a decision problem and its possible consequences in a tree-like graph. It is very suitable for a decision that involves possible chance event outcomes, resource costs, and utility. Decision trees are commonly used in decision analysis to help identify the strategy that is most likely to reach a goal. In applications, a decision tree or consequences can contain fuzzy numbers or linguistic terms and are therefore called *fuzzy decision trees*.

5.3.6 Fuzzy Sets and Systems

Whatever decision techniques are used, a critical issue is to deal with is uncertainty. Decision environments and data sources often have various uncertain factors, resulting in uncertain relations among decision objectives and decision entities. For example, an individual's preference for alternatives and judgment for criteria are often expressed by linguistic terms such as "low" and "high," which are uncertain expressions. Precise mathematical and inference approaches are not efficient enough to tackle such uncertainty.

Various uncertain information processing techniques have therefore been developed by using fuzzy sets, fuzzy numbers, and fuzzy logic in decision-making activities. Research results include new methodologies and algorithms of fuzzy multi-objective decision making, fuzzy multi-criteria decision making, fuzzy case-based reasoning, fuzzy decision trees, fuzzy data retrieval, and fuzzy association rules. Various applications of fuzzy decision making have been developed as well.

5.4 Decision-Support Systems

Decision-support systems (DSSs) enable decisions based on the data collected through the various systems across the enterprise.

5.4.1 Multi-Source Driven DSSs

1. Data-Driven DSSs: Data-driven DSSs emphasize access to and manipulation of a time series of internal company data and sometimes external and real-time data. Simple file systems accessed by query and retrieval tools provide the most elementary level of functionality. Data warehouse systems that allow the manipulation of data by computerized tools tailored to a specific task and setting or by more general tools and operators provide additional functionality. Data-driven DSSs with online analytical processing provide the highest level of functionality and decision support that is linked to analysis of large collections of historical data.

2. Model-Driven DSSs: Model-driven DSSs emphasize access to and manipulation of financial, optimization, and/or simulation models. Simple quantitative models provide the most elementary level of functionality. Model-driven DSSs use limited data and parameters provided by decision makers to aid decision makers in analyzing a situation, but in general, large databases are not needed for model-driven DSSs. In 1978, Dan Bricklin and Bob Frankston co-invented the software program VisiCalc (visible calculator). VisiCalc provided managers the opportunity for hands-on computer-based analysis and decision support at a reasonably low cost. VisiCalc was the first killer application for personal computers and made possible the development of many model-oriented, personal DSSs for use by managers.

3. Communications-Driven DSSs: Communications-driven DSSs use network and communications technologies to facilitate decision-relevant collaboration and communication. In these systems, communication technologies are the dominant architectural component. Tools used include groupware, videoconferencing, and computer-based bulletin boards. D. Engelbart's 1962 paper "Augmenting human intellect: A conceptual framework" is the anchor for much of the later work related to communications-driven DSSs. In 1989, Lotus introduced a groupware product called Notes and broadened the focus of Group DSSs (GDSSs) to include enhancing communication, collaboration, and coordination among groups of people. Notes had its roots in a product called PLATO Notes, written at the Computer-based Education Research Laboratory (CERL) at the University of Illinois in 1973 by David R. Woolley.

   In general, groupware, bulletin boards, audioconferencing, and videoconferencing are the primary technologies for communications-driven decision support. In the past few years, voice and video delivered using the Internet protocol have greatly expanded the possibilities for synchronous communications-driven DSSs.

4. Knowledge-Driven DSSs: Knowledge-driven DSSs can suggest or recommend actions to managers. These DSSs are person-computer systems

with specialized problem-solving expertise. The expertise consists of knowledge about a particular domain, understanding of problems within that domain, and skill at solving some of these problems. In 1965, a Stanford University research team led by Edward Feigenbaum created the DENDRAL expert system. DENDRAL led to the development of other rule-based reasoning programs including MYCIN, which helped physicians diagnose blood diseases based on sets of clinical symptoms. The MYCIN project resulted in development of the first expert-system shell. In 1983, Dustin Huntington established EXSYS. That company and product made it practical to use PC-based tools to develop expert systems.

Artificial Intelligence (AI) systems have been developed to detect fraud and expedite financial transactions, many additional medical diagnostic systems have been based on AI, and expert systems have been used for scheduling in manufacturing operation and web-based advisory systems. In recent years, connecting expert systems technologies to relational databases with Web-based front ends has broadened the deployment and use of knowledge-driven DSSs.

5. Document-Driven DSSs: A document-driven DSS uses computer storage and processing technologies to provide document retrieval and analysis. Large document databases may include scanned documents, hypertext documents, images, sounds, and video. Examples of documents that might be accessed by a document-driven DSS are policies and procedures, product specifications, catalogs, and corporate historical documents, including minutes of meetings and correspondence. A search engine is a primary decision-aiding tool associated with a document-driven DSS. These systems have also been called text-oriented DSSs. The precursor for this type of DSS is Vannevar Bush's (1945) article titled "As we may think." Bush wrote "Consider a future device for individual use, which is a sort of mechanized private file and library. It needs a name, and to coin one at random, 'memex' will do." Bush's memex is a much broader vision than that of today's document-driven DSS.

By 1995, T. Berners-Lee's World Wide Web was recognized by a number of software developers and academics as a serious platform for implementing all types of decision-support systems.

Beginning in approximately 1995, the World Wide Web and global Internet provided a technology platform for further extending the capabilities and deployment of computerized decision support. The release of the HTML 2.0 specifications with form tags and tables was a turning point in the development of Web-based DSS. New handheld PCs, wireless networks, expanding parallel processing coupled with very large databases, and visualization tools are continuing to encourage the development of innovative decision-support applications.

5.4.2 Generic DSS Architecture

DSSs are defined in terms of the roles they play in decision processes; they enhance the processes and/or outcomes of decision making. They provide knowledge and/or knowledge processing capability that is instrumental in making decisions or in making sense of decision situations.

Generic architecture furnishes a unifying framework for guiding explorations of the multitude of issues related to designing, using, and evaluating these systems. The general architecture of houses identifies such important elements as a plumbing system, an electrical system, an air-treatment system, and a system of rooms. It also identifies relationships among these elements. Similarly, the architecture of DSSs can be described by a generic framework that identifies essential elements of a DSS and their interrelationships.

Structurally, a DSS has four essential components:

1. A language system (LS) consists of all messages the DSS can accept.
2. A presentation system (PS) consists of all messages the DSS can emit.
3. A knowledge system (KS) consists of all knowledge the DSS has stored and retained.
4. A problem-processing system (PPS) is what tries to recognize and solve problems (i.e., process problems) during the making of a decision.

The original discussion of the architecture emphasized the importance of knowledge representation and processing in the functioning of a DSS and advanced the idea of a generalized problem-processing system. This is a PPS that is invariant across a large array of DSSs and decision-making applications, with all variations being accommodated by different KSs that all work with the same PPS.

Even though a relatively generalized problem processor can exist, DSSs can also differ by having diverse PPSs. All PPSs possess the first-order abilities of acquisition, selection, assimilation, and emission. Many have a knowledge-generation ability too. The exact character of each ability can differ widely from one problem-processing system to the next. When a PPS employs a spreadsheet processing approach, the DSS's knowledge system uses a corresponding spreadsheet approach to knowledge representation. In contrast, if a DSS's problem processor relies on a database-management technique for processing knowledge, then its KS must contain knowledge represented in terms of databases. In other words, DSSs can differ with respect to the knowledge-management techniques with which their PPSs are equipped and that govern the usable representations held in their KSs.

Many special cases of the generic DSS architecture can be identified by viewing KS contents and PPS abilities is in terms of the knowledge-management techniques employed by a DSS:

1. *Text-oriented DSSs*: In the 1970s and especially in the 1980s, text management emerged as an important, widely used computerized means for representing and processing pieces of text. The LS contains requests corresponding to the various allowed manipulations. It may also contain requests that let a user ask for assistance in covering some aspect of the DSS. The PS consists of images of stored text that can be emitted, plus messages that can help the decision maker use the DSS. The PPS consists of software that can perform various manipulations on contents of any of the stored documents. It may also involve software that can help a user in making requests.

   A text-oriented DSS supports a decision maker by electronically keeping track of textually represented knowledge that could have a bearing on decisions. It allows documents to be electronically created, revised, and reviewed by a decision maker on an as-needed basis. The viewing can be exploratory browsing in search of stimulation or a focused search for some particular piece of knowledge needed in the manufacture of a decision.

   However, there is a problem with traditional text management: it is not convenient to trace a flow of ideas through separate pieces of text. There is no explicit relationship or connection between the knowledge held in one text file and the knowledge in another.

2. *Hypertext-oriented DSSs*: This problem is remedied by a technique known as *hypertext*. Each piece of text is linked to other pieces of text that are conceptually related to it. In addition to the PPS capabilities of a traditional text-oriented DSS, a user can request the creation, deletion, and traversal of links. In traversing a link, the PPS shifts its focus (and the user's) from one piece of text to another. This ad hoc traversal through associated pieces of text continues at your discretion, resembling a flow of thoughts through the many associated concepts in your own mind.

   The benefit of this hypertext kind of DSS is that it supplements a decision maker's own capabilities by accurately storing and recalling large volumes of concepts and connections that he or she is not inclined personally to memorize

   Web-oriented DSSs comprise a large portion of the class of hypertext-oriented DSSs.

3. *Database-oriented DSSs*: The knowledge handled by database-oriented DSSs tends to be primarily descriptive, rigidly structured, and often extremely voluminous. Like text-oriented DSSs, these systems aid decision makers by accurately tracking and selectively recalling knowledge that satisfies a particular need or serves to stimulate ideas. Rather than treating data as streams of text, these systems are organized in a highly structured, tabular fashion. The processing of these data tables is designed to take advantage of their high degree of structure.

   The PPS has three kinds of software: a database control system, an interactive query processing system, and various custom-built processing systems.

One—but not both—of the latter two could be omitted from the DSS. The database control system consists of capabilities for manipulating table structures and contents (e.g., defining or revising table structures, finding or updating records, creating or deleting records, and building new tables from existing ones). These capabilities are used by the query processor and by custom-built processors in their efforts at satisfying user requests.

For a variety of reasons, rather than dealing with the standard query processors, users may prefer to deal with custom-built processors or application programs because

- They may give responses more quickly to requests a standard query could not handle, presenting responses in a specially tailored fashion without requiring the user to learn the syntax of a query language or to use as many keystrokes.
- They may give the logic to interpret some custom-designed set of requests.
- They may give commands to the database control system, telling it what database manipulations to perform for each possible request.
- They may also give the logic necessary for packaging responses in a customized manner.
- They may even perform some calculation(s) to generate new knowledge based on values from the database. Calculation results can be included in an emitted response and/or assimilated into the KS for subsequent use.

By the 1990s, a special class of database systems known as *data warehouses* had emerged. A data warehouse is a large collection of data integrated from multiple operational systems, oriented toward a particular subject domain, whose content is not over-written or discarded but is time-stamped as it is assimilated. A data warehouse may have the look of a relational database or a multi-dimensional database. Data warehouse technology was specifically conceived to devise KSs for high-performance support of decision-making processes.

In the case of a database-oriented DSS, extensive procedural knowledge cannot be readily represented in the KS. However, the application programs that form part of the PPS can contain instructions for analyzing data selected from the database. By carrying out these procedures, the PPS can emit new knowledge (e.g., a sales forecast) that has been generated from KS contents (e.g., records of past sales trends). But, because they are part of the PPS, a user cannot readily view, modify, or create such procedures, as can be done in the text-oriented case.

4. *Spreadsheet-oriented DSSs*: Using the spreadsheet technique for knowledge management, a DSS user not only can create, view, and modify procedural knowledge assimilated in the KS but also can tell the PPS to carry out the

instructions they contain. This gives DSS users much more power in handling procedural knowledge than is achievable with either text management or database management. In addition, spreadsheet management is able to deal with descriptive knowledge.

 However, spreadsheet-oriented DSSs are not nearly as convenient as database management systems in handling large volumes of descriptive knowledge, nor do they allow a user to readily represent and process data in textual passages.

Spreadsheet-oriented DSSs are typically used for what-if analyses in order to see the implications of some set of assumptions embodied in the cell definitions. They support a decision maker by giving a rapid means of revaluating various alternatives.

5. *Rule-oriented DSSs*: DSS architecture is based on a knowledge-management technique that involves representing and processing rules. This technique evolved within the field of artificial intelligence, giving computers the ability to manage reasoning knowledge. Recall that reasoning knowledge tells us what conclusions are valid when a certain situation exists. Rules offer a straightforward, convenient means for representing such fragments of knowledge. A rule has the basic form:

> If: Description of a possible situation (premise)
> Then: Indication of actions to take (conclusion)
> Because: Justification for taking those actions (reason)

This format says that if the possible situation can be determined to exist, then the indicated actions should be carried out for the reasons given. In other words, if the premise is true, then the conclusion is valid.

The KS of a rule-oriented DSS holds one or more rule sets, where each rule set pertains to reasoning about what recommendation to give a user seeking advice on some subject Additionally, a KS can contain descriptions of the current state of affairs (e.g., current machine settings, locations of competing outlets, an investor's present financial situation). Such state descriptions can be thought of as values that have been assigned to variables.

Aside from requests for help and for editing state descriptions, users of a rule-oriented DSS can issue various types of requests for decision-support purposes:

a. The LS can contain requests for advice and requests for explanation.
b. The problem processor for a rule-oriented DSS has capabilities for creating, revising, and deleting state descriptions. Of greater interest is the capability to do logical inference (i.e., to reason) with a set of rules to produce advice sought by a user. The problem processor examines pertinent

rules in a rule set, looking for those whose premises are true for the present situation. This situation is defined by current state descriptions (e.g., machine settings) and the user's request for advice (e.g., citing the nature of the quality defect). When the PPS finds a true premise, it takes the actions specified in that rule's conclusion. This action sheds further light on the situation, which allows premises of still other rules to be established as true, causing actions in their conclusions to be taken. Reasoning continues in this way until some action is taken that yields the requested advice or the PPS gives up due to insufficient knowledge in its KS. The PPS also has the ability to explain its behavior both during and after conducting the inference. There are many possible variations for the inference process for both the forward-reasoning approach just outlined and the alternative reverse-reasoning approach, which involves goal seeking.

A rule-oriented DSS is also known as an *expert system* because it emulates the nature of a human expert from whom we may seek advice in the course of making a decision. Its rule sets are built to embody reasoning knowledge similar to what its human counterpart uses. Because its inference mechanisms process those rules using basic principles of logic, the PPS for this kind of decision-support system is often called an *inference engine*. This special kind of DSS is particularly valuable when human experts are unavailable, too expensive, or perhaps erratic. Rather than asking the human expert for a recommendation and explanation, the expert system is asked.

6. *Compound DSSs*: Each generic DSS framework tends to emphasize one knowledge-management technique; however, a decision maker would like the kinds of support offered by multiple knowledge-management techniques. One can use multiple DSSs, each oriented toward a particular technique, or one can use a single DSS that encompasses multiple techniques. The first option is akin to having multiple staff assistants, each of whom is well versed in a single knowledge-management technique. When results of using one technique need to be processed via another technique, it is the decision maker's responsibility to translate responses from one DSS into requests to another DSS. The second option is akin to having a staff assistant who is adept at multiple knowledge-management techniques. There is one LS and one PS for the decision maker to learn. Although they are probably more extensive than those of a particular single-technique DSS, they are likely less demanding than coping with the sum total of LSs and PSs for all corresponding single-technique DSSs. The effort required of a decision maker who wants to use results of one technique in the processing of another technique varies depending on the way in which the multiple techniques have been integrated into a single compound DSS.

5.5 Analytics

With recent technological advances and the reduced costs of collecting, transferring, and storing digital information, companies are accumulating increasingly larger repositories of e-mails, documents, customer loyalty transactions, sensor data, financial information, Internet footprints, and more.

The combination of intuition and domain knowledge has and will always be instrumental in driving businesses' decisions; intuition and instinct are still the most commonly used basis for important and sometimes critical decisions by senior executives and managers. Intuition-based decision making is prone to serious inaccuracies and errors, while data-backed decision making, being immune to such failings, is much more powerful. Data hold the promise of providing more accurate documentation of the past. Such objective documentation is necessary for improving awareness, enhancing understanding, and detecting unusual events in the past. Armed with a better understanding of the past, there is a better chance of improving decision making in the future.

Analytics can be used for improving performance, driving sustainable growth through innovation, speeding up response time to market and environmental changes, and anticipating and planning for change while managing and balancing risk. These benefits are achieved through a framework that deploys automated data analysis within the business context. The paradigm shift is from intuition-driven decision making to data-driven, computer-assisted decision making that takes advantage of large amounts of data or data from multiple sources.

Generating insights from data requires transforming the data in its raw form into information that is comprehensible to humans. Humans excel in detecting patterns in data when the data are provided in manageable size. For example, a domain expert may be able to uncover a trend or pattern in a spreadsheet that includes information on several hundreds of consumers' shop card transactions with a dozen columns of measurements. Even with small samples, it is often difficult for humans to detect patterns and to distinguish real patterns from random ones. However, in the more typical scenario of thousands to millions of customers (rows) and hundreds to thousands of measurements (columns), human experts, no matter how much domain expertise and experience they possess, do not have the capacity to extract patterns or insights from such large amounts of data without the aid of analytics software and knowledge.

Analytics can be defined as the skills, technologies, applications, and practices for continuous iterative exploration and investigation of past business performance, based on data and statistical methods, to gain insight and drive business planning for the future.

Analytics differs from business intelligence in terms of the following:

- Analytics is system-generated intelligence based on automated data analysis.
- Analytics loops the output assessment back into the business process and system, enabling the measurement and further fine tuning of the business benefits.
- Analytics, unlike traditional business intelligence (BI), does not employ a consistent set of metrics to both measure past performance and guide business planning for the future.

5.5.1 Descriptive Analytics

Descriptive analytics summarizes and describes what happened in the past. Descriptive analytics includes the various forms of reporting—standard or ad hoc reports, queries, scorecards, and alerts. They simply describe what has happened in the past. Descriptive analytics may also be used to classify customers or other business entities into groups that are similar on certain dimensions.

5.5.2 Predictive Analytics

Predictive analytics predicts what will happen in the future. Predictive analytics models are very popular in predicting the behavior of customers based on past buying history and perhaps some demographic variables. They typically use multiple variables to predict a particular dependent variable. Examples include using various measures of growing season rainfall and temperatures to predict the price of Bordeaux wine, or using variables about your credit history to predict the likelihood that you will repay loans in the future.

5.5.3 Prescriptive Analytics

Prescriptive analytics determines actions to take to make the future happen. Randomized testing, in which a test group is compared to a control group with random assignment of subjects to each group, is a powerful method to establish cause. On comparison of the groups, if one is better than the other with statistical significance, the thing that's being tested in the test group should be prescribed. Optimization is another form of prescriptive analytics. Based on a statistical model, it prescribes what the optimum level of key variables is for maximizing a particular outcome variable. For instance, for maximizing profitability, pricing optimization prescribes the price to charge for your products and services.

5.6 Data Science Techniques

Doing data science means implementing flexible, scalable, extensible systems for data preparation, analysis, visualization, and modeling.

Many firms are moving away from internally owned, centralized computing systems and toward distributed cloud-based services. Distributed hardware and software systems, including database systems, can be expanded more easily as the data-management needs of organizations grow. Doing data science means being able to gather data from the full range of database systems: relational and non-relational, commercial and open source. We employ database query and analysis tools, gathering information across distributed systems, collating information, creating contingency tables, and computing indices of relationship across variables of interest. We use information technology and database systems as far as they can take us, and then we do more, applying what we know about statistical inference and the modeling techniques of predictive analytics.

5.6.1 Database Systems

Relational databases have a row-and-column table structure, similar to a spreadsheet. We access and manipulate these data using structured query language (SQL). Because they are transaction-oriented with enforced data integrity, relational databases provide the foundation for sales order processing and financial accounting systems.

Non-relational databases focus on availability and scalability. They may employ key-value, column-oriented, document-oriented, or graph structures. Some are designed for online or real-time applications, where fast response times are key. Others are well suited for massive storage and offline analysis, with map reduce providing a key data aggregation tool.

5.6.2 Statistical Inference

Statistics are functions of sample data and are more credible when samples are representative of the concerned population. Typically, large random samples, small standard errors, and narrow confidence intervals are preferred. Formal scientific method suggests that we construct theories and test those theories with sample data. The process involves drawing statistical inferences as point estimates, interval estimates, or tests of hypotheses about the population. Whatever the form of inference, we need sample data relating to questions of interest.

Classical and Bayesian statistics represent alternative approaches to inference—alternative ways of measuring uncertainty about the world.

1. Classical hypothesis testing involves making null hypotheses about population parameters and then rejecting or not rejecting those hypotheses based on sample data. Typical null hypotheses (as the word *null* would imply) states

that there is no difference between proportions or groups or no relationship between variables.

To test a null hypothesis, we compute a special statistic called a *test statistic* along with its associated p-value. Assuming that the null hypothesis is true, we can derive the theoretical distribution of the test statistic. We obtain a p-value by referring the sample test statistic to this theoretical distribution. The p-value, itself a sample statistic, gives the probability of rejecting the null hypothesis under the assumption that it is true. Let us assume that the conditions for valid inference have been satisfied. Then, when we observe a very low p-value (0.05, 0.01, or 0.001, for instance), this indicates that either of these two things must be true:

- An event of very low probability has occurred under the assumption that the null hypothesis is true.
- The null hypothesis is false.

A low p-value leads us to reject the null hypothesis, and we say the research results are statistically significant. Some results are statistically significant and meaningful.

2. Bayesian approach treats parameters as random variables having probability distributions representing of our uncertainty about the world, which can be reduced by collecting relevant sample data. Sample data and Bayes' theorem is used to derive posterior probability distributions for these same parameters, which in turn is used to obtain conditional probabilities.

5.6.3 Regression and Classification

Data science involves a search for meaningful relationships between variables. We look for relationships between pairs of continuous variables using scatter plots and correlation coefficients. We look for relationships between categorical variables using contingency tables and the methods of categorical data analysis. We use multivariate methods and multi-way contingency tables to examine relationships among many variables. There are two main types of predictive models: regression and classification. Regression is prediction of a response of meaningful magnitude. Classification involves prediction of a class or category.

The most common form of regression is least-squares regression, also called ordinary least-squares regression, linear regression, or multiple regression. When we use ordinary least-squares regression, we estimate regression coefficients so that they minimize the sum of the squared residuals, where residuals are differences between the observed and predicted response values. For regression problems, we think of the response as taking any value along the real number line, although in practice the response may take a limited number of distinct values. The important thing for regression is that the response values have meaningful magnitude.

Poisson regression is useful for counts. The response has meaningful magnitude but takes discrete (whole number) values with a minimum value of zero. Log-linear models for frequencies, grouped frequencies, and contingency tables for cross-classified observations fall within this domain.

Most traditional modeling techniques involve linear models or linear equations. The response or transformed response is on the left-hand side of the linear model. The linear predictor is on the right-hand side. The linear predictor involves explanatory variables and is linear in its parameters. That is, it involves the addition of coefficients or the multiplication of coefficients by the explanatory variables. The coefficients we fit to linear models represent estimates of population parameters.

Generalized linear models, as their name would imply, are generalizations of the classical linear regression model. They include models for choices and counts, including logistic regression, multinomial logit models, log-linear models, ordinal logistic models, Poisson regression, and survival data models. To introduce the theory behind these important models, we begin by reviewing the classical linear regression model. Generalized linear models help us model what are obvious nonlinear relationships between explanatory variables and responses.

Linear regression is a special generalized linear model. It has normally distributed responses and an identity link relating the expected value of responses to the linear predictor. Linear regression coefficients may be estimated by ordinary least squares. For other members of the family of generalized linear models, we use maximum likelihood estimation. With the classical linear model, we have analysis of variance and F-tests. With generalized linear models, we have analysis of deviance and likelihood ratio tests, which are asymptotic chi-square tests.

The method of logistic regression, although called "regression," is actually a classification method. It involves the prediction of a binary response. Ordinal and multinomial logit models extend logistic regression to problems involving more than two classes. Linear discriminant analysis is another classification method from the domain of traditional statistics.

5.6.4 Data Mining and Machine Learning

Machine learning refers to the methods or algorithms used as an alternative to traditional statistical methods. When we apply these methods in the analysis of data, it is termed *data mining*. Recommender systems, collaborative filtering, association rules, optimization methods based on heuristics, as well as a myriad of methods for regression, classification, and clustering, are all examples of machine learning. With traditional statistics, we define the model specification prior to working with the data and also make assumptions about the population distributions from which the data have been drawn. Machine learning, on the other hand, is data adaptive: model specification is defined by applying algorithms to the data. With machine learning, a few assumptions are made about the underlying distributions of the data.

Cluster analysis is referred to as unsupervised learning to distinguish it from classification, which is supervised learning, guided by known, coded values of a response variable or class. Association rules modeling, frequent item sets, social network analysis, link analysis, recommender systems, and many multivariate methods employed in data science represent unsupervised learning methods.

An important multivariate method, principal component analysis, draws on linear algebra and provides a way to reduce the number of measures or quantitative features we use to describe domains of interest. Long a staple of measurement experts and a prerequisite of factor analysis, principal component analysis has seen recent applications in latent semantic analysis, a technology for identifying important topics across a document corpus.

5.6.5 Data Visualization

Statistical summaries fail to tell the story of data. To understand data, we must look beyond data tables, regression coefficients, and the results of statistical tests. Visualization tools help us learn from data. We explore data, discover patterns in data, and identify groups of observations that go together and unusual observations or outliers. Data visualization is critical to the work of data science in the areas of discovery (exploratory data analysis), diagnostics (statistical modeling), and design (presentation graphics).

R is particularly strong in data visualization.

5.6.6 Text Analytics

Text analytics is an important and growing area of predictive analytics. Text analytics draws from a variety of disciplines, including linguistics, communication and language arts, experimental psychology, political discourse analysis, journalism, computer science, and statistics.

The output from these processes, such as crawling, scraping, and parsing, is a document collection or text corpus. This document collection or corpus is in the natural language. The two primary ways of analyzing a text corpus are the bag-of-words approach and natural language processing. We parse the corpus further, creating commonly formatted expressions, indices, keys, and matrices that are more easily analyzed by computer. This additional parsing is sometimes referred to as *text annotation*. We extract features from the text and then use those features in subsequent analyses. Natural language processing is more than a collection of individual words: Natural language conveys meaning.

Natural language documents contain paragraphs, paragraphs contain sentences, and sentences contain words. There are grammatical rules, with many ways to convey the same idea, along with exceptions to rules and rules about exceptions. Words used in combination and the rules of grammar comprise the linguistic foundations of text analytics. Linguists study natural language, the words and the rules that we use to form meaningful utterances. *Generative grammar* is a general term for the rules; *morphology, syntax,* and *semantics* are more specific terms. Computer programs for natural language processing use linguistic rules to mimic human communication and convert natural language into structured text for further analysis.

A key step in text analysis is the creation of a terms-by-documents matrix (sometimes called a *lexical table*). The rows of this data matrix correspond to words or word stems from the document collection, and the columns correspond to documents in the collection. The entry in each cell of a terms-by-documents matrix could be a binary indicator for the presence or absence of a term in a document, a frequency count of the number of times a term is used in a document, or a weighted frequency indicating the importance of a term in a document. After being created, the terms-by-documents matrix is like an index, a mapping of document identifiers to terms (keywords or stems) and vice versa. For information retrieval systems or search engines, we might also retain information regarding the specific location of terms within documents.

 An alternative system might distinguish among parts of speech, permitting more sophisticated syntactic searches across documents.

Typical text analytics applications:

1. Spam filtering has long been a subject of interest as a classification problem, and many e-mail users have benefited from the efficient algorithms that have evolved in this area. In the context of information retrieval, search engines classify documents as being relevant to the search or not. Useful modeling techniques for text classification include logistic regression, linear discriminant function analysis, classification trees, and support vector machines. Various ensemble or committee methods may be employed.

2. Automatic text summarization is an area of research and development that can help with information management. Imagine a text-processing program with the ability to read each document in a collection and summarize it in a sentence or two, perhaps quoting from the document itself. Today's search engines are providing partial analysis of documents prior to their being displayed. They create automated summaries for fast information retrieval. They recognize common text strings associated with user requests. These applications of text analysis comprise tools of information search that we take for granted as part of our daily lives.

3. Sentiment analysis is measurement-focused text analysis. Sometimes called *opinion mining*, one approach to sentiment analysis is to draw on positive and negative word sets (lexicons, dictionaries) that convey human emotion or feeling. These word sets are specific to the language being spoken and the context of application. Another approach to sentiment analysis is to work directly with text samples and human ratings of those samples, developing text-scoring methods specific to the task at hand. The objective of sentiment analysis is to score text for affect, feelings, attitudes, or opinions. Sentiment

analysis and text measurement in general hold promise as technologies for understanding consumer opinion and markets. Just as political research-ers can learn from the words of the public, press, and politicians, business researchers can learn from the words of customers and competitors. There are customer service logs, telephone transcripts, and sales call reports, along with user group, listserv, and blog postings. And we have ubiquitous social media from which to build document collections for text and sentiment analysis.

4. Text measures flow from a measurement model (algorithms for scoring) and a dictionary, both defined by the researcher or analyst. A dictionary in this context is not a traditional dictionary; it is not an alphabetized list of words and their definitions. Rather, the dictionary used to construct text measures is a repository of word lists, such as synonyms and antonyms, positive and negative words, strong and weak sounding words, bipolar adjectives, parts of speech, and so on. The lists come from expert judgments about the meaning of words. A text measure assigns numbers to documents according to rules, with the rules being defined by the word lists, scoring algorithms, and model-ing techniques in predictive analytics.

5.6.7 Time Series and Market Research Models

Sales and marketing data are organized by observational unit, time, and space. The observational unit is typically an economic agent (individual or firm) or a group of such agents as in an aggregate analysis. It is common to use geographical areas as a basis for aggregation. Alternatively, space (longitude and latitude) can be used directly in spatial data analyses. Time considerations are especially important in macro-economic analysis, which focuses upon nationwide economic measures.

The term *time-series regression* refers to regression analysis in which the organizing unit of analysis is time. We look at relationships among economic measures organized in time. Much economic analysis concerns time-series regression. Special care must be taken to avoid what might be called spurious relationships, as many economic time series are correlated with one another because they depend upon underlying fac-tors, such as population growth or seasonality. In time-series regression, we use stan-dard linear regression methods. We check the residuals from our regression to ensure that they are not correlated in time. If they are correlated in time (auto-correlated), then we use a method such as generalized least squares as an alternative to ordinary least squares. That is, we incorporate an error data model as part of our modeling pro-cess. Longitudinal data analysis or panel data analysis is an example of a mixed data method with a focus on data organized by cross-sectional units and time.

Sales forecasts can build on the special structure of sales data as they are found in business. These are data organized by time and location, where location might refer to geographical regions or sales territories, stores, departments within stores, or product lines. Sales forecasts are a critical component of business planning and a first step in the budgeting process. Models and methods that provide accurate forecasts can be of great benefit to management. They help managers to understand the determinants of sales, including promotions, pricing, advertising, and distribution. They reveal competitive position and market share. There are many approaches to forecasting. Some are judgmental, relying on expert opinion or consensus. There are top-down and bottom-up forecasts and various techniques for combining the views of experts. Other approaches depend on the analysis of past sales data.

1. *Forecasting by time periods*: These may be days, weeks, months, or whatever intervals make sense for the problem at hand. Time dependencies can be noted in the same manner as in traditional time-series models. Auto-regressive terms are useful in many contexts. Time-construed covariates, such as day of the week or month of the year, can be added to provide additional predictive power. An analyst can work with time-series data, using past sales to predict future sales, noting overall trends and cyclical patterns in the data. Exponential smoothing, moving averages, and various regression and econometric methods may be used with time-series data.
2. *Forecasting by location*: Organizing data by location contributes to a model's predictive power. Location may itself be used as a factor in models. In addition, we can search for explanatory variables tied to location. With geographic regions, for example, we might include consumer and business demographic variables known to relate to sales.

Sales dollars per time period is the typical response variable of interest in sales forecasting studies. Alternative response variables include sales volume and time-to-sale. Related studies of market share require information about the sales of other firms in the same product category.

When we use the term *time-series analysis*, however, we are not talking about time-series regression. We are talking about methods that start by focusing on one economic measure at a time and its pattern across time. We look for trends, seasonality, and cycles in that individual time series. Then, after working with that single time series, we look at possible relationships with other time series. If we are concerned with forecasting or predicting the future, as we often are in predictive analytics, then we use methods of time-series analysis. Recently, there has been considerable interest in state space models for time series, which provide a convenient mechanism for incorporating regression components into dynamic time-series models.

There are myriad applications of time-series analysis in marketing, including marketing mix models and advertising research models. Along with sales forecasting, these fall under the general class of market response models. Marketing mix models look at the effects of price, promotion, and product placement in retail establishments. These are multiple time-series problems. Advertising research looks for cumulative effectiveness of advertising on brand and product awareness as well as sales.

Much of this research employs defined measures such as "advertising stock," which attempt to convert advertising impressions or rating points to a single measure in time. The thinking is that messages are most influential immediately after being received, decline in influence with time, but do not decline completely until many units in time later. Viewers or listeners remember advertisements long after initial exposure to those advertisements. Another way of saying this is to note that there is a carry-over effect from one time period to the next. Needless to say, measurement and modeling on the subject of advertising effectiveness present many challenges for the marketing data scientist.

5.7 Snapshot of Data Analysis Techniques and Tasks

There is no universally accepted best data-analysis method; choosing particular data analytic tool(s) or some combination with traditional methods is entirely dependent on the particular application, and it requires human interaction to decide on the suitability of a blended approach. Depending on the desired outcome, several data-analysis techniques with different goals may be applied successively to achieve a desired result. For example, to determine which customers are likely to buy a new product, a business analyst may need first to use cluster analysis to segment the customer database, then apply regression analysis to predict buying behavior for each cluster.

Table 5.2 presents a selection of analysis techniques and tasks.

A useful selection of data analysis techniques:

1. *Descriptive* and *visualization* include simple descriptive statistics such as
   a. Averages and measures of variation
   b. Counts and percentages
   c. Cross-tabs and simple correlations
   They are useful for understanding the structure of the data. Visualization is primarily a discovery technique and is useful for interpreting large amounts of data; visualization tools include histograms, box plots, scatter diagrams, and multi-dimensional surface plots.
2. *Correlation analysis* measures the relationship between two variables. The resulting correlation coefficient shows if changes in one variable will result in changes in the other. When comparing the correlation between two variables, the goal is to see if a change in the independent variable will result in a change in the dependent variable. This information helps in understanding an independent variable's predictive abilities. Correlation findings, like regression findings, can be useful in analyzing causal relationships, but they do not by themselves establish causal patterns.
3. *Cluster analysis* seeks to organize information about variables so that relatively homogeneous groups, or "clusters," can be formed. The clusters formed with

Table 5.2 Analysis Techniques versus Tasks

Data Analysis Techniques	Data Summarization	Segmentation	Classification	Prediction	Dependency Analysis
Descriptive and visualization	◆	◆			◆
Correlation analysis					◆
Cluster analysis		◆			
Discriminant analysis			◆		
Regression analysts				◆	◆
Neural networks		◆	◆	◆	◆
Case-based reasoning			◆	◆	
Decision trees					
Association rules					◆

this family of methods should be highly internally homogenous (members are similar to one another) and highly externally heterogeneous (members are not like members of other clusters).

4. *Discriminant analysis* is used to predict membership in two or more mutually exclusive groups from a set of predictors when there is no natural ordering on the groups. Discriminant analysis can be seen as the inverse of a one-way multivariate analysis of variance (MANOVA), in that the levels of the independent variable (or factor) for MANOVA become the categories of the dependent variable for discriminant analysis, and the dependent variables of the MANOVA become the predictors for discriminant analysis.

5. *Regression analysis* is a statistical tool that uses the relation between two or more quantitative variables so that one variable (dependent variable) can be predicted from the other(s) (independent variables). But no matter how strong the statistical relations are between the variables, no cause-and-effect pattern is necessarily implied by the regression model. Regression analysis comes in many flavors, including simple linear, multiple linear, curvilinear, and multiple curvilinear regression models, as well as logistic regression, which is discussed next.

6. *Neural networks* (NN) are a class of systems modeled after the human brain. As the human brain consists of millions of neurons that are inter-connected by synapses, NN are formed from large numbers of simulated neurons, connected to each other in a manner similar to brain neurons. As in the human brain, the strength of neuron inter-connections may change (or be changed by the learning algorithm) in response to a presented stimulus or an obtained output, which enables the network to "learn."

    A disadvantage of NN is that building the initial neural network model can be especially time-intensive because input processing almost always means that raw data must be transformed. Variable screening and selection requires large amounts of the analysts' time and skill. Also, for the user without a technical background, figuring out how neural networks operate is far from obvious.

7. *Case-based reasoning* (CBR) is a technology that tries to solve a given problem by making direct use of past experiences and solutions. A case is usually a specific problem that was encountered and solved previously. Given a particular new problem, CBR examines the set of stored cases and finds similar ones. If similar cases exist, their solution is applied to the new problem, and the problem is added to the case database for future reference.

    A disadvantage of CBR is that the solutions included in the case database may not be optimal in any sense because they are limited to what was actually done in the past, not necessarily what should have been done under similar circumstances. Therefore, using them may simply perpetuate earlier mistakes.

8. *Decision trees* (DTs) are like those used in decision analysis where each non-terminal node represents a test or decision on the data item considered. Depending on the outcome of the test, one chooses a certain branch. To classify a particular data item, one would start at the root node and follow the assertions down until a terminal node (or leaf) is reached; at that point, a decision is made. DTs can also be interpreted as a special form of a rule set characterized by their hierarchical organization of rules.

A disadvantage of DTs is that trees use up data very rapidly in the training process. They should never be used with small data sets. They are also highly sensitive to noise in the data, and they try to fit the data exactly, which is referred to as *overfitting*. Overfitting means that the model depends too strongly on the details of the particular data set used to create it. When a model suffers from overfitting, it is unlikely to be externally valid (i.e., it won't hold up when applied to a new data set).

9. *Association rules* (ARs) are statements about relationships between the attributes of a known group of entities and one or more aspects of those entities that enable predictions to be made about aspects of other entities who are not in the group but who possess the same attributes. More generally, ARs state a statistical correlation between the occurrences of certain attributes in a data item or between certain data items in a dataset. The general form of an AR is $X1...Xn => Y[C,S]$ which means that the attributes $X1,... ,Xn$ predict Y with a confidence C and a significance S.

A useful selection of data analysis tasks:

1. *Data summarization* gives the user an overview of the structure of the data and is generally carried out in the early stages of a project. This type of initial exploratory data analysis can help to understand the nature of the data and to find potential hypotheses for hidden information. Simple descriptive statistical and visualization techniques generally apply.

2. *Segmentation* separates the data into interesting and meaningful sub-groups or classes. In this case, the analyst can hypothesize certain sub-groups as relevant for the business question based on prior knowledge or based on the outcome of data description and summarization. Automatic clustering techniques can detect previously unsuspected and hidden structures in data that allow segmentation. Clustering techniques, visualization, and neural nets generally apply.

3. *Classification* assumes that a set of objects—characterized by some attributes or features—belong to different classes. The class label is a discrete qualitative identifier, for example, large, medium, or small. The objective is to build classification models that assign the correct class to previously unseen and unlabeled objects. Classification models are mostly used for predictive modeling.

Discriminant analysis, DT methods, rule induction methods, and genetic algorithms generally apply.

4. *Prediction* is very similar to classification. The difference is that in prediction, the class is not a qualitative discrete attribute but a continuous one. The goal of prediction is to find the numerical value of the target attribute for unseen objects; this problem type is also known as *regression*, and if the prediction deals with time-series data, then it is often called *forecasting*. Regression analysis, decision trees, and neural nets generally apply.

5. *Dependency analysis* deals with finding a model that describes significant dependencies (or associations) between data items or events. Dependencies can be used to predict the value of an item given information on other data items. Dependency analysis has close connections with classification and prediction because the dependencies are implicitly used for the formulation of predictive models. Correlation analysis, regression analysis, association rules, case-based reasoning, and visualization techniques generally apply.

5.8 Summary

This chapter then introduces the generic DSS architecture. From the perspective of this framework, a DSS can be studied in terms of four interrelated elements: a language system, a presentation system, a knowledge system, and a problem-processing system. The first three of these are systems of representation: the set of all requests a user can make, the set of all responses the DSS can present, and the knowledge representations presently stored in the DSS. The problem processor is a dynamic system that can accept any request in the LS and react with a corresponding response from the PS. Each special case of the generic DSS architecture characterizes a distinct class of DSS, including text, hypertext, database, spreadsheet, rule, and compound DSSs.

The chapter then presents the basics of analytics, which is an essential component of any performance intelligence project. The chapter describes the various kinds of analytics like descriptive, predictive, and prescriptive analytics. The chapter then provides an overview of data science and related techniques.

Chapter 6

Cloud Computing Basics

Many motivating factors have led to the emergence of cloud computing. Businesses require services that include both infrastructure and application workload requests, while meeting defined service levels for capacity, resource tiering, and availability. Information technology (IT) delivery often necessitates costs and efficiencies that create a perception of IT as a hindrance, not a strategic partner. Issues include underutilized resources, over-provisioning or under-provisioning of resources, lengthy deployment times, and lack of cost visibility. Virtualization is the first step toward addressing some of these challenges by enabling improved utilization through server consolidation, workload mobility through hardware independence, and efficient management of hardware resources.

The virtualization system is a key foundation for the cloud computing system. We stitch together computer resources so as to appear as one large computer behind which the complexity is hidden. By coordinating, managing, and scheduling resources such as central processing units (CPUs), network, storage, and firewalls in a consistent way across internal and external premises, we create a flexible cloud infrastructure platform. This platform includes security, automation and management, interoperability and openness, self-service, pooling, and dynamic resource allocation. In the view of cloud computing we are advocating, applications can run within an external provider, in internal IT premises, or in combination as a hybrid system—it matters how they are run, not where they are run.

Cloud computing builds on virtualization to create a service-oriented computing model. This is done through the addition of resource abstractions and controls to create dynamic pools of resources that can be consumed through the network. Benefits include economies of scale, elastic resources, self-service provisioning, and cost transparency. Consumption of cloud resources is enforced through resource metering and pricing models that shape user behavior. Consumers benefit through leveraging allocation models such as pay-as-you-go to gain greater cost-efficiency, lower barrier to entry, and immediate access to infrastructure resources.

6.1 Cloud Definition

Here is the National Institute of Standards and Technology (NIST) working definition:

Cloud computing is a model for enabling convenient, on-demand network access to a shared pool of configurable computing resources (e.g., networks, servers, storage, applications, and services) that can be rapidly provisioned and released with minimal management effort or service provider interaction. This cloud model promotes availability and is composed of five essential characteristics, three delivery models, and four deployment models.

The five essential characteristics are

- On-Demand Self-service
- Broad Network Access
- Resource Pooling
- Rapid Elasticity
- Measured Service

The three delivery models are

1. Infrastructure as a Service (IaaS)
2. Platform as a Service (PaaS)
3. Software as a Service (SaaS)

The four deployment models are

1. Public Cloud
2. Private Cloud
3. Hybrid Cloud
4. Community Cloud

Cloud computing is the IT foundation for cloud services and it consists of technologies that enable cloud services. The key attributes of cloud computing are shown in Table 6.1. Key attributes of cloud services are described in Table 6.2.

6.2 Cloud Characteristics

Large organizations such as IBM, Dell, Microsoft, Google, Amazon, and Sun have already started to take strong positions with respect to cloud computing provision.

Table 6.1 Key Attributes of Cloud Computing

Attributes	Description
Offsite, third-party provider	In the cloud execution, it is assumed that third party provides services. There is also a possibility of in-house cloud service delivery.
Accessed via the Internet	Services are accessed via standard-based, universal network access. It can also include security and quality-of-service options.
Minimal or no IT skill required	There is a simplified specification of requirements.
Provisioning	It includes self-service requesting, near real-time deployment, and dynamic and fine-grained scaling.
Pricing	Pricing is based on usage-based capability and it is fine grained.
User interface	User interface includes browsers for a variety of devices and with rich capabilities.
System interface	System interfaces are based on Web Services APIs providing a standard framework for accessing and integrating among cloud services.
Shared resources	Resources are shared among cloud services users; however, via configuration options with the service, there is the ability to customize.

Table 6.2 Key Attributes of Cloud Services

Attributes	Description
Infrastructure systems	It includes servers, storage, and networks that can scale as per user demand.
Application software	It provides Web-based user interface, Web Services APIs, and a rich variety of configurations.
Application development and deployment software	It supports the development and integration of cloud application software.
System and application management software	It supports rapid self-service provisioning and configuration and usage monitoring.
IP networks	They connect end users to the cloud and the infrastructure components.

They are so much behind this latest paradigm that the success is virtually guaranteed. The essential characteristics of cloud environment include

1. On-demand self-service that enables users to consume computing capabilities (e.g., applications, server time, network storage) as and when required
2. Rapid elasticity and scalability that allows functionalities and resources to be rapidly, elastically, and automatically scaled out or in, as demand rises or drops

According to the current demand requirement, automatic services are provided. This is done automatically using software automation, enabling the expansion and contraction of service capability as needed. This dynamic scaling needs to be done while maintaining high levels of reliability and security.

These characteristics show the following features:

1. An economical model of cloud computing that enables consumers to order required services (computing machines and/or storage devices). The service requested could scale rapidly upward or downward on demand.
2. It is a machine responsibility that does not require any human to control the requested services. The cloud architecture manages on-demand requests (increase or decrease in service requests), availability, allocation, subscription, and the customer's bill.
3. Broad network access. Capabilities are available over the network and are accessed through standard mechanisms that promote use by heterogeneous thin or thick client platforms (e.g., mobile phones, tablets, laptops, and workstations).

    Capabilities are available over the network, and a continuous Internet connection is required for a broad range of devices such as PCs, laptops, and mobile devices, using standards-based APIs (e.g., ones based on HTTP). Deployments of services in the cloud include everything from using business applications to the latest application on the newest smart phones.
4. Multi-tenancy and resource pooling that allows combining heterogeneous computing resources (e.g., hardware, software, processing, servers, network bandwidth) to serve multiple consumers—such resources being dynamically assigned.

    A virtualized software model is used, which enables the sharing of physical services, storage, and networking capabilities. Regardless of deployment model, whether it be a public cloud or private cloud, the cloud infrastructure is shared across a number of users.

    A cloud vendor provides a pool of resources (e.g., computing machines, storage devices, and network) to customers. The cloud architecture manages all available resources via global and local managers for different sites and local sites, respectively.

This feature allows Big Data to be distributed on different servers, which is not possible in traditional models, such as supercomputing systems.

5. Measured provision to automatically control and optimize resource allocation and to provide a metering capability to determine the usage for billing purpose, allowing easy monitoring, controlling, and reporting.

Resource usage can be monitored, controlled, and reported, providing transparency for both the provider and consumer of the utilized service. It uses metering for managing and optimizing the service and to provide reporting and billing information. In this way, consumers are billed for services according to how much they have actually used during the billing period.

Thus, in summation, cloud computing allows for the sharing and scalable deployment of services, as needed, from almost any location, and for which the customer can be billed based on actual usage.

6.2.1 Cloud Storage Infrastructure Requirements

Data is growing at an immense rate, and the combination of technology trends such as virtualization with increased economic pressures, the exploding growth of unstructured data, and regulatory environments that are requiring enterprises to keep data for longer periods of time makes it easy to see the need for a trustworthy and appropriate storage infrastructure. Storage infrastructure is the backbone of every business. Whether a cloud is public or private, the key to success is creating a storage infrastructure in which all resources can be efficiently utilized and shared. Because all data resides on the storage systems, data storage becomes even more crucial in a shared infrastructure model.

The most important cloud infrastructure requirements are as follows:

1. Elasticity: Cloud storage must be elastic so that it can quickly adjust its underlying infrastructure according to changing requirements of customer demands and comply with service-level agreements (SLAs).
2. Automatic: Cloud storage must have the ability to be automated so that policies can be leveraged to make underlying infrastructure changes such as placing user and content management in different storage tiers and geographic locations quickly and without human intervention.
3. Scalability: Cloud storage needs to scale quickly up and down according to the requirement of customer. This is one of the most important requirements that make cloud so popular.
4. Recovery Performance: Cloud storage infrastructure must provide fast and robust data recovery as an essential element of a cloud service.

5. Reliability: As more and more users are depending on the services offered by a cloud, reliability becomes increasingly important. Various users of the cloud storage want to make sure that their data is reliably backed up for disaster recovery purposes, and cloud should be able to continue to run in the presence of hardware and software failures.

6. Operational Efficiency: Operational efficiency is a key to successful business enterprise that can be ensured by better management of storage capacities and cost benefit. Both these features should be the integral part of the cloud storage.

7. Latency: Cloud storage models are not suitable for all applications, especially for real-time applications. It is important to measure and test network latency before committing to a migration. Virtual machines can introduce additional latency through the time-sharing nature of the underlying hardware, and unanticipated sharing and reallocation of machines can significantly affect run times.

8. Data Retrieval: Once the data is stored on the cloud, it can be easily accessed from anywhere at any time where the network connection is available. Ease of access to data in the cloud is critical in enabling seamless integration of cloud storage into existing enterprise workflows and minimizing the learning curve for cloud storage adoption.

9. Data Security: Security is one of the major concerns of the cloud users. As different users store more of their own data in a cloud, they want to ensure that their private data is not accessible to other users who are not authorized to see it. If this is the case, than the user can have a private clouds because security is assumed to be tightly controlled in case of private cloud. But in case of public clouds, data should either be stored on a partition of a shared storage system, or cloud storage providers must establish multi-tenancy policies to allow multiple business units or separate companies to securely share the same storage hardware.

Storage is the most important component of IT Infrastructure. Unfortunately, it is almost always managed as a scarce resource because it is relatively expensive, and the consequences of running out of storage capacity can be severe. Nobody wants to take the responsibility of storage manager; thus, the storage management suffers from slow provisioning practices.

6.3 Cloud Delivery Models

Cloud computing is not a completely new concept for the development and operation of Web applications. It allows for the most cost-effective development of scalable Web portals on highly available and fail-safe infrastructures. In the cloud computing system, we have to address different fundamentals like virtualization,

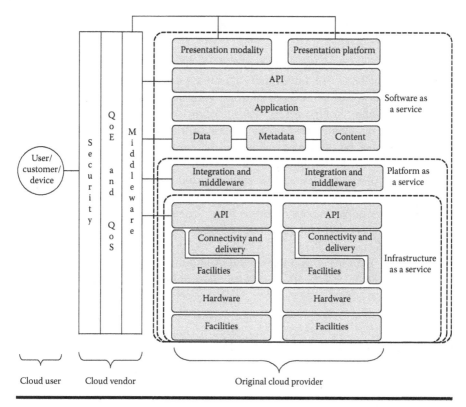

Figure 6.1   The cloud reference model.

scalability, interoperability, quality of service, failover mechanism, and the cloud deployment models (private, public, hybrid) within the context of the taxonomy. The taxonomy of cloud includes the different participants involved in the cloud along with the attributes and technologies that are coupled to address their needs and the different types of services like "XaaS" offerings, where X is software, hardware, platform, infrastructure, data, and business. (Figure 6.1)

6.3.1 Infrastructure as a Service (IaaS)

The IaaS model is about providing compute and storage resources as a service. According to the National Institute of Standards and Technology (NIST), IaaS is defined as follows:

The capability provided to the consumer is to provision processing, storage, networks, and other fundamental computing resources where the consumer is able to deploy and run arbitrary software, which can include operating systems and applications. The consumer does not manage or control the underlying cloud infrastructure but has control over operating systems, storage, and deployed applications; and possibly limited control of select networking components (e.g., host firewalls).

The user of IaaS has single ownership of the hardware infrastructure allotted to him (this may be a virtual machine) and can use it as if it is his own machine on a remote network, and he has control over the operating system and software on it. IaaS is illustrated in Figure 13.1. The IaaS provider has control over the actual hardware and the cloud user can request allocation of virtual resources, which are then allocated by the IaaS provider on the hardware (generally without any manual intervention). The cloud user can manage the virtual resources as desired, including installing any desired OS, software, and applications. Therefore, IaaS is well suited for users who want complete control over the software stack that they run; for example, the user may be using heterogeneous software platforms from different vendors, and they may not like to switch to a PaaS platform where only selected middleware is available. Well-known IaaS platforms include Amazon EC2, Rackspace, and Rightscale. Additionally, traditional vendors such as HP, IBM, and Microsoft offer solutions that can be used to build private IaaS. (Figure 6.2)

6.3.2 Platform as a Service (PaaS)

The PaaS model is to provide a system stack or platform for application deployment as a service. NIST defines PaaS as follows:

The capability provided to the consumer is to deploy onto the cloud infrastructure consumer-created or acquired applications created using programming languages and tools supported by the provider. The consumer does not manage or control the underlying cloud infrastructure including network, servers, operating systems, or storage, but has control over the deployed applications and possibly application hosting environment configurations.

Figure 7.2 shows a PaaS model diagrammatically. The hardware, as well as any mapping of hardware to virtual resources, such as virtual servers, is controlled by the PaaS provider. Additionally, the PaaS provider supports selected middleware, such as a database, Web application server, and so on, as shown in the figure. The cloud user can configure and build on top of this middleware, such as by defining a new database table in a database. The PaaS provider maps this new table onto their cloud infrastructure. Subsequently, the cloud user can manage the database as needed and develop applications on top of this database. PaaS platforms are well suited to those cloud users who find that the middleware they are using matches the middleware provided by one of the PaaS vendors. This enables them to focus on the application. Windows Azure, Google App Engine, and Hadoop are some well-known PaaS platforms. As in the case of IaaS, traditional vendors such as HP, IBM, and Microsoft offer solutions that can be used to build private PaaS.

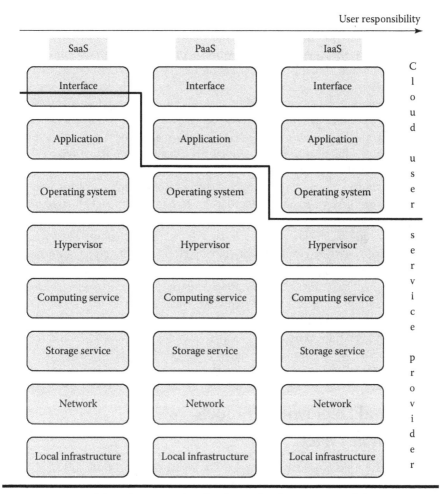

Figure 6.2   Portfolio of services for the three cloud delivery models.

6.3.3 *Software as a Service (SaaS)*

SaaS is about providing the complete application as a service. SaaS has been defined by NIST as follows:

The capability provided to the consumer is to use the provider's applications running on a cloud infrastructure. The applications are accessible from various client devices through a thin client interface such as a web browser (e.g., Web-based e-mail). The consumer does not manage or control the underlying cloud infrastructure including network, servers, operating systems, storage, or even individual application capabilities, with the possible exception of limited user-specific application configuration settings.

Any application that can be accessed using a Web browser can be considered as SaaS. These points are illustrated in Figure 7.2. The SaaS provider controls all the layers apart from the application. Users who log in to the SaaS service can both use the application and configure the application for their use. For example, users can use Salesforce.com to store their customer data. They can also configure the application, for example, by requesting additional space for storage or adding additional fields to the customer data that is already being used. When configuration settings are changed, the SaaS infrastructure performs any management tasks needed (such as allocation of additional storage) to support the changed configuration. SaaS platforms are targeted toward users who want to use the application without any software installation (in fact, the motto of Salesforce.com, one of the prominent SaaS vendors, is "No Software"). However, for advanced usage, some small amount of programming or scripting may be necessary to customize the application for usage by the business (e.g., adding additional fields to customer data). In fact, SaaS platforms like Salesforce.com allow many of these customizations to be performed without programming, but by specifying business rules that are simple enough for non-programmers to implement. Prominent SaaS applications include Salesforce.com for CRM, Google Docs for document sharing, and Web e-mail systems like Gmail, Hotmail, and Yahoo! Mail. IT vendors such as HP and IBM also sell systems that can be configured to set up SaaS in a private cloud; SAP, for example, can be used as an SaaS offering inside an enterprise.

Table 6.3 presents a comparison of the three cloud delivery models.

6.4 Cloud Deployment Models

6.4.1 Private Clouds

A private cloud has an exclusive purpose for a particular organization. The cloud resources may be located on or off premises and could be owned and managed by the consuming organization or a third party. This may be an example of an organization that has decided to adopt the infrastructure cost-saving potential of a virtualized architecture on top of existing hardware. The organization feels unable to remotely host their data, so they are looking to the cloud to improve their resource utilization and automate the management of such resources. Alternatively, an organization may wish to extend its current IT capability by using an exclusive, private cloud that is remotely accessible and provisioned by a third party. Such an organization may feel uncomfortable with their data being held alongside a potential competitor's data in the multi-tenancy model.

6.4.2 Public Clouds

A public cloud, as its name implies, is available to the general public and is managed by an organization. The organization may be a business (such as Google), academic,

Table 6.3 Comparison of Cloud Delivery Models

Service Type	IaaS	PaaS	SaaS
Service category	VM rental; online storage	Online operating environment, online database, online message queue	Application and software rental
Service customization	Server template	Logic resource template	Application template
Service provisioning	Automation	Automation	Automation
Service accessing and use	Remote console, Web 2.0	Online development and debugging, integration of offline development tools and cloud	Web 2.0
Service monitoring	Physical resource monitoring	Logic resource monitoring	Application monitoring
Service-level management	Dynamic orchestration of physical resources	Dynamic orchestration of logic resources	Dynamic orchestration of application
Service resource optimization	Network visualization, server visualization, storage visualization	Large-scale distributed file system. Database, middleware, etc.	Multi-tenancy
Service measurement	Physical resource metering	Logic resource usage metering	Business resource usage metering
Service integration and combination	Load balance	SOA	SOA, mashup
Service security	Storage encryption and isolation, VM isolation, VLAN; SSL/SSH	Data isolation, operating environment isolation, SSL	Data isolation, operating environment isolation, SSL; Web authentication and authorization

or a governmental department. The cloud-computing provider owns and manages the cloud infrastructure. The existence of many different consumers within one cloud architecture is referred to as a *multi-tenancy model.*

6.4.3 Hybrid Clouds

Hybrid clouds are formed when more than one type of cloud infrastructure is utilized for a particular situation. For instance, an organization may utilize a public cloud for some aspect of its business yet also have a private cloud on the premises for data that is sensitive. As organizations start to exploit cloud service models, it is increasingly likely that a hybrid model is adopted as the specific characteristics of each of the different service models are harnessed. The key enabler here is the open standards by which data and applications are implemented, since if portability does not exist, then vendor lock-in to a particular cloud-computing provider becomes likely. Lack of data and application portability has been a major hindrance for the widespread uptake of grid computing, and this is one aspect of cloud computing that can facilitate much more flexible, abstract architectures.

6.4.4 Community Clouds

Community clouds are a model of cloud computing where the resources exist for a number of parties who have a shared interest or cause. This model is very similar to the single-purpose grids that collaborating research and academic organizations have created to conduct large-scale scientific experiments (e-science). The cloud is owned and managed by one or more of the collaborators in the community, and it may exist either on or off premises.

6.5 Cloud Benefits

Cloud computing is an attractive paradigm that promises numerous benefits, inherent in the characteristics mentioned above. These include:

- Optimization of a company's capital investment by reducing costs of purchasing hardware and software, resulting in a much lower total cost of ownership and, ultimately, a whole new way of looking at the economics of scale and operational IT
- Simplicity and agility of operations and use, requiring minimal time and effort to provision additional resources
- Enabling an enterprise to tap into a talent pool, as and when needed, for a fraction of the cost of hiring staff or retaining the existing staff and, thus, enabling the key personnel in the organizations to focus more on producing value and innovation for the business

■ Enabling small organizations to access the IT services and resources that would otherwise be out of their reach, thus placing large organizations and small businesses on a level playing field

■ Providing novel and complex computing architectures and innovation potential

■ Providing mechanisms for disaster recovery and business continuity through a variety of fully outsourced ICT services and resources

Cloud computing can be massively scalable, and there are built-in benefits of efficiency, availability, and high utilization that, in turn, result in reduced capital expenditure and reduced operational costs. It permits seamless sharing and collaboration through virtualization. In general, cloud computing promises cost savings, agility, innovation, flexibility, and simplicity. The offerings from vendors, in terms of services of the application, platform, and infrastructure nature, are continuing to mature, and the cost savings are becoming particularly attractive in the current competitive economic climate. Another broader aim of cloud technology is to make supercomputing available to the enterprises, in particular, and the public, in general.

The major benefits of the cloud paradigm can be distilled to its inherent flexibility and resiliency, potential for reducing costs, availability of very large amounts of centralized data storage, means to rapidly deploy computing resources, and scalability.

1. Flexibility and Resiliency: A major benefit of cloud computing is the flexibility, though cloud providers cannot provide infinite configuration and provisioning flexibility and will seek to offer structured alternatives. They might offer a choice among a number of computing and storage resource configurations at different capabilities and costs, and the cloud customer will have to adjust his or her requirements to fit one of those models.

   The flexibility offered by cloud computing can be in terms of
   – Automated provisioning of new services and technologies
   – Acquisition of increased resources on an as-needed basis
   – Ability to focus on innovation instead of maintenance details
   – Device independence
   – Freedom from having to install software patches
   – Freedom from concerns about updating servers

   Resiliency is achieved through the availability of multiple redundant resources and locations. As autonomic computing becomes more mature, self-management and self-healing mechanisms can ensure the increased reliability and robustness of cloud resources. Also, disaster recovery and business continuity planning are inherent in using the provider's cloud-computing platforms.

2. Reduced Costs: Cloud computing offers reductions in system administration, provisioning expenses, energy costs, software licensing fees, and

hardware costs. The cloud paradigm, in general, is a basis for cost savings because capability and resources can be paid for incrementally without the need for large investments in computing infrastructure. This model is especially true for adding storage costs for large database applications. Therefore, capital costs are reduced and replaced by manageable, scalable operating expenses.

There might be some instances, particularly for long-term, stable computing configuration usage, where cloud computation might not have a cost advantage over using one's internal resources or directly leasing equipment. For example, if the volume of data storage and computational resources required are essentially constant and there is no need for rapid provisioning and flexibility, an organization's local computational capabilities might be more cost-effective than using a cloud.

Resources are used more efficiently in cloud computing, resulting in substantial support and energy cost savings. The need for highly trained and expensive IT personnel is also reduced; client organizational support and maintenance costs are reduced dramatically because these expenses are transferred to the cloud provider, including 24/7 support that, in turn, is spread onto a much larger base of multiple tenants or clients.

Another reason for migrating to the cloud is the drastic reduction in the cost of power and energy consumption.

3. Centralized Data Storage: Many data centers are an ensemble of legacy applications, operating systems, hardware, and software and are a support and maintenance nightmare. This situation requires more specialized maintenance personnel, entails increased costs because of lack of standardization, and carries a higher risk of crashes. The cloud not only offers larger amounts of data storage resources than are normally available in local, corporate computing systems but also enables a decrease or increase in the resources used per requirements—with the corresponding adjustments in operating cost. This centralization of storage infrastructure results in cost efficiencies in utilities, real estate, and trained personnel. Also, data-protection mechanisms are much easier to implement and monitor in a centralized system than on large numbers of computing platforms that might be widely distributed geographically in different parts of an organization.

4. Reduced time to deployment: In a competitive environment where rapid evaluation, development, and deployment of new approaches, processes, solutions, or offerings is critical, the cloud offers the means to use powerful computational or large storage resources on short notice within a short period of time, without requiring sizable initial investments of finances, efforts, or

time (in hardware, software, and personnel). Thus, this rapid provisioning of the latest technologically upgraded and enhanced resources can be accomplished at relatively small cost (with minimal cost of replacing discontinued resources) and offers the client access to advanced technologies that are constantly being acquired by the cloud provider. Improved delivery of services obtained by rapid cloud provisioning improves time to market and, hence, market growth.

5. Scalability: Cloud computing provides the means, within limits, for a client to rapidly provision computational resources to meet increases or decreases in demand. Cloud scalability provides for optimal resources so that computing resources are provisioned per requirements, seamlessly ensuring maximum cost benefit to the clients. Since, the cloud provider operates on a multi-tenancy utility model, the client organization has to pay only for the resources it is using at any particular time.

6.6 Cloud Technologies

Virtualization is widely used to deliver customizable computing environments on demand. Virtualization technology is one of the fundamental components of cloud computing. Virtualization allows the creation of a secure, customizable, and isolated execution environment for running applications without affecting other users' applications. The basis of this technology is the ability of a computer program—or a combination of software and hardware—to emulate an executing environment separate from the one that hosts such programs. For instance, we can run Windows OS on top of a virtual machine, which itself is running on Linux OS. Virtualization provides a great opportunity to build elastically scalable systems that can provision additional capability with minimum costs.

6.6.1 Virtualization

Resource virtualization is at the heart of most cloud architectures. The concept of virtualization allows an abstract, logical view on the physical resources and includes servers, data stores, networks, and software. The basic idea is to pool physical resources and manage them as a whole. Individual requests can then be served as required from these resource pools. For instance, it is possible to dynamically generate a certain platform for a specific application at the very moment when it is needed—instead of a real machine, a virtual machine is instituted.

Resource management grows increasingly complex as the scale of a system, as well as the number of users and the diversity of applications using the system, increases. Resource management for a community of users with a wide range of applications running under different operating systems is a very difficult problem. Resource management becomes even more complex when resources are oversubscribed and users are uncooperative. In addition to external factors, resource management is affected by internal factors, such as the heterogeneity of the hardware and software systems, the ability to approximate the global state of the system and to redistribute the load, and the failure rates of different components. The traditional solution for these in a data center is to install standard operating systems on individual systems and to rely on conventional OS techniques to ensure resource sharing, application protection, and performance isolation. System administration, accounting, security, and resource management are very challenging for the providers of service in this setup; application development and performance optimization are equally challenging for the users.

The alternative is resource virtualization, a technique analyzed in this chapter. Virtualization is a basic tenet of cloud computing—which simplifies some of the resource management tasks. For instance, the state of a virtual machine (VM) running under a virtual machine monitor (VMM) can be saved and migrated to another server to balance the load. At the same time, virtualization allows users to operate in environments with which they are familiar rather than forcing them to work in idiosyncratic environments. Resource sharing in a virtual machine environment requires not only ample hardware support and, in particular, powerful processors but also architectural support for multilevel control. Indeed, resources such as central processing unit (CPU) cycles, memory, secondary storage, and I/O and communication bandwidth are shared among several virtual machines; for each VM, resources must be shared among multiple instances of an application. There are two distinct approaches for virtualization:

■ Full virtualization: Full virtualization is feasible when the hardware abstraction provided by the VMM is an exact replica of the physical hardware. In this case, any operating system running on the hardware will run without modifications under the VMM.
■ Paravirtualization: Paravirtualization requires some modifications of the guest operating systems because the hardware abstraction provided by the VMM does not support all the functions the hardware does.

One of the primary reasons that companies have implemented virtualization is to improve the performance and efficiency of processing of a diverse mix of workloads. Rather than assigning a dedicated set of physical resources to each set of tasks, a pooled set of virtual resources can be quickly allocated as needed across all workloads. Reliance on the pool of virtual resources allows companies to improve latency. This increase in service delivery speed and efficiency is a function of the distributed nature of virtualized environments and helps to improve overall time-to-realize value. Using a distributed set of physical resources, such as servers, in a more flexible and efficient way delivers significant benefits in terms of cost savings and improvements in productivity:

1. Virtualization of physical resources (such as servers, storage, and networks) enables substantial improvement in the utilization of these resources.
2. Virtualization enables improved control over the usage and performance of the IT resources.
3. Virtualization provides a level of automation and standardization to optimize your computing environment.
4. Virtualization provides a foundation for cloud computing.

Virtualization increases the efficiency of the cloud, making many complex systems easier to optimize. As a result, organizations have been able to achieve the performance and optimization to be able to access data that were previously either unavailable or very hard to collect. Big Data platforms are increasingly used as sources of enormous amounts of data about customer preferences, sentiment, and behaviors (see Chapter 7, Section 7.1.1 "What Is Big Data?"). Companies can integrate this information with internal sales and product data to gain insight into customer preferences to make more targeted and personalized offers.

6.6.1.1 Characteristics of Virtualized Environment

In a virtualized environment, there are three major components: guest, host, and virtualization layer. The guest represents the system component, which interacts with the virtualization layer rather than with the host, as would normally happen. The host represents the original environment where the guest is supposed to be managed. The virtualization layer is responsible for recreating the same or a different environment where the guest will operate.

Virtualization has three characteristics that support the scalability and operating efficiency required for Big Data environments:

1. Partitioning: In virtualization, many applications and operating systems are supported in a single physical system by partitioning (separating) the available resources.
2. Isolation: Each virtual machine is isolated from its host physical system and other virtualized machines. Because of this isolation, if one virtual instance crashes, the other virtual machines and the host system are not affected. In addition, data are not shared between one virtual instance and another.
3. Encapsulation: A virtual machine can be represented (and even stored) as a single file, so you can identify it easily based on the services it provides. For example, the file containing the encapsulated process could be a complete business service. This encapsulated virtual machine could be presented to an application as a complete entity. Thus, encapsulation could protect each application so that it does not interfere with another application.

Virtualization abstracts the underlying resources and simplifies their use, isolates users from one another, and supports replication, which, in turn, increases the elasticity of the system. Virtualization is a critical aspect of cloud computing, equally important to the providers and consumers of cloud services, and it plays an important role in

- System security, because it allows isolation of services running on the same hardware
- Portable performance and reliability, because it allows applications to migrate from one platform to another
- Development and management of services offered by a provider
- Performance isolation

6.6.1.1.1 Virtualization Advantages

Virtualization—the process of using computer resources to imitate other resources—is valued for its capability to increase IT resource utilization, efficiency, and scalability. One obvious application of virtualization is server virtualization, which helps organizations to increase the utilization of physical servers and potentially save on infrastructure costs; companies are increasingly finding that virtualization is not limited only to servers but is valid and applicable across the entire IT infrastructure, including networks, storage, and software. For instance, one of the most important requirements for success with Big Data is having the right level of performance to support the analysis of large volumes and varied types of data. If a company only virtualizes the servers, they may experience bottlenecks from other infrastructure elements such as storage and networks; furthermore, they are less likely to achieve the latency and efficiency that they need and more likely to expose the company to higher costs and increased security risks. As a result, a company's entire IT environment needs to be optimized at every layer from the network to the databases, storage, and servers—virtualization adds efficiency at every layer of the IT infrastructure.

For a provider of IT services, the use of virtualization techniques has a number of advantages:

1. Resource usage: Physical servers rarely work to capacity because their operators usually allow for sufficient computing resources to cover peak usage. If virtual machines are used, any load requirement can be satisfied from the resource pool. In case the demand increases, it is possible to delay or even avoid the purchase of new capacities.
2. Management: It is possible to automate resource pool management. Virtual machines can be created and configured automatically as required.
3. Consolidation: Different application classes can be consolidated to run on a smaller number of physical components. Besides server or storage consolidation, it is also possible to include entire system landscapes, data and databases,

networks, and desktops. Consolidation leads to increased efficiency and thus to cost reduction.

4. Energy consumption: Supplying large data centers with electric power has become increasingly difficult, and seen over its lifetime, the cost of energy required to operate a server is higher than its purchase price. Consolidation reduces the number of physical components. This, in turn, reduces the expenses for energy supply.

5. Less space required: Each and every square yard of data-center space is scarce and expensive. With consolidation, the same performance can be obtained on a smaller footprint, and the costly expansion of an existing data center might possibly be avoided.

6. Emergency planning: It is possible to move virtual machines from one resource pool to another. This ensures better availability of the services and makes it easier to comply with service-level agreements. Hardware maintenance windows are inherently no longer required.

6.6.1.1.2 Virtualization Benefits

Since the providers of cloud services tend to build very large resource centers, virtualization leads not only to a size advantage but also to a more favorable cost situation. This results in the following benefits for the customer:

1. Dynamic behavior: Any request can be satisfied just in time and without any delays. In case of bottlenecks, a virtual machine can draw on additional resources (such as storage space and I/O capabilities).

2. Availability: Services are highly available and can be used day and night without stop. In the event of technology upgrades, it is possible to hot-migrate applications because virtual machines can easily be moved to an up-to-date system.

3. Access: The virtualization layer isolates each virtual machine from the others and from the physical infrastructure. This way, virtual systems feature multi-tenant capabilities and, using a roles concept, it is possible to safely delegate management functionality to the customer. Customers can purchase IT capabilities from a self-service portal (customer emancipation).

The most direct benefit of virtualization is to ensure that MapReduce engines work better. Virtualization will result in better scale and performance for MapReduce. Each one of the map and reduce tasks needs to be executed independently. If the MapReduce engine is parallelized and configured to run in a virtual environment, you can reduce management overhead and allow for expansions and contractions in the task workloads. MapReduce itself is inherently parallel and distributed. By encapsulating the MapReduce engine in a virtual container, you can run what you need whenever you need it. With virtualization, you can increase your utilization of the assets you have already paid for by turning them into generic pools of resources.

6.6.1.1.3 Virtualization Challenges

There are side effects of virtualization, notably the performance penalty and the hardware costs. All privileged operations of a VM must be trapped and validated by the VMM, which ultimately controls system behavior; the increased overhead has a negative impact on performance. The cost of the hardware for a VM is higher than the cost for a system running a traditional operating system because the physical hardware is shared among a set of guest operating systems, and it is typically configured with faster and/or multi-core processors, more memory, larger disks, and additional network interfaces compared with a system running a traditional operating system.

A drawback of virtualization is the fact that the operation of the abstraction layer itself requires resources. Modern virtualization techniques, however, are so sophisticated that this overhead is not too significant: due to the particularly effective interaction of current multicore systems with virtualization technology, this performance loss plays only a minor role in today's systems. In view of possible savings and the quality benefits perceived by the customers, the use of virtualization pays off in nearly all cases.

6.6.2 Service-Oriented Computing

Service-oriented computing (SOA) introduces a flexible architectural style that provides an integration framework through which software architects can build applications using a collection of reusable functional units (services) with well-defined interfaces, which it combines in a logical flow. Applications are integrated at the interface (contract) and not at the implementation level. This allows greater flexibility since applications are built to work with any implementation of a contract rather than take advantage of a feature or idiosyncrasy of a particular system or implementation. For example, different service providers (of the same interface) can be dynamically chosen based on policies, such as price, performance, or other quality of system (QoS) guarantees, current transaction volume, and so on.

Another important characteristic of an SOA is that it allows many-to-many integration; that is, a variety of consumers across an enterprise can use and reuse applications in a variety of ways. This ability can dramatically reduce the cost/complexity of integrating incompatible applications and increase the ability of developers to quickly create, reconfigure, and repurpose applications as business needs arise. Benefits include reduced IT administration costs, ease of business-process integration across organizational departments and with trading partners, and increased business adaptability.

SOA is a logical way of designing a software system to provide services to either end-user applications or to other services distributed in a network via published and discoverable interfaces. To achieve this, SOA reorganizes a portfolio of previously siloed software applications and support infrastructure in an organization into an interconnected collection of services, each of which is discoverable and accessible through standard interfaces and messaging protocols. Once all the elements of an SOA are in place, existing and future applications can access the SOA-based services as necessary. This architectural approach is particularly applicable when multiple applications running on varied technologies and platforms need to communicate with each other.

The essential goal of an SOA is to enable general-purpose interoperability among existing technologies and extensibility to future purposes and architectures. SOA lowers interoperability hurdles by converting monolithic and static systems into modular and flexible components, which it represents as services that can be requested through an industry-standard protocol. Much of SOA's power and flexibility derives from its ability to leverage standards-based functional services, calling them when needed on an individual basis or aggregating them to create composite applications or multistage business processes. The building-block services might employ pre-existing components that are reused and can also be updated or replaced without affecting the functionality or integrity of other independent services. In this latter regard, the services model offers numerous advantages over large monolithic applications, in which modifications to some portions of the code can have unintended and unpredictable effects on the rest of the code to which it is tightly bundled. Simply put, an SOA is an architectural style, inspired by the service-oriented approach to computing, for enabling extensible interoperability.

SOA as a design philosophy is independent of any specific technology, for example, Web Services or J2EE. Although the concept of SOA is often discussed in conjunction with Web Services, these two are not synonymous. In fact, SOA can be implemented without the use of Web Services, for example, using Java, C#, or J2EE. However, Web Services should be seen as a primary example of a message delivery model that makes it much easier to deploy an SOA. Web Services standards are key to enabling interoperability as well as key issues including QoS, system semantics, security, management, and reliable messaging.

6.6.2.1 Advantages of SOA

Enterprises may use SOA for the following:

1. Implementing end-to-end collaborative business processes: The term *end-to-end business process* signifies that a succession of automated business processes and information systems in different enterprises (which are typically

involved in intercompany business transactions) are successfully integrated. The aim is to provide seamless interoperation and interactive links between all the relevant members in an extended enterprise—ranging from product designers, suppliers, trading partners, and logistics providers to end customers. At this stage, an organization moves into the highest strategic level of SOA implementation. Deployment of services becomes ubiquitous, and federated services collaborate across enterprise boundaries to create complex products and services. Individual services in this extended enterprise may originate from many providers, irrespective of company-specific systems or applications.

2. Implementing enterprise service orchestrations: This basic SOA entry point focuses on a typical implementation within a department or between a small number of departments and enterprise assets, and it comprises two steps. The first step is transforming enterprise assets and applications into an SOA implementation. This can start by service enabling existing individual applications or creating new applications using Web Services technology. This can begin by specifying a Web Service interface into an individual application or application element (including legacy systems). The next step after this basic Web Service implementation is implementing service orchestrations out of the service-enabled assets or newly created service applications.

3. Service enabling the entire enterprise: The next stage in the SOA entry-point hierarchy is when an enterprise seeks to provide a set of common services based on SOA components that can be used across the entire organization. Enterprise-wide service integration is achieved on the basis of commonly accepted standards. This results in achieving service consistency across departmental boundaries and is a precursor to integrating an organization with its partners and suppliers. Consistency is an important factor for this configuration as it provides both a uniform view to the enterprise and its customers as well as ensuring compliance with statutory or business policy requirements.

One problem when implementing an SOA at the enterprise level or implementing a cross-enterprise collaborative SOA is how to manage the SOA model, how to categorize the elements in this model, and how to organize them in such a way that the different stakeholders reviewing the model can understand it. Toward this end, it is often convenient to think of the SOA as comprising a number of distinct layers of abstraction that emphasize service interfaces, service realizations, and compositions of services into higher-level business processes. Each of these describes a logical separation of concerns by defining a set of common enterprise elements; each layer uses the functionality of the layer below it, adding new functionality, to accomplish its objective. The logical flow employed in the layered SOA development model may focus on a top-down development approach, which emphasizes how business processes are decomposed into a collection of business services and how these services are implemented in terms of pre-existing enterprise assets.

6.6.2.2 Layers in SOA

SOA can be considered to be comprised of the following six distinct layers:

1. Domains: A business domain is a functional domain comprising a set of current and future business processes that share common capabilities and functionality and can collaborate with each other to accomplish a higher-level business objective, such as loans, insurance, banking, finance, manufacturing, marketing, and human resources.
2. Business processes: This layer is formed by subdividing a business domain, such as distribution, into a small number of core business processes, such as purchasing, order management, and inventory, which are made entirely standard for use throughout the enterprise; having a large number of fine-grained processes leads to tremendous overhead and inefficiency, and hence, having a small collection of coarser-grained processes that are usable in multiple scenarios is a better option.
3. Business services: For any process, the right approach to business services is to subdivide it into increasingly smaller sub-processes until the process cannot be divided any further. The resulting sub-processes then become candidate indivisible (singular) business services for implementation. Business services automate generic business tasks that provide value to an enterprise and are part of standard business process. The more processes that an enterprise decomposes in this way, the more commonality across these sub-processes can be achieved. In this way, an enterprise has the chance of building an appropriate set of reusable business services.

   This layer relies on the orchestration interface of a collection of business-aligned services to realize reconfigurable end-to-end business processes. Individual services or collections of services that exhibit various levels of granularity are combined and orchestrated to produce new composite services that not only introduce new levels of reuse but also allow the reconfiguration of business processes.

   The interfaces get exported as service descriptions in this layer using a service description language, such as WSDL. The service description can be implemented by a number of service providers, each offering various choices of qualities of service based on technical requirements in the areas of availability, performance, scalability, and security.

During the exercise of defining business services, it is also important to take existing utility logic, ingrained in code, and expose it as services, which themselves become candidate services that specify not the overall business process but rather the mechanism for implementing the process. This exercise should thus yield two categories of services: business functionality services, which are reusable across multiple processes; and a collection of fine-grained utility (or commodity) services, which provide value to and are shared by business services across the organization. Examples of utility services include services implementing calculations, algorithms, and directory management services.

4. Infrastructure services: Infrastructure services are subdivided into technical utility services, access services, management and monitoring services, and interaction services; these are not specific to a single line of business but are reusable across multiple lines of business. They also include mechanisms that seamlessly interlink services that span enterprises. This can, for example, include the policies, constraints, and specific industry messages and interchange standards (such as the need to conform to specific industry message and interchange standards like EDIFACT, SWIFT, xCBL, ebXML BPSS, or RosettaNet) that an enterprise, say within a particular vertical marketplace, must conform to in order to work with other similar processes. Access services are dedicated to transforming data and integrating legacy applications and functions into the SOA environment. This includes the wrapping and service enablement of legacy functions.

5. Service realizations: This layer is the component realization layer that uses components for implementing services out of pre-existing applications and systems found in the operational systems layer. Components comprise autonomous units of software that may provide a useful service or a set of functionality to a client (business service) and have meaning in isolation from other components with which they interoperate.

6. Operational systems: This layer is used by components to implement business services and processes. This layer contains existing enterprise systems or applications, including customer relationship management (CRM) and ERP systems and applications, legacy applications, database systems and applications, and other packaged applications. These systems are usually known as *enterprise information systems.*

6.6.3 Business Processes with SOA

Every enterprise has unique characteristics that are embedded in its business processes. Most enterprises perform a similar set of repeatable routine activities that may include the development of manufacturing products and services, bringing these products and services to market, and satisfying the customers who purchase them. Automated business processes can perform such activities. We may view an automated business process as a precisely choreographed sequence of activities systematically directed toward performing a certain business task and bringing it to completion. Examples of typical processes in manufacturing firms include new product development (which cuts across research and development, marketing, and manufacturing); customer order fulfillment (which combines sales, manufacturing, warehousing, transportation, and billing); and financial asset management. The possibility to design, structure, and measure processes and determine their contribution to customer value makes them an important starting point for business improvement and innovation initiatives.

The largest possible process in an organization is the value chain. The value chain is decomposed into a set of core business processes and support processes necessary to produce a product or product line. These core business processes are subdivided into activities. An activity is an element that performs a specific function within a process. Activities can be as simple as sending or receiving a message or as complex as coordinating the execution of other processes and activities. A business process may encompass complex activities, some of which run on back-end systems, such as a credit check, automated billing, a purchase order, stock updates and shipping, or even such frivolous activities as sending a document and filling a form. A business process activity may invoke another business process in the same or a different business system domain. Activities will inevitably vary greatly from one company to another and from one business analysis effort to another.

At runtime, a business process definition may have multiple instantiations, each operating independently of the other, and each instantiation may have multiple activities that are concurrently active. A process instance is a defined thread of activity that is being enacted (managed) by a workflow engine. In general, instances of a process, its current state, and the history of its actions will be visible at runtime and expressed in terms of the business process definition so that

- Users can determine the status of business activities and business
- Specialists can monitor the activity and identify potential improvements to the business process definition

6.6.3.1 Process

A process is an ordering of activities with a beginning and an end; it has inputs (in terms of resources, materials, and information) and a specified output (the results it produces). We may thus define a process as any sequence of steps that is initiated by an event; transforms information, materials, or commitments; and produces an output. A business process is typically associated with operational objectives and business relationships, for example, an insurance claims process or an engineering development process. A process may be wholly contained within a single organizational unit or may span different enterprises, such as in a customer–supplier relationship. Typical examples of processes that cross organizational boundaries are purchasing and sales processes jointly set up by buying and selling organizations, supported by EDI and value-added networks. The Internet is now a trigger for the design of new business processes and the redesign of existing ones.

A business process is a set of logically related tasks performed to achieve a well-defined business outcome. A (business) process view implies a horizontal view of a business organization and looks at processes as sets of interdependent activities designed and structured to produce a specific output for a customer or a market. A business process defines the results to be achieved, the context of the activities, the relationships between the activities, and the interactions with other processes and resources. A business process may receive events that alter the state of the process and the sequence of activities. A business process may produce events for input to other applications or processes. It may also invoke applications to perform computational functions, and it may post assignments to human work lists to request actions by human actors. Business processes can be measured, and different performance measures apply, such as cost, quality, time, and customer satisfaction.

A business process has the following behavior:

◼ It may contain defined conditions triggering its initiation in each new instance (e.g., the arrival of a claim) and defined outputs at its completion.
◼ It may involve formal or relatively informal interactions between participants.
◼ It has a duration that may vary widely.
◼ It may contain a series of automated activities and/or manual activities. Activities may be large and complex, involving the flow of materials, information, and business commitments.
◼ It exhibits a very dynamic nature, so it can respond to demands from customers and to changing market conditions.
◼ It is widely distributed and customized across boundaries within and between enterprises, often spanning multiple applications with very different technology platforms.
◼ It is usually long running—a single instance of a process such as order to cash may run for months or even years.

Every business process implies processing: A series of activities (processing steps) leading to some form of transformation of data or products for which the process exists. Transformations may be executed manually or in an automated way. A transformation will encompass multiple processing steps. Finally, every process delivers a product, like a mortgage or an authorized invoice. The extent to which the end product of a process can be specified in advance and can be standardized impacts the way that processes and their workflows can be structured and automated.

Processes have decision points. Decisions have to be made with regard to routing and allocation of processing capacity. In a highly predictable and standardized environment, the trajectory in the process of a customer order will be established in advance in a standard way. Only if the process is complex and if the conditions of the process are not predictable will routing decisions have to be made on the spot. In general, the customer orders will be split into a category that is highly proceduralized (and thus automated) and a category that is complex and uncertain. Here, human experts will be needed, and manual processing is a key element of the process.

6.6.3.2 Workflow

A workflow system automates a business process, in whole or in part, during which documents, information, or tasks are passed from one participant to another for action, according to a set of procedural rules. Workflows are based on document life cycles and form-based information processing, so generally they support well-defined, static, clerical processes. They provide transparency, since business processes are clearly articulated in the software, and they are agile because they produce definitions that are fast to deploy and change.

A workflow can be defined as the sequence of processing steps (execution of business operations, tasks, and transactions), during which information and physical objects are passed from one processing step to another. Workflow is a concept that links together technologies and tools able to automatically route events and tasks with programs or users.

Process-oriented workflows are used to automate processes whose structure is well defined and stable over time, which often coordinate sub-processes executed by machines and which only require minor user involvement (often only in specific cases). An order management process or a loan request is an example of a well-defined process. Certain process-oriented workflows may have transactional properties. The process-oriented workflow is made up of tasks that follow routes, with checkpoints represented by business rules, for example, a pause for a credit approval. Such business process rules govern the overall processing of activities, including the routing of requests, the assignment or distribution of requests to designated roles, the passing of workflow data from activity to activity, and the dependencies and relationships between business process activities.

A workflow involves activities, decision points, rules, routes, and roles. These are briefly described later. Just like a process, a workflow normally comprises a number of logical steps, each of which is known as an *activity*. An activity is a set of actions that are guided by the workflow. An activity may involve manual interaction with a user or workflow participant or may be executed using diverse resources such as application programs or databases. A work item or data set is created and is processed and changed in stages at a number of processing or decision points to meet specific business goals. Most workflow engines can handle very complex series of processes.

A workflow can depict various aspects of a business process, including automated and manual activities, decision points and business rules, parallel and sequential work routes, and how to manage exceptions to the normal business process. A workflow can have logical decision points that determine which branch of the flow a work item may take in the event of alternative paths. Every alternate path within the flow is identified and controlled through a bounded set of logical decision points. An instantiation of a workflow to support a work item includes all possible paths from beginning to end.

Within a workflow, business rules at each decision point determine how workflow-related data are to be processed, routed, tracked, and controlled. Business rules are core business policies that capture the nature of an enterprise's business model and define the conditions that must be met in order to move to the next stage of the workflow. Business rules are represented as compact statements about an aspect of the business that can be expressed within an application, and, as such, they determine the route to be followed. For instance, for a health-care application, business rules may include policies on how new claim validation, referral requirements, or special procedure approvals are implemented. Business rules can represent, among other things, typical business situations such as escalation ("send this document to a supervisor for approval") and managing exceptions ("this loan is more than $50,000; send it to the MD").

6.6.3.3 Business Process Management (BPM)

BPM is a commitment to expressing, understanding, representing, and managing a business (or the portion of business to which it is applied) in terms of a collection of business processes that are responsive to a business environment of internal or external events. The term *management of business processes* includes process analysis, process definition and redefinition, resource allocation, scheduling, measurement of process quality and efficiency, and process optimization. Process optimization includes collection and analysis of both real-time measures (monitoring) and strategic measures (performance management) and their correlation as the basis for process improvement and innovation. A BPM solution is a graphical productivity tool for modeling, integrating, monitoring, and optimizing process flows of all sizes, crossing any application, company boundary, or human interaction. BPM codifies value-driven processes and institutionalizes their execution within the enterprise. This implies that BPM tools can help analyze, define, and enforce process standardization. BPM provides a modeling tool to visually construct, analyze, and execute cross-functional business processes.

BPM is more than process automation or traditional workflow. BPM within the context of EAI and e-business integration provides the flexibility necessary to automate cross-functional processes. It adds conceptual innovations and technology from EAI and e-business integration and reimplements it on an e-business infrastructure based on Web and XML standards. Conventional applications provide traditional workflow features that work well only within their local environment. However, integrated process management is then required for processes spanning enterprises. Automating cross-functional activities, such as checking or confirming inventory between an enterprise and its distribution partners, enables corporations to manage processes by exception based on real-time events driven from the integrated environment. Process execution then becomes automated, requiring human intervention only in situations where exceptions occur; for example, if inventory level has fallen below a critical threshold or manual tasks and approvals are required.

The distinction between BPM and workflow is mainly based on the management aspect of BPM systems: BPM tools place considerable emphasis on management and business functions. Although BPM technology covers the same space as workflow, its focus is on the business user and it provides more sophisticated management and analysis capabilities. With a BPM tool, the business user is able to manage all the processes of a certain type, for example, claim processes, and should be able to study them from historical or current data and produce costs or other business measurements. In addition, the business user should also be able to analyze and compare the data or business measurements based on the different types of claims. This type of functionality is typically not provided by modern workflow systems.

6.6.3.4 Business Processes via Web Services

Business processes management and workflow systems today support the definition, execution, and monitoring of long-running processes that coordinate the activities of multiple business applications. However, because these systems are activity oriented and not communication (message) oriented, they do not separate internal implementation from external protocol description. When processes span business boundaries, loose coupling based on precise external protocols is required because the parties involved do not share application and workflow implementation technologies and will not allow external control over the use of their back-end applications. Such business interaction protocols are by necessity message-centric; they specify the flow of messages representing business actions among trading partners without requiring any specific implementation mechanism. With such applications, the loosely coupled, distributed nature of the Web enables exhaustive and full orchestration, choreography, and monitoring of the enterprise applications that expose the Web Services participating in the message exchanges.

Web Services provide a standard and interoperable means of integrating loosely coupled Web-based components that expose well-defined interfaces while abstracting the implementation and platform-specific details. Core Web Service standards such as SOAP, WSDL, and UDDI provide a solid foundation to accomplish this. However, these specifications primarily enable the development of simple Web Service applications that can conduct simple interactions. However, the ultimate goal of Web Services is to facilitate and automate business process collaborations both inside and outside enterprise boundaries. Useful business applications of Web Services in EAI and business-to-business environments require the ability to compose complex and distributed Web Service integrations and the ability to describe the relationships between the constituent low-level services. In this way, collaborative business processes can be realized as Web Service integrations.

A business process specifies the potential execution order of operations originating from a logically interrelated collection of Web Services, each of which performs a well-defined activity within the process. A business process also specifies the shared data passed between these services, the external partners' roles with respect to the process, joint exception handling conditions for the collection of Web Services, and other factors that may influence how Web Services or organizations participate in a process. This would enable long-running transactions between Web Services in order to increase the consistency and reliability of business processes that are composed out of these Web Services.

The orchestration and choreography of Web Services are enabled under three specification standards, namely, the Business Process Execution Language for Web Services (BPEL4WS or BPEL for short), WS-Coordination (WS-C), and WS-Transaction (WS-T). These three specifications work together to form the bedrock for reliably choreographing Web Service–based applications, providing BPM, transactional integrity, and generic coordination facilities. BPEL is a workflow-like definition language that describes sophisticated business processes that can orchestrate Web Services. WS-C and WS-T complement BPEL to provide mechanisms for defining specific standard protocols for use by transaction processing systems, workflow systems, or other applications that wish to coordinate multiple Web Services.

6.6.3.4.1 Service Composition

The platform-neutral nature of services creates the opportunity for building composite services by combining existing elementary or complex services (the component services) from different enterprises and in turn offering them as high-level services or processes. Composite services (and, thus, processes) integrate multiple services—and put together new business functions—by combining new and existing application assets in a logical flow.

The definition of composite services requires coordinating the flow of control and data between the constituent services. Business logic can be seen as the ingredient that sequences, coordinates, and manages interactions among Web Services. By programming a complex cross-enterprise workflow task or business transaction, it is possible to logically chain discrete Web Services activities into cross-enterprise business processes. This is enabled through orchestration and choreography (because Web Services technologies support coordination and offer an asynchronous and message-oriented way to communicate and interact with application logic).

1. Orchestration: Orchestration describes how Web Services can interact with each other at the message level, including the business logic and execution order of the interactions from the perspective and under the control of a single endpoint. This is, for instance, the case of the process flow where the business process flow is seen from the vantage point of a single supplier. Orchestration refers to an executable business process that may result in a long-lived, transactional, multi-step process model. With orchestration, business process interactions are always controlled from the (private) perspective of one of the business parties involved in the process.

2. Choreography: Choreography is typically associated with the public (globally visible) message exchanges, rules of interaction, and agreements that occur between multiple business process endpoints, rather than a specific business process that is executed by a single party. Choreography tracks the sequence of messages that may involve multiple parties and multiple sources, including customers, suppliers, and partners, where each party involved in the process describes the part it plays in the interaction, and no party owns the conversation. Choreography is more collaborative in nature than orchestration. It is described from the perspectives of all parties (common view) and, in essence, defines the shared state of the interactions between business entities. This common view can be used to determine specific deployment implementations for each individual entity. Choreography offers a means by which the rules of participation for collaboration can be clearly defined and agreed to, jointly. Each entity may then implement its portion of the choreography as determined by their common view.

6.7 Summary

This chapter introduces the concept of cloud computing. It describes its definition, presents the cloud delivery and deployment models, and highlights its benefits for enterprises; we discussed the primary challenges faced while provisioning cloud services, namely, scalability, multi-tenancy, and availability. The later part of the chapter describes virtualization technology, which is one of the fundamental components of cloud computing. Virtualization allows the creation of a secure, customizable, and isolated execution environment for running applications without affecting other users' applications. One of the primary reasons companies implement virtualization is to improve the performance and efficiency of processing of a diverse mix of workloads. Rather than assigning a dedicated set of physical resources to each set of tasks, a pooled set of virtual resources can be quickly allocated as needed across all workloads. Virtualization provides a great opportunity to build elastically scalable systems that can provision additional capability with minimum costs. The chapter introduced Service-Oriented Architecture (SOA) to explain the realization of processes in terms of Web Services.

Chapter 7

Big Data Computing

The rapid growth of the Internet and World Wide Web has led to vast amounts of information available online. In addition, business and government organizations create large amounts of both structured and unstructured information, which needs to be processed, analyzed, and linked. It is estimated that the amount of information currently stored in a digital form in 2007 is at 281 exabytes and the overall compound growth rate is at 57%, with information in organizations growing at even a faster rate. It is also estimated that 95% of all current information exists in unstructured form with increased data processing requirements compared to structured information. The storing, managing, accessing, and processing of this vast amount of data represents a fundamental need and an immense challenge in order to satisfy needs to search, analyze, mine, and visualize this data as information.

The Web is believed to have well over a trillion Web pages, of which at least 50 billion have been catalogued and indexed by search engines such as Google, making them searchable by all of us. This massive Web content spans well over 100 million domains (i.e., locations where we point our browsers, such as <http://www.wikipedia.org>). These are themselves growing at a rate of more than 20,000 net domain additions daily. Facebook and Twitter each have over 900 million users, who between them generate over 300 million posts a day (roughly 250 million tweets and over 60 million Facebook updates). Added to this are over 10,000 credit-card payments made per second, well over 30 billion point-of-sale transactions per year (via dial-up POS devices), and finally over 6 billion mobile phones, of which almost 1 billion are smartphones, many of which are GPS-enabled; these access the Internet for e-commerce, for tweets, and to post updates on Facebook. Last but not least, there are the images and videos on YouTube and other sites, which by themselves outstrip all these put together in terms of the sheer volume of data they represent.

7.1 Big Data

This deluge of data, along with emerging techniques and technologies used to handle it, is commonly referred to today as *Big Data*. Such Big Data is both valuable and challenging, because of its sheer volume, so much so that the volume of data being created in the current 5 years from 2010 to 2015 will far exceed all the data generated in human history. The Web, where all this data is being produced and resides, consists of millions of servers, with data storage soon to be measured in zettabytes.

Cloud computing provides the opportunity for organizations with limited internal resources to implement large-scale Big Data computing applications in a cost-effective manner. The fundamental challenges of Big Data computing are managing and processing exponentially growing data volumes; significantly reducing associated data analysis cycles to support practical, timely applications; and developing new algorithms that can scale to search and process massive amounts of data. The answer to these challenges is a scalable, integrated computer systems hardware and software architecture designed for parallel processing of Big Data computing applications. This chapter explores the challenges of Big Data computing.

7.1.1 What Is Big Data?

Big Data can be defined as volumes of data available in varying degrees of complexity, generated at different velocities and varying degrees of ambiguity that cannot be processed using traditional technologies, processing methods, algorithms, or any commercial off-the-shelf solutions. Data defined as Big Data includes weather, geospatial, and geographic information system (GIS) data; consumer-driven data from social media; enterprise-generated data from legal, sales, marketing, procurement, finance and human-resources departments; and device-generated data from sensor networks, nuclear plants, X-ray and scanning devices, and airplane engines (Figures 7.1 and 7.2).

7.1.1.1 Data Volume

The most interesting data for any organization to tap into today is social media data. The amount of data generated by consumers every minute provides extremely important insights into choices, opinions, influences, connections, brand loyalty, brand management, and much more. Social media sites not only provide consumer perspectives but also competitive positioning, trends, and access to communities formed by common interest. Organizations today leverage the social media pages to personalize marketing of products and services to each customer.

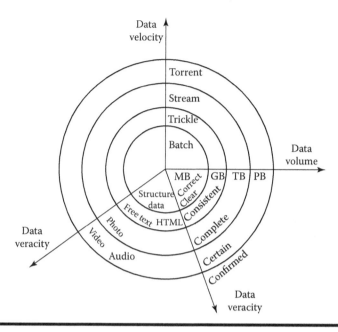

Figure 7.1   4V characteristics of Big Data.

Many additional applications are being developed and are slowly becoming a reality. These applications include using remote sensing to detect underground sources of energy, environmental monitoring, traffic monitoring and regulation by automatic sensors mounted on vehicles and roads, remote monitoring of patients using special scanners and equipment, and tighter control and replenishment of inventories using radio-frequency identification (RFID) and other technologies. All these developments will have associated with them a large volume of data. Social networks such as Twitter and Facebook have hundreds of millions of subscribers worldwide who generate new data with every message they send or post they make.

Every enterprise has massive amounts of e-mails that are generated by its employees, customers, and executives on a daily basis. These e-mails are all considered an asset of the corporation and need to be managed as such. After Enron and the collapse of many audits in enterprises, the US government mandated that all enterprises should have a clear life-cycle management of e-mails, and that e-mails should be available and auditable on a case-by-case basis. There are several examples that come to mind, like insider trading, intellectual property, competitive analysis, and many more, to justify governance and management of e-mails.

If companies can analyze petabytes of data (equivalent to 20 million four-drawer file cabinets filled with text files or 13.3 years of HDTV content) with acceptable performance to discern patterns and anomalies, businesses can begin to make sense of data in new ways. Table 7.1 indicates the escalating scale of data.

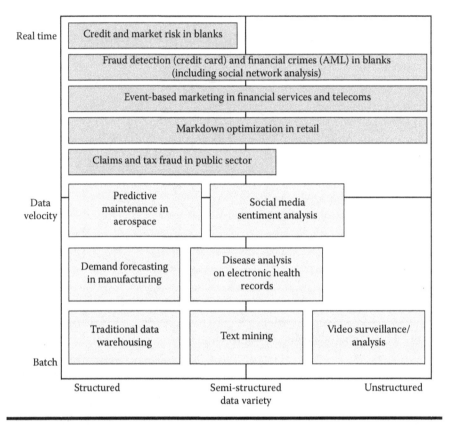

Figure 7.2   Use cases for Big Data computing.

Table 7.1   Scale of Data

Size of Data	Scale of Data
1,000 megabytes	1 gigabyte (GB)
1,000 gigabytes	1 terabyte (TBJ)
1,000 terabytes	1 petabyte (PB)
1,000 petabytes	1 exabyte (EB)
1,000 exabytes	1 zettabyte (ZBJ)
1,000 zettabytes	1 yottabyte (YB)

The list of features for handling data volume includes the following:

- Non-traditional and unorthodox data processing techniques need to be innovated for processing this data type.
- Metadata is essential for processing this data successfully.
- Metrics and key performance indicators (KPIs) are key to provide visualization.
- Raw data does not need to be stored online for access.
- Processed output is needed to be integrated into an enterprise-level analytical ecosystem to provide better insights and visibility into the trends and outcomes of business exercises, including customer relationship management (CRM), optimization of inventory, and clickstream analysis.
- The enterprise data warehouse (EDW) is needed for analytics and reporting.

7.1.1.2 Data Velocity

The business models adopted by Amazon, Facebook, Yahoo!, and Google, which became the *de facto* business models for most Web-based companies, operate on the fact that by tracking customer clicks and navigations on the website, you can deliver personalized browsing and shopping experiences. In this process of clickstreams, there are millions of clicks gathered from users at every second, amounting to large volumes of data. This data can be processed, segmented, and modeled to study population behaviors based on time of day, geography, advertisement effectiveness, click behavior, and guided navigation response. The result sets of these models can be stored to create a better experience for the next set of clicks exhibiting similar behaviors. The velocity of data produced by user clicks on any website today is a prime example for Big Data velocity. Real-time data and streaming data are accumulated by the likes of Twitter and Facebook at a very high velocity. Velocity is helpful in detecting trends among people that are tweeting a million tweets every 3 minutes. Processing of streaming data for analysis also involves the velocity dimension. Similarly, high velocity is attributed to data associated with the typical speed of transactions on stock exchanges; this speed reaches billions of transactions per day on certain days. If these transactions must be processed to detect potential fraud, or billions of call records on cell phones daily must be processed to detect malicious activity, we are dealing with the velocity dimension.

The most popular way to share pictures, music, and data today is via mobile devices. The sheer volume of data that is transmitted by mobile networks provides insights to the providers on the performance of their network; the amount of data processed at each tower; the time of day; the associated geographies; user demographics, location, and latencies; and much more. The velocity of data movement is unpredictable and sometimes can cause a network to crash. The data movement and its study have enabled mobile service providers to improve the QoS (quality of service), and associating this data with social media inputs has enabled insights into competitive intelligence.

The list of features for handling data velocity includes the following:

- System must be elastic for handling data velocity along with volume.
- System must scale up and scale down as needed without increasing costs.
- System must be able to process data across the infrastructure in the least processing time.
- System throughput should remain stable independent of data velocity.
- System should be able to process data on a distributed platform.

7.1.1.3 Data Variety

Data comes in multiple formats as it ranges from e-mails to tweets to social media and sensor data. There is no control over the input data format or the structure of the data. The processing complexity associated with a variety of formats is the availability of appropriate metadata for identifying what is contained in the actual data. This is critical when we process images, audio, video, and large chunks of text. The absence of metadata or partial metadata means processing delays from the ingestion of data to producing the final metrics and, more importantly, in integrating the results with the data warehouse (Tables 7.2 and 7.3). Sources of data in traditional applications were mainly transactions involving financial, insurance, travel, healthcare, retail industries, and governmental and judicial processing. The types of sources have expanded dramatically and include Internet data (e.g., clickstream and social media), research data (e.g., surveys and industry reports), location data (e.g., mobile device data and geospatial data), images (e.g., surveillance, satellites, and medical scanning), e-mails, supply-chain data (e.g., EDI—electronic data interchange, vendor catalogs), signal data (e.g., sensors and RFID devices), and videos (YouTube enters hundreds of minutes of video every minute). Big Data includes structured, semi-structured, and unstructured data in different proportions based on context.

The list of features for handling data variety includes the following:

- Scalability
- Distributed processing capabilities
- Image processing capabilities
- Graph processing capabilities
- Video and audio processing capabilities

7.1.1.4 Data Veracity

The veracity dimension of Big Data is a more recent addition than the advent of the Internet.

Veracity has two built-in features: the credibility of the source and the suitability of data for its target audience. It is closely related to trust; listing veracity as one of the dimensions of Big Data amounts to saying that data coming into the

Table 7.2 Value of Big Data Across Industries

	Volume of Data	Velocity of Data	Variety of Data	Underutilized Data (Dark Data)	Big Data Value Potential
Banking and securities	High	High	Low	Medium	High
Communications and media services	High	High	High	Medium	High
Education	Very low	Very low	Very low	High	Medium
Government	High	Medium	High	High	High
Healthcare providers	Medium	High	Medium	Medium	High
Insurance	Medium	Medium	Medium	Medium	Medium
Manufacturing	High	High	High	High	High
Chemicals and natural resources	High	High	High	High	Medium
Retail	High	High	High	Low	High
Transportation	Medium	Medium	Medium	High	Medium
Utilities	Medium	Medium	Medium	Medium	Medium

so-called Big Data applications have a variety of trustworthiness, and therefore before we accept the data for analytical or other applications, it must go through some degree of quality testing and credibility analysis. Many sources of data generate data that is uncertain, incomplete, and inaccurate, therefore making its veracity questionable.

7.1.2 Common Characteristics of Big Data Computing Systems

There are several important common characteristics of Big Data computing systems that distinguish them from other forms of computing.

1. Principle of co-location of the data and programs or algorithms to perform the computation: to achieve high performance in Big Data computing, it is important to minimize the movement of data. This principle—"move the code to the data"—which was designed into the data-parallel processing architecture implemented by Seisint in 2003, is extremely effective since

Table 7.3   Industry Use Cases for Big Data

Manufacturing	*Retail*
Product research	Customer relationship management
Engineering analysis	Store location and layout
Predictive maintenance	Fraud detection and prevention
Process and quality metrics	Supply-chain optimization
Distribution optimization	Dynamic pricing
Media and telecommunications	**Financial services**
Network optimization	Algorithmic trading
Customer scoring	Risk analysis
Churn prevention	Fraud detection
Fraud prevention	Portfolio analysis
Energy	**Advertising and public relations**
Smart grid	Demand signaling
Exploration	Targeted advertising
Operational modeling	Sentiment analysis
Power-line sensors	Customer acquisition
Healthcare and life sciences	**Government**
Pharmacogenomics	Market governance
Bioinformatics	Weapon systems and counter terrorism
Pharmaceutical research	Econometrics
Clinical outcomes research	Health informatics

program size is usually small in comparison to the large datasets processed by Big Data systems and results in much less network traffic since data can be read locally instead of across the network. In direct contrast to other types of computing and supercomputing that utilize data stored in a separate repository or servers and transfer the data to the processing system for computation, Big Data computing uses distributed data and distributed file systems in which data is located across a cluster of processing nodes, and instead of moving the data, the program or algorithm is transferred to the nodes with the data that needs to be processed. This characteristic allows processing algorithms to execute on the nodes where the data resides, reducing system overhead and increasing performance.

2. Programming model utilized: Big Data computing systems utilize a machine-independent approach in which applications are expressed in terms of high-level operations on data, and the runtime system transparently controls the scheduling, execution, load balancing, communications, and movement of programs and data across the distributed computing cluster. The programming abstraction and language tools allow the processing to be expressed in terms of dataflows and transformations incorporating new dataflow programming languages and shared libraries of common data manipulation algorithms such as sorting. Conventional supercomputing and distributed computing systems typically utilize machine-dependent programming models that can require low-level programmer control of processing and node communications using conventional imperative programming languages and specialized software packages that add complexity to the parallel programming task and reduce programmer productivity. A machine-dependent programming model also requires significant tuning and is more susceptible to single points of failure.

3. Focus on reliability and availability: Large-scale systems with hundreds or thousands of processing nodes are inherently more susceptible to hardware failures, communications errors, and software bugs. Big Data computing systems are designed to be fault resilient. This includes redundant copies of all data files on disk, storage of intermediate processing results on disk, automatic detection of node or processing failures, and selective recomputation of results. A processing cluster configured for Big Data computing is typically able to continue operation with a reduced number of nodes following a node failure with automatic and transparent recovery of incomplete processing.

4. Scalability: A final important characteristic of Big Data computing systems is the inherent scalability of the underlying hardware and software architecture. Big Data computing systems can typically be scaled in a linear fashion to accommodate virtually any amount of data or to meet time-critical performance requirements by simply adding additional processing nodes to a system configuration in order to achieve billions of records per second processing rates (BORPS). The number of nodes and processing tasks assigned for a specific application can be variable or fixed depending on the hardware, software, communications, and distributed file system architecture. This scalability allows computing problems that were once considered to be intractable due to the amount of data required or amount of processing time required to now be feasible, and it affords opportunities for new breakthroughs in data analysis and information processing.

 One of the key characteristics of the cloud is elastic scalability: Users can add or subtract resources in almost real time based on changing requirements. The cloud plays an important role within the Big Data world. Dramatic changes happen when these infrastructure components are combined with the advances in data management. Horizontally expandable and optimized infrastructure supports the practical implementation of Big Data. Cloudware technologies like virtualization increase the efficiency of the cloud, making many complex systems easier to optimize. As a result, organizations have the performance and optimization to be able to access data that was previously either unavailable or very hard to collect. Big Data platforms are increasingly used as sources of enormous amounts of data about customer preferences, sentiment, and behaviors. Companies can integrate this information with internal sales and product data to gain insight into customer preferences to make more targeted and personalized offers.

7.1.3 Big Data Appliances

Big Data analytics applications combine the means for developing and implementing algorithms that must access, consume, and manage data. In essence, the framework relies on a technology ecosystem of components that must be combined in a variety of ways to address each application's requirements, which can range from general information technology (IT) performance scalability to detailed performance improvement objectives associated with specific algorithmic demands. For example, some algorithms expect that massive amounts of data are immediately available quickly, necessitating large amounts of core memory. Other applications may need numerous iterative exchanges of data between different computing nodes, which would require high-speed networks.

The Big Data technology ecosystem stack may include the following:

1. Scalable storage systems that are used for capturing, manipulating, and analyzing massive datasets
2. A computing platform, sometimes configured specifically for large-scale analytics, often composed of multiple (typically multicore) processing nodes connected via a high-speed network to memory and disk storage subsystems. These are often referred to as *appliances*.
3. A data management environment, whose configurations may range from a traditional database management system scaled to massive parallelism to databases configured with alternative distributions and layouts to newer graph-based or other Not only SQL (NoSQL) data management schemes
4. An application development framework to simplify the process of developing, executing, testing, and debugging new application code. This framework should include programming models, development tools, program execution and scheduling, and system configuration and management capabilities.

5. Methods of scalable analytics (including statistical and data mining models) that can be configured by the analysts and other business consumers to help improve the ability to design and build analytical and predictive models
6. Management processes and tools that are necessary to ensure alignment with the enterprise analytics infrastructure and collaboration among the developers, analysts, and other business users

7.2 Tools and Techniques of Big Data

7.2.1 Processing Approach

Current Big Data computing platforms use a "divide and conquer" parallel processing approach combining multiple processors and disks in large computing clusters. These clusters are connected using high-speed communications switches and networks that allow the data to be partitioned among the available computing resources and processed independently to achieve performance and scalability based on the amount of data. We define a *cluster* as "a type of parallel and distributed system, which consists of a collection of interconnected standalone computers working together as a single integrated computing resource."

This approach to parallel processing is often referred to as a *shared nothing* approach, since each node consisting of processor, local memory, and disk resources shares nothing with other nodes in the cluster. In parallel computing, this approach is considered suitable for data-processing problems that are "embarrassingly parallel," that is, where it is relatively easy to separate the problem into a number of parallel tasks and there is no dependency or communication required between the tasks other than overall management of the tasks. These types of data-processing problems are inherently adaptable to various forms of distributed computing, including clusters and data grids and cloud computing. Analytical environments are deployed in different architectural models. Even on parallel platforms, many databases are built on a shared everything approach, in which the persistent storage and memory components are all shared by the different processing units. Parallel architectures are classified by what shared resources each processor can directly access. One typically distinguishes shared memory, shared disk, and shared nothing architectures (as depicted in Figure 7.3).

1. In a shared memory system, all processors have direct access to all memory via a shared bus. Typical examples are the common symmetric multi-processor systems, where each processor core can access the complete memory via the shared memory bus. To preserve the abstraction, processor caches, buffering a subset of the data closer to the processor for fast access, have to be kept consistent with specialized protocols. Because disks are typically accessed via the memory, all processes also have access to all disks.

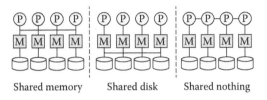

Shared memory   Shared disk   Shared nothing

Figure 7.3   Parallel architectures.

2. In a shared disk architecture, all processes have their own private memory, but all disks are shared. A cluster of computers connected to a SAN is a representative for this architecture.
3. In a shared nothing architecture, each processor has its private memory and private disk. The data is distributed across all disks, and each processor is responsible only for the data on its own connected memory and disks. To operate on data that spans the different memories or disks, the processors have to explicitly send data to other processors. If a processor fails, data held by its memory and disks is unavailable. Therefore, the shared nothing architecture requires special considerations to prevent data loss.

When scaling out the system, the two main bottlenecks are typically the bandwidth of the shared medium and the overhead of maintaining a consistent view of the shared data in the presence of cache hierarchies. For that reason, the shared nothing architecture is considered the most scalable one, because it has no shared medium and no shared data. While it is often argued that shared disk architectures have certain advantages for transaction processing, the shared nothing is the undisputed architecture of choice for analytical queries.

A shared disk approach may have isolated processors, each with its own memory, but the persistent storage on disk is still shared across the system. These types of architectures are layered on top of symmetric multi-processing (SMP) machines. While there may be applications that are suited to this approach, there are bottlenecks that exist because of the sharing, because all I/O and memory requests are transferred (and satisfied) over the same bus. As more processors are added, the synchronization and communication needs increase exponentially, and therefore the bus is less able to handle the increased need for bandwidth. This means that unless the need for bandwidth is satisfied, there will be limits to the degree of scalability.

In contrast, in a shared nothing approach, each processor has its own dedicated disk storage. This approach, which maps nicely to a massively parallel processing (MPP) architecture, is not only more suitable to discrete allocation and distribution of the data but also enables more effective parallelization and consequently does not introduce the same kind of bus bottlenecks from which the SMP/shared-memory and shared disk approaches suffer. Most Big Data appliances use a collection of computing resources, typically a combination of processing nodes and storage nodes.

7.2.2 *Big Data System Architecture*

A variety of system architectures have been implemented for Big Data and large-scale data analysis applications, including parallel and distributed relational database management systems that have been available to run on shared nothing clusters of processing nodes for more than two decades. These include database systems from Teradata, Netezza, Vertica, and Exadata/Oracle and others that provide high-performance parallel database platforms. Although these systems have the ability to run parallel applications and queries expressed in the SQL language, they are typically not general-purpose processing platforms and usually run as a back-end to a separate front-end application processing system.

Although this approach offers benefits when the data utilized is primarily structured in nature and fits easily into the constraints of a relational database, and it often excels for transaction processing applications, most data growth is with data in unstructured form and new processing paradigms with more flexible data models were needed. Internet companies such as Google, Yahoo!, Microsoft, Facebook, and others required a new processing approach to effectively deal with the enormous amount of Web data for applications such as search engines and social networking. In addition, many government and business organizations were overwhelmed with data that could not be effectively processed, linked, and analyzed with traditional computing approaches.

Several solutions have emerged, including the MapReduce architecture pioneered by Google and now available in an open-source implementation called Hadoop, used by Yahoo!, Facebook, and others (see KALE 2017).

7.2.2.1 *Brewer's CAP (Consistency Availability Partition) Theorem*

Techniques for achieving atomicity, consistency, isolation, and durability (ACID) properties in a database system are explained in the note below. However, applying these techniques in large-scale scenarios such as data services in the cloud leads to scalability problems: the amount of data to be stored and processed and the transaction and query load to be managed are usually too large to run the database services on a single machine. To overcome this data storage bottleneck, the database must be stored on multiple nodes, for which horizontal scaling is the typically chosen approach.

The database is partitioned across the different nodes, either tablewise or by sharding (see Chapter 7 Sub-section 7.2.3, "Row Partitioning or Sharding"). Both cases result in a distributed system for which Eric Brewer has formulated the famous consistency availability partition (CAP) theorem, which characterizes three of the main properties of such a system:

1. Consistency: All clients have the same view, even in the case of updates. For multisite transactions, this requires all-or-nothing semantics. For replicated data, this implies that all replicas have always consistent states.

2. Availability: Availability implies that all clients always find a replica of data even in the presence of failures.
3. Partition tolerance: In the case of network failures that split the nodes into groups (partitions), the system is still able to continue the processing.

The CAP theorem further states that in a distributed, shared data system, these three properties cannot be achieved simultaneously in the presence of failures. In order to understand the implications, we have to consider possible failures. For scalability reasons, the database is running on two sites, S1 and S2, sharing a data object o, for example, a flight booking record. This data sharing should be transparent to client applications, that is, an application AS1 connected to site A and AS2 accessing the database via site S2. Both clients should always see the same state of o even in the presence of an update. Hence, in order to ensure a consistent view, any update performed for instance by AS1 and changing o to a new state o' has to be propagated by sending a message m to update o at S2 so that AS2 reads o'.

To understand why the CAP theorem holds, we consider the scenario where the network connecting S1 and S2 fails, resulting in a network partitioning, and examine whether all three properties can be simultaneously fulfilled. In this situation, m cannot be delivered, resulting in an inconsistent (outdated) value of o at site S2. If we want to avoid this to ensure consistency, m has to be sent synchronously, that is, in an atomic operation with the updates. However, this procedure sacrifices the availability property: if m cannot be delivered, the update on node S1 cannot be performed. However, sending m asynchronously does not solve the problem, because then S1 does not know when S2 receives the message. Therefore, any approach trying to achieve a strong consistent view such as locking and centralized management would either violate availability or partition tolerance.

In order to address these restrictions imposed by CAP, the system designer has to choose to relax or give up one of these three properties:

■ Consistency: If we want to preserve availability and partition tolerance, the only choice is to give up or relax consistency. The data can be updated on both sites, and both sites will converge to the same state when the connection between them is re-established and a certain time has elapsed.
■ Availability: Availability is given up by simply waiting when a partition event occurs until the nodes come back and the data are consistent again. The service is unavailable during the waiting time. Particularly, for large settings with many nodes, this could result in long downtimes.
■ Partition tolerance: Basically, this means avoiding network partitioning in the case of link failures. Partition tolerance can be achieved by ensuring that all nodes are connected to each other or making a single atomically failing unit, but obviously, this limits scalability.

The CAP theorem implies that consistency guarantees in large-scale distributed systems cannot be as strict as those in centralized systems. Specifically, it suggests that distributed systems may need to provide BASE guarantees instead of the ACID guarantees provided by traditional database systems (see next subsection). The CAP theorem states that no distributed system can provide more than two of the following three guarantees: consistency, availability, and partitioning tolerance. Here, consistency is defined as in databases; that is, if multiple operations are performed on the same object (which is actually stored in a distributed system), the results of the operations appear as if the operations were carried out in some definite order on a single system. Availability is defined to be satisfied if each operation on the system (e.g., a query) returns some result. The system provides partitioning tolerance if the system is operational even when the network between two components of the system is down.

Since distributed systems can satisfy only two of the three properties due to the CAP theorem, there are three types of distributed systems. CA (consistent, available) systems provide consistency and availability but cannot tolerate network partitions. An example of a CA system is a clustered database, where each node stores a subset of the data. Such a database cannot provide availability in the case of network partitioning, since queries to data in the partitioned nodes must fail. CA systems may not be useful for cloud computing, since partitions are likely to occur in medium to large networks (including the case in which latency is very high). If there is no network partitioning, all servers are consistent, and the value seen by both clients is the correct value.

However, if the network is partitioned, it is no longer possible to keep all the servers consistent in the face of updates. There are then two choices. One choice is to keep both servers up and ignore the inconsistency. This leads to AP (available, partition-tolerant) systems where the system is always available but may not return consistent results. The other possible choice is to bring one of the servers down, to avoid inconsistent values. This leads to CP (consistent, partition-tolerant) systems where the system always returns consistent results but may be unavailable under partitioning—including the case in which latency is very high. AP systems provide weak consistency. An important sub-class of weakly consistent systems is those that provide eventual consistency. A system is defined as being eventually consistent if the system is guaranteed to reach a consistent state in a finite amount of time if there are no failures (e.g., network partitions) and no updates are made. The inconsistency window for such systems is the maximum amount of time that can elapse between the time that the update is made and the time that the update is guaranteed to be visible to all clients. If the inconsistency window is small compared to the update rate, then one method of dealing with stale data is to wait for a period greater than the inconsistency window and then retry the query.

Classic database systems focus on guaranteeing the ACID properties and, therefore, favor consistency over partition tolerance and availability. This is achieved by employing techniques like distributed locking and two-phase commit protocols.

In certain circumstances, data needs are not transactionally focused, and at such times, the relational model is not the most appropriate one for what we need to do with the data we are storing. However, giving up availability is often not an option in the Web business, where users expect a 24/7 or always-on operation.

Most traditional RDBMS would guarantee that all the values in all our nodes are identical before it allows another user to read the values. But as we have seen, that is at a significant cost in terms of performance. Relational databases, with their large processing overhead in terms of maintaining the ACID attributes of the data they store and their reliance on potentially processor-hungry joins, are not the right tool for the task they have before them: quickly finding relevant data from terabytes of unstructured data (Web content) that may be stored across thousands of geographically disparate nodes. In other words, relational model does not scale well for this type of data. Thus, techniques for guaranteeing strong consistency in large distributed systems limit scalability and results in latency issues. To cope with these problems, essential for Big Data, BASE was proposed as an alternative to ACID.

 A transaction represents a sequence of database operations (insert, update, delete, select) for which the system guarantees four properties also known as ACID:

1. Atomicity: A transaction is executed completely or not at all, thus exhibiting the characteristics of atomicity. As a consequence, all changes to the data made by this transaction become visible only if the transaction reaches a commit successfully. Otherwise, if the transaction was terminated abnormally before reaching a commit, the original state of the data from the beginning is restored.

2. Consistency: The property of consistency guarantees that all defined integrity or consistency constraints are preserved at the end of a transaction, that is, a transaction always moves the database from one consistent state to another consistent state. This has two consequences: in case a consistency constraint is violated, the transaction may be abnormally terminated; and secondly, constraints can be temporarily violated during transaction execution but must be preserved upon the commit.

3. Isolation: A transaction behaves as if it runs alone on the database without any concurrent operations. Furthermore, it only sees effects from previously committed transactions.

4. Durability: When a transaction reaches the commit, it is guaranteed that all changes made by this transaction will survive subsequent system and disk failures.

7.2.2.2 BASE (Basically Available, Soft State, Eventual Consistency)

BASE follows an optimistic approach, accepting stale data and approximate answers while favoring availability. Some ways to achieve this are by supporting partial failures without total system failures, decoupling updates on different tables (i.e., relaxing consistency), and item-potent operations that can be applied multiple times with the same result. In this sense, BASE describes more a spectrum of architectural styles than a single model. The eventual state of consistency can be provided as a result of a read repair, where any outdated data is refreshed with the latest version of the data as a result of the system detecting stale data during a read operation. Another approach is that of weak consistency. In this case, the read operation will return the first value found, not checking for staleness. Any stale nodes discovered are simply marked for updating at some stage in the future. This is a performance-focused approach but has the associated risk that data retrieved may not be the most current. In the following sections, we will discuss several techniques for implementing services following the BASE principle.

Conventional storage techniques may not be adequate for Big Data and, hence, the cloud applications. To scale storage systems to cloud-scale, the basic technique is to partition and replicate the data over multiple independent storage systems. The word *independent* is emphasized, since it is well known that databases can be partitioned into mutually dependent sub-databases that are automatically synchronized for reasons of performance and availability. Partitioning and replication increase the overall throughput of the system, since the total throughput of the combined system is the aggregate of the individual storage systems. To scale both the throughput and the maximum size of the data that can be stored beyond the limits of traditional database deployments, it is possible to partition the data and store each partition in its own database. For scaling the throughput only, it is possible to use replication. Partitioning and replication also increase the storage capacity of a storage system by reducing the amount of data that needs to be stored in each partition. However, this creates synchronization and consistency problems, and discussion of this aspect is out of scope for this book.

The other technology for scaling storage is known by the name Not only SQL (NoSQL). NoSQL was developed as a reaction to the perception that conventional databases, focused on the need to ensure data integrity for enterprise applications, were too rigid to scale to cloud levels. As an example, conventional databases enforce a schema on the data being stored, and changing the schema is not easy. However, changing the schema may be a necessity in a rapidly changing environment like the cloud. NoSQL storage systems provide more flexibility and simplicity compared to relational databases. The disadvantage, however, is greater application complexity. NoSQL systems, for example, do not enforce a rigid schema. The trade-off is that applications have to be written to deal with data records of varying formats (schema). BASE is the NoSQL operating premise, in the same way that traditional transactionally focused databases use ACID: one moves from a world of certainty in terms of data consistency to a world where all we are promised is that all copies of the data will, at some point, be the same.

Partitioning and replication techniques used for scaling are as follows:

1. The first possible method is to store different tables in different databases (as in multi-database systems [MDBS]).
2. The second approach is to partition the data within a single table onto different databases. There are two natural ways to partition the data from within a table: to store different rows in different databases and to store different columns in different databases (more common for NoSQL databases).

7.2.2.3 Functional Decomposition

As stated previously, one technique for partitioning the data to be stored is to store different tables in different databases, leading to the storage of the data in a MDBS.

7.2.2.4 Master–Slave Replication

To increase the throughput of transactions from the database, it is possible to have multiple copies of the database. A common replication method is master–slave replication. The master and slave databases are replicas of each other. All writes go to the master, and the master keeps the slaves in sync. However, reads can be distributed to any database. Since this configuration distributes the reads among multiple databases, it is a good technology for read-intensive workloads. For write-intensive workloads, it is possible to have multiple masters, but then ensuring consistency if multiple processes update different replicas simultaneously is a complex problem. Additionally, time to write increases due to the necessity of writing to all masters, and the synchronization overhead between the masters rapidly becomes a limiting overhead.

7.2.3 Row Partitioning or Sharding

In cloud technology, *sharding* is used to refer to the technique of partitioning a table among multiple independent databases by row. However, partitioning of data by row in relational databases is not new and is referred to as *horizontal partitioning* in parallel database technology. The distinction between sharding and horizontal partitioning is that horizontal partitioning is done transparently to the application by the database, whereas sharding is explicit partitioning done by the application. However, the two techniques have started converging, since traditional database vendors have started offering support for more sophisticated partitioning strategies. Since sharding is similar to horizontal partitioning, we first discuss different horizontal partitioning techniques. It can be seen that a good sharding technique depends on both the organization of the data and the type of queries expected.

The different techniques of sharding are as follows:

1. Round-robin partitioning: The round-robin method distributes the rows in a round-robin fashion over different databases. In the example, we could partition the transaction table into multiple databases so that the first transaction is stored in the first database, the second in the second database, and so on. The advantage of round-robin partitioning is its simplicity. However, it also suffers from the disadvantage of losing associations (say) during a query, unless all databases are queried. Hash partitioning and range partitioning do not suffer from the disadvantage of losing record associations.

2. Hash partitioning method: In this method, the value of a selected attribute is hashed to find the database into which the tuple should be stored. If queries are frequently made on an attribute, say Customer_Id, then associations can be preserved by using this attribute as the attribute that is hashed, so that records with the same value of this attribute can be found in the same database.

3. Range partitioning: The range partitioning technique stores records with "similar" attributes in the same database. For example, the range of Customer_Id could be partitioned between different databases. Again, if the attributes chosen for grouping are those on which queries are frequently made, record association is preserved and it is not necessary to merge results from different databases. Range partitioning can be susceptible to load imbalance, unless the partitioning is chosen carefully. It is possible to choose the partitions so that there is an imbalance in the amount of data stored in the partitions (data skew) or in the execution of queries across partitions (execution skew). These problems are less likely in round-robin and hash partitioning, since they tend to uniformly distribute the data over the partitions.

Thus, hash partitioning is particularly well suited to large-scale systems. Round robin simplifies a uniform distribution of records but does not facilitate the restriction of operations to single partitions. While range partitioning does supports this, it requires knowledge about the data distribution in order to properly adjust the ranges.

7.2.4 Row versus Column-Oriented Data Layouts

Most traditional database systems employ a row-oriented layout, in which all the values associated with a specific row are laid out consecutively in memory. That layout may work well for transaction processing applications that focus on updating specific records associated with a limited number of transactions (or transaction steps) at a time. These are manifested as algorithmic scans performed using multi-way joins; accessing whole rows at a time when only the values of a smaller set of columns are needed may flood the network with extraneous data that is not immediately needed and ultimately will increase the execution time.

Big Data analytics applications scan, aggregate, and summarize over massive datasets. Analytical applications and queries will only need to access the data elements needed to satisfy join conditions. With row-oriented layouts, the entire record must be read in order to access the required attributes, with significantly more data read than is needed to satisfy the request. Also, the row-oriented layout is often misaligned with the characteristics of the different types of memory systems (core, cache, disk, etc.), leading to increased access latencies. Subsequently, row-oriented data layouts will not enable the types of joins or aggregations typical of analytic queries to execute with the anticipated level of performance.

Hence, a number of appliances for Big Data use a database management system that uses an alternate, columnar layout for data that can help to reduce the negative performance impacts of data latency that plague databases with a row-oriented data layout. The values for each column can be stored separately, and because of this, for any query, the system is able to selectively access the specific column values requested to evaluate the join conditions. Instead of requiring separate indexes to tune queries, the data values themselves within each column form the index. This speeds up data access while reducing the overall database footprint and dramatically improving query performance. The simplicity of the columnar approach provides many benefits, especially for those seeking a high-performance environment to meet the growing needs of extremely large analytic datasets.

7.2.5 NoSQL Data Management

NoSQL suggests environments that combine traditional SQL (or SQL-like query languages) with alternative means of querying and access. NoSQL data systems hold out the promise of greater flexibility in database management while reducing the dependence on more formal database administration. NoSQL databases have more relaxed modeling constraints, which may benefit both the application developer and the end-user analysts when their interactive analyses are not throttled by the need to cast each query in terms of a relational table-based environment.

Different NoSQL frameworks are optimized for different types of analyses. For example, some are implemented as key-value stores, which nicely align to certain Big Data programming models, while another emerging model is a graph database, in which a graph abstraction is implemented to embed both semantics and connectivity within its structure. In fact, the general concepts for NoSQL include schemaless modeling, in which the semantics of the data are embedded within a flexible connectivity and storage model; this provides for automatic distribution of data and elasticity with respect to the use of computing, storage, and network bandwidth in ways that do not force specific binding of data to be persistently stored in particular physical locations. NoSQL databases also provide for integrated data caching, which helps reduce data access latency and speed performance.

> The key_value store does not impose any constraints about data typing or data structure—the value associated with the key is the value, and it is up to the consuming business applications to assert expectations about the data values and their semantics and interpretation. This demonstrates the schemaless property of the model.

A relatively simple type of NoSQL data store is a key_value store, a schemaless model in which distinct character strings called *keys* are associated with values (or sets of values, or even more complex entity objects)—not unlike hash table data structure. If you want to associate multiple values with a single key, you need to consider the representations of the objects and how they are associated with the key. For example, you may want to associate a list of attributes with a single key, which may suggest that the value stored with the key is yet another key_value store object itself.

Key_value stores are essentially very long and presumably thin tables (in that there are not many columns associated with each row). The table's rows can be sorted by the key value to simplify finding the key during a query. Alternatively, the keys can be hashed using a hash function that maps the key to a particular location (sometimes called a "bucket") in the table. The representation can grow indefinitely, which makes it good for storing large amounts of data that can be accessed relatively quickly, as well as allowing massive amounts of indexed data values to be appended to the same key_value table, which can then be sharded or distributed across the storage nodes. Under the right conditions, the table is distributed in a way that is aligned with the way the keys are organized, so that the hashing function that is used to determine where any specific key exists in the table can also be used to determine which node holds that key's bucket (i.e., the portion of the table holding that key).

NoSQL data management environments are engineered for the following two key criteria:

1. Fast accessibility, whether that means inserting data into the model or pulling it out via some query or access method
2. Scalability for volume, so as to support the accumulation and management of massive amounts of data

The different approaches are amenable to extensibility, scalability, and distribution, and these characteristics blend nicely with programming models (like MapReduce) with straightforward creation and execution of many parallel processing threads. Distributing a tabular data store or a key_value store allows many queries/accesses to be performed simultaneously, especially when the hashing of the keys maps to different data storage nodes. Employing different data allocation strategies will allow the tables to grow indefinitely without requiring significant rebalancing. In other words, these data organizations are designed for high-performance computing of reporting and analysis.

 The model will not inherently provide any kind of traditional database capabilities (such as atomicity of transactions or consistency when multiple transactions are executed simultaneously)—those capabilities must be provided by the application itself.

7.2.6 In-Memory Computing

The idea of running databases in memory was used by business intelligence (BI) product company QlikView. In-memory allows the processing of massive quantities of data in main memory to provide immediate results from analysis and transaction. The data to be processed is ideally real-time data or as close to real time as is technically possible. Data in main memory (RAM) can be accessed 100,000 times faster than data on a hard disk; this can dramatically decrease access time to retrieve data and make it available for the purpose of reporting, analytics solutions, or other applications.

The medium used by a database to store data, that is, RAM, is divided into pages. In-memory databases save changed pages in savepoints, which are asynchronously written to persistent storage in regular intervals. Each committed transaction generates a log entry that is written to non-volatile storage—this log is written synchronously. In other words, a transaction does not return before the corresponding log entry has been written to persistent storage—in order to meet the durability requirement that was described earlier—thus ensuring that in-memory databases meet (and pass) the ACID test. After a power failure, the database pages are restored from the savepoints; the database logs are applied to restore the changes that were not captured in the savepoints. This ensures that the database can be restored in memory to exactly the same state as before the power failure.

7.2.7 Developing Big Data Applications

For most Big Data appliances, the ability to achieve scalability to accommodate growing data volumes is predicated on multi-processing—distributing the computation across the collection of computing nodes in ways that are aligned with the distribution of data across the storage nodes. One of the key objectives of using a multi-processing nodes environment is to speed application execution by breaking up large "chunks" of work into much smaller ones that can be farmed out to a pool of available processing nodes. In the best of all possible worlds, the datasets to be consumed and analyzed are also distributed across a pool of storage nodes. As long as there are no dependencies forcing any one specific task to wait to begin until another specific one ends, these smaller tasks can be executed at the same time, that is, *task parallelism*. More than just scalability, it is the concept of "automated scalability" that has generated the present surge of interest in Big Data analytics (with corresponding optimization of costs).

A good development framework will simplify the process of developing, executing, testing, and debugging new application code, and this framework should include the following:

1. A programming model and development tools
2. Facility for program loading, execution, and for process and thread scheduling
3. System configuration and management tools

The context for all of these framework components is tightly coupled with the key characteristics of a Big Data application—algorithms that take advantage of running lots of tasks in parallel on many computing nodes to analyze lots of data distributed among many storage nodes. Typically, a Big Data platform will consist of a collection (or a "pool") of processing nodes; the optimal performances can be achieved when all the processing nodes are kept busy, and that means maintaining a healthy allocation of tasks to idle nodes within the pool. Any big application that is to be developed must map to this context, and that is where the programming model comes in. The programming model essentially describes two aspects of application execution within a parallel environment:

■ How an application is coded
■ How that code maps to the parallel environment

MapReduce programming model is a combination of the familiar procedural/imperative approaches used by Java or C++ programmers embedded within what is effectively a functional language programming model, such as the one used within languages like Lisp and APL. The similarity is based on MapReduce's dependence on two basic operations that are applied to sets or lists of data value pairs:

1. Map, which describes the computation or analysis applied to a set of input key-value pairs to produce a set of intermediate key-value pairs
2. Reduce, in which the set of values associated with the intermediate key-value pairs output by the Map operation are combined to provide the results

A MapReduce application is envisioned as a series of basic operations applied in a sequence to small sets of many (millions, billions, or even more) data items. These data items are logically organized in a way that enables the MapReduce execution model to allocate tasks that can be executed in parallel.

Combining both data and computational independence means that both the data and the computations can be distributed across multiple storage and processing units and automatically parallelized. This parallelizability allows the programmer to exploit scalable massively parallel processing resources for increased processing speed and performance.

7.3 NoSQL Databases

NoSQL databases have been classified into four subcategories:

1. *Column family stores*: An extension of the key–value architecture with columns and column families; the overall goal was to process distributed data over a pool of infrastructure, for example, HBase and Cassandra.
2. *Key–value pairs*: This model is implemented using a hash table where there is a unique key and a pointer to a particular item of data creating a key–value pair, for example, Voldemort.
3. *Document databases*: This class of databases is modeled after Lotus Notes and is similar to key–value stores. The data is stored as a document and is represented in JSON or XML formats. The biggest design feature is the flexibility to list multiple levels of key–value pairs, for example, Riak and CouchDB.
4. *Graph databases*: Based on the graph theory, this class of database supports the scalability across a cluster of machines. The complexity of representation for extremely complex sets of documents is evolving, for example, Neo4J.

7.3.1 Column-Oriented Stores or Databases

Hadoop HBase is the distributed database that supports the storage needs of the Hadoop distributed programming platform. HBase is designed by taking inspiration from Google BigTable; its main goal is to offer real-time read/write operations for tables with billions of rows and millions of columns by leveraging clusters of commodity hardware. The internal architecture and logic model of HBase is very similar to Google BigTable, and the entire system is backed by the Hadoop Distributed File System (HDFS), which mimics the structure and services of GFS.

7.3.2 Key–Value Stores (K–V Store) or Databases

Apache Cassandra is a distributed object store from large amounts of aging structured data spread across many commodity servers. The system is designed to avoid a single point of failure and to offer a highly reliable service. Cassandra was initially developed by Facebook; now, it is part of the Apache incubator initiative. Facebook in the initial years had used a leading commercial database solution for their internal architecture in conjunction with some Hadoop. Eventually, the tsunami of users led the company to start thinking in terms of unlimited scalability and to focus on availability and distribution. The nature of the data and its producers and consumers did not mandate consistency but needed unlimited availability and scalable performance.

The team at Facebook built an architecture that combines the data-model approaches of BigTable and the infrastructure approaches of Dynamo with scalability and performance capabilities, named *Cassandra*. Cassandra is often referred to as hybrid architecture since it combines the column-oriented data model from BigTable with Hadoop MapReduce jobs, and it implements the patterns from Dynamo like eventually consistent, gossip protocols, a master–master way of serving both read and write requests. Cassandra supports a full replication model based on NoSQL architectures.

The Cassandra team had a few design goals to meet, considering that the architecture at the time of first development and deployment was primarily being done at Facebook. The goals included

- High availability
- Eventual consistency
- Incremental scalability
- Optimistic replication
- Tunable trade-offs between consistency, durability, and latency
- Low cost of ownership
- Minimal administration

Amazon Dynamo is the distributed key–value store that supports the management of information of several of the business services offered by Amazon Inc. The main goal of Dynamo is to provide an incrementally scalable and highly available storage system. This goal helps in achieving reliability at a massive scale, where thousands of servers and network components build an infrastructure serving 10 million requests per day. Dynamo provides a simplified interface based on get/put semantics, where objects are stored and retrieved with a unique identifier (key). The main goal of achieving an extremely reliable infrastructure has imposed some constraints on the properties of these systems. For example, ACID properties on data have been sacrificed in favor of a more reliable and efficient infrastructure. This creates what it is called an eventually consistent model (i.e., in the long term, all the users will see the same data).

7.3.3 Document-Oriented Databases

Document-oriented databases or document databases can be defined as a schema-less and flexible model of storing data as documents rather than relational structures.

The document will contain all the data it needs to answer specific query questions. Benefits of this model include

- Ability to store dynamic data in unstructured, semi-structured, or structured formats
- Ability to create persisted views from a base document and store the same for analysis
- Ability to store and process large datasets

The design features of document-oriented databases include

- Schema-free—There is no restriction on the structure and format of how the data need to be stored. This flexibility allows an evolving system to add more data and allows the existing data to be retained in the current structure.
- Document store—Objects can be serialized and stored in a document, and there is no relational integrity to enforce and follow.
- Ease of creation and maintenance—A simple creation of the document allows complex objects to be created once, and there is minimal maintenance once the document is created.
- No relationship enforcement—Documents are independent of each other, and there is no foreign key relationship to worry about when executing queries. The effects of concurrency and performance issues related to the same are not a bother here.
- Open formats—Documents are described using JSON, XML, or some derivative, making the process standard and clean from the start.
- Built-in versioning—Documents can get large and messy with versions. To avoid conflicts and keep processing efficiencies, versioning is implemented by most solutions available today.

Document databases express the data as files in JSON or XML formats. This allows the same document to be parsed for multiple contexts and the results scrapped and added to the next iteration of the database data.

Apache CouchDB and MongoDB are two examples of document stores. Both provide a schema-less store whereby the primary objects are documents organized into a collection of key–value fields. The value of each field can be of type string, integer, float, date, or an array of values. The databases expose a RESTful interface and represent data in JSON format. Both allow querying and indexing data by using the MapReduce programming model, expose JavaScript as a base language for data querying and manipulation rather than SQL, and support large files as documents. From an infrastructure point of view, the two systems support data replication and high availability. CouchDB ensures ACID properties on data. MongoDB supports sharding, which is the ability to distribute the content of a collection among different nodes.

7.3.4 Graph Stores or Databases

Social media and the emergence of Facebook, LinkedIn, and Twitter have accelerated the emergence of the most complex NoSQL database, the graph database. The graph database is oriented toward modeling and deploying data that is graphical by construct. For example, to represent a person and their friends in a social network, we can either write code to convert the social graph into key–value pairs on a Dynamo or Cassandra or simply convert them into a node-edge model in a graph database, where managing the relationship representation is much more simplified.

A graph database represents each object as a node and the relationships as an edge. This means person is a node and household is a node and the relationship between them is an edge. Like the classic ER model for RDBMS, we need to create an attribute model for a graph database. We can start by taking the highest level in a hierarchy as a root node (similar to an entity) and connect each attribute as its sub-node. To represent different levels of the hierarchy, we can add a subcategory or sub-reference and create another list of attributes at that level. This creates a natural traversal model like a tree traversal, which is similar to traversing a graph. Depending on the cyclic property of the graph, we can have a balanced or skewed model. Some of the most evolved graph databases include Neo4J, InfiniteGraph, GraphDB, and AllegroGraph.

7.4 Aadhaar Project

The Aadhaar project, undertaken by the Unique Identification Authority of India (UIDAI), has the mission of identifying 1.2 billion citizens of India uniquely and reliably to build the largest biometric identity repository in the world (while eliminating duplication and fake identities) and provide an online, anytime anywhere, multi-factor authentication service. This makes it possible to identify any individual and get this identity authenticated at any time, from any place in India, in less than a second.

The UIDAI project is a Hadoop-based program that is well into production. At the time of this writing, over 700 million people have been enrolled and their identity information has been verified. The target is to reach a total of at least 1 billion enrolments during 2015. Currently, the enrolment rate is about 10 million people every 10 days, so the project is well positioned to meet that target.

In India, there is no social security card, and much of the population lacks a passport. Literacy rates are relatively low, and the population is scattered across hundreds of thousands of villages. Without adequately verifiable identification, it has been difficult for many citizens to set up a bank account or otherwise participate in a modern economy.

For India's poorer citizens, this problem has even more dire consequences. The government has extensive programs to provide widespread relief for the poor—for example, through grain subsidies to those who are underfed and through government-sponsored work programs for the unemployed. Yet many who need help do not have access to benefit programs, in part because of the inability to verify who they are and whether they qualify for the programs. In addition, there is a huge level of so-called "leakage" of government aid that disappears to apparent fraud. For example, it has been estimated that over 50% of funds intended to provide grain to the poor goes missing, and that fraudulent claims for "ghost workers" siphon off much of the aid intended to create work for the poor.

There are clearly immense benefits from a mechanism that uniquely identifies a person and ensures instant identity verification. The need to prove one's identity only once will bring down transaction costs. A clear identity number can transform the delivery of social welfare programs by making them more inclusive of those communities now cut off from such benefits due to their lack of identification. It also enables the government to shift from indirect to direct benefit delivery by directly reaching out to the intended beneficiaries. A single universal identity number is also useful in eliminating fraud and duplicate identities, since individuals can no longer represent themselves differently to different agencies. This results in significant savings to the state exchequer.

Aadhaar is in the process of creating the largest biometric database in the world, one that can be leveraged to authenticate identities for each citizen, even on site in rural villages. A wide range of mobile devices from cell phones to micro-scanners can be used to enroll people and to authenticate their identities when a transaction is requested. People will be able to make payments at remote sites via micro-ATMs. Aadhaar ID authentication will be used to verify qualification for relief food deliveries and to provide pension payments for the elderly. Implementation of this massive digital identification system is expected to save the equivalent of millions and perhaps billions of dollars each year by thwarting efforts at fraud. While the UIDAI project will have broad benefits for Indian society as a whole, the greatest impact will be for the poorest people.

All application components are built using open-source components and open standards.

Aadhaar software currently runs across two of the data centers within India managed by UIDAI and handles 1 million enrolments a day, at the peak doing about 600 trillion biometric matches a day. The current system already has about 4 PB (4,000 terabytes) of raw data and continues grow as new enrolments come in. The Aadhaar Authentication service is built to handle 100 million authentications a day across both the data centers in an active-active fashion and is benchmarked to provide sub-second response time. Central to the Aadhaar system is its biometric subsystem, which performs de-duplication and authentication in an accurate way.

Figure 7.4 presents the solution architecture for the Aadhaar project.

Application modules are built on a common technology platform that contains frameworks for persistence, security, messaging, and so on. The platform

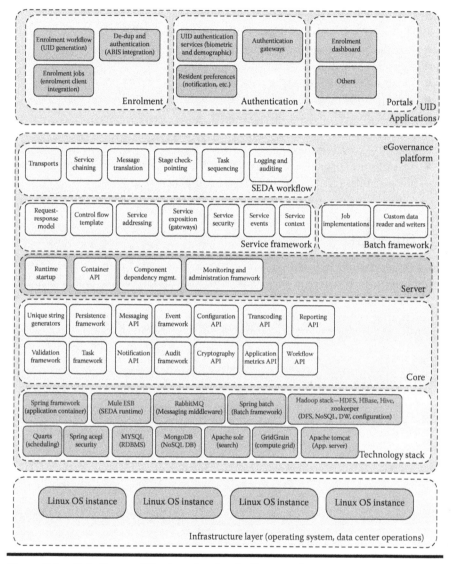

Figure 7.4   Solution architecture for the Aadhaar project.

standardizes on a technology stack based on open standards and using open source where prudent. A list of extensively used open-source technology stacks is as follows:

- Spring Framework—Application container for all components and runtime
- Spring Batch—Runtime for various batch jobs
- Spring Security—For all application security needs
- Mule ESB—Runtime for loosely coupled SEDA stages of enrolment flow

- RabbitMQ—Messaging middleware
- Hadoop Stack—HDFS, Hive, HBase, Pig, and Zookeeper
- Pentaho—Open-source BI Solution
- Quartz—Scheduling of batch jobs
- MongoDB—NoSQL Document Database
- MySQL—RDBMS for storing relational data
- Apache Solr—Index for full text search
- Apache Tomcat—Web container
- Liferay—Portal framework
- Several other open-source libraries for random number generation, hashing, advanced data structures, HTML UI components, and others.

7.5 Summary

This chapter introduces Big Data systems that are associated with big volume, variety, and velocity. It describes the characteristic features of such systems, including Big Data architecture, row versus column-oriented data layouts, NoSQL data management, in-memory computing, and developing Big Data applications.

Chapter 8

Web Applications

Retail organizations are performing log analysis, website optimization, and customer loyalty programs by using brand and sentiment analysis and market-basket analysis. Dynamic pricing, website real-time customization, and product recommendations are the results of this analysis. The finance industry is using Big Data for fraud-pattern detection and to perform analyses for corruption, bribery, risk modeling, and trade analytics. This enables them to improve their customer risk evaluation and fraud detection, as well as to design programs for real-time upsell and cross-marketing offers. Energy is doing analyses of grid failure, soil analytics, predictive mechanical failure, chemical analysis, and smart meters, to name a few. Manufacturing is performing supply-chain analysis, customer-churn analysis, and part replacement, as well as layout and design of manufacturing plants and factories. Telecommunication firms use Big Data information for customer profiling, cell-tower analysis, optimizing customer experience, monitoring equipment status, and network analysis. This improves hardware maintenance, product recommendations, and location-based advertising. Healthcare uses electronic medical records (EMR) and RFID to perform hospital design, patient treatment, clinical decision support, clinical-trial analysis, and real-time instrument and patient monitoring and analysis. Government is using Big Data for areas such as threat identification, government program analysis, and person-of-interest discovery. It's the power of the data that is disrupting business and the IT industry.

8.1 Web-Based Applications

Java Enterprise Edition (J2EE) is the result of Sun's effort to integrate the assortment of Java technologies and application programming interfaces (APIs) together into a cohesive Java development platform for developing complex distributed Java applications. Sun's enhancement of the n-tier development model for Java, combined with the introduction of specific functionalities to permit easier development of the server-side scalable Web-based enterprise applications, has led to a wide adoption of Java for Web-centric application development.

Enterprise application development entails expertise in a host of areas like interprocess communications, memory management, security issues, and database-specific access queries. J2EE provides built-in support for services in all these areas, enabling developers to focus on implementing business logic rather than intricate code that supports basic application support infrastructure.

There are numerous advantages of application development in the J2EE area:

- J2EE offers support for componentization of enterprise applications that enable higher productivity via reusability of components, rapid development of functioning applications via prebuilt functional components, higher-quality test-driven development via pretested components, and easier maintenance via cost-effective upgrades to individual components.
- J2EE offers support for hardware and operating systems (OS) independence by enabling system services to be accessed via Java and J2EE rather than directly via APIs specific to the underlying systems.
- J2EE offers a wide range of APIs to access and integrate with third-party products in a consistent manner, including databases, mail systems, and messaging platforms.
- J2EE offers clear-cut segregation between system development, deployment, and execution, thus enabling independent development, integration, and upgradation of components.
- J2EE offers specialized components that are optimized for specific types of roles in an enterprise application, like Entity Beans for handling persistent data and Session Beans for handling processing.

All the aforementioned features make possible rapid development of complex, distributed applications by enabling developers to focus on developing business logic, implementing the system without being impacted by prior knowledge of the target execution environment(s) and creating systems that can be ported more easily between different hardware platforms and operating systems (OS).

8.1.1 Reference Architecture

The objective of the flexibility and reusability can be achieved primarily at two levels: the application architecture level and the application component design level. The reference architecture is the vision of the application architecture that integrates common elements into a component structure modeling the current business and also positioning it to meet the challenges of the future. From a technical point of view, the architecture positions the development organization to automatically meet the benchmark requirements on time to market, flexibility, and performance.

A set of key elements drive the definition of the reference architecture, which is comprised of three layers, namely, business objects, process-oriented or service-based objects, and a user interface layer.

The defining elements of enterprise applications are as follows:

■ Business entities are the foci of the enterprise applications. These range from top-level entities such as a customer or a supplier down to bottom-level entities such as purchase orders, sales orders, or even individual level line items of these orders. Entities participate in the business processes, have attributes or properties, have methods for responding to requests for information, and have different sets of enforceable policies or rules applicable to them. The latter include the requirement for persistence of the state of the entities as reflected in the snapshot of all attributes.

■ Business processes carry out the tasks of the enterprise. They have some kind of specified workflow and essentially involve one or more business entities. They must be executed in a secure manner and must also be accessible via a host of user interfaces or devices or clients.

■ User interactions carry out the access and display of information related to business entities as an outcome of some business processes for scrutiny by the users of the enterprise application. This essentially involves some kind of screen flow or page navigation, attributes for presentation, user requests, or generated responses, that is, static or dynamic content, form-oriented processing, and error handling. The user interaction could be via a host of user interfaces or devices or clients.

Each of these elements gives rise to the three primary architecture layers of the reference architecture. These layers could reside on the same physical layer or be distributed across a network. Figure 8.1 presents the three architecture layers constituting the reference architecture.

8.1.1.1 User Interaction Architecture

User interactions are modeled by user interface components that comprise the User Interaction Architecture. In the J2EE platform, this is typically implemented as a combination of servlets and Java Server Pages (JSP). In a Web-based application, this layer would process HTML form submissions, manage state within an application, generate Web-page content, and control navigation between pages. Many of the functions within this layer can be automated through configurable foundation components.

8.1.1.2 Service-Based Architecture

Business processes are modeled by service components that comprise the Service-Based Architecture. In the J2EE platform, this is typically implemented as a

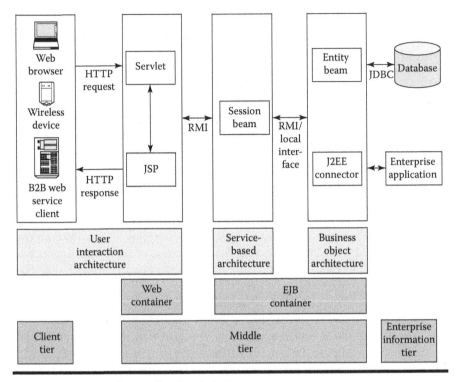

Figure 8.1 **Enterprise application in J2EE.**

process-oriented object wrapped with a stateless Session Bean. The concept of services allows the front end to be decoupled from the back-end business object components. The service-based layer adds tremendous value in terms of flexibility, reusability, and component design.

8.1.1.3 Business Object Architecture

Business entities are modeled by object components that comprise the Business Object Architecture. Each of these components manages the data and business logic associated with a particular entity, including persistence of that data into a relational database. In the J2EE platform, this is typically implemented as a combination of regular Java classes and Entity Beans in the J2EE application. The database access can be implemented by the container in the case of CMP (Container-Managed Persistence) Entity Beans or by the developer in the case of BMP (Bean-Managed Persistence) Entity Beans or regular Java classes. The persistence of each business object is abstracted out to the extent possible so that separate data objects, persistent frameworks, or CMP services can be used to affect the data object persistence in the database.

A major portion of the reference architecture is a generic and configurable implementation of the Model 2 architecture discussed later in the following section.

8.1.2 Realization of the Reference Architecture in J2EE

The J2EE platform provides a component-based approach to implement n-tier distributed enterprise applications. Figure 15.1 shows how the J2EE components provide the implementations for the different layers of the reference architecture.

The components that make up the application are executed in runtime environments called *containers*. Containers are used to provide infrastructure-type services such as life-cycle management, distribution, and security. Containers and components in the J2EE application are broadly divided into three tiers. The client tier is typically a Web browser or alternatively a Java application client. The middle tier contains two primary containers of the J2EE application, namely, Web container and EJB container. The function of the Web container is to process client requests and generate corresponding responses, while the function of the EJB container is to implement the business logic of the application. The EIS tier primarily consists of data sources and a number of interfaces and APIs to access the resources and other existing or legacy applications.

8.1.2.1 JavaServer Pages and Java Servlets as the User Interaction Components

JSPs and Java Servlets are meant to process and respond to Web user request. Servlet provides a Java-centric programming approach for implementing Web tier functionality. The Servlet API provides an easy-to-use set of objects that process HTTP requests and generate HTML/XML responses. JSPs provide an HTML-centric version of the Java Servlets. JSP components are document based rather than object based and possess built-in access to Servlet API request and response objects as also the user session object. JSPs also provide a powerful custom tag mechanism, enabling the encapsulation of reusable Java presentation code that can be placed directly into the JSP document.

8.1.2.2 Session Bean EJBs as Service-Based Components

Session Beans are meant for representing services provided to a client. Unlike Entity Beans, Session Beans do not share data across multiple clients—each user requesting a service or executing a transaction invokes a separate Session Bean to process the request. A stateless Session Bean, after processing a request, goes on to the next request or next client without maintaining or sharing any data. On the other hand, stateful Session Beans are often constructed for a particular client and maintain a state across method invocations for a single client until the component is removed.

8.1.2.3 Entity Bean EJBs as the Business Object Components

Entity Beans are meant for representing persistent data entities within an enterprise application. One of the major component services provided to the Entity Beans is that of Container-Managed Persistence (CMP). However, in EJB 2.0 specification, CMP persistence is limited to one table only. Any object-relational mapping involving more than a one-to-one table-object mapping is supported only through Bean-Managed Persistence (BMP).

8.1.2.4 Distributed Java Components

Java Naming and Directory Interface (JNDI) enables naming and distribution of Java components within the reference architecture. JNDI can be used to store and retrieve any Java object. However, JNDI is usually used to look up for component (home or remote) interfaces to enterprise beans. The client uses JNDI to look up the corresponding EJB Home interface, which enables creation, access, or removal of instances of Session and Entity Beans. In case of a local Entity Bean, a method invocation is proxied directly to the bean's implementation, while in case of remote Entity Beans, the Home interface is used to obtain access to the remote interface to invoke the exposed methods using Remote Method Invocation (RMI). The remote interface takes the local method call, serializes the objects that will be passed as arguments, and invokes the corresponding remote method on the distributed object. These serialized objects are converted back into normal objects to invoke the method to return the resulting value upon which the process is reversed to revert the value back to the remote interface client.

8.1.2.5 J2EE Access to the EIS (Enterprise Information Systems) Tier

J2EE provides a number of interfaces and APIs to access resources in the EIS tier. The use of JDBC API is encapsulated primarily in the data access layer or within the CMP classes of the Entity Bean. Data sources that map to a database are defined in JDBC, which can be looked up by a client searching for a resource using the JNDI. This enables the J2EE application server to provide connection pooling to different data resources, which should appropriately be closed as soon as the task is over to prevent bottlenecks.

The various J2EE interfaces and APIs available are as follows:

■ Java Connector Architecture provides a standard way to build adapters to access existing enterprise applications.
■ JavaMail API provides a standard way to access mail server applications.
■ Java Message Service (JMS) provides a standard interface to enterprise messaging systems. JMS enables reliable asynchronous communication with other distributed components. JMS is used by Message-Driven Beans (MDBs) to perform asynchronous or parallel processing of messages.

8.1.3 Model–View–Controller Architecture

The Model 2 architecture is based on the Model–View–Controller (MVC) design pattern. A generic MVC implementation is a vital element of the reference architecture as it provides a flexible and reusable foundation for very rapid Web-based application development.

The components of the MVC architecture are as follows:

- *View* deals with the display on the screens presented to the user.
- *Controller* deals with the flow and processing of user actions.
- *Model* deals with the business logic.

MVC architecture modularizes and isolates screen logic, control logic, and business logic in order to achieve greater flexibility and opportunity for reuse. A critical isolation point is between the presentation objects and the application backend objects that manage the business logic and data. This enables the user interface to affect major changes on the display screens without impacting the business logic and data components.

View does not contain the source of data and relies on the model to furnish the relevant data. When the model updates the data, it notifies and also furnishes the changed data to the view so that it can re-render the display to the user with the up-to-date data and correct data.

The controller channels information from the view on the user actions for processing by the business logic in the model. The controller enables an application design to flexibly handle things such as page navigation and access to the functionality provided by the application model in case of form submissions. Thus, the controller provides an isolation point between the model and the view, resulting in a more loosely coupled front end and back end.

Figure 8.2 gives a complete picture of how objects in the MVC architecture are mapped to the reference architecture in J2EE.

8.2 Evolution of the Web

8.2.1 Web 1.0

To start with, most websites were just a collection of static Web pages. The *Shallow Web*, also known as the *Static Web*, is primarily a collection of static HTML Web pages providing information about products or services offered. After a while, the Web became dynamic, delivering Web pages created on the fly. The ability to create Web pages from the content stored on databases enabled Web developers to provide customized information to visitors. These sites are known as the *Deep Web* or the *Dynamic Web*. Though a visitor to such Web sites gets information attuned

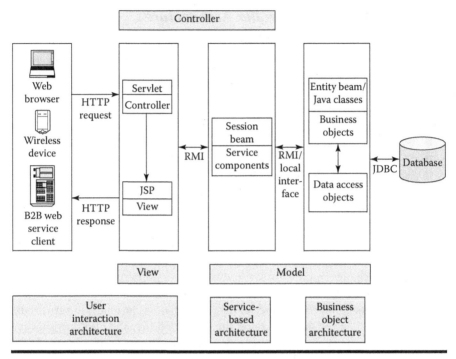

Figure 8.2   MVC and enterprise application architecture.

to his or her requirements, these sites provide primarily one-way interaction and limited user interactivity. The users have no role in content generation and no means to access content without visiting the sites concerned. The Shallow Web sites and Deep Web sites, which have none or minimal user interaction, are now generally termed *Web 1.0*.

8.2.2 Web 2.0

In the last few years, a new class of Web applications, known as Web 2.0 (or Service-Oriented Applications), has emerged. These applications let people collaborate and share information online in seemingly new ways—examples include social networking sites such as myspace.com, media sharing sites such as YouTube.com, and collaborative authoring sites such as Wikipedia. These second-generation Web applications offer smart user interfaces and built-in facilities for users to generate and edit content presented on the Web and thereby enrich the content base. Besides leveraging the users' potential in generating content, Web 2.0 applications provide facilities to keep the content under the user's own categories (tagging feature) and access it easily (Web feed tool). These new versions of Web applications are also able to integrate multiple services under a rich user interface.

With the incorporation of new Web technologies such as AJAX (Asynchronous JavaScript and XML), Ruby, blog, wiki, social bookmarking, and tagging, the Web is fast becoming more dynamic and highly interactive, where users can not only pick content from a site but can also contribute to it. The Web feed technology allows users to keep up with a site's latest content without having to visit it. Another feature of the new Web is the proliferation of Web sites with APIs. An API from a Web service facilitates Web developers in collecting data from the service and creating new online applications based on these data.

The Web 2.0 is a collection of technologies, business strategies, and social trends. The Web 2.0 is a highly interactive and dynamic application platform that is more dynamic than its predecessor, Web 1.0.

a. Weblogs or Blogs: With the advent of software like Wordpress and Typepad, along with blog service companies like blogger.com, the weblog is fast becoming the communication medium of the new Web. Unlike traditional Hypertext Markup Language (HTML) Web pages, blogs offer the ability for the non-programmer to communicate on a regular basis. Traditional HTML-style pages required knowledge of style, coding, and design in order to publish content that was basically read only from the consumer's point of view. Weblogs remove much of the constraints by providing a standard user interface that does not require customization. Weblogs originally emerged as a repository for linking but soon evolved to the ability to publish content and allow readers to become content providers. The essence of a blog can be defined by the format, which includes small chunks of content referred to as posts, date stamped and maintained in the reverse chronological order; and content expanded to include links, text and images.

The biggest advancement made with weblogs is the permanence of the content, which has a unique Universal Resource Locator (URL). This allows the content to be posted and, along with the comments, to define a permanent record of information. This is critical in that having a collaborative record that can be indexed by search engines will increase the utility of and spread the information to a larger audience.

b. Wikis: A wiki is a website that promotes the collaborative creation of content. Wiki pages can be edited by anyone at any time. Informational content can be created and easily organized within the wiki environment and then reorganized as required. Wikis are currently in high demand in a large variety of fields, due to their simplicity and flexibility. Documentation, reporting, project management, online glossaries and dictionaries, discussion groups, or general information applications are just a few examples of where the end user can provide value. While stating that anyone can alter content, some large-scale wiki environments have extensive role definitions that define who can perform functions of update, restore, delete, and creation. Wikipedia, like many wiki-type projects, has readers, editors, administrators, patrollers, policy makers, subject-matter experts, content maintainers, software developers, and system operators, all of whom create an environment open to sharing information and knowledge to a large group of users.

 The major difference between a wiki and blog is that the wiki user can alter the original content, while the blog user can only add information in the form of comments.

c. RSS Technologies: Originally developed by Netscape, RSS was intended to publish news-type information based upon a subscription framework. Many Internet users have experienced the frustration of searching Internet sites for hours at a time to find relevant information. RSS is an XML-based content-syndication protocol that allows websites to share information as well as aggregate information based upon the user's needs. In the simplest form, RSS shares the metadata about the content without actually delivering the entire information source. An author might publish the title, description, publication date, and copyrights to anyone that subscribes to the feed. The end user is required to have an application called an *aggregator* in order to receive the information. By having the RSS aggregator application, end users are not required to visit each site in order to obtain information.

From an end-user perspective, the RSS technology changes the communication method from a search and discover to a notification model. Users can locate content that is pertinent to their job and subscribe to the communication that enables a much faster communication stream.

d. Social Tagging: Social tagging describes the collaborative activity of marking shared online content with keywords or tags as a way to organize content for future navigation, filtering, or search. Traditional information architecture utilized a central taxonomy or classification scheme in order to place in formation into a specific pre-defined bucket or category. The assumption was that trained librarians understood more about information content and context than the average user. While this might have been true for the local library, the enormous amount of content on the Internet makes this type of system unmanageable.

Tagging offers a number of benefits to the end-user community. Perhaps the most important feature to the individual is able to bookmark the information in a way that is easier for them to recall at a later date. The idea of social tagging is to allow multiple users to tag content in a way that makes sense to them; by combining these tags, users create an environment where the opinions of the majority define the appropriateness of the tags themselves. The act of creating a collection of popular tags is referred to as a *folksonomy*, which is defined as a folk taxonomy of important and emerging content within the user community. The vocabulary problem is defined by the fact that different users define content in different ways. The disagreement can lead to missed information or inefficient user interactions.

One of the best examples of social tagging is Flickr, which allows users to upload images and "tag" them with appropriate metadata keywords. Other users who view your images can also tag them with their concept of appropriate keywords. After a critical mass has been reached, the resulting tag collection will identify images correctly and without bias. Other sites like iStockPhoto have also utilized this technology but more along the sales channel versus the community one.

e. Mashups: Integrating Information: The final Web 2.0 technology describes the efforts around information integration, commonly referred to as *mashups*. These applications can be combined to deliver additional value that the individual parts could not on their own:

1. HousingMaps.com combines the Google mapping application with a real-estate listing service on Craiglists.com.

2. Chicagocrime.org overlays local crime statistics on top of Google Maps so end users can see what crimes wre committed recently in the neighborhood.

3. Another site synchronizes Yahoo! Inc.'s real-time traffic data with Google Maps.

   Much of the work with Web services will enable greater extensions of mashups and combine many different businesses and business models. Organizations like Amazon and Microsoft are embracing the mashup movement by offering developers easier access to their data and services. Moreover, they're programming their services so that more computing tasks, such as displaying maps onscreen, get done on the users' Personal Computers rather than on their far-flung servers.

f. User Contributed Content: One of the basic themes of Web 2.0 is user contributed information. The value derived from the contributed content comes not from a subject-matter expert but rather from individuals whose small contributions add up. One example of user-contributed content is the product review systems like Amazon.com and the reputation systems used with ebay.com. A common practice of online merchants is to enable their customers to review or to express opinions on the products they have purchased. Online reviews are a major source of information for consumers and have demonstrated enormous implications for a wide range of management activities, such as brand building, customer acquisition and retention, product development, and quality assurance.

   A person's reputation is a valuable piece of information that can be used when deciding whether or not to interact or do business with them. A

Table 8.1 Comparison between Web 1.0 and Web 2.0

Web 1.0 Characteristics	Web 2.0 Characteristics
Static Content	Dynamic Content
Producer Based Information	Participatory Based Information
Messages Pushed to Consumer	Messages Pulled by Consumer
Institutional Control	Individual Enabled
Top Down Implementation	Bottom-up Implementation
Users Search and Browse	Users Publish and Subscribe
Transactional Based Interactions	Relationship Based Interactions
Goal of Mass Adoption	Goal of Niche Adoption
Taxonomy	Folksonomy

reputation system is a bi-directional medium where buyers post feedback on sellers and vice versa. For example, eBay buyers voluntarily comment on the quality of service, their satisfaction with the item traded, and promptness of shipping. Sellers comment about the prompt payment from buyers or respond to comments left by the buyer. Reputation systems may be categorized in three basic types: ranking, rating, and collaborative. Ranking systems use quantifiable measures of users' behavior to generate a rating. Rating systems use explicit evaluations given by users in order to define a measure of interest or trust. Finally, collaborative filtering systems determine the level of relationship between the two individuals before placing a weight on the information. For example, if a user has reviewed similar items in the past, then the relevancy of a new rating will be higher.

Table 8.1 presents a comparison between Web 1.0 and Web 2.0.

8.2.3 Web 3.0

In current Web applications, information is presented in natural language, which humans can process easily, but computers can't manipulate natural language information on the Web meaningfully. The Semantic Web is an extension of the current Web in which information is given a well-defined meaning, better enabling computers and universal mediums for information exchange by putting documents with computer-processable meaning (semantics) on the Web. Adding semantics radically changes the nature of the Web—from a place where information is merely displayed to one where it is interpreted, exchanged, and processed. Associating meaning with content or establishing a layer of machine-understandable data enables a higher degree of automation and more intelligent applications and also facilitates interoperable services.

Semantic Web technologies will enhance Web 2.0 tools and its associated data with semantic annotations and semantic knowledge representations, thus enabling a better automatic processing of data, which, in turn, will enhance search mechanisms, management of the tacit knowledge and the overall efficiency of the actual Knowledge Management (KM) tools. The benefits of semantic blogging, semantic wikis or semantic Wikipedia, semantic-enhanced social networks, semantic-enhanced KM and semantic-enhanced user support will increase its benefits multi-fold.

The ultimate goal of the Semantic Web is to support machine-facilitated global information exchange in a scalable, adaptable, extensible manner, so that information on the Web can be used for more effective discovery, automation, integration, and reuse across various applications. The three key ingredients that constitute the Semantic Web and help achieve its goals are semantic markup, ontology, and intelligent software agents.

8.2.4 Mobile Web

Advances in mobile computing and wireless communications and widespread worldwide adoption of mobile devices, such as smart mobile, access the Web using handheld devices. Mobile Web applications could offer some additional features compared to traditional desktop Web applications, such as location-aware services, context-aware capabilities, and personalization.

8.2.5 The Semantic Web

While the Web keeps growing at an astounding pace, most Web pages are still designed for human consumption and cannot be processed by machines. Similarly, while Web search engines help retrieve Web pages, they do not offer support to interpret the results—for that, human intervention is still required. As the size of search results is often just too big for humans to interpret, finding relevant information on the Web is not as easy as we would desire. The existing Web has evolved as a medium for information exchange among people, rather than machines. As a consequence, the semantic content, that is, the meaning of the information on a Web page, is coded in a way that is accessible to human beings only. Today's Web may be defined as the Syntactic Web, where information presentation is carried out by computers, and the interpretation and identification of relevant information is delegated to human beings. With the volume of available digital data growing at an exponential rate, it is becoming virtually impossible for human beings to manage the complexity and volume of the available information. This phenomenon, often referred to as information overload, poses a serious threat to the continued usefulness of today's Web.

As the volume of Web resources grows exponentially, researchers from industry, government, and academia are now exploring the possibility of creating a Semantic Web in which meaning is made explicit, allowing machines to process and integrate Web resources intelligently. Biologists use a well-defined taxonomy, the Linnaean taxonomy, adopted and shared by most of the scientific community worldwide. Likewise, computer scientists are looking for a similar model to help structure Web content. In 2001, T. Berners-Lee, J. Hendler, and O. Lassila published a revolutionary article in *Scientific American* titled "The Semantic Web: A New Form of Web Content That Is Meaningful to Computers Will Unleash a Revolution of New Possibilities"*

The semantic Web is an extension of the current Web in which information is given well-defined meaning, enabling computers and people to work in cooperation. In the lower part of the architecture, we find three building blocks that can be used to encode text (Unicode), to identify resources on the Web (URIs) and to structure and exchange information (XML). Resource Description Framework (RDF) is a simple yet powerful data model and language for describing Web resources. The SPARQL Protocol and RDF Query Language (SPARQL) is the de facto standard used to query RDF data. While RDF and the RDF Schema provide a model for representing Semantic Web data and for structuring semantic data using simple hierarchies of classes and properties, respectively, the SPARQL language and protocol provide the means to express queries and retrieve information from across diverse Semantic Web data sources. The need for a new language is motivated by the different data models and semantics at the level of XML and RDF, respectively.

Ontology is a formal, explicit specification of a shared conceptualization of a particular domain—concepts are the core elements of the conceptualization corresponding to entities of the domain being described, and properties and relations are used to describe interconnections between such concepts. Web Ontology Language (OWL) is the standard language for representing knowledge on the Web. This language was designed to be used by applications that need to process the content of information on the Web instead of just presenting information to human users. Using OWL, one can explicitly represent the meaning of terms in vocabularies and the relationships between those terms. The Rule Interchange Format (RIF) is the W3C Recommendation that defines a framework to exchange rule-based languages on the Web. Like OWL, RIF defines a set of languages covering various aspects of the rule layer of the Semantic Web.

8.2.6 Rich Internet Applications

Rich Internet applications (RIA) are Web-based applications that run in a Web browser and do not require software installation, but still have the features and

---

* Berners-Lee, T.; Lassila, O.; Hendler, J. (2001) The semantic web: A new form of Web content that is meaningful to computers will unleash a revolution of new possibilities. *Scientific American*, 284(5), pp. 34–43.

functionality of traditional desktop applications. The term *RIA* was introduced in a Macromedia whitepaper in March 2002. RIA represents the evolution of the browser from a static request–response interface to a dynamic, asynchronous interface. Broadband proliferation, consumer demand, and enabling technologies, including the Web 2.0, are driving the proliferation of RIAs. RIAs promise a richer user experience and benefits—interactivity and usability that are lacking in many current applications. Some prime examples of RIA frameworks are Adobe's Flex and AJAX, and examples of RIA include Google's Earth, Mail, and Finance applications.

Enterprises are embracing the promises of RIAs by applying them to user tasks that demand interactivity, responsiveness, and richness. Predominant techniques such as HTML, forms, and CGI are being replaced by other programmer or user-friendly approaches such as AJAX and Web services. Building a Web application using fancy technology, however, doesn't ensure a better user experience. To add real value, developers must address the dimension of usability.

8.3 Web Applications

Web applications' operational environment and their development approach and the faster pace in which these applications are developed and deployed differentiate Web applications from those of traditional software.

Characteristics of Web applications:

- Web-based systems, in general, demand good aesthetic appeal—"look and feel"—and easy navigation.
- Web-based applications demand presentation of a variety of content—text, graphics, images, audio, and/or video—and the content may also be integrated with procedural processing. Hence, their development includes the creation and management of the content and their presentation in an attractive manner, as well as a provision for subsequent content management (changes) on a continual basis after the initial development and deployment.
- Web applications are meant to be used by a vast, diverse, remote community of users who have different requirements, expectations, and skill sets. Therefore, the user interface and usability features have to meet the needs of a diverse, anonymous user community. Furthermore, the number of users accessing a Web application at any time is problematic—there could be a "flash crowd" triggered by major events or promotions.
- Web applications, especially those meant for a global audience, need to adhere to many different social and cultural sentiments and national standards—including multiple languages and different systems of units.
- Ramifications of failure or dissatisfaction of users of Web-based applications can be much worse than conventional IT systems. Also, Web applications could fail for many different reasons.

■ Successfully managing the evolution, change, and newer requirements of Web applications is a major technical, organizational, and management challenge. Most Web applications are evolutionary in their nature, requiring (frequent) changes of content, functionality, structure, navigation, presentation, or implementation on an ongoing basis. The frequency and degree of change of information content can be quite high; they particularly evolve in terms of their requirements and functionality, especially after the system is put into use. In most Web applications, frequency and degree of change are much higher than in traditional software applications, and in many applications, it is not possible to specify fully their entire requirements at the beginning.

■ There is a greater demand on the security of Web applications; the security and privacy needs of Web-based systems are in general more demanding than those of traditional software.

■ Web applications need to cope with a variety of display devices and formats and support hardware, software, and networks with vastly varying access speeds.

■ Proliferation of new Web technologies and standards and competitive pressure to use them bring its own advantages and also additional challenges to the development and maintenance of Web applications.

■ The evolving nature of Web applications necessitates an incremental developmental process.

8.3.1 Web Applications Dimensions

1. Presentation: Presentation technologies have advanced over time, such as in terms of multimedia capabilities, but the core technology of the Web application platform, the Hypertext Markup Language (HTML), has remained relatively stable. Consequently, application user interfaces have to be mapped to document-oriented markup code, resulting in an impedance or a gap between the design and the subsequent implementation.

   The task of communicating content in an appropriate way combines both artistic visual design and engineering disciplines. Usually, based on the audience of the website, there are numerous factors to be considered. For example, in the international case, cultural differences may have to be accounted for, affecting not only languages but also, for example, the perception of color schemes. Further restrictions may originate from the publishing organizations themselves, which aim at reflecting the company's brand with a corresponding corporate design or legal obligations with respect to accessibility.

2. Dialogue: Interactive elements in Web applications often appear in the shape of forms that allow users to enter data that is used as input for further processing. More generally, the dialogue concern covers not only interaction between humans and the application but also between arbitrary actors (including other programs) and the manipulated information space. The flow

of information is governed by the Web's interaction model, which, due to its distributed nature, differs considerably from other platforms. The interaction model is subject to variations, as in the context of recent trends toward more client-sided application logic and asynchronous communication between client and server like in the case of AJAX, focusing on user interfaces that provide a look and feel that resembles desktop applications.

3. Navigation: In addition to the challenge of communicating information, there exists the challenge of making it easily accessible to the user without ending in the "lost in hyperspace" syndrome. This holds true even though the Web makes use of only a sub-set of the rich capabilities of hypertext concepts, for example, allowing only unidirectional links. Over time, a set of common usage patterns have evolved that aids them in navigating through new Web sites that may not have been visited before. Applied to Web application development, navigation concepts can be extended for accessing not only static document content but also application functionality.

4. Process: The process dimensions relates to the operations performed on the information space that are generally triggered by the user via the Web interface and whose execution is governed by the business policy. Particular challenges arise from scenarios with frequently changing policies, demanding agile approaches with preferably dynamic wiring between loosely coupled components. Beneath the user interface of a Web application lies the implementation of the actual application logic, for which the Web acts as a platform to make it available to the concerned stakeholders. In case the application is not distributed, the process dimension is hardly affected by Web-specific factors, allowing for standard non-Web approaches like Component-Based Software Engineering to be applied. Otherwise, service-oriented approaches account for cases where the wiring extends over components that reside on the Web.

5. Data: Data are the content of the documents to be published; although content can be embedded in the Web documents together with other dimensions like presentation or navigation, the evolution of Web applications often demands a separation, using data sources such as XML files, databases, or Web services. Traditional issues include, for example, the structure of the information space as well as the definition of structural linking. In the context of the dynamic nature of Web applications, one can distinguish between static information that remains stable over time and dynamic information that is subject to changes. Depending on the media type being delivered, either the data can be persistent, that is, accessible independently of time; or it can be transient, that is, accessible as a flow, as in the case of a video stream. Moreover, metadata can also describe other data facilitating the usefulness of the data within the global information space established by the Web. Similarly, the machine-based processing of information is further supported by Semantic Web approaches that apply technologies like RDF to

make metadata statements (e.g., about Web-page content) and express the semantics about associations between arbitrary resources worldwide.

8.4 Search Analysis

Exploiting the data stored in search logs of Web search engines, intranets, and websites provides important insights into understanding the information-searching habits and tactics of online searchers. Web search engine companies use search logs (also referred to as *transaction logs*) to investigate searching trends and effects of system improvements. This understanding can inform information system design, interface development, and information architecture construction for content collections. Search logs are an unobtrusive method of collecting significant amounts of searching data on a sizable number of system users.

A search log is an electronic record of interactions that have occurred during a searching episode between a Web search engine and users searching for information on that Web search engine. The users may be humans or computer programs acting on behalf of humans. Interactions are the communication exchanges that occur between users and the system initiated either by the user or the system. Most search logs are server-side recordings of interactions; the server software application can record various types of data and interactions depending on the file format that the server software supports. The search log format is typically an extended file format, which contains data such as the client computer's Internet Protocol (IP) address, user query, search engine access time, and referrer site, among other fields.

Search Log Analysis (SLA) is defined as the use of data collected in a search log to investigate particular research questions concerning interactions among Web users, the Web search engine, or the Web content during searching episodes. Within this interaction context, SLA could use the data in search logs to discern attributes of the search process, such as the searcher's actions on the system, the system responses, or the evaluation of results by the searcher. From this understanding, one achieves some stated objective, such as improved system design, advanced searching assistance, or better understanding of some user information-searching behavior.

There are methodological issues with SLA like execution, conception, and communication. SLA can be difficult to execute due to collection, storage, and analysis problems associated with the huge volume and complexity of the dataset (i.e., significant number of variables). With complex datasets, it is sometimes difficult to develop a conceptual methodology for analyzing the dependent variables. Communication problems occur when researchers do not define terms and metrics in sufficient detail to allow other researchers to interpret and verify their results. The Big Data computing environment coupled with the accompanying cloud computing environment expressly address these issues.

8.4.1 SLA Process

SLA involves the following three major stages:

1. Data Collection involves the process of collecting the interaction data for a given period in a search log. Search logs provide a good balance between collecting a robust set of data and unobtrusively collecting that data. Collecting data from real users pursuing needed information while interacting with real systems on the Web affects the type of data that one can realistically assemble. On a real-life system, the method of data monitoring and collecting should not interfere with the information searching process. Not only may a data collection method that interferes with the information searching process unintentionally alter that process, but such a non-permitted interference may also lead to a loss of a potential customer.

    A search log typically consists of data such as
    - User Identification: The IP address of the customer's computer
    - Date: The date of the interaction as recorded by the search engine server
    - The Time: The time of the interaction as recorded by the search engine server

    Additionally, it could also consist of data such as
    - Results Page: The code representing a set of result abstracts and URLs returned by the search engine in response to a query
    - Language: The user preferred language of the retrieved Web pages
    - Source: The federated content collection searched
    - Page Viewed: The URL that the searcher visited after entering the query and viewing the results page, which is also known as *click-thru* or *click-through*

2. Data Preparation involves the process of cleaning and preparing the search log data for analysis. For data preparation, the focus is on importing the search log data into a relational or NoSQL database, assigning each record a primary key, cleaning the data (i.e., checking each field for bad data), and calculating standard interaction metrics that will serve as the basis for further analysis.

Data preparation consists of steps like

1. Cleaning data: Records in search logs can contain corrupted data. These corrupted records can be as a result of multiple reasons, but they are mostly related to errors when logging the data.

2. Parsing data: Using the three fields of The Time, User Identification, and Search URL common to all Web search logs, the chronological series of actions in a searching episode is recreated. The Web query search logs usually contain queries from both human users and agents. Depending on the research objective, one may be interested in only individual human interactions, those from common user terminals, or those from agents.

3. Normalizing searching episodes: When a searcher submits a query, then views a document, and returns to the search engine, the Web server typically logs this second visit with the identical user identification and query but with a new time (i.e., the time of the second visit). This is beneficial information in determining how many of the retrieved results pages the searcher visited from the search engine, but unfortunately, it also skews the results of the query-level analysis. In order to normalize the searching episodes, one must first separate these result page requests from query submissions for each searching episode.

4. Data Analysis involves the process of analyzing the prepared data. There are three common levels of analysis for examining search logs:

   a. *Session Analysis*: A searching episode is defined as a series of interactions within a limited duration to address one or more information needs. This session duration is typically short, with Web researchers using between 5 and 120 min as a cutoff. Each choice of time has an impact on the results; the searcher may be multitasking within a searching episode, or the episode may be an instance of the searcher engaged in successive searching.

   This session definition is similar to the definition of a unique visitor used by commercial search engines and organizations to measure website traffic. The number of queries per searcher is the session *length*. Session *duration* is the total time the user spent interacting with the search engine, including the time spent viewing the first and subsequent Web documents, except the final document. Session duration can therefore be measured from the time the user submits the first query until the user departs the search engine for the last time (i.e., does not return). This viewing time of the final Web document is not available since the Web search engine server does not record the time stamp.

   A *Web document* is the Web page referenced by the URL on the search engine's results page. A Web document may be text or multimedia and, if viewed hierarchically, may contain a nearly unlimited number of sub-Web documents. A Web document may also contain URLs linking to other Web documents. From the results page, a searcher may click on a URL, (i.e., visit) one or more results from the listings on the result page. This is *click-through analysis* and measures the page viewing behavior of Web searchers.

b. *Query Analysis*: The query level of analysis uses the query as the base metric. A *query* is defined as a string list of one or more terms submitted to a search engine. This is a mechanical definition as opposed to an information-searching definition. The first query by a particular searcher is the *initial query*. A subsequent query by the same searcher that is different than any of the searcher's other queries is a *modified query*. There can be several occurrences of different modified queries by a particular searcher. A *unique query* refers to a query that is different from all other queries in the transaction log, regardless of the searcher. A *repeat query* is a query that appears more than once within the dataset by two or more searchers.

    Query complexity examines the query syntax, including the use of advanced searching techniques such as Boolean and other query operators.

c. *Term Analysis*: The term level of analysis naturally uses the term as the basis for analysis. A *term* is a string of characters separated by some delimiter such as a space or some other separator. At this level of analysis, one focuses on measures such as *term occurrence*, which is the frequency that a particular term occurs in the transaction log. Total terms is High Usage Terms are those terms that occur most frequently in the dataset. *Term co-occurrence* measures the occurrence of term pairs within queries in the entire search log. One can also calculate degrees of association of term pairs using various statistical measures

The mutual information formula measures term association and does not assume mutual independence of the terms within the pair. One can calculate the mutual information statistic for all term pairs within the data set. Many times, a relatively low-frequency term pair may be strongly associated (i.e., if the two terms always occur together). The mutual information statistic identifies the strength of this association:

$$I(w_1, w_2) = \ln \frac{P(w_1, w_2)}{P(w_1) * P(w_2)}$$

Where $P(w_1)$, $P(w_2)$ are probabilities estimated by relative frequencies of the two words and $P(w_1, w_2)$ is the relative frequency of the word pair (ignoring the order sequence).

Relative frequencies are observed frequencies (F) normalized by the number of the queries:

$$P(w_1) = \frac{F_1}{Q}; P(w_1) = \frac{F_2}{Q}; P(w_1, w_2) = \frac{F_{12}}{Q},$$

Both the frequency of term occurrence and the frequency of term pairs are the occurrence of the term or term pair within the set of queries. However, since a one-term query cannot have a term pair, the set of queries for the frequency base differs. The number of queries for the terms is the number of non-duplicate queries in the data set.

The number of queries for term pairs is defined as

$$Q' = \sum_{n}^{m} (2n - 3) Qn$$

where Qn is the number of queries with n words (n > 1), and m is the maximum query length. So, queries of length one have no pairs. Queries of length two have one pair. Queries of length three have three possible pairs. Queries of length four have five possible pairs. This continues up to the queries of maximum length in the data set. The formula for queries of term pairs (Q') account for this term pairing.

8.5 Web Analysis

Effective website management requires a way to map the behavior of the visitors to the site against the particular objectives and purpose of the site. Web analysis or log file analysis is the study of the log files from a particular Website. The purpose of log file analysis is to assess the performance of the Website.

Every time a browser hits a particular Web page, the server computer on which the website is hosted registers and records data called log files for every action a visitor at that particular website takes. Log files data includes information on

- Who is visiting the website (the visitor's URL or Web address)
- The IP address (numeric identification) of the computer the visitor is browsing from
- The date and time of each visit
- Which pages the visitor viewed; how long the visitor viewed the site
- Other relevant data

Log files contain potentially useful information for anyone working with a website—from server administrators to designers to marketers—who needs to assess website usability and effectiveness.

1. Website administrators use the data in log files to monitor the availability of a website to make sure the site is online, available, and without technical errors that might prevent easy access and use. Administrators can also predict and plan for growth in server resources and monitor for unusual and possibly malicious activity. For example, by monitoring past Web usage logs for visitor activity, a site administrator can predict future activity during holidays

and other spikes in usage and plan to add more servers and bandwidth to accommodate the expected traffic. In order to watch for potential attacks on a website, administrators can also monitor Web usage logs for abnormal activity on the website such as repetitive login attempts, unusually large numbers of requests from a single IP address, and so forth.

2. Marketers can use the log files to understand the effectiveness of various on- and offline marketing efforts. By analyzing the Web logs, marketers can determine which marketing efforts are the most effective. Marketers can track the effectiveness of online advertising, such as banner ads and other links, through the use of the referrer logs ("referring URLs"). Examination of the referring URLs indicates how visitors got to the website, showing, say, whether they typed the URL (Web address) directly into their Web browser or whether they clicked through from a link at another site.

Web logs can also be used to track the amount of activity from offline advertising, such as magazine and other print ads, by utilizing a unique URL in each offline ad that is run. Unlike online advertising, which shows results in log information about the referring Website, offline advertising requires a way to track whether or not the ad generated a response from the viewer. One way to do this is to use the ad to drive traffic to a particular Website especially established only for tracking that source.

3. Website designers use log files to assess the user experience and site usability. Understanding the user environment provides Web designers with the information they need to create a successful design. While ensuring a positive user experience on a Website requires more than merely good design, log files do provide readily available information to assist with the initial design as well as continuous improvement of the website. Web designers can find useful information about

- The type of operating system (e.g., Windows XP or Linux)
- The screen settings (e.g., screen resolution)
- The type of browser (e.g., Internet Explorer or Mozilla) used to access the site

This information allows designers to create Web pages that display well for the majority of users.

Click trail can show how a viewer navigates through the various pages of a given website; the corresponding clickstream data can show

- What products a customer looked at on an e-commerce site
- Whether the customer purchased those products
- What products a customer looked at but did not purchase
- What ads generated many click-throughs but resulted in few purchases
- And so on

By giving clues as to which Website features are successful and which are not, log files assist website designers in the process of continuous improvement by adding new features, improving upon current features, or deleting unused features. Then, by monitoring the Web logs for the impact on the user reaction and making suitable adjustments based on those reactions, the website designer can improve the overall experience for website visitors on a continuous basis.

 Internet technologies relevant for Web analysis

1. Proxy server is a network server which acts as an intermediary between the user's computer and the actual server on which the website resides; they are used to improve service for groups of users. First, it saves the results of all requests for a particular Web page for a certain amount of time. Then, it intercepts all requests to the real server to see if it can fulfill the request itself. Say user A requests a certain Web page (called Page 1); some time later, user B requests the same page. Instead of forwarding the request to the Web server where Page 1 resides, which can be a time-consuming operation, the proxy server simply returns the Page 1 that it already fetched for user A. Since the proxy server is often on the same network as the user, this is a much faster operation. If the proxy server cannot serve a stored page, then it forwards the request to the real server. Importantly, pages served by the proxy server are not logged in the log files, resulting in inaccuracies in counting site traffic.

   Major online services (such as Facebook, MSN, and Yahoo) and other large organizations employ an array of proxy servers in which all user requests are made through a single IP address. This situation causes Web log files to significantly under-report unique visitor traffic. On the other hand, sometimes home users with an Internet Service Provider get assigned a new IP address each time they connect to the Internet. This causes the opposite effect of inflating the number of unique visits in the Web logs.

2. Firewalls: For the purpose of security rather than efficiency, acting as an intermediary device, a proxy server can also function as a firewall in an organization. Firewalls are used by organizations to protect internal users from outside threats on the Internet or to prevent employees from accessing a specific set of websites. Firewalls hide the actual IP address for specific user computers and instead present a single generic IP address to the Internet for all its users. Hence, this contributes to under-reporting unique visitor traffic in Web analytics.

3. Caching refers to the technique in which most Web browser software keeps a copy of each Web page, called a *cache*, in its memory. So, rather than requesting the same page again from the server (e.g., if the user clicks the "back" button), the browser on the computer will display a copy of the page rather than make another new request to the server. Many Internet Service Providers and large organizations cache Web pages in an effort to serve content more quickly and reduce bandwidth usage. As with the use of proxy servers, caching poses a problem because Web log files don't report these cached page views. Again, as a result, Web log files can significantly under-report the actual visitor count.

8.5.1 *Veracity of Log Files data*

Despite the wealth of useful information available in log files, the data also suffer from limitations.

8.5.1.1 *Unique Visitors*

One of the major sources of inaccuracy arises from the way in which unique visitors are measured. Traditional Web log reports measure unique visitors based on the IP address, or network address, recorded in the log file. Because of the nature of different Internet technologies, IP addresses do not always correspond to an individual visitor in a one-to-one relationship. In other words, there is no accurate way to identify each individual visitor. Depending upon the particular situation, this causes the count of unique visitors to be either over or under-reported.

Cookies are small bits of data that a website leaves on a visitor's hard drive after that visitor has hit a website. Then, each time the user's Web browser requests a new Web page from the server, the cookie on the user's hard drive can be read by the server. These cookie data benefit in several ways:

■ A unique cookie gets generated for each user even if multiple viewers access the same website through the same proxy server; consequently, a unique session is recorded and a more accurate visitor count can be obtained.

■ Cookies also make it possible to track users across multiple sessions (i.e., when they return to the site subsequently), thus enabling a computation of new versus returning visitors.

■ Third-party cookies enable the website to assess what other sites the visitor has visited; this enables personalization of the website in terms of the content that is displayed.

Cookies are not included in normal log files. Therefore, only a Web analytics solution that supports cookie tracking can utilize the benefits.

8.5.1.2 Visitor Count

Another source of inaccuracy is in visitor count data. Most Web log reports give two possible ways to count visitors—hits and unique visits. The very definition of hits is a source of unreliability. By definition, each time a Web page is loaded, each element of the Web page (i.e., different graphics on the same page) is counted as a separate "hit." Therefore, even with one page view, multiple hits are recorded as a function of the number of different elements on a given Web page. The net result is that hits are highly inflated numbers.

In contrast, the under-reporting of visitors is a serious issue for online advertising. If the ad is cached, nobody knows that the ad was delivered. As a result, the organization delivering the ad doesn't get paid. Log files cannot track visitor activity from cached pages because the Web server never acknowledges the request. This deficiency is remedied by using page tagging. This technique has its origins in the hit counter, which, like a car odometer, increases by one count with each additional page view. Page tagging embeds a small piece of JavaScript software code on the Web page itself. Then, when the website user visits the Web page, the Java code is activated by the computer user's browser software. Since page tagging is located on the Web page itself rather than on the server, each time the page is viewed, it is "tagged"; while server logs cannot keep track of requests for a cached page, a "tagged" page will still acknowledge and record a visit. Moreover, rather than recording a visit in a Web log file that is harder to access, page tagging records visitor information in a database, offering increased flexibility to access the information more quickly and with more options to further manipulate the data.

8.5.1.3 Visit Duration

Web logs do not provide an accurate way to determine visit duration. Visit duration is calculated based on the time spent between the first page request and the last page request. If the next page request never occurs, duration can't be calculated and will be under-reported. Web logs also can't account for the user who views a page, leaves the computer for 20 minutes, and comes back and clicks to the next page. In this situation, the visit duration would be highly inflated.

8.5.2 Web Analysis Tools

New tools in Web analytics like Google Analytics provide a stronger link between online technologies and online marketing, giving marketers more essential information lacking in earlier versions of Web analytics software. For many years, Web analytics programs that delivered only simple measurements such as hits, visits, referrals, and search-engine queries were not well linked to an organization's marketing efforts to drive online traffic. As a result, they provided very little insights to help the organization track and understand its online marketing efforts.

Trends in Web analytics specifically improve both the method of data collection as well as the analysis of the data, providing significantly more value from a marketing perspective. These newer tools attempt to analyze the entire marketing process, from a user clicking an advertisement through to the actual sale of a product or service. This information helps to identify not merely which online advertising is driving traffic (number of clicks) to the website and which search terms lead visitors to the site, but also which advertising is most effective in actually generating sales (conversion rates) and profitability. This integration of the Web log files with other measures of advertising effectiveness is critical to provide guidance into further advertising spending.

Web analytics software has the capability to perform more insightful, detailed reporting on the effectiveness of common online marketing activities such as search-engine listings, pay-per-click advertising, and banner advertising. Marketing metrics to assess effectiveness can include

- Cost-per-click: The total online expenditure divided by the number of click-throughs to the site
- Conversion rate: The percentage of the total number of visitors who make a purchase, signup for a service, or complete another specific action
- Return on marketing investment: The advertising expense divided by the total revenue generated from the advertising expense
- Bounce rate: The number of users that visit only a single page divided by the total number of visits—one indicator of the "stickiness" of a Web page

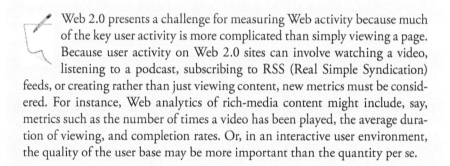

Web 2.0 presents a challenge for measuring Web activity because much of the key user activity is more complicated than simply viewing a page. Because user activity on Web 2.0 sites can involve watching a video, listening to a podcast, subscribing to RSS (Real Simple Syndication) feeds, or creating rather than just viewing content, new metrics must be considered. For instance, Web analytics of rich-media content might include, say, metrics such as the number of times a video has been played, the average duration of viewing, and completion rates. Or, in an interactive user environment, the quality of the user base may be more important than the quantity per se.

8.5.3 Common Analysis and Reports

The following are some of the most common types of analyses:

1. *Trend analysis* looks at data along the time dimension and shows the chronological changes of selected metrics. For example, data can show how the percentage of mobile client access has changed for the past two years.

2. *Distribution analysis* is about metric value breakdown. Values are usually calculated as percentages of the total by one or more dimensions. It is often used to analyze visitor and client profiles. For example, the percentages of browser types for the past month give information about client diversity. Other commonly used dimensions in this type of analysis are traffic source (e.g., referral source analysis reveals the campaign effectiveness); location; technical data that includes information about browser, OS, device, screen resolution, and color depth; client technology support; and so on.

3. *User activity or behavior analysis* analyzes how users interact with websites. Typical examples are engagement analysis, clickstream analysis, and in-page analysis.

4. *Engagement analysis* is one of the most frequently used analyses in the industry. It measures the following factors:

   How many pages were visited per session?

   What is the duration of a visit?

   How often do new visitors become returning visitors?

   How often do visitors return to the site (loyalty)?

   The goal of visitor engagement analysis is to find out why the multitude of operations performed on a website did not end in conversion. There were several attempts to create engagement calculators that will distinguish between user visits. For example, one user came from Google search, visited two pages in 5 minutes, and downloaded a necessary document. Another user came from the main site, visited 20 pages in 40 minutes, and downloaded five documents.

5. *Clickstream analysis*, also known as *click paths*, analyzes the navigation path a visitor browsed through a website. A clickstream is a list of all the pages viewed by a visitor presented in the viewing order, also defined as the "succession of mouse clicks" that each visitor makes. Clickstream analysis helps to improve the navigation and information architecture of websites.

6. *Visitor interest/attention analysis* (in-page analysis) analyzes users' attentions on a web page. It uses client script to track user mouse movements and clicks and shows results in a heat map. It can also show how far down visitors scroll the page. Analysis of link popularity and areas of attention helps to develop content placement strategies. For example, it helps determine what navigational items should be placed on the top of the page or find the best places for advertisements.

7. *Conversion analysis* is one of the key analyses in e-commerce and other sectors. Conversion rate is calculated by dividing the number of completed targeted actions (e.g., purchases) by the number of unique users visited the site. All Web analytics providers strive to improve conversion tracking. For example, Google Analytics provides Multi-Channel Funnels conversion reports that show what campaigns, sources, or channels have contributed to a visitor's multi-visit conversion.

8. *Performance analysis* helps reveal website performance issues (such as loading time) or linking errors. For example, after a website redesign, indirect traffic volume needs to be watched. If there is less indirect traffic, then some links from other sites and/or bookmarks were potentially broken after the redesign.

8.6 Summary

This chapter introduced the concept of a Web-based application. It then sketched the reference architecture along with the realization of this architecture in J2EE. In the later part of the chapter, it discussed the details and characteristics of Web log analysis. It then traced the development of Web-based applications from Web 1.0 to Web 2.0 on to developments envisaged in future in Web 3.0, Mobile Web, Semantic Web, and Rich Internet Applications.

Chapter 9

Social Networks

Social computing is the use of social software, which is based on creating or recreating online social conversations and social contexts through the use of software and technology. An example of social computing is the use of e-mail for maintaining social relationships. Social Networks (SNs) are social structures made up of nodes and ties; they indicate the relationships between individuals or organizations and how they are connected through social contexts. SNs operate on many levels; they play an important role in solving problems and in how organizations are run, and they help individuals succeed in achieving their targets and goals. Computer-based social networks enable people in different locations to interact with each other socially (e.g., chat, view photos, etc.) over a network. SNs are very useful for visualizing patterns: A social network structure is made up of nodes and ties; there may be few or many nodes in the networks or one or more different types of relations between the nodes. Building a useful understanding of a social network is to sketch a pattern of social relationships, kinships, community structure, and so forth. The use of mathematical and graphical techniques in social network analysis is important to represent the descriptions of networks compactly and more efficiently.

Social Networks operate on many different levels, from families up to nations, and they play a critical role in determining the way problems are solved, how organizations are run, and the degree to which people succeed in achieving their goals.

9.1 Networks

Networks have become the basic conceptual building blocks of the computational sciences, especially triggered by the burgeoning growth of the Internet and fueled by the rising significance of cloud computing, Big Data, mobile computing, and social networking solutions and applications.

This sub-section presents a quick overview of the concept of networks and enterprises based on characteristics of networks, namely, network enterprises that are likely to swamp the business environment in the future.

9.1.1 Concept of Networks

At its most basic level, a network is any system or structure of interconnected elements that can be represented by a graph of nodes (the elements) connected by some kind of links (whatever ties them together). The nodes of a network may be anything from land masses to cells in a body, political institutions, or people. The links between the nodes might be physical connections, biochemical interactions, relationships of power and authority, or reciprocal social ties such as friendship.

The concept of a network first arose in a field of mathematics known as *graph theory*, pioneered by Swiss-born mathematician Leonhard Euler in 1736. In a seminal paper, Euler solved a long-standing puzzle of geography known as the Konigsberg Bridge problem: Could someone cross each of the seven bridges of that Baltic seaport without repeating once? Euler found the solution (which was in the negative) by treating the city's islands and river banks as featureless nodes and Konigsberg's bridges as links connecting them. By reducing urban geography to a simple mathematical graph, the puzzle was easily solved, and the mathematics of networks was born.

In the mid-twentieth century, Hungarian mathematicians Paul Erdos and Alfred Renyi greatly expanded the theory of nodes and links in eight papers exploring the topology and behavior of randomly generated networks. In the late twentieth century, the mathematics of graph theory gave birth to a new inter-disciplinary science of networks, devoted to examining the common principles of network graphs that are found across domains ranging from engineering to information science to biology to sociology.

Decades before the arrival of websites like Facebook, sociologists attempted to map the social ties within groups via the field of social network analysis. Different typologies of networks were seen to represent varying organizational structures, from the hierarchical models of companies and traditional militaries to the more distributed, centerless topologies of voluntary organizations whose numerous cells are only loosely connected to one another. Similarly, social network analysis has often focused on how and why certain innovations spread rapidly, be their new technologies (use of smartphones), new language (Twitter), or new ideas (video call). In all these cases, a network model has allowed for new insights to be gained into the behavior and properties of extremely complex systems—insights that may not be visible by simply observing the actions of the individual constituent parts.

In the field of communications, networks were used to map telephone systems, with their wires (links) connecting phone lines and exchanges (the nodes). Later, these same phone networks began to link computers into the Internet. In terms of communications content (rather than communications hardware), the World Wide Web has been mapped as a network of interconnected Web pages linked together by hyperlinks. Transportation systems have been mapped as networks, starting with Euler's bridges of Konigsberg and continuing later as train networks, with stations (the nodes) linked by lines of track; road networks, with cities connected by interstate highways; and air traffic networks, with airports linked by the airline routes that crisscross our globe. In biology, network science has been used to map out the relationships of nerve cells connected by the dendrites and axons that transmit and receive their messages. Networks are used to map molecules in an organism by how they are linked through biochemical reactions. Network maps have also been applied to tracking the spread of infectious diseases, with patients representing the nodes and vectors of disease transmission being the links between them.

9.1.2 Principles of Networks

9.1.2.1 Metcalfe's Law

Robert Metcalfe, the inventor of the Ethernet and founder of 3Com, evaluated that the value of a network increases as the square of the number of users; consequently, additional users are attracted to connect to the network resulting in a virtuous cycle of positive feedback. Considering that the original observation was inspired by telephonic systems that are typically bi-lateral, the value associated with computer networks that admit multi-lateralism is manyfold. Thus, for computer networks with n number of nodes allowing conversations of m users simultaneously, the value of the computer network may increase as $nm!$ This phenomenon has important implications for corporations competing in network markets.

While in the traditional economy, value is derived from scarcity, in the network economy, critical mass supersedes scarcity as a source of value. Positive feedback works to the advantage of big networks and to the detriment of smaller networks. Consequently, the bigger networks continue to grow bigger, while the smaller networks are sucked into a vortex of negative feedback and shrink to insignificance. The classic examples of this phenomenon are the rapid ascendancy of Microsoft Windows to market domination against other alternatives like Apple or UNIX operating systems, or the VHS-versus-Betamax standard battle.

9.1.2.2 Power Law

Many natural phenomena, such as the height of a species, follow the random distribution known as a *bell curve*: most animals grow to be quite close to the average height of their species, and those that deviate will be only slightly taller or shorter. But among phenomena that follow a power law curve, there is no clustering around the average; instead, there are a few extremely high values and then many, many more increasingly small values. Power law distributions are seen in the distribution of wealth, as famously observed by Vilfredo Pareto's principle (also termed as the 80–20 rule) that 80% of the wealth is held by 20% of the population. Network enterprises (network customers) follow this kind of power law distribution as well: some enterprises (customers) are much more or less connected or active within a network than the average enterprise (customer).

9.1.2.3 Small Worlds Networks (SWNs)

The phenomenon of networks is pervasive, and they deeply affect all aspects of human life and relationships. Networks matter because local actions have global consequences, and the relationship between local and global dynamics depends on the network structure. The idea of small worlds is applicable to diverse problems— community of prospects or customers, organizations, national markets, global economy, flying routes, postal services, food chains, electrical power grids, disease propagation, ecosystems, language, or firing of neurons. In 1998, Cornell mathematician Duncan Watts, with his advisor, Steve Strogatz, recognized the structural similarity between graph problems describing any collection of dots connected by lines and the co-ordinated lightning of fireflies. The 1967 idea of sociologist Stanley Milgram states that the world's six billion people are all connected by six degrees of separation; that is, the average number of steps needed to get from one selected person to another is six.

They showed that when networks of connected dots have a degree of order to their clustering, the degree of separation is correspondingly high, but adding random links shrinks the degree of separation rapidly. Real-world networks are far from being a bunch of nodes randomly linked to each other; instead, a few well-connected hubs keep most of the networks together. They showed that networks operate on the *power law*, the notion that a few large interactions carry the most action, or the rich get richer! This explains why the Internet is dominated by a few highly connected nodes or large hubs such as Yahoo!, Google, or Amazon.com, and also the dominance of Microsoft Windows on desktops. Similarly, in a separate context, a few individuals with extraordinary ability to make friendships keep a society together.

Thus, networks combine order and randomness to reveal two defining characteristics of the small worlds networks: local robustness and global accessibility. Local robustness results from the fact that excepting the hubs, malfunctioning at other smaller nodes does not disrupt or paralyze the network; it continues to function normally. However, paradoxically, the elegance and efficiency of these structures also make them vulnerable to infiltration, failures, sabotage, and, in case of the Internet, virus attacks.

9.2 Computer Networks

Two computers are said to be networked if they are able to exchange information. The connection need not be via a copper wire; fiber optics, microwaves, infrared, and communication satellites can also be used. Networks come in many sizes, shapes, and forms, as we will see later. They are usually connected together to make larger networks, with the Internet being the most well-known example of a network of networks.

Computer Network and a Distributed System: The key distinction between them is that in a distributed system, a collection of independent computers appears to its users as a single coherent system. Usually, it has a single model or paradigm that it presents to the users. Often, a layer of software on top of the operating system, called *middleware*, is responsible for implementing this model. A well-known example of a distributed system is the World Wide Web (WWW). It runs on top of the Internet and presents a model in which everything looks like a document (Web page). On the other hand, in a computer network, coherence, model, and software are absent. Users are exposed to the actual machines, without any attempt by the system to make the machines look and act in a coherent way. If the machines have different hardware and different operating systems, that is fully visible to the users. If a user wants to run a program on a remote machine, it entails logging onto that machine and running it there. In effect, a distributed system is a software system built on top of a network. The software gives it a high degree of cohesiveness and transparency.

Thus, the distinction between a network and a distributed system lies with the software (especially the operating system), rather than with the hardware. Nevertheless, there is considerable overlap between the two subjects. For example, both distributed systems and computer networks need to move files around. The difference lies in who invokes the movement, the system or the user.

9.2.1 Internet

The origins of the Internet can be traced to the US government support of the ARPANET project. Computers in several US universities were linked via packet switching, and this allowed messages to be sent between the universities that were part of the network. The use of ARPANET was limited initially to academia and to the US military, and in the early years, there was little interest from industrial companies.

However, by the mid-1980s, there were over 2000 hosts on the TCP/ IP-enabled network, and the ARPANET was becoming more heavily used and congested. It was decided to shut down the network by the late 1980s, and the National Science Foundation in the United States commenced work on the NSFNET. This work commenced in the mid-1980s, and the network consisted of multiple regional networks connected to a major backbone. The original links in NSFNET were 56 Kbps, but these were later updated to the faster T1 (1.544 Mbps) links. The NSFNET T1 backbone initially connected 13 sites, but this increased due to a growing interest from academic and industrial sites in the United States and from around the world. The NSF began to realize from the mid-1980s onward that the Internet had significant commercial potential.

9.2.2 *World Wide Web (WWW)*

The WWW was invented by Tim Berners-Lee in 1990 at CERN in Geneva, Switzerland. One of the problems that scientists at CERN faced was that of keeping track of people, computers, documents, databases, and so on. This problem was more acute due to the international nature of CERN, as the center had many visiting scientists from overseas who spent several months there. Berners-Lee essentially created a system to give every page on a computer a standard address. This standard address is called the universal resource locator and is better known by its acronym URL. Each page is accessible via the hypertext transfer protocol (HTTP), and the page is formatted with the hypertext markup language (HTML). Each page is visible using a Web browser.

Inventors tend to be influenced by existing inventions and especially inventions that are relevant to their areas of expertise. The Internet was a key existing invention, and it allowed worldwide communication via electronic e-mail, the transfer of files electronically via FTP, and newsgroups that allowed users to make postings on various topics. Another key invention that was relevant to Berners-Lee was that of hypertext. This was invented by Ted Nelson in the 1960s, and it allows links to be present in text. For example, a document such as a book contains a table of contents, an index, and a bibliography. These are all links to material that is either within the book itself or external to the book. The reader of a book is able to follow the link to obtain the internal or external information. The other key invention that was relevant to Berners-Lee was that of the mouse. This was invented by Doug Engelbart in the 1960s, and it allowed the cursor to be steered around the screen. The major leap that Berners-Lee made was essentially a marriage of the Internet, hypertext, and the mouse into what has become the World Wide Web.

The invention of the WWW by Berners-Lee was a revolution in the use of the Internet. Users could now surf the Web, that is, hyperlink among the millions of computers in the world and obtain information easily. The WWW creates a space in which users can access information easily in any part of the world. This is done using only a Web browser and simple Web addresses. Browsers are used to connect to remote computers over the Internet and to request, retrieve, and display the Web pages on the local machine. The user can then click on hyperlinks on Web pages to access further relevant information that may be on an entirely different continent. Berners-Lee developed the first Web browser, called the *World Wide Web* browser. He also wrote the first browser program, and this allowed users to access Web pages throughout the world. The invention of the WWW was announced in August 1991, and the growth of the Web has been phenomenal since then.

The WWW is revolutionary in that

- No single organization is controlling the Web
- No single computer is controlling the Web
- Millions of computers are interconnected
- It is an enormous market place of millions (billions) of users
- The Web is not located in one physical location
- The Web is a space and not a physical thing

The WWW has been applied to many areas including

- Travel industry (booking flights, train tickets, and hotels)
- E-marketing
- Portal sites (such as Yahoo! and Hotmail)
- Ordering books and CDs over the Web (such as www.amazon.com)
- Recruitment services (such as www.jobserve.com)
- Internet banking
- Online casinos (for gambling)
- Newspapers and news channels
- Online shopping and shopping malls

9.3 Social Networks

The study of social networks really began to take off as an inter-disciplinary specialty only after 1970, when modern discrete combinatorics (particularly graph theory) experienced rapid development and relatively powerful computers became readily available. Since then, it has found important applications in organizational behavior, inter-organizational relations, the spread of contagious diseases, mental health, social support, the diffusion of information, and animal social organization.

German sociologist F. Tönnies was a major contributor to sociological theory, and it was he who initially highlighted that social groups exist by containing individuals that are linked together through shared beliefs and values. E. Durkheim gave a non-individualistic explanation of social facts, arguing that social phenomena arise when interacting individuals constitute a reality that can no longer be accounted for in terms of the properties of individual actors. He distinguished between a traditional society—"mechanical solidarity"—which prevails if individual differences are minimized; and the modern society— "organic solidarity"—that develops out of co-operation between differentiated individuals with independent roles. By the turn of the twentieth century, another major German sociologist, Georg Simmel, became the first scholar to think appropriately in social network terms. Simmel produced a series of essays that pinpointed the nature of network size. He further displayed an understanding of social networking with his writings as he highlighted that social interaction existed within loosely knit networks as opposed to groups. The next real significant growth of social networking didn't really commence until the 1930s, when three main social networking traditions emerged. The first tradition to emerge was pioneered by Jacob Levy Moreno, who was recognized as one of the leading social scientists. Moreno began the systematic recording and analysis of social interaction in smaller groups such as work groups and classrooms. The second tradition was founded by a Harvard group that began to focus specifically on inter-personal relations at work. The third tradition originated from Alfred Radcliffe-Brown, an English social anthropologist.

Social groups can exist as personal and direct social ties that link individuals who either share values and beliefs or impersonal, formal, and instrumental social links. Durkheim gave a non-individualistic explanation of social facts, arguing that social phenomena arise when interacting individuals constitute a reality that can no longer be accounted for in terms of the properties of individual actors. He distinguished between a traditional society—"mechanical solidarity"—which succeeds if individual differences are lessened, and a modern society that develops out of support between differentiated individuals with independent roles. Social network analysis has emerged as a key technique in modern sociology and has also gained a following in anthropology, biology, communication studies, economics, geography, information science, organizational studies, social psychology, and sociolinguistics.

Efforts to support social networks via computer-mediated communication were made in many early online services, including Usenet, ARPANET, listserv, and bulletin board services (BBS). Many prototypical features of social networking sites were also present in online services such as America Online, Prodigy, and CompuServe. Early social networking on the WWW began in the form of generalized online communities such as TheGlobe.com in 1995, Geocities in 1994, and Tripod.com in 1995. Many of these early communities focused on bringing people together to interact with each other through chat rooms, and they encouraged users to share personal information and ideas via personal Web pages by providing easy-to-use publishing tools and free or inexpensive Web space. Some communities— such as Classmates.com—took a different approach by simply having people link to each other via e-mail addresses. In the late 1990s, user profiles became a central feature of social networking sites, allowing users to compile lists of "friends" and to search for other users with similar interests.

New social networking methods were developed by the end of the 1990s, and many sites began to develop more advanced features for users to find and manage friends. Web-based social networking services make it possible to connect people who share interests and activities across political, economic, and geographic borders. Through e-mail and instant messaging, online communities are created where a gift economy and mutual unselfishness are encouraged through collaboration. Information is particularly suited to a gift economy, as information is a non-rival good and can be gifted at practically no cost. The newer generation of social networking sites began to flourish with the emergence of Makeoutclub in 2000, followed by Friendster in 2002, and they soon became part of the Internet mainstream. Friendster was followed by MySpace and LinkedIn a year later, and finally Bebo and Facebook in 2004. Attesting to the rapid increase in social networking sites' popularity, by 2005, MySpace was reportedly getting more page views than Google. Facebook launched in 2004, has since become the largest social networking site in the world. Today, it is estimated that there are now over 200 active sites using a wide variety of social networking models.

Social networks differ from most other types of networks, including technological and biological networks, in two important ways. First, they have non-trivial clustering or network transitivity and second, they show positive correlations between the degrees of adjacent vertices. Social networks are often divided into groups or communities, and it has recently been suggested that this division could account for the observed clustering. Furthermore, group structure in networks can also account for degree correlations. Hence, assortative mixing in such networks with a variation in the sizes of the groups provides the predicted level and compares well with that observed in real-world networks.

A definition of social networks that is merely based on their structure: "a social network is an organized set of people that consists of two kinds of elements: human beings and the connections between them." The online social network in that case is the tool or the platform that facilitates the development and maintenance of this relationship, which may stem from different needs of the participants.

The current metrics for social network analysis are as follows:

■ Bridge: An edge is said to be a bridge if deleting it would cause its endpoints to lie in different components of a graph.
■ Centrality: This measure gives a rough indication of the social power of a node based on how well they "connect" the network. *Betweenness*, *Closeness*, and *Degree* are all measures of centrality.

- Betweenness: The extent to which a node lies between other nodes in the network. This measure takes into account the connectivity of the node's neighbors, giving a higher value for nodes that bridge clusters. The measure reflects the number of people who a person is connecting indirectly through their direct links.
- Closeness: The degree an individual is near all other individuals in a network (directly or indirectly). It reflects the ability to access information through the "grapevine" of network members. Thus, closeness is the inverse of the sum of the shortest distances between each individual and every other person in the network. The shortest path may also be known as the *geodesic distance.*
- Centralization: The difference between the number of links for each node divided by maximum possible sum of differences. A centralized network will have many of its links dispersed around one or a few nodes, while a decentralized network is one in which there is little variation between the number of links each node possesses.
- Clustering Coefficient: A measure of the likelihood that two associates of a node are associates. A higher clustering coefficient indicates a greater "cliquishness."
- Density: The degree a respondent's ties know one another/the proportion of ties among an individual's nominees. Network or global-level density is the proportion of ties in a network relative to the total number possible (sparse vs. dense networks).
- Degree: The count of the number of ties to other actors in the network.
- Cohesion: The degree to which actors are connected directly to each other by cohesive bonds. Groups are identified as *cliques* if every individual is directly tied to every other individual, and *social circles* if there is less stringency of direct contact, which is imprecise, or as structurally cohesive blocks if precision is wanted.
- Eigenvector Centrality: A measure of the importance of a node in a network. It assigns relative scores to all nodes in the network based on the principle that connections to nodes having a high score contribute more to the score of the node in question.
- Prestige: In a directed graph, *prestige* is the term used to describe a node's centrality. Degree Prestige, Proximity Prestige, and Status Prestige are all measures of Prestige.
- Reach: The degree to which any member of a network can reach other members of the network.
- Structural hole: Static holes that can be strategically filled by connecting one or more links to link together other points. This is linked to ideas of social capital: if you link to two people who are not linked, you can control their communication.

The most important centrality measures are degree centrality, closeness centrality, and betweenness centrality.

1. Degree centrality: Degree of a node is the number of direct connections a node has. Degree centrality is the sum of all other actors who are directly connected to ego. It signifies activity or popularity. Lots of ties coming in and lots of ties coming out of an actor would increase degree centrality.
2. Betweenness centrality: This type of centrality is the number of times a node connects pairs of other nodes who otherwise would not be able to reach one another. It is a measure of the potential for control, as an actor who is high in "betweenness" is able to act as a gatekeeper controlling the flow of resources (e.g., information, money, power) between the alters that he or she connects. This measurement of centrality is a purely structural measure of popularity, efficiency, and power in a network; in other words, the more connected or centralized actor is more popular, efficient, or powerful.
3. Closeness centrality: Closeness centrality is based on the notion of distance. If a node or actor is close to all others in the network, a distance of no more than one, then it is not dependent on any other to reach everyone in the network. Closeness measures independence or efficiency. With disconnected networks, closeness centrality must be calculated for each component.

As indicated earlier, the two basic elements of social networks are links and nodes. Links are connections, or ties, between individuals or groups, and nodes are the individuals or groups involved in the network. A node's importance in a social network refers to its centrality. Central nodes have the potential to exert influence over less central nodes. A network that possesses just a few or perhaps even one node with high centrality is a centralized network. In this type of network, all nodes are directly connected to each other. Subordinate nodes direct information to the central node, and the central node distributes it to all other nodes. Centralized networks are susceptible to disruption because they have few central nodes, and damage to a central node could be devastating to the entire network.

Decentralized networks are those that do not possess one central hub but rather possess several important hubs. Each node is indirectly tied to all others, and therefore the network has more elasticity. Consequently, these networks are more difficult to disrupt due to their loose connections and ability to replace damaged nodes. Consequently, terror networks choose this type of structure whenever possible.

The term *degrees* is used in reference to the number of direct connections that a node enjoys. The node that possesses the largest number of connections is the hub of the network. The term *betweenness* refers to the number of groups that a node is indirectly tied to through the direct links that it possesses. Therefore, nodes with high a degree of betweenness act as liaisons or bridges to other nodes in the structure. These nodes are known as brokers because of the power that they wield. However, these brokers represent a single point of failure, because if their communication flows are disrupted then they will be cut off to the nodes that it connects. Closeness measures the trail that a node would take in order to reach all other nodes in a network. A node with high closeness does not necessarily have the most direct connections; but because they are "close" to many members they maintain rapid access to most other nodes through both direct and indirect ties.

9.3.1 Popular Social Networks

This section briefly describes popular social networks like LinkedIn, Facebook, Twitter, and Google+.

9.3.1.1 LinkedIn

LinkedIn is currently considered the *de facto* source of professional networking. Launched in 2003, it is the largest business-oriented social network with more than 260 million users. This network allows users to find the key people they may need to make introductions into the office of the job they may desire. Users can also track friends and colleagues during times of promotion and hiring to congratulate them if they choose; this results in a complex social web of business connections. In 2008, LinkedIn introduced their mobile app as well as the ability for users to not only endorse each other but also to specifically attest to individual skills that they may hold and have listed on the site. LinkedIn now supports more than 20 languages.

Users cannot upload their resumes directly to LinkedIn. Instead, a user adds skills and work history to their profile. Other users inside that social network can verify and endorse each attribute. This essentially makes a user's presence on LinkedIn only as believable as the people they connect with.

9.3.1.2 Facebook

Facebook was created by Mark Zuckerberg at Harvard College. Launched in 2004, it grew rapidly and now has more than a billion and half users. In 2011, Facebook introduced personal timelines to complement a user's profile; timelines show chronological placement of photos, videos, links, and other updates made by a user and his or her friends. Though a user can customize their timeline as well as the kind of content and profile information that can be shared with individual users, Facebook networks rely heavily on people posting comments publically and also tagging people in photos. Tagging is a very common practice that places people and events together, though, if required, a user can always untag himself or herself.

Conceptually, timeline is a chronological representation of a person's life from birth until his or her death, or present day if you are still using Facebook. A user's life can be broken up into pieces or categories that can be more meaningfully analyzed by the algorithms run by Facebook. These categories include Work and Education, Family and Relationships, Living, Health and Wellness, and Milestones and Experiences. Each category contains four to seven sub-categories. Users have granular control over who sees what content related to them but less so over what they see in relation to other people.

Facebook is often accused of selling user information and not fully deleting accounts after users choose to remove them. Because Facebook has such a generalized privacy policy, they can get away with handling user information in almost any way that they see fit. Facebook has done many things to improve security in recent years.

Facebook has provided users with a detailed list of open sessions under their account name and given them the ability to revoke them at will. This is to say that, if an unauthorized person accesses a user's account or the user forgets to log out of a computer, they can force that particular connection to close. Location and time of access are listed for each open session, so a user can easily determine if their account is being accessed from somewhere unexpected.

When viewed through a Web browser, Facebook supports https. This protocol is considered secure; however, it is not supported by mobile devices. Data transmitted by Facebook to mobile devices has been proven to be in plain text, meaning if it is intercepted it is easily humanly readable. However, GPS (Global Positioning System) coordinates and information about your friends require special permission. Default access granted to any Facebook app includes user ID, name, profile picture, gender, age range, locale, networks, list of friends, and any information set as public. Any of this information can be transmitted between devices at any time without a user's express permission, and, in the case of mobile devices, in plain, unencrypted text.

Facebook has partially solved this problem by releasing a separate app for messaging. It provides more granular control for mobile device permissions, such as contact syncing and specific profile information. The only problem with this solution is that it relies on every user to not only know about and download the separate app but to also carefully take the considerable amount of time to properly read through and set all the new permissions properly.

9.3.1.3 Twitter

Twitter's original idea was to design a system for individuals to share short SMS messages with a small group of people. Hence, tweets were designed to be short and led to the limit of 144 characters per tweet. By 2013, Twitter had 200 million users sending 500 million tweets a day.

Twitter was originally designed to work with text messages. This is why the 140 character limit was put into the original design, to comply with text message rates. Twitter's original design was to create a service that a person could send a text to, and that text would not only be available online but it would then be able to resend that text to other people using the service. Subsequently, Twitter has incorporated many different sources of media. In 2010, Twitter added facility for online video and photo viewing without redirection to third-party sites. In 2013, Twitter added its own music service as an iPhone app. Despite Twitter's continued expansion of supported content, the language used in modern tweets along with some other helpful additions has continued to adhere to the 140-character limit.

> When Twitter was first implemented, tweets were handled by a server running Ruby on Rails and stored in a shared MySQL database. As the number of Twitter users grew rapidly and the number of tweets being made skyrocketed past the throughput capacity of the system, the MySQL database could not keep up, resulting in read and write errors that prevented tweets from being handled properly. Eventually, Rails components were replaced with the corresponding Scala implementations, leading to improvement of throughput by more than 50 times.

9.3.1.4 Google+

Google+ is the only social network to rival Facebook's user base with more than a billion users. The main feature of Google+ is circles; by being part of the same circle, people create focused social networks. Circles allow networks to center around ideas and products; circles are also the way that streaming content is shared between people. Circles generate content for users and help organize and segregate with whom information is shared. A user makes circles by placing other Google+ users into them. This is done through an interface built very similarly to Gmail and Google Maps.

When Circles create content for a user, it is accumulated and displayed on their Stream. A user's Stream is a prioritized list of any content from that user's circles that they have decided to display. A user can control how much of a Circle's content is included in their Stream. Circles can also be shared, either with individual users or other circles. This action being a single time share means that there is no subsequent syncing after the share takes place. The lack of synchronous updates without sharing a Circle again means that it is simply very easy for others to have incorrect information about Circles that change on a regular basis. If frequent updates are made and a user wants his or her network to stay up to date, a user may have to share a Circle quite frequently.

Google+ Pages are essentially profiles for businesses, organizations, publications, or other entities that are not related to a single individual. They can be added to Circles like normal users and share updates to user Streams in the same way. The real distinction is that Pages do not require a legal name to be attached to the associated Google account.

Google+ has a large amount of additional services and support owing to its high level of integration with Google accounts including games, messenger, photo editing and saving, mobile upload and diagnostics, apps, calendars, and video streaming. Hangouts, which is Google's video-streaming application, is available free for use and supports up to 10 simultaneous users in a session. Hangouts can be used as a conference call solution or to create instant webcasts. Functionally, Hangouts is similar to programs like Skype.

9.3.1.5 Other Social Networks

Here are some of the other notable social networks:

1. Classmates was established in 1995 by Randy Conrads as a means for class reunions, and it has more than 50 million registered users. By linking together people from the same school and class year, Classmates.com provides individuals with a chance to "walk down memory lane" and get reacquainted with old classmates that have also registered with the site. With a minimum age limit of 18 years, registration is free, and anyone may search the site for classmates that they may know. Purchasing a gold membership is required to communicate with other members through the site's e-mail system. User e-mail addresses are private, and communication for paying members is handled through a double-blind e-mail system, which ensures that only paying members can make full use of the site, allowing unlimited communication and orchestration of activities for events like reunions.

2. Friendster was launched in 2002 by Jonathan Abrams as a generic social network in Malaysia. Friendster is a social network made primarily of Asian users. Friendster was redesigned and re-launched as a gaming platform in 2011, from where it would grow to its current user base of more than 115 million. Friendster filed many of the fundamental patents related to social networks. Eighteen of these patents were acquired by Facebook in 2011.

3. hi5 is a social network developed by Ramu Yalamanchi in 2003 in San Francisco, California, and was acquired by Tagged in 2011. All of the normal social network features were included like friend networks, photo sharing, profile information, and groups. In 2009, hi5 was redesigned as a purely

social gaming network with a required age of 18 years for all new and exist-ing users. Several hundred games were added, and Application Programming Interfaces (APIs) were created that include support for Facebook games. This popular change boosted hi5's user base, and at the time of acquisition, its user base was more than 80 million.

4. Orkut was a social network almost identical to Facebook that was launched in 2004 and was shut down by the end of September 2014. Orkut obtained more than 100 million users, most of which were located in India and Brazil.

5. Flickr is a photo-sharing website that was created in 2004 and was acquired by Yahoo in 2005; photos and videos can also be accessed via Flickr. It has tens of millions of members sharing billions of images.

6. YouTube is a video-sharing website that was created in 2005 and was acquired by Google in 2006. Members as well as corporations and organizations post videos of themselves as well as various events and talks. Movies and songs are also posted on this website.

9.4 Social Network Analysis (SNA)

In social science, the structural approach, which is based on the study of interaction among social actors, is called *social network analysis* (SNA). The relationships that social network analysts study are usually those that link individual human beings, since these social scientists believe that besides individual characteristics, relational links or social structure are necessary and indispensable to fully understand social phenomena.

SNA is used to understand the social structure that exists among entities in an organization. The defining feature of SNA is its focus on the structure of rela-tionships, ranging from casual acquaintance to close bonds. This is in contrast with other areas of the social sciences where the focus is often on the attributes of agents rather than on the relations between them. SNA maps and measures the formal and informal relationships to understand what facilitates or impedes the knowledge flows that bind the interacting units, that is, who knows whom and who shares what information and how. SNA is focused on uncovering the pattern-ing of people's interaction. SNA is based on the intuition that these patterns are important features of the lives of the individuals who display them. The network analysts believe that how an individual lives depends in large part on how that individual is tied into larger web of social connections. Moreover, many believe that the success or failure of societies and organizations often depends on the pattern-ing of their internal structure, which is guided by formal concept analysis, which is grounded in systematic analysis of the empirical data. With the availability of pow-erful computers and discrete combinatorics (especially graph theory) after 1970, the study of SNA took off as an inter-disciplinary specialty; the applications are found many folds that include: organizational behavior, inter-organizational relations, the spread of contagious diseases, mental health, social support, the diffusion of information, and animal social organization. SNA software provides the researcher with data that can be analyzed to determine the centrality, betweenness, degree, and closeness of each node.

An individual's social network influences his/her social attitude and behavior. Before collecting network data, typically through interviews, it must first be decided as to the kinds of networks and kinds of relations that will be studied:

1. One-mode versus two-mode networks: The former involve relations among a single set of similar actors, while the latter involve relations among two different sets of actors. An example of a two-mode network would be the analysis of a network consisting of private, for-profit organizations and their links to non-profit agencies in a community. Two-mode networks are also used to investigate the relationship between a set of actors and a series of events. For example, although people may not have direct ties to each other, they may attend similar events or activities in a community, and in doing so, this sets up opportunities for the formation of "weak ties."

2. Complete/whole versus ego networks: Complete/whole or Socio-centric networks consist of the connections among members of a single, bounded community. Relational ties among all of the teachers in a high school represent an example of a whole network. Ego/Ego-centric or personal networks are referred to as the ties directly connecting the focal actor, or ego to others, or ego's alters in the network, plus ego's views on the ties among his or her alters. If we asked a teacher to nominate the people he/she socializes with outside of school, and then asked that teacher to indicate who in that network socializes with the others nominated, it is a typical ego network.

   a. Ego-centric network data focus on the network surrounding one node, or in other words, the single social actor. Data are on nodes that share the chosen relation(s) with the ego and on relations between those nodes. Ego network data can be extracted from whole network data by choosing a focal node and examining only nodes connected to this ego. Ego network data, like whole network data, can also include multiple relations; these relations can be collapsed into single networks, as when ties to people who provide companionship and emotional aid are collapsed into a single support network. Unlike whole-network analyses, which commonly focus on one or a small number of networks, ego network analyses typically sample large numbers of egos and their networks.

   b. Complete/whole networks focus on all social actors rather than focusing on the network surrounding any particular actor. These networks begin from a list of included actors and include data on the presence or absence of relations between every pair of actors. When researcher adopts the *whole network* perspective, he/she will inquire each social actor and all other individuals to collect relational data.

Using a network perspective, Mark Granovetter put forward the theory of the "strength-of-weak-ties." Granovetter found in one study that more numerous weak ties can be important in seeking information and innovation. Because cliques have a tendency to have more homogeneous opinions and common traits, individuals in the same cliques would also know more or less what the other members know. To gain new information and opinion, people often look beyond the clique to their other friends and acquaintances.

9.5 Text Analysis

Text analysis is a new and exciting research area that tries to solve the information overload problem by using techniques from data mining, machine learning, natural language processing (NLP), information retrieval (IR), and knowledge management. Text analysis involves the pre-processing of document collections (text categorization, information extraction, term extraction); the storage of the intermediate representations; the techniques to analyze these intermediate representations (such as distribution analysis, clustering, trend analysis, and association rules); and visualization of the results. Text analysis draws on advances made in other computer-science disciplines concerned with the handling of natural language because of the centrality of natural language text to its mission; text analysis exploits techniques and methodologies from the areas of information retrieval, information extraction, and corpus-based computational linguistics.

Since text analysis derives much of its inspiration and direction from seminal research on data mining, there are many high-level architectural similarities between the two systems. For instance, text analysis adopts many of the specific types of patterns in its core knowledge discovery operations, which were first introduced and vetted in data mining research. Further, both types of systems rely on pre-processing routines, pattern-discovery algorithms, and presentation-layer elements such as visualization tools to enhance the browsing of answer sets.

Regarding pre-processing, because data mining assumes that data have already been stored in a structured format, much of its pre-processing focus falls on two critical tasks:

Scrubbing and normalizing data; creating extensive numbers of table joins.

In contrast, for text-analysis systems, pre-processing operations center on the identification and extraction of representative features for natural language documents. These pre-processing operations are responsible for transforming unstructured data stored in document collections into a more explicitly structured intermediate format, which is not a concern relevant for most data mining systems.

The sheer size of document collections makes manual attempts to correlate data across documents, map complex relationships, or identify trends at best extremely labor intensive and at worst nearly impossible to achieve. Automatic methods for identifying and exploring inter-document data relationships dramatically enhance the speed and efficiency of research activities. Indeed, in some cases, automated exploration techniques like those found in text analysis are not just a helpful adjunct but a baseline requirement for researchers to be able, in a practicable way, to recognize subtle patterns across large numbers of natural language documents. Text-analysis systems, however, usually do not run their knowledge discovery algorithms on unprepared document collections. Considerable emphasis in text analysis is devoted to what are commonly referred to as pre-processing operations.

Text-analysis pre-processing operations include a variety of different types of techniques culled and adapted from information retrieval, information extraction, and computational linguistics research that transform raw, unstructured, original-format content (like that which can be downloaded from document collections) into a carefully structured, intermediate data format. Knowledge discovery operations, in turn, are operated against this specially structured intermediate representation of the original document collection.

9.5.1 Defining Text Analysis

Text analysis can be broadly defined as a knowledge-intensive process in which a user interacts with a document collection over time by using a suite of analysis tools. In a manner analogous to data mining, text analysis seeks to extract useful information from data sources through the identification and exploration of interesting patterns. In the case of text analysis, however, the data sources are document collections, and interesting patterns are found not among formalized database records but in the unstructured textual data in the documents in these collections.

9.5.1.1 Document Collection

A document collection can be any grouping of text-based documents. Practically speaking, however, most text-analysis solutions are aimed at discovering patterns across very large document collections. The number of documents in such collections can range from the many thousands to the tens of millions.

Document collections can be either static, in which case the initial complement of documents remains unchanged; or dynamic, which is a term applied to document collections characterized by their inclusion of new or updated documents over time.

Extremely large document collections, as well as document collections with very high rates of document change, can pose performance optimization challenges for various components of a text-analysis system.

9.5.1.2 Document

A document can be very informally defined as a unit of discrete textual data within a collection that usually correlates with some real-world document such as a business report, legal memorandum, e-mail, research paper, manuscript, article, press release, or news story. Within the context of a particular document collection, it is usually possible to represent a class of similar documents with a prototypical document. But a document can (and generally does) exist in any number or type of collections—from the very formally organized to the very ad hoc. A document can also be a member of different document collections or different subsets of the same document collection, and it can exist in these different collections at the same time.

1. A document, as a whole, is seen as a structured object.
2. Documents with extensive and consistent format elements in which field-type metadata can be inferred—such as some e-mail, HTML Web pages, PDF files, and word-processing files with heavy document templating or style-sheet constraints—are described as *semi-structured* documents.
3. Documents that have relatively little in the way of strong typographical, layout, or markup indicators to denote structure—like most scientific research papers, business reports, legal memoranda, and news stories—are referred as *free format* or *weakly structured* documents.

Some text documents, like those generated from a WYSIWYG HTML editor, actually possess from their inception more overt types of embedded metadata in the form of formalized markup tags. On the other hand, even a rather innocuous document demonstrates a rich amount of semantic and syntactical structure, although this structure is implicit and hidden in its textual content. In addition, typographical elements such as punctuation marks, capitalization, numerics, and special characters—particularly when coupled with layout artifacts such as white spacing, carriage returns, underlining, asterisks, tables, columns, and so on—can often serve as a kind of "soft markup" language, providing clues to help identify important document sub-components such as paragraphs, titles, publication dates, author names, table records, headers, and footnotes. Word sequence may also be a structurally meaningful dimension to a document.

9.5.1.3 Document Features

An essential task for most text-analysis systems is the identification of a simplified sub-set of document features that can be used to represent a particular document as a whole. Such a set of features is referred as the *representational model* of a document; features required to represent a document collection tend to become very large, affecting every aspect of a text-analysis system's approach, design, and performance.

The high dimensionality of potentially representative features in document collections is a driving factor in the development of text-analysis pre-processing operations aimed at creating more streamlined representational models. This high dimensionality also indirectly contributes to other conditions that separate text-analysis systems from data mining systems such as greater levels of pattern over-abundance and more acute requirements for post-query refinement techniques. The feature sparsity of a document collection reflects the fact that some features often appear in only a few documents, which means that the support of many patterns is quite low; furthermore, only a small percentage of all possible features for a document collection as a whole appears in any single document.

While evaluating optimal set of features for the representational model for a document collection, the trade-off is between the following two conflicting objectives:

■ To achieve the correct calibration of the volume and semantic level of features to portray the meaning of a document accurately, which tends toward evaluating relatively a larger set of features
■ To identify features in a way that is most computationally efficient and practical for pattern discovery, which tends toward evaluating a smaller set of features

Commonly used document features are described below.

1. Characters: A character-level representation can include the full set of all characters for a document or some filtered sub-set, and this feature space is the most complete of any representation of a real-world text document. The individual component-level letters, numerals, special characters, and spaces are the building blocks of higher-level semantic features such as words, terms, and concepts. Character-based representations that include some level of positional information (e.g., bigrams or trigrams) are more useful and common. Generally, character-based representations can often be unwieldy for some types of text-processing techniques because the feature space for a document is fairly unoptimized.
2. Words: These are word-level features existing in the native feature space of a document. A word-level representation of a document includes a feature for each word within that document—that is the "full text," where a document is represented by a complete and unabridged set of its word-level features. However, most word-level document representations exhibit at least some minimal optimization and therefore consist of sub-sets of representative features devoid of items such as stop words, symbolic characters, meaningless numerics, and so on.
3. Terms: Terms are single words and multi-word phrases selected directly from the corpus of a native document by means of term-extraction methodologies. Term-level features, in the sense of this definition, can only be made up of

specific words and expressions found within the native document for which they are meant to be generally representative. Hence, a term-based representation of a document is necessarily composed of a sub-set of the terms in that document.

Several term-extraction methodologies can convert the raw text of a native document into a series of normalized terms—that is, sequences of one or more tokenized and lemmatized word forms associated with part-of-speech tags. Sometimes an external lexicon is also used to provide a controlled vocabulary for term normalization. Term-extraction methodologies employ various approaches for generating and filtering an abbreviated list of most meaningful candidate terms from among a set of normalized terms for the representation of a document. This culling process results in a smaller but relatively more semantically rich document representation than that found in word-level document representations.

4. Concepts: Concepts are features generated for a document by means of manual, statistical, rule-based, or hybrid categorization methodologies. Concept-level features can be manually generated for documents but are now more commonly extracted from documents using complex pre-processing routines that identify single words, multi-word expressions, whole clauses, or even larger syntactical units that are then related to specific concept identifiers.

Many categorization methodologies involve a degree of cross-referencing against an external knowledge source; for some statistical methods, this source might simply be an annotated collection of training documents. For manual and rule-based categorization methods, the cross-referencing and validation of prospective concept-level features typically involve interaction with a "gold standard" such as a pre-existing domain ontology, lexicon, or formal concept hierarchy—or even just the mind of a human domain expert. Unlike word and term-level features, concept-level features can consist of words not specifically found in the native document.

Term and concept-based representations exhibit roughly the same efficiency but are generally much more efficient than character or word-based document models. Terms and concepts reflect the features with the most condensed and expressive levels of semantic value, and there are many advantages to their use in representing documents for text-analysis purposes. Term-level representations can sometimes be more easily and automatically generated from the original source text (through various term-extraction techniques) than concept-level representations, which, as a practical matter, have often entailed some level of human intervention.

Concept-based representations can be processed to support very sophisticated concept hierarchies and arguably provide the best representations for leveraging the domain knowledge afforded by ontologies and knowledge bases. They are much better than any other feature-set representation at handling synonymy and polysemy and are clearly best at relating a given feature to its various hyponyms and hypernyms. Possible disadvantages of using concept-level features to represent documents include the relative complexity of applying the heuristics, during pre-processing operations, required to extract and validate concept-type features the domain dependence of many concepts.

There are also hybrid approaches to the generation of feature-based document representations. For instance, a particular text-analysis system's pre-processing operations could first extract terms using term-extraction techniques and then match or normalize these terms, or do both, by pruning them against a list of meaningful entities and topics (i.e., concepts) extracted through categorization. However, such hybrid approaches need careful planning, testing, and optimization to avoid a dramatic surge in the feature dimensionality of individual document representations without a corresponding increase in system effectiveness.

9.5.1.4 Domain Knowledge

Text analysis can leverage information from formal external knowledge sources for these domains to greatly enhance elements of their pre-processing, knowledge discovery, and presentation layer operations. A *domain* is defined as a specialized area of interest with dedicated ontologies, lexicons, and taxonomies of information. Domain Knowledge can be used in text-analysis pre-processing operations to enhance concept extraction and validation activities; domain knowledge can play an important role in the development of more meaningful, consistent, and normalized concept hierarchies.

Advanced text-analysis systems can create fuller representations of document collections by relating features by way of lexicons and ontologies in pre-processing operations and can support enhanced query and refinement functionalities. Domain knowledge can be used to inform many different elements of a text-analysis system:

- Domain knowledge is an important adjunct to classification and concept-extraction methodologies in pre-processing operations.
- Domain knowledge can also be leveraged to enhance core mining algorithms and browsing operations.
- Domain-oriented information serves as one of the main bases for search refinement techniques.
- Domain knowledge may be used to construct meaningful constraints in knowledge discovery operations.
- Domain knowledge may also be used to formulate constraints that allow users greater flexibility when browsing large result sets.

9.5.1.5 Search for Patterns and Trends

The problem of pattern over-abundance can exist in all knowledge discovery activities. It is simply aggravated when interacting with large collections of text documents, and, therefore, text-analysis operations must necessarily be conceived to provide not only relevant but also manageable result sets to a user. Although text-analysis pre-processing operations play the critical role of transforming the unstructured content of a raw document collection into a more tractable concept-level data representation, the core functionality of a text-analysis system resides in the analysis of concept co-occurrence patterns across documents in a collection. Indeed, text-analysis systems rely on algorithmic and heuristic approaches to consider distributions, frequent sets, and various associations of concepts at an inter-document level in an effort to enable a user to discover the nature and relationships of concepts as reflected in the collection as a whole.

Text-analysis methods—often based on large-scale, brute-force search directed at large, high-dimensionality feature sets—generally produce very large numbers of patterns. This results in an over-abundance problem with respect to identified patterns that is usually much more severe than that encountered in data-analysis applications aimed at structured data sources. A main operational task for text-analysis systems is to enable a user to limit pattern over-abundance by providing refinement capabilities that key on various specifiable measures of "interestingness" for search results. Such refinement capabilities prevent system users from getting overwhelmed by too many uninteresting results.

9.5.1.6 Results Presentation

Several types of functionality are commonly supported within the front ends of text-analysis systems:

- Browsing: Most contemporary text-analysis systems support browsing that is both dynamic and content-based, for the browsing is guided by the actual textual content of a particular document collection and not by anticipated or rigorously pre-specified structures; user browsing is usually facilitated by the graphical presentation of concept patterns in the form of a hierarchy to aid interactivity by organizing concepts for investigation.
- Navigation: Text-mining systems must enable a user to move across these concepts in such a way as to always be able to choose either a "big picture" view of the collection *in toto* or to drill down on specific concept relationships.
- Visualization: Text-analysis systems use visualization tools to facilitate navigation and exploration of concept patterns; these use various graphical approaches to express complex data relationships. While basic visualization tools generate static maps or graphs that are essentially rigid snapshots of patterns or carefully generated reports displayed on the screen or printed by

an attached printer, state-of-the-art text-analysis systems increasingly rely on highly interactive graphic representations of search results that permit a user to drag, pull, click, or otherwise directly interact with the graphical representation of concept patterns.

■ Query: Languages have been developed to support the efficient parameterization and execution of specific types of pattern discovery queries; these are required because the presentation layer of a text-analysis system really serves as the front end for the execution of the system's core knowledge discovery algorithms. Instead of limiting a user to running only a certain number of fixed, pre-programmed search queries, text-analysis systems are increasingly designed to expose much of their search functionality to the user by opening up direct access to their query languages by means of query language interfaces or command-line query interpreters.

■ Clustering: Text-analysis systems enable clustering of concepts in ways that make the most cognitive sense for a particular application or task.

■ Refinement constraints: Some text-mining systems offer users the ability to manipulate, create, or concatenate refinement constraints to assist in producing more manageable and useful result sets for browsing.

9.6 Sentiment Analysis

Social media systems on the Web have provided excellent platforms to facilitate and enable audience participation, engagement, and community, which has resulted in our new participatory culture. From reviews and blogs to YouTube, Facebook, and Twitter, people have embraced these platforms enthusiastically because they enable their users to freely and conveniently voice their opinions and communicate their views on any subject across geographic and spatial boundaries. They also allow people to easily connect with others and to share their information. This participatory Web and communications revolution has transformed our everyday lives and society as a whole. It has also popularized two major research areas, namely, *social network analysis* and *sentiment analysis*.

Although social network analysis is not a new research area, as it started in the 1940s and 1950s when management science researchers began to study social actors (people in organizations) and their interactions and relationships, social media has certainly fueled its explosive growth in the past 15 years. Sentiment analysis essentially grew out of social media on the Web, which has been very active since the year 2002. Apart from the availability of a large volume of opinion data in social media, opinions and sentiments also have a very wide range of applications simply because opinions are central to almost all human activities. Whenever we need to make a decision, we often seek out others' opinions. This is true not only for individuals but also for organizations. It is thus no surprise that the industry and applications surrounding sentiment analysis have flourished since around 2006.

Because a key function of social media is for people to express their views and opinions, sentiment analysis is right at the center of research and application of social media itself. It is now well recognized that, to extract and exploit information in social media, sentiment analysis is a necessary technology. One can even take a sentiment-centric view of social network analysis, and, in turn, social media content analysis, because the most important information that one wants to extract from the social network or social media content is what people talk about and what their opinions are. These are exactly the core tasks of sentiment analysis.

Social media also allows us to study the participants themselves. We can produce a sentiment profile of each social media participant based on his or her topical interests and opinions about these interests expressed in the users' posts, because a person's topical interests and opinions reflect the nature and preferences of the person. Such information can be used in many applications, for example, recommending products and services and determining which political candidates to vote for. Additionally, social media participants can not only post messages but also interact with one another through discussions and debates, which involve sentiments such as agreement and disagreement (or contention). Discovery of such information is also of great importance. For example, contentious social and political issues and views of opposing positions can be exploited to frame political issues and to predict election results. This necessitates highlighting another attendant problem of imposters gaming the system by posting fake or deceptive opinions to promote some target products, services, and ideological agendas. Detecting such fake or deceptive opinions is an important challenge.

9.6.1 Sentiment Analysis and Natural Language Processing (NLP)

Sentiment analysis, also called *opinion mining*, is the field of study that analyzes people's opinions, sentiments, appraisals, attitudes, and emotions toward entities and their attributes expressed in written text. The entities can be products, services, organizations, individuals, events, issues, or topics. The field represents a large problem space. The term *opinion* is taken to mean the whole concept of sentiment, evaluation, appraisal, or attitude and associated information, such as the opinion target and the person who holds the opinion; and the term *sentiment* is taken to mean the underlying *positive* or *negative* feeling implied by opinion. Sentiment analysis or opinion mining aims to identify positive and negative opinions or sentiments expressed or implied in text and also the targets of these opinions or sentiments.

Sentiment analysis mainly focuses on opinions that express or imply positive or negative or sentiments, also called *positive* or *negative* or *neutral* opinions respectively in everyday language. This type of opinion is similar to the concept of *attitude* in social psychology. Apart from sentiment and opinion, there are also the concepts of *affect*, *emotion*, and *mood*, which are psychological states of mind. Sentences expressing opinions or sentiments, being inherently subjective, are usually subjective sentences, as opposed to objective sentences, which state facts. However, objective sentences can imply positive or negative sentiments of their authors too, because they may describe desirable or undesirable facts.

Sentiment analysis is a semantic analysis problem, but it is highly focused and confined because a sentiment analysis system does not need to fully "understand" each sentence or document; it only needs to comprehend some aspects of it, for example, positive and negative opinions and their targets. Owing to some special characteristics of sentiment analysis, it allows much deeper language analyses to be performed to gain better insights into NLP than in the general setting because the complexity of the general setting of NLP is simply overwhelming. Although general natural language understanding is still far from us, with the concerted effort of researchers from different NLP areas, we may be able to solve the sentiment analysis problem, which, in turn, can give us critical insight into how to deal with general NLP.

The experience in the past 15 years seems to indicate that rather than being a sub-area of NLP, sentiment analysis is actually more like a mini version of the full NLP or a special case of the full-fledged NLP, the reason for this being that sentiment analysis touches every core area of NLP, such as lexical semantics, co-reference resolution, word sense disambiguation, discourse analysis, information extraction, and semantic analysis.

Sentiment analysis is mainly carried out at three levels:

1. Document level: Assuming that each document expresses opinions on a single entity (e.g., a single product or service), document-level sentiment classification indicates whether a whole opinion document expresses a positive or negative sentiment. For instance, given a product review, the system determines whether the review expresses an overall positive or negative opinion about the product.
2. Sentence level: Sentence-level sentiment classification indicates whether each sentence expresses a positive, negative, or neutral opinion. This level of analysis is closely related to subjectivity classification, which distinguishes sentences that express factual information (called *objective sentences*) from sentences that express subjective views and opinions (called *subjective sentences*).
3. Aspect level: If a sentence has multiple opinions, It does not make much sense to classify this sentence as positive or negative because it is positive about one entity but negative about another. To obtain this level of fine-grained

results, we need to go to the aspect level. Instead of looking at language units (documents, paragraphs, sentences, clauses, or phrases), aspect-level analysis directly looks at opinion and its target (called opinion target). Thus, the goal of this level of analysis is to discover sentiments on entities and/or their aspects. On the basis of this level of analysis, a summary of opinions about entities and their aspects can be produced.

There are two different types of opinions:

■ A regular opinion expresses a sentiment about a particular entity or an aspect of the entity; for example, "Orange tastes very good" expresses a positive sentiment or opinion on the aspect taste of Orange. This is the most common type of opinion.
■ A comparative opinion compares multiple entities based on some of their shared aspects, for example, "Mango tastes better than Orange" compares Mango and Orange based on their tastes (an aspect) and expresses a preference for Mango.

Sentiment analysis involves addressing the problems of opinion searching and opinion summarization at appropriate levels.

Sentiment words, also called *opinion words*, are words in a language that indicate desirable or undesirable states. For example, *good*, *great*, and *beautiful* are positive sentiment words, and *bad*, *awful*, and *dreadful* are negative sentiment words. Sentiment words and phrases are instrumental to sentiment analysis. A list of such words and phrases is called a *sentiment lexicon*. Sentiment analysis is usually undertaken in the context of a pre-defined lexicon.

 Initial work in the area of sentiment analysis usually tends to focus on document and sentence-level sentiment and subjectivity classification, which is insufficient for real-life applications. Practical applications almost always demand aspect-level analysis.

9.6.2 Applications

Individuals, organizations, and government agencies are increasingly using the content in social media for decision making. If an individual wants to buy a consumer product, he or she is no longer limited to asking his or her friends and family for opinions because there are many user reviews and discussions in public forums on the Web about the product. For an organization, it may no longer be necessary to conduct surveys, opinion polls, or focus groups to gather public or consumer opinions about the organization's products and services because an abundance of such information is publicly available. Governments can also easily obtain public opinions about their policies and measure the pulses of other nations simply by monitoring their social media.

Sentiment analysis applications have spread to almost every possible domain, from consumer products, healthcare, tourism, hospitality, and financial services to social events and political elections. There are now hundreds of companies in this space, start-up companies and established large corporations, that have built or are in the process of building their own in-house capabilities, such as Google, Microsoft, Hewlett-Packard, Amazon, eBay, SAS, Oracle, Adobe, Bloomberg, and SAP.

A popular application of sentiment analysis is stock-market prediction. The system identifies opinions from message board posts by classifying each post into one of three sentiment classes: bullish (optimistic), bearish (pessimistic), or neutral (neither bullish nor bearish). The resulting sentiments across all stocks were then aggregated and used to predict the stock Index. Instead of using bullish and bearish sentiments, an alternate approach is to identify positive and negative public moods on Twitter and used them to predict the movement of stock market indices such as the Dow Jones, S&P 500, and NASDAQ. The analysis shows that when emotions on Twitter fly high, that is, when people express a lot of hope, fear, or worry, the Dow goes down the next day. When people have less hope, fear, or worry, the Dow goes up.

9.7 Summary

This chapter discussed the characteristics of social media applications and technologies. It started with an introduction to the concept and principles of networks; this was followed with a description of the Internet and the World Wide Web, which enabled the phenomenon of social networks and, consequently, social network analysis. After describing the social networks and the characteristics of social network analysis, it focused on textual analytics as a pre-requisite for sentiment analysis, which is discussed in the later part of the chapter.

Chapter 10

Mobile Applications

A mobile environment is different from traditional distributed environments due to its unique characteristics such as the mobility of users or computers, the limitation of the computing capacity of mobile devices, and the frequent and unpredictable disconnection of wireless networks. Therefore, development of mobile systems is different from development of distributed systems. In other words, when designing a mobile system, we have to overcome challenges due to physical mobility of the clients, the portability features of mobile devices, and the fact that the communication is wireless. Thus, it is important that these issues are examined carefully when considering the system requirements, in terms of both functional and non-functional requirements.

 Functional requirements include all the logical and specific behaviors of a system, while non-functional requirements concern the overall characteristics of the system—like performance, reliability, and security.

The process to identify the requirements of a mobile client server–based system is very different from a non-mobile one. This is due to the unique characteristics of mobile environments, which are the mobility of users or computers, the limitation of the computing capacity of mobile devices, and the frequent and unpredictable disconnections of wireless networks.

10.1 Mobile Computing Applications

A wireless mobile application is defined as a software application, a wireless service, or a mobile service that can be either pushed to users' handheld wireless devices or downloaded and installed, over the air, on these devices.

Such applications must work within the daunting constraints of the mobile devices themselves:

■ Memory: Wireless devices such as cellular phones and two-way pagers have limited amounts of memory, obliging developers to consider memory management most carefully when designing application objects.
■ Processing power: Wireless devices also have limited processing power (16-bit processors are typical).
■ Input: Input capabilities are limited. Most cell phones provide only a one-hand keypad with 12 buttons: the ten numerals, an asterisk (*), and a pound sign (#).
■ Screen: The display might be as small as 96 pixels wide by 54 pixels high and 1 bit deep (black and white). The amount of information that can be squeezed into such a tight screen is severely limited.

The wireless environment itself imposes further constraints:

1. Wireless networks are unreliable and expensive, and bandwidth is low.
2. They tend to experience more network errors than wired networks.
3. The very mobility of wireless devices increases the risk that a connection will be lost or degraded.

In order to design and build reliable wireless applications, designers need to keep these constraints in mind and as also the impact wireless devices with limited resources have on application design.

Wireless applications themselves can be classified into three streams:

1. Browser-based: Applications were developed using a markup language. This is similar to the current desktop browser model where the device is equipped with a browser. The wireless application protocol or WAP follows this approach.
2. Native applications: Compiled applications where the device has a runtime environment to execute applications. Highly interactive wireless applications are only possible with the latter model. Interactive applications, such as mobile computer games, are a good example. Such applications can be developed using the fast growing Java 2 Micro Edition (J2ME) platform, and they are known as MIDlets.
3. Hybrid applications: Applications that aim at incorporating the best aspects of both streams above: the browser is used to allow the user to enter URLs to download native applications from remote servers, and the runtime environment is used to let these applications run on the device.

10.1.1 Generations of Communication Systems

10.1.1.1 1st Generation: Analog

The first generation analog cell phone was a rather bulky piece of equipment. This invention nonetheless was the exciting beginning to cellular technology for the consumer and business marketplace. Though the concept of "mobile" devices for voice communication was truly nothing new in early 1980s, the important technology of leveraging a distinct network of "cells" to enable wireless voice communication was a revolution. The "cell" technology works by assigning multiple base stations to a subset of users, thereby increasing the system's capacity exponentially while reducing power requirements for the user terminals, namely, the analog cell phones. Analog networks can only carry voice and not data. So, it's impossible to send an e-mail or any other type of data element that requires the movement of digital information.

10.1.1.2 2nd Generation: CDMA, TDMA and GSM

The second generation (2G) of wireless and mobile phone technology gave users the capability to send and receive data in a digital format. Digital technology offers many benefits over analog by offering better service to customers (a service operator can fit more information in a transmission), much improved clarity of sound (during voice conversations), higher security, and access to future generation features.

However, it led to the creation of three mutually incompatible networks:

1. CDMA: Code Division Multiple Access (CDMA) is actually a military technology first used during World War II by the English allies to foil German attempts at jamming transmissions. Because Qualcomm Inc. created communications chips for CDMA technology, it was privy to the classified information and became the first to patent and commercialize it. CDMA is a digital cellular technology that uses spread-spectrum techniques. CDMA does not assign a specific frequency to each user; instead, every channel uses the full available spectrum. Individual conversations are encoded with a pseudo-random digital sequence. The architecture of CDMA is such that multiple conversations are transpiring at the same time, sharing the same frequency as other CDMA conversations. The CDMA systems decipher each of the conversations so that each listener understands whom he or she is listening to.

    Advantages of CDMA over analog systems include:
    a. Enhanced privacy through the spreading of voice signals
    b. Improved coverage characteristics, allowing for fewer cell sites
    c. Increased talk time for portables

d. Improved call quality, with better and more consistent sound as compared to AMPS systems
e. Capacity gains of 8–10 times that of AMPS analog systems
f. Simplified system planning through the use of the same frequency in every sector of every cell

2. TDMA: Time Division Multiple Access (TDMA) was released in 1984. It uses the frequency bands available to the wireless network and divides them into time slots, with each phone user having access to one time slot at regular intervals. TDMA exists in North America at both the 800 and 1900 MHz bands. Major US carriers using TDMA are AT&T Wireless Services, BellSouth, and Southwestern Bell. The TDMA architecture works in a "timeslot" format. In other words, one person speaks, and another is listening. For another person to speak, a timeslot (channel) must open up. Only one subscriber is assigned a channel at one time, and no other subscriber can access that same channel until the call is ended. Consequently, the total requirement for the number of channels is very high.

Advantages of TDMA include that

a. TDMA is the most cost-effective technology for upgrading a current analog system to digital.
b. TDMA is the only technology that offers an efficient utilization of hierarchical cell structures (HCSs) offering picocells, microcells, and macrocells. HCSs allow coverage for the system to be tailored to support specific traffic and service needs. By using this approach, system capacities of more than 40 times AMPS can be achieved in a cost-efficient way.
c. Because of its inherent compatibility with analog systems, TDMA allows service compatibility with dual-mode handsets.
d. Unlike spread-spectrum techniques like CDMA, which can suffer from interference among the users all of whom are on the same frequency band and transmitting at the same time, TDMA's technology, which separates users in time, ensures that they will not experience interference from other simultaneous transmissions.
e. TDMA provides the user with extended battery life and talk time because the mobile is only transmitting a portion of the time (from 1/3 to 1/10) of the time during conversations.
f. TDMA installations offer substantial savings in base-station equipment, space, and maintenance, an important factor as cell sizes grow ever smaller.

3. GSM: Global System for Mobile Communications (GSM) is actually based on an improved version of TDMA technology. In 1982, the Conference of European Posts and Telecommunications (CEPT) began the process of creating a digital cellular standard that would allow users to roam from country to country in Europe. By 1987, the GSM standard was created based on a hybrid of FDMA (analog) and TDMA (digital) technologies. GSM engineers

decided to use wider 200 kHz channels instead of the 30 kHz channels that TDMA used, and instead of having only three slots like TDMA, GSM channels had eight slots. This allowed for fast bit rates and more natural-sounding voice-compression algorithms. GSM is currently the only one of the three technologies that provide data services such as e-mail, fax, Internet browsing, and intranet/LAN wireless access, and it's also the only service that permits users to place a call from either North America or Europe. The GSM standard was accepted in the United States in 1995. GSM-1900 cellular systems have been operating in the United States since 1996, with the first network being in the Washington, D.C. area. Major carriers of GSM 1900 include Pacific Bell, BellSouth, and Sprint Spectrum.

 Analog networks still exist today because digital networks like CDMA, TDMA, and GSM cannot readily communicate and interchange information directly with each other. For interchangeable communication, 2G networks have to fall back on 1G analog communication.

10.1.1.3 2.5 Generation: GPRS, EDGE and CDMA 2000

Third-generation networks require a complete overhaul of the wireless network, and the expense to complete the implementation is very high. The 2.5G is actually more of an intermediate solution to third-generation networks. 2.5G networks provide additional functions like

■ Speed of data access
■ Identification of location of the wireless device
■ Ability to access customized information based upon location
■ Ability to store information such as addresses and credit card numbers within personal profiles
■ Ability to facilitate mobile online shopping
■ Full mobility on the Internet
■ Ability to provide business users with access to intranets

2.5G networks are of three types:

1. GPRS: General Packet Radio Services (GPRS) enables true "always-on" capability in the wireless network. Similar to a modem dialing for service to an Internet service provider, in today's cell network, a phone call must be initiated to connect to a network, Similarly, "always-on" can be compared with broadband-wired connections such as DSL (Digital Subscriber Line) or T1 lines and faster connections. However, GPRS only enables speeds in the range of 115 Kbps.

2. EDGE: Enhanced Data Rate for GSM Evolution (EDGE) can simply be defined as a faster version of the GSM wireless service. EDGE technology enables data to be delivered at rates up to 384 Kbps on broadband connections. The standard is based on the GSM standard and uses TDMA multiplexing technology. In essence, the EDGE may enable higher functionality such as the downloading of music and videos over mobile devices.

3. CDMA 2000: Code Division Multiple Access 2000 (CDMA 2000) is essentially a migration or upgrade of the CDMA standard discussed in the second generation section. CDMA 2000 is also an "always-on" technology that offers transmission speeds around 100 Kbps.

10.1.1.4 3rd Generation: wCDMA, UMTS, and iMode

3G mobile communication systems support data rates of over 153.6 Kbps. 3G systems provide the ability to transfer both voice data such as a phone call and non-voice data such as uploading and downloading information, e-mail exchange, and instant messaging. They provide better quality of experience for the users and support multi-media data transfers such as transfer of audio, video, text, and pictures.

3G enables receiving wired Internet features and services at ISDN-like speeds over a mobile handset. Examples of 3G technology include the wideband-CDMA (wCDMA) and Universal Mobile Telecommunication System (UMTS).

10.1.1.5 4th Generation

4G is a fully IP-based integrated system and the Internet work is accomplished with the union of wired and wireless networks, including computers, consumer electronics, communication technology; and the capability to provide 100 Mbps and 1 Gbps, respectively, in outdoor and indoor environments with better quality of service (QoS) and improved security, facilitating any kind of services anytime, anywhere, at affordable cost and single billing (Table 10.1).

10.1.2 Mobile Operating Systems

An Operating System (OS) is a set of programs making the link between the hardware and the software. They manage the processor, the file system, the memory, and the peripherals.

Most of these OS developed for the mobile devices adopt a layered architecture. Some of the common layers are as follows:

■ The Application Suite contains the majority of the applications available in the system. Here we can find browsers, configuration menus, the calendar, and games, among others.

Table 10.1 Evolution of Wireless Networks

Generation	1G	2G	2.5G	3G	4G
Starting time	1985	1992	1995	2002	2010–2012
Driven technique	Analogue signal Processing	Digital signal processing	Packet switching	Intelligent signal processing	Intelligent software auto configuration
Representative standard	AMPS, TAGS, NMT	GSM, TDMA	GPRS, I-Mode, HSCSD, EDGE	IMT-2000 (UMTS, wCDMA CDMA2000)	OFDM, UWB
Radio frequency (Hz)	400 M–800 M	800 M–900 M	1800 M–1900 M	2G	3G–5G
Bandwidth (bps)	2.4 kbps–30 kbps	9.6 kbps–14.4 kbps	171 kbps–384 kbps	2 Mbps–5 Mbps	10 Mbps–20 Mbps
Multi-address technique	FDMA	TDMA, CDMA	TDMA, CDMA	CDMA	FDMA, TDMA, CDMA
Cellular coverage	Large area	Medium area	Medium area	Small area	Mini area
Core networks	Telecom networks	Telecom networks	Telecom networks	Telecom networks, some IP networks	All-IP networks
Service type	Voice Mono-service Person-to-person	Voice, SMS Mono-media Person-to-person	Data service	Voice, data Some multimedia Person-to-machine	Multimedia Machine-to-machine

- The User Interface layer furnishes the graphical environment of each system.
- The Application Execution Environment offers Application Programming Interfaces (API) for the development of new applications.
- The Middleware is a transparent layer making the link to the peripherals through software libraries.
- The Kernel is the core of the operating system where, among others, we can find the hardware, memory, and file system drivers. It is also responsible for proper process management.

10.1.2.1 Symbian

The Symbian Foundation it is a non-profit organization that started its activity in 1998, supported by a set of manufacturers with the goal of licensing a software platform (which is based on Symbian OS) for mobile devices.

This OS supports 2G and 3G technology and communications protocols like WAP (Wireless Application Protocol), TCP, IPv4, and IPv6. At the PAN level, Symbian OS supports irDA, Bluetooth, and USB. It provides also multi-task and multi-thread and the ability to work with the different types of phones, either they be numeric, alpha-numeric or touch screen. In addition to the telephony services, Symbian OS also supports others as Short Message Service (SMS), Enhanced Messaging Service (EMS), and Multimedia Messaging Service (MMS), videoconferencing, and the ability to switch between networks.

Navigation, agenda, e-mail, fax, and a word processor are some of the applications developed for this OS.

10.1.2.2 BlackBerry OS

Research In Motion® (RIM) is a Canadian designer, manufacturer, and marketer of wireless solutions for the worldwide mobile communications market. Products include the BlackBerry wireless e-mail solution, wireless handhelds, and wireless modems. RIM is the driving force behind BlackBerry smart phones and the BlackBerry solution. RIM provides a proprietary multi-tasking OS for the BlackBerry, which makes heavy use of the device's specialized input devices, particularly the scroll wheel or, more recently, the trackball.

BlackBerry offers the best combination of mobile phone, server software, push e-mail, and security from a single vendor. It integrates well with other platforms, it works with several carriers, and it can be deployed globally for the sales force that is on the move. It is easy to manage, has a longer than usual battery life, and has a small form-factor with an easy-to-use keyboard. BlackBerry is good for access to some of the simpler applications, such as contact list, time management, and field force applications.

10.1.2.3 Google Android

Google's Android Mobile platform is the latest mobile platform on the block. This open-source development platform is built on the Linux kernel, and it includes an operating system (OS), middleware stack, and a number of mobile applications. Enterprises will benefit from Android because the availability of open-source code for the entire software stack will allow the existing army of Linux developers to create special-purpose applications that will run on a variety of mobile devices.

The Android is the open-source mobile OS launched by Google. It is intuitive, user friendly, and graphically similar to the iPhone and BlackBerry. Being open source, the Android applications may be cheaper and the spread of the Android possibly will increase. The Kernel is based on the Linux v 2.6 and supports 2G, 3G, Wi-Fi, IPv4, and IPv6.

At the multimedia level, Android works with OpenGL and several image, audio, and video formats. The persistence is assured with the support of the SQLite. Regarding security, the Android uses SSL and encryption algorithms.

If Android makes it into phones designed specifically for the enterprise, those products will have to include technology from the likes of Sybase, Intellisync, or another such company to enable security features like remote data wipe functionality and forced password changes.

10.1.2.4 Apple iOS

iPhone OS is the Apple proprietary OS used in the Macintosh machines; an optimized version is used in the iPhone and iPod Touch.

The simplicity and robustness provided either in the menus navigation or in the application' navigation are two of the main potentialities of the OS. iPhone OS is also equipped with good quality multimedia software, including games, music, and video players. It has also a good set of tools, including imaging editing and word processor.

10.1.2.5 Windows Phone

The Windows Mobile, variant of the Windows CE (also known officially as Windows Embedded Compact), was developed initially for the Pocket PCs but by 2002 was incorporated in HTC2 mobile phones. This OS was engineered to offer data and multimedia services. By 2006, Windows Mobile had become available for the developers' community. Many new applications started using the system, turning Windows Mobile in one of the most used systems.

Windows Mobile comes in two flavors. A smartphone edition is good for wireless e-mail, calendaring, and voice notes. A Pocket PC edition adds mobile versions of Word, Excel, PowerPoint, and Outlook. Palms Treo 700w, with the full functionality of the Pocket PC edition, is a better choice for sales-force professionals. The main draw of the Windows Mobile operating system is its maker Microsoft.

Windows Mobile also actively syncs to the Exchange and SQL servers. This augurs very well for use by the sales force. Mobile sales-force solutions for Windows Mobile are available from companies like SAP, Siebel, PeopleSoft, and Salesforce.com as well as other leading solution providers.

Windows Mobile permits Bluetooth connections through the interface Winsock. It also allows 902.11x, IPv4, IPv6, VoIP (Voice over IP), GSM and CDMA (Code Division Multiple Access) connections.

Some of the main applications available are the Pocket Outlook (adapted version of the Outlook for Desktops), Word, and Excel. It provides also Messenger, Browser and remote desktop. The remote desktop is an easy way of access to other mobile or fixed terminals. ActiveSync application facilitates the synchronization between the mobile devices and the desktops. At the multimedia level, Windows Mobile reproduces music, video, and 3D applications. Security is also a concern, so Secure Socket Layer (SSL), Kerberos and the use of encryption algorithms are available (Table 10.2).

Table 10.2 Comparison of Mobile Operating Systems

Mobile OS	Android	BlackBerry OS	iOS	Windows Phone
Provider (Major Company)	Open Handheld Alliance	RIM	Apple	Microsoft
Development Language	Java	Java	Objective C/C++	Visual C++
Kernel Type	Linux	Unix	Hybrid	Windows CE 6/7
IDLs, Libraries, Frameworks	Android SDK; ADT plug-in for Eclipse	BlackBerry IDE	iPhone SDK	Windows Phone SDK (works with Visual Studio)
Source Model	Open	Closed	Closed (open for the core)	Closed
Initial release	2008	1999	2007	2010
Latest Version as of December 2013	4.4 KitKat	7.1	7	8
Mobile Application Store	Google Play	BlackBerry World	App Store	Windows Phone Store

10.2 Mobile Web Services

Web Services (WS) are the cornerstone toward building a global distributed information system, in which many individual applications will take part; building a powerful application whose capability is not limited to local resources will unavoidably require interacting with other partner applications through WSs across the Internet. The strengths of WSs come from the fact that WSs use XML and related technologies connecting business applications based on various computers and locations with various languages and platforms. The counterpart of the WS in the context of mobile business processes would be mobile WS (MWS).

The proposed MWS are to be the base of the communications between the Internet network and wireless devices such as mobile phones, PDAs, and so forth. The integration between wireless device applications and other applications would be a very important step toward global enterprise systems. Similar to WS, MWS is also based on the industry-standard language XML and related technologies such as SOAP, WSDL, and UDDI.

Many constraints make the implementation of WSs in a mobile environment very challenging. The challenge comes from the fact that mobile devices have smaller power and capacities as follows:

- Small power limited to a few hours
- Small memory capacity
- Small processors not big enough to run larger applications
- Small screen size, especially in mobile phones, which requires developing specific websites with suitable size
- Small keypad that makes it harder to enter data
- Small hard disk
- The speed of the data communication between the device and the network, and that varies

The most popular MWS is a proxy-based system where the mobile device connects to the Internet through a proxy server. Most of the processing of the business logic of the mobile application will be performed on the proxy server, which transfers the results to the mobile device that is mainly equipped with a user interface to display output on its screen. The other important advantage a proxy server provides in MWS is that, instead of connecting the client application residing on the mobile device to many service providers and consuming most of the mobile processor and the bandwidth, the proxy will communicate with service providers, do some processing, and send back only the final result to the mobile device. In the realistic case where the number of mobile devices becomes in the range of tens of millions, the proxy server would be on the cloud and the service providers would be the cloud service providers.

MWS use existing industry-standard XML-based WS architecture to expose mobile network services to the broadest audience of developers. Developers will be able to access and integrate mobile network services such as messaging, location-based content delivery, syndication, personalization, identification, authentication, and billing services into their applications. This will ultimately enable solutions that work seamlessly across stationary networks and mobile environments. Customers will be able to use MWS from multiple devices on both wired and wireless networks.

The aim of the MWS effort is twofold:

1. To create a new environment that enables the IT industry and the mobile industry to create products and services that meet customer needs in a way not currently possible within the existing WS practices. With WSs being widely deployed as the SOA of choice for internal processes in organizations, there is also an emerging demand for using WS-enabling mobile working and e-business. By integrating WS and mobile computing technologies, consistent business models can be enabled on a broad array of endpoints, not just on mobile devices operating over mobile networks but also on servers and computing infrastructure operating over the Internet. To make this integration happen at a technical level, mechanisms are required to expose and leverage existing mobile network services. Also, practices for how to integrate the various business needs of the mobile network world and their associated enablers such as security must be developed. The result is a framework, such as the Open Mobile Alliance, that demonstrates how the WS specifications can be used and combined with mobile computing technology and protocols to realize practical and interoperable solutions.

   Successful mobile solutions that help architect customers' service infrastructures need to address security availability and scalability concerns both at the functional level and at the end-to-end solution level, rather than just offering fixed-feature products. What is required is a standard specification and an architecture that tie together service discovery, invocation, authentication, and other necessary components—thereby adding context and value to WS. In this way, operators and enterprises will be able to leverage the unique capabilities of each component of the end-to-end network and shift the emphasis of service delivery from devices to the human user. Using a combination of wireless, broadband, and wireline devices, users can then access any service on demand with a single identity and single set of service profiles, personalizing service delivery as dictated by the situation. There are three important requirements to accomplish user (mobile subscriber)–focused delivery of mobile services: federated identity, policy, and federated context.

   Integrating identity, policy, and context into the overall mobile services architecture enables service providers to differentiate the user from the device and to deliver the right service to the right user on virtually any device:

a. Federated identity: In a mobile environment, users are not seen as individuals (e.g., mobile subscribers) to software applications and processes who are tied to a particular domain but rather as entities that are free to traverse multiple service networks. This requirement demands a complete federated network identity model to tie the various personas of an individual without compromising privacy or loss of ownership of the associated data. The federated network identity model allows the implementation of seamless single sign-on for users interacting with applications (Nokia 2004). It also ensures that user identity, including transactional information and other personal information, is not tied to a particular device or service but rather is free to move with the user between service providers. Furthermore, it guarantees that only appropriately authorized parties are able to access protected information.

b. Policy: User policy, including roles and access rights, is an important requirement for allowing users not only to have service access within their home network but also to move outside it and still receive the same access to services. Knowing who the user is and what role they fulfill at the moment they are using a particular service is essential to providing the right service at the right instance. The combination of federated identity and policy enables service providers and users to strike a balance between access rights and user privacy

c. Federated context: Understanding what the user is doing, what they ask, why it is being requested, where they are, and what device they are using is an essential requirement. The notion of federated context means accessing and acting upon a user's current location, availability, presence, and role, for example, at home, at work, on holiday, and other situational attributes. This requires the intelligent synthesis of information available from all parts of the end-to-end network and allows service providers and enterprises to deliver relevant and timely applications and services to end users in a personalized manner. For example, information about the location and availability of a user's device may reside on the wireless network, the user's calendar may be on the enterprise intranet, and preferences may be stored in a portal.

2. To help create WS standards that will enable new business opportunities by delivering integrated services across stationary (fixed) and wireless networks. MWS use existing industry-standard XML-based WS architecture to expose mobile network services to the broadest audience of developers. Developers will be able to access and integrate mobile network services such as messaging, location-based content delivery, syndication, personalization, identification, authentication, and billing services into their applications. This will ultimately enable solutions that work seamlessly across stationary networks and mobile environments. Customers will be able to use mobile WS from multiple devices on both wired and wireless networks.

Delivering appealing, low-cost mobile data services, including ones that are based on mobile Internet browsing and mobile commerce, is proving increasingly difficult to achieve. The existing infrastructure and tools as well as the interfaces between Internet/Web applications and mobile network services remain largely fragmented, characterized by tightly coupled, costly, and close alliances between value-added service providers and a complex mixture of disparate and sometimes overlapping standards (WAP, MMS, Presence, Identity, etc.) and proprietary models (e.g., propriety interfaces). This hinders inter-operability solutions for the mobile sector and at the same time drives up the cost of application development and ultimately the cost of services offered to mobile users. Such problems have given rise to initiatives for standardizing mobile WS. The most important of these initiatives are the Open Mobile Alliance and the mobile WS frameworks that are examined below:

The Open Mobile Alliance (www.openmobilealliance.org) is a group of wireless vendors, IT companies, mobile operators, and application and content providers who have come together to drive the growth of the mobile industry. The objective of OMA is to deliver open technical specifications for the mobile industry, based on market requirements, that enable interoperable solutions across different devices, geographies, service providers, operators, and networks. OMA includes all key elements of the wireless value chain and contributes to the timely availability of mobile service enablers. For enterprises already using a multi-tiered network architecture based on open technologies such as WS, which implement wireless services, OMA is a straightforward extension of existing wireline processes and infrastructures. In this way, wireless services become simply another delivery channel for communication, transactions, and other value-added services. Currently, the OMA is defining core services such as location, digital rights, and presence services and is using cases involving mobile subscribers, mobile operators, and service providers; an architecture for the access and deployment of core services; and a WS framework for using secure SOAP.

The technical working groups within OMA address the need to support standardized interactions. To achieve this, the OMA is currently addressing how mobile operators can leverage WS and defines a set of common protocols, schemas, and processing rules using WS technologies that are the elements that can be used to create or interact with a number of different services. The OMA Web Services Enabler (OWSER) specification capitalizes on all the benefits of WS technologies to simplify the task of integrators, developers, and implementers of service enablers by providing them with common mechanisms and protocols for interoperability of service enablers. Examples of functionality common across service enablers range from transport and message encoding definitions to security concerns, service discovery, charging, definition, and management of Service Level Agreements (SLAs), as well as management, monitoring, and provisioning of the service enablers that exist within a service provider's network.

The OMA WS interfaces are intended to enhance a service provider's data for a particular mobile subscriber. A common scenario starts with a data request from some application (perhaps a mobile browser) to a service provider. The service provider then uses WS to interact with a subscriber's mobile operator to retrieve some relevant data about the subscriber, such as location or presence. This data can be used to enhance the service provider's response to the initial request. Mobile WS are envisioned to support server-to-server, server-to-mobile terminal, mobile terminal-to-server, and mobile terminal-to-mobile terminal (or peer-to-peer) interactions.

Similarly, the objective of the MWS framework is to meet the requirements for bridging stationary enterprise infrastructure and the mobile world, and it enables the application of WS specifications, SOA implementations, and tools to the problem of exposing mobile network services in a commercially viable way to the mass market of developers. The focus of the work concentrates on mechanisms to orchestrate the calls to MWS.

The MWS framework places particular emphasis on core mechanisms such as security, authentication, and payment. Core security mechanisms are offered that apply WS-Security to mobile network security services, such as the use of a GSM-style SIM security device within a WS end point to provide a means for authentication. In addition, a set of core payment mechanisms within the WS architecture have been proposed that understand how to interact with the participating WS end points. It is expected that a number of services dependent on the mobile WS framework and that rely on its core mechanisms will be developed. SMS services, MMS services, and location-based services have been identified as common services that are candidates for specification activity. Specification work will include profiling and optimization of the core WS protocols so that they can easily be realized over any bearer, on any device, or both. This addresses the inefficiencies that current WS specifications exhibit when used over a narrowband and possibly intermittent bearer or when being processed by a low-performance mobile device.

10.2.1 Mobile Field Cloud Services

Companies that can outfit their employees with devices like PDAs, laptops, multifunction smartphones, or pagers will begin to bridge the costly chasm between the field and the back office. For example, transportation costs for remote employees can be significantly reduced, and productivity can be significantly improved by eliminating needless journeys back to the office to file reports, collect parts, or simply deliver purchase orders.

Wireless services are evolving toward the goal of delivering the right cloud service to whoever needs it, for example, employees, suppliers, partners, and customers, at the right place, at the right time, and on any device of their choice. The combination of wireless handheld devices and cloud service delivery technologies poses the opportunity for an entirely new paradigm of information access that, in the enterprise context, can substantially reduce delays in the transaction and fulfillment process and lead to improved cash flow and profitability.

A field cloud services solution automates, standardizes, and streamlines manual processes in an enterprise and helps centralize disparate systems associated with customer service life-cycle management including customer contact, scheduling and dispatching, mobile workforce communications, resource optimization, work order management, time, labor, material tracking, billing, and payroll. A field WS solution links seamlessly all elements of an enterprise's field service operation—customers, service engineers, suppliers, and the office—to the enterprise's stationary infrastructure, wireless communications, and mobile devices. Field WS provide real-time visibility and control of all calls and commitments, resources, and operations. They effectively manage business activities such as call taking and escalation, scheduling and dispatching, customer entitlements and SLAs, work orders, service contracts, time sheets, labor and equipment tracking, pre-invoicing, resource utilization, reporting, and analytics.

> Cloud service optimization solutions try to automatically match the most cost-effective resource with each service order based on prioritized weightings assigned to every possible schedule constraint. To accommodate evolving business priorities, most optimization solutions allow operators to reorder these weightings and to execute *ad hoc* what-if scenario analyses to test the financial and performance impacts of scheduling alternatives. In this way, they help enhance supply-chain management by enabling real-time response to changing business conditions.

Of particular interest to field services are location-based services, notification services, and service disambiguation, as these mechanisms enable developers to build more sophisticated cloud service applications by providing accessible interfaces to advanced features and intelligent mobile features:

1. Location-based services provide information specific to a location using the latest positioning technologies and are a key part of the mobile Web Services suite. Dispatchers can use GPS or network-based positioning information to determine the location of field workers and optimally assign tasks (push model) based on geographic proximity. Location-based services and applications enable enterprises to improve operational efficiencies by locating, tracking, and communicating with their field workforce in real time. For example, location-based services can be used to keep track of vehicles and employees, whether they are conducting service calls or delivering products. Trucks

could be pulling in or out of a terminal, visiting a customer site, or picking up supplies from a manufacturing or distribution facility. With location-based services, applications can get such things such as real-time status alerts, for example, estimated time of approach, arrival, and departure; duration of stop; and current information on traffic, weather, and road conditions for both home-office and en-route employees.

2. Notification services allow critical business to proceed uninterrupted when employees are away from their desks by delivering notifications to their preferred mobile device. Employees can thus receive real-time notification when critical events occur, such as when incident reports are completed. The combination of location-based and notification services provides added value by enabling such services as proximity-based notification and proximity-based actuation. Proximity-based notification is a push or pull interaction model that includes targeted advertising, automatic airport check-in, and sightseeing information. Proximity-based actuation is a push–pull interaction model whose most typical example is payment based on proximity, for example, toll watch.

3. Service instance disambiguation helps distinguish between many similar candidate service instances, which may be available inside close perimeters. For instance, there may be many on-device payment services in proximity of a single point of sale. Convenient and natural ways for identifying appropriate service instances are then required, for example, relying on closeness or pointing rather than identification by cumbersome unique names.

10.3 Context-Aware Mobile Applications

A mobile application is context aware if it uses context to provide relevant information to users or to enable services for them; relevancy depends on a user's current task (and activity) and profile (and preferences). Apart from knowing who the users are and where they are, we need to identify what they are doing, when they are doing it, and which object they focus on. The system can define user activity by taking into account various sensed parameters like location, time, and the object used. In outdoor applications, and depending on the mobile devices that are used, satellite-supported technologies like GPS or network-supported cell information like GSM, IMTS, and WLAN are applied. Indoor applications use RFID, IrDA, and Bluetooth technologies in order to estimate the users' position in space. While time is another significant parameter of context that can play an important role in order to extract information on user activity, the objects that are used in mobile applications are the most crucial context sources.

In mobile applications, the user can use mobile devices, like mobile phones and PDAs and objects that are enhanced with computing and communication abilities. Sensors attached to artifacts provide applications with information about what the user is utilizing. In order to present the user with the requested information in the best possible form, the system has to know the physical properties of the artifact that will be used (e.g., the artifact screen's display characteristics); the types of interaction interfaces that an artifact provides to the user need to be modeled (e.g., whether the artifact can be handled by both speech and touch techniques); and the system must know how it is designed. Thus, the system has to know the number of each artifact's sensors and their position in order to gradate context information with a level of certainty. Based on information on the artifact's physical properties and capabilities, the system can extract information on the services that they can provide to the user.

In the context-aware mobile applications, artifacts are considered as context providers. They allow users to access context in a high-level abstracted form, and they inform other application's artifacts so that context can be used according to the application needs. Users are able to establish associations between the artifacts based on the context that they provide; keep in mind that the services enabled by artifacts are provided as context. Thus, users can indicate their preferences, needs, and desires to the system by determining the behavior of the application via the artifacts they create. The set of sensors attached to an artifact measure various parameters such as location, time, temperature, proximity, and motion—the raw data given by its sensors determine the low-level context of the artifact. The aggregation of such low-level context information from various homogenous and non-homogenous sensors results in a high-level context information.

10.3.1 Ontology-Based Context Model

This ontology is divided into two layers: a common one that contains the description of the basic concepts of context-aware applications and their interrelations representing the common language among artifacts, and a private one that represents an artifact's own description as well as the new knowledge or experience acquired from its use. The common ontology defines the basic concepts of a context-aware application; such an application consists of a number of artifacts and their associations. The concept of artifact is described by its physical properties and its communication and computational capabilities; the fact that an artifact has a number of sensors and actuators attached is also defined in our ontology. Through the sensors, an artifact can perceive a set of parameters based on which the state of the artifact is defined; an artifact may also need these parameters in order to sense its interactions with other artifacts as well as with the user. The ontology also defines the interfaces via which artifacts may be accessed in order to enable the selection of the appropriate one. The common ontology represents an abstract form of the concepts represented, especially of the context parameters, as more detailed descriptions are stored in each artifact's private ontology. For instance, the private ontology of an artifact that represents a car contains a full description of the different components in a car as well as their types and their relations.

The basic goal of the proposed ontology-based context model is to support a context management process based on a set of rules that determine the way in which a decision is made and are applied to existing knowledge represented by this ontology. The rules that can be applied during such a process belong to the following categories: rules for an artifact's state assessment that define the artifact's state based on its low and high-level contexts, rules for local decisions that exploit an artifact's knowledge only in order to decide the artifact's reaction (like the request or the provision of a service), and, finally, rules for global decisions that take into account various artifacts' states and their possible reactions in order to preserve a global state defined by the user.

10.3.2 Context Support for User Interaction

The ontology-based context model that we propose empowers users to compose their own personal mobile applications. In order to compose their applications, they first have to select the artifacts that will participate and establish their associations. They set their own preferences by associating artifacts, denoting the sources of context that artifacts can exploit, and defining the interpretation of this context through rules in order to enable various services. As the context acquisition process is decoupled from the context management process, users are able to create their own mobile applications, avoiding the problems emerging from the adaptation and customization of applications like disorientation and system failures.

The goal of context in computing environments is to improve interaction between users and applications. This can be achieved by exploiting context, which works like implicit commands and enables applications to react to users or surroundings without the users' explicit commands. Context can also be used to interpret explicit acts, making interaction much more efficient. Thus, context-aware computing completely redefines the basic notions of interface and interaction. In this section, we present how our ontology-based context model enables the use of context in order to assist human–computer interaction in mobile applications and to achieve the selection of the appropriate interaction technique. Mobile systems have to provide multi-modal interfaces so that users can select the most suitable technique based on their context. The ontology-based context model that we presented in the previous section captures the various interfaces provided by the application's artifacts in order to support and enable such selections. Similarly, the context can determine the most appropriate interface when a service is enabled. Ubiquitous and mobile interfaces must be proactive in anticipating needs, while at the same time working as a spatial and contextual filter for information so that the user is not inundated with requests for attention.

Context can also assist designers to develop mobile applications and manage various interfaces and interaction techniques that would enable more satisfactory and faster closure of transactions. Easiness is an important requirement for mobile applications; by using context according to our approach, designers are abstracted from the difficult task of context acquisition and have merely defined how context is exploited from various artifacts by defining simple rules. Our approach presents an infrastructure capable of handling, substituting, and combining complex interfaces when necessary. The rules applied to the application's context and the reasoning process support the application's adaptation. The presented ontology-based context model is easily extended; new devices, new interfaces, and novel interaction techniques can be exploited into a mobile application by simply incorporating their descriptions in the ontology.

10.4 Mobile Web 2.0

Mobile Web 2.0 results from the convergence of the Web 2.0 services and the proliferation of Web-enabled mobile devices. Web 2.0 enables to facilitate interactive information sharing, inter-operability, user-centered design, and collaboration among users. This convergence is leading to a new communication paradigm, where mobile devices act not only as mere consumers of information but also as complex carriers for getting and providing information and as platforms for novel services.

Mobile Web 2.0 represents both an opportunity for creating novel services and an extension of Web 2.0 applications to mobile devices. The management of user-generated content, of content personalization, and of community and information sharing is much more challenging in a context characterized by devices with limited capabilities in terms of display, computational power, storage, and connectivity. Furthermore, novel services require support for real-time determination and communication of the user position.

Mobile Web 2.0 are constituted of

1. Sharing services that are characterized by the publication of contents to be shared with other users. Sharing services offer the users the capability to store, organize, search, and manage heterogeneous contents. These contents may be rated, commented on, tagged, and shared with specified users or groups that can usually visualize the stored resources chronologically; by category, rating, or tags; or via a search engine. Multimedia sharing services are related to sharing of multimedia resources, such as photos or videos. These resources are typically generated by the users who exploit the sharing service to upload and publish their own contents. Popular examples of Web portals offering a multimedia sharing service include Flickr, YouTube, Mocospace, and so on.
2. Social services, which refer to the management of social relationships among the users. This is constituted of services like
   a. Community management services enable registered users to maintain a list of contact details of people they know. Their key feature is the possibility of creating and updating a personal profile, including information such as user preferences and his or her list of contacts. These contacts

may be used in different ways depending on the purpose of the service, which may range from the creation of a personal network of business and professional contacts (e.g., LinkedIn) to the management of social events (e.g., Meetup) and up to the connection with old and new friends (e.g., Facebook).

b. Blogging services enable a user to create and manage a blog, that is, a sort of personal online journal, possibly focused on a specific topic of interest. Blogs are usually created and managed by an individual or a limited group of people, namely author(s), through regular entries of heterogeneous content, including text, images, and links to other resources related to the main topic, such as other blogs, Web pages, or multimedia contents. A blog is not a simple online journal, because the large majority of blogs allow external comments on the entries. The final effect is the creation of a discussion forum that engages readers and builds a social community around a person or a topic. Other related services may also include blogrolls (i.e., links to other blogs that the author reads) to indicate social relationships to other bloggers. Among the most popular portals that allow users to manage their own blog, we cite BlogSpot, Wordpress, and so on.

c. Microblogging services are characterized by very short message exchanges among the users. Although this class of services originates from the blogging category, there are important differences between microblogging and traditional blogs, namely, the size of the exchanged messages is significantly smaller, the purpose of microblogging is to capture and communicate instantaneous thoughts or feelings of the users, and the recipient of the communication may differ from that of traditional blogs because microblogging allows authors to interact with a group of selected friends. Twitter is an example of portals providing microblogging services.

3. Location services that tailor information and contents on the basis of the user location. The knowledge of the user's current location may be exploited in several ways to offer value-added services.

a. People discovery services, which enable locating user friends; usually these services plot the position of the user and his or her friends on a map; the geographical location of the users is uploaded to the system by means of a positioning system installed on the user mobile devices.

b. Points of interest (POIs) discovery exploits geographical information to locate POIs, such as events, restaurants, museums, and any kind of attractions that may be useful or interesting for a user. These services offer the users a list of nearby POIs selected on the basis of their personal preferences and specifications. POIs are collected by exploiting collaborative recommendations from other users that may add a new POI by uploading its geographical location, possibly determined through a GPS positioning system installed on the mobile device. Users may also upload short descriptions, comments, tags, and images or videos depicting the place.

10.5 Mobile Analytics

The objectives of mobile analytics are twofold: prediction and description—prediction of unknown or future values of selected variables, such as interests or location of mobiles; and description in terms of human behavior patterns. Description involves gaining "insights" into mobile behaviors, whereas prediction involves improving decision making for brands, marketers, and enterprises. This can include the modeling of sales, profits, effectiveness of marketing efforts, and the popularity of apps and a mobile site. The key is to realize the data that is being aggregated and determining how to not only create and issue metrics on mobile activity, but also, more importantly, how to leverage it via the data mining of mobile devices to improve sales and revenue.

For years, retailers have been testing new marketing and media campaigns, new pricing promotions, and the merchandizing of new products with freebies and half-price deals, as well as a combination of all of these offers, in order to improve sales and revenue. With mobiles, it has become increasingly easy to generate the data and metrics for mining and precisely calibrating consumer behaviors.

Brands and companies leveraging mobile analytics can be more adept at identifying, co-opting, and shaping consumer behavior patterns to increase profits. Brands and mobile marketers that figure out how to induce new habits can enhance their bottom lines. Inducing a new habit loop can be used to introduce new products, services, and content via the offer of coupons or deals based on the location of mobiles.

10.5.1 Mobile Site Analytics

Mobile site analytics can help the brand and companies solve the mystery of how mobile consumers are engaging and interacting with their site. Without dedicated customer experience metrics, brands, marketers, and companies cannot tell whether the mobile site experience actually got better or how changes in the quality of that experience affected the site's business performance. Visitors tend to focus on three basic things when evaluating a mobile site: usefulness, ease of use, and how enjoyable it is. Metrics should measure these criteria with completion rates and survey questions.

10.5.2 Mobile Clustering Analysis

Clustering is the partition of a dataset into subsets of "similar" data, without using a priori knowledge about properties or existence of these subsets. For example, a clustering analysis of mobile site visitors might discover a high propensity for Android devices to make higher amounts of purchases of, say, Apple mobiles. Clusters can be mutually exclusive (disjunct) or overlapping. Clustering can lead to the autonomous discovery of typical customer profiles.

Clustering detection is the creation of models that find mobile behaviors that are similar to each other; these clumps of similarity can be discovered using SOM software to find previously unknown patterns in mobile datasets. Unlike classification software, which analyzes for predicting mobile behaviors, clustering is different in that the software is "let loose" on the data; there are no targeted variables. Instead, it is about exploratory autonomous knowledge discovery. The clustering software automatically organizes itself around the data with the objective of discovering some meaningful hidden structures and patterns of mobile behaviors. This type of clustering can be done to discover key words or mobile consumer clusters, and it is a useful first step for mining mobiles. It allows for the mapping of mobiles into distinct clusters of groups without any human bias.

Clustering is often performed as a prelude to the use of classification analysis using rule-generating or decision-tree software for modeling mobile device behaviors.

Market-basket analysis using a SOM is useful in situations where the marketer or brand wants to know what items or mobile behaviors occur together or in a particular sequence or pattern. The results are informative and actionable because they can lead to the organization of offers, coupons, discounts, and the offering of new products or services that, prior to the analysis, were unknown.

Clustering analyses can lead to answers to such questions as why products or services sell together, or who is buying what combinations of products or services; they can also map what purchases are made and when. Unsupervised knowledge discovery occurs when one cluster is compared to another and new insight is revealed. For example, SOM software can be used to discover clusters of locations, interests, models, operating systems, mobile site visitors, and app downloads, thus enabling a marketer or developer to discover unique features of different consumer mobile groupings.

10.5.3 Mobile Text Analysis

Another technology that can be used for data mining mobile devices is text mining, which refers to the process of deriving, extracting, and organizing high-quality information from unstructured content, such as texts, e-mails, documents, messages, comments, and so on. Text mining means extracting meaning from social media and customer comments about a brand or company in mobile sites and app reviews.

This is a different variation of clustering programs; text-mining software is commonly used to sort through unstructured content that can reside in millions of e-mails, chat, Web forums, texts, tweets, blogs, and so on that daily and continuously accumulate in mobile sites and mobile servers.

Text analytics generally includes such tasks as

■ Categorization of taxonomies
■ Clustering of concepts
■ Entity and information extraction
■ Sentiment analysis
■ Summarization

Text analytics is important to the data mining of mobile devices because, increasingly, companies, networks, mobile sites, enterprises, and app servers are accumulating a large percentage of their data in unstructured formats, which is impossible to analyze and categorize manually. Text mining refers to the process of deriving an understanding from unstructured content through the division of clustering patterns and the extraction of categories or mobile trends using machine learning algorithms for the organization of key concepts from unstructured content.

Text mining can be used to gain new insight into unstructured content from multiple data sources, such as a social network of a mobile site or an app platform. Text analytical tools can convert unstructured content and parse it over to a structure format that is amenable to data mining of mobile devices via classification software. For example, all the daily e-mails or visits that a mobile site accumulates on a daily basis can be organized into several groupings, such as those mobiles seeking information, service assistance, or those complaining about specific products, services, or brands. Text mining can also be used to gauge sentiment regarding a brand or company.

Mobile marketers, developers, and brands need to consider how to incorporate time, demographics, location, interests, and other mobile available variables into their analytics models. Clustering, text, and classification software can be used to accomplish this for various marketing and brand goals. Clustering software analyses can be used to discover and monetize mobile mobs. Text software analyses can discover important brand value and sentiment information being bantered about in social networks. Finally, classification software can pinpoint important attributes about profitable and loyal mobiles. Classification often involves the use of rule-generating decision-tree programs for the segmentation of mobile data behaviors.

10.5.4 Mobile Classification Analysis

There are two major objectives to classification via the data mining of mobile devices: description and prediction. Description is an understanding of a pattern of mobile behaviors and aims to gain insight—for example, what devices are the most profitable to a mobile site and app developer. Prediction, on the other hand, is the creation of models to support, improve, and automate decision making, such as what highly profitable mobiles to target in an ad marketing campaign via a mobile site or app. Both description and prediction can be accomplished using classification software, such as rule-generator and decision-tree programs. This type of data mining analysis is also known as *supervised learning*.

For example, a mobile analyst or marketer can take advantage of segmenting the key characteristics of mobile behaviors over time to discover hidden trends and patterns of purchasing behaviors. Machine learning technology can discover the core features of mobiles by automatically learning to recognize complex patterns and make intelligent decisions based on mobile data, such as what, when, where, and why certain mobiles have a propensity to make a purchase or download an app, while others do not. Classifying mobiles enables the positioning of the right product, service, or content to these moving devices via precise messages on a mobile site, or the targeting of an e-mail, text, or the creation of key features to an app.

The marketer or developer will need to use classification software known as *rule-generators* or *decision-tree* programs. Decision trees are powerful classification and segmentation programs that use a tree-like graph of decisions and their possible consequences. Decision-tree programs provide a descriptive means of calculating conditional probabilities. Trained with historical data samples, these classification programs can be used to predict future mobile behaviors.

A decision tree takes as input an objective, such as what type of app to offer, described by a set of properties from historical mobile behaviors or conditions, such as geo-location, operating system, and device model. These mobile features can then be used to make a prediction, such as what type of app to offer to a specific mobile. The prediction can also be a continuous value, such as total expected coupon sales, or what price to offer for an app. When a developer or marketer needs to make a decision based on several consumer factors, such as their location, device being used, total log-in time, and so on, a decision tree can help identify which factors to consider and how each factor has historically been associated with different outcomes of that decision—such as what products or services certain mobiles are likely to purchase based on observed behavioral patterns over time.

One common advantage of using decision trees is to eliminate a high number of noisy and ineffective consumer attributes for predicting, say, "high customer loyalty" or "likely to buy" models. Developers and marketers can start with hundreds of mobile attributes from multiple data sources and, through the use of decision trees, they can eliminate many of them in order to focus simply on those with the highest information gain as they pertain to predicting high loyalty or potential revenue growth from mobile features and behaviors.

10.5.5 *Mobile Streaming Analysis*

The data mining of mobile devices may require the use of both deductive and inductive "streaming analytical" software that is event driven to link, monitor, and analyze mobile behaviors. These new streaming analytical software products react to mobile consumer events in real time. There are two main types of streaming analytical products:

1. Deductive streaming programs operate based on user-defined business rules and are used to monitor multiple streams of data, reacting to consumer events as they take place.
2. Inductive streaming software products use predictive rules derived from the data itself via clustering, text, and classification algorithms. These inductive streaming products build their rules from global models involving the segmentation and analysis from multiple and distributed mobile data clouds and networks.

These deductive and inductive software products can work with different data formats, from different locations, to make real-time predictions using multiple models from massive digital data streams.

10.6 Summary

The potential of mobile experience can be judged from the fact that consumers are spending almost half of the media time available to them on mobile, the other half being spent watching TV. Unlike print advertising, mobile marketing can be precisely calibrated to reach and persuade consumers by the data mining of their mobile devices. In short, despite the fact that mobile advertising is growing, the platform is far from getting rational levels of spending compared to other media. There is really no modeling of mobile Big Data taking place aside from mobile site reports and the counting of app downloads, although several companies are developing new mobile analytic strategies and tools.

Chapter 11

Internet of Things (IoT) Technologies

Internet of Things (IoT) refers to a network of inter-connected things, objects, or devices on a massive scale connected to the Internet. These objects, being smart, sense their surroundings and gather and exchange data with other objects. Based on the gathered data, the objects make intelligent decisions to trigger an action or send the data to a server over the Internet and wait for its decision. The most common nodes in IoT are

- Sensors used in many areas from industrial process control
- Sensors used inside ovens and refrigerators
- Radio Frequency Identification (RFID) chips used as tags in many products of everyday use

Almost all of these smart devices have a short communication range and require very little power to operate. Bluetooth and IEEE ZigBee are the most common communication technologies used in this regard.

A single smart device (e.g., in a refrigerator) will communicate to a router installed in the house or with a cellular tower, and the same thing will happen for similar devices installed in other equipment and places. But in places where a large number of these devices are used, an aggregation point might be required to collect the data and then send it to a remote server. Examples of such deployment can be industrial process control; monitoring of utilities supply lines, such as oil pipelines or water sewage lines; or product-supply chain in a warehouse or some secured area.

Just like the Internet and Web connects humans, the Internet of Things (IoT) is a revolutionary way of architecting and implementing systems and services based on evolutionary changes. The Internet as we know it is transforming radically, from an academic network in the 1980s and early 1990s to a mass-market, consumer-oriented network. Now, it is set to become fully pervasive, connected, interactive, and intelligent. Real-time communication is possible not only by humans but also by things at any time and from anywhere.

It is quite likely that, sooner or later, the majority of items connected to the Internet will not be humans but things. IoT will primarily expand communication from the 7 billion people around the world to the estimated 50–70 billion machines. This would result in a world where everything is connected and can be accessed from anywhere—this has a potential to connect 100 trillion things that are deemed to exist on Earth. With the advent of IoT, the physical world itself will become a connected information system. In the world of the IoT, sensors and actuators embedded in physical objects are linked through wired and wireless networks that connect the Internet. These information systems churn out huge volumes of data that flow to computers for analysis. When objects can both sense the environment and communicate, they become tools for understanding the complexity of the real world and responding to it swiftly.

The increasing volume, variety, velocity, and veracity of data produced by the IoT will continue to fuel the explosion of data for the foreseeable future. With estimates ranging from 16 to 50 billion Internet-connected devices by 2020, the hardest challenge for large-scale, context-aware applications and smart environments is to tap into disparate and ever-growing data streams originating from everyday devices and to extract hidden but relevant and meaningful information and hard-to-detect behavioral patterns. To reap the full benefits, any successful solution to build context-aware data-intensive applications and services must be able to make this valuable or important information transparent and available at a much higher frequency to substantially improve the decision-making and prediction capabilities of the applications and services.

11.1 Internet of Things

"Internet of Things" was originally introduced by Auto-ID research center at MIT (Massachusetts Institute of Technology), where an important effort was made on the unique identification of products named EPC (Electronic Product Code) which was then commercialized by EPCglobal. EPCglobal was created to follow the Auto ID objectives in the industry, with EAN.UCC (European Article Numbering—Uniform Code Council), now called GS1, as a partner to commercialize Auto-ID research, mainly the electronic product code.

IoT aims to integrate, collect information from, and offer services to a very diverse spectrum of physical things used in different domains. "Things" are everyday objects for which IoT offers a virtual presence on the Internet, allocates a specific identity and virtual address, and adds capabilities to self-organize and communicate with other things without human intervention. To ensure a high quality of services, additional capabilities can be included, such as context awareness, autonomy, and reactivity.

> Very simple things, like books, can have RFID tags that help them to be tracked without human intervention. For example, in an electronic commerce system, a RFID sensor network can detect when a thing has left the warehouse and can trigger specific actions like inventory update or customer rewarding for buying a high-end product. RFIDs enable the automatic identification or things, the capture of their context (e.g., the location) and the execution of corresponding actions if necessary. Sensors and actuators are used to transform real things into virtual objects with digital identities. In this way, things may communicate, interfere, and collaborate with each other over the Internet.

Adding part of application logic to things transforms them into smart objects, which have additional capabilities to sense, log, and understand the events occurring in the physical environment; autonomously react to context changes; and intercommunicate with other things and people. A tool endowed with such capabilities could register when and how the workers used it and produce a financial cost figure. Similarly, smart objects used in the e-health domain could continuously monitor the status of a patient and adapt the therapy according to their needs. Smart objects can also be general-purpose portable devices, like smartphones and tablets, that have processing and storage capabilities and are endowed with different types of sensors for time, position, temperature, and so on. Both specialized and general-purpose smart objects have the capability to interact with people.

The IoT includes a hardware, software, and services infrastructure for things networking. IoT infrastructure is event driven and real time, supporting the context sensing, processing, and exchange with other things and the environment. The infrastructure is very complex due to the huge number (50–100 trillion) of heterogeneous and (possibly) mobile things that dynamically join and leave the IoT and generate and consume billions of parallel and simultaneous events geographically distributed all over the world. The complexity is augmented by the difficulty to represent, interpret, process, and predict the diversity of possible contexts. The infrastructure must have important characteristics such as reliability, safety, survivability, security, and fault tolerance. Also, it must manage the communication, storage, and compute resources.

The main function of the IoT infrastructure is to support communication among things (and other entities such as people, applications, etc.). This function must be flexible and adapted to the large variety of things, from simple sensors to sophisticated smart objects. More specifically, things need a communication infrastructure that is low data rate, low power, and low complexity. Actual solutions are based on short-range radio frequency (RF) transmissions in *ad-hoc* wireless per-sonal area networks (WPANs). A main concern of the IoT infrastructure develop-ers is supporting heterogeneous things by adopting appropriate standards for the physical and media access control (MAC) layers and for communication protocols. The protocol and compatible interconnection for simple wireless connectivity with relaxed throughput (2–250 Kbps), low range (up to 100 m), moderate latency (10–50 ms) requirements, and low cost, adapted to devices previously not connected to the Internet, were defined in IEEE 802.15.4. The main scope of IoT specialists is the worldwide network of inter-connected virtual objects that are uniquely address-able and communicating through standard protocols. The challenge here is coping with a huge number of (heterogeneous) virtual objects.

Table 11.1 presents a comparison of conventional Internet with IoT.

Characteristics of successful IoT deployments are

- Distributivity: IoT will likely evolve in a highly distributed environment. In fact, data might be gathered from different sources and processed by several entities in a distributed manner.
- Interoperability: Devices from different vendors will have to cooperate in order to achieve common goals. In addition, systems and protocols will have to be designed in a way that allows objects (devices) from different manufac-turers to exchange data and work in an interoperable way.
- Scalability: In IoT, billions of objects are expected to be part of the network. Thus, systems and applications that run on top of them will have to manage this unprecedented amount of generated data.
- Resources scarcity: Both power and computation resources will be highly scarce.
- Security: Users' feelings of helplessness and being under some unknown external control could seriously hinder IoT's deployment.

11.1.1 IoT Building Blocks

The IoT architecture supports physical things' integration into the Internet and the complex interaction flow of services triggered by events occurrence. The main concepts involved the basis for the development of independent cooperative services and applications are:

1. Sensing technologies: RFID and Wireless Sensor Networks (WSN) are the two main building blocks of sensing and communication technologies for IoT. However, these technologies suffer from different constraints (e.g., energy limitation, reliability of wireless medium, security and privacy). In particular, the scarcity of energy resources available in the embedded devices is a sensitive issue. Consequently, to increase energy efficiency, a number of solutions have been introduced in the literature. For instance, lightweight

Table 11.1 Comparison of Conventional Internet with Internet of Things (IoT)

Internet	Internet of Things (IoT)
In the Internet, the end-nodes are full-computers ranging from workstations to smart phones, with regular access to the public power-supply networks.	In the IoT, the end-nodes are very small electronic devices with low energy consumption. Compared to Internet computers their functionality is limited and they cannot interact directly with humans.
In the Internet, the number of connected devices are envisaged to be in billions.	In the IoT, the number of connected devices are envisaged to be in trillions.
In the Internet, not only the long-distance connection but also the last-mile connection has become very fast (in the range of megabits/sec).	In the IoT, the speed of the last-mile to an RFID tag is quite slow ((in the range of kilobits/sec).
In the Internet, there are globally accepted identification and address schemes (e.g., IP and MAC addresses).	In the IoT, such standards cannot be employed devices because they require too much energy. Many vendor-specific solutions exists, but they prevent objects from being globally identified and addressed.
In the Internet, the major share of functionality is addressed to human users like World Wide Web (www), e-mail, chat and e-commerce.	In the IoT, devices usually interact directly, not via human intervention.
Internet enabled a breakthrough in human communication and interaction	IoT enabled a breakthrough in sensing the physical environment; sensing enables measurement, which in turn enables their management.

MAC protocols, energy-efficient routing protocols, and tailored security protocols have been proposed to mitigate the impact of resources' scarcity on sensing technologies. Nevertheless, their limited autonomy remains a considerable obstacle to their widespread deployment in our daily lives.

a. RFID): An RFID is a tiny microchip (e.g., 0.4 mm × 0.4 mm × 0.15 mm) attached to an antenna (called *tags*), which is used for both receiving the reader signal and transmitting the tag identity, which can be appended to an object of our daily life. As in an electronic barcode, stored data in these tags can automatically be used to identify and extract useful information about the object. RFID devices are classified into two categories: passive and active. The passive RFID tags are not battery powered; they use the power of the readers' interrogation signal to communicate their data. They are also used in bank cards and road-toll tags as a means to control access; they are also used in many retail, supply-chain management, and transportation applications.

b. WSN: WSN, along with RFID systems, enable one to better track the status of things (e.g., their location, temperature, and movements). Sensor networks consist of a large number of sensing nodes communicating in a wireless multi-hop fashion, reporting their sensing results into a small number of special nodes called *sinks* (or *base stations*).

The main issues of concern are
   i. Energy efficiency (which is a limited resource in WSN)
  ii. Scalability (the number of nodes can rise significantly)
 iii. Reliability (the system might be involved in critical applications)
  iv. Robustness (nodes might be subject to failure)

c. Integration: Integration of heterogeneous technologies like sensing technologies into passive RFID tags would bring completely new applications into the IoT context. Sensing RFID systems will allow the construction of RFID sensor networks, which consist of small RFID-based sensing and computing devices. RFID readers would constitute the sinks of data generated by sensing RFID tags. Moreover, they would provide the power for the different network operations. Efficiently networking tag readers with RFID sensors would allow real-time queries on the physical world, leading to better forecasts, new business models, and improved management techniques.

2. Compute technologies: The middleware is a software interface between the physical layer (i.e., hardware) and the application one. It provides the required abstraction to hide the heterogeneity and the complexity of the underlying technologies involved in the lower layers. Indeed, the middleware is essential to spare both users and developers from the exact knowledge of the heterogeneous set of technologies adopted by the lower layers. The service-based approaches lying on a cloud infrastructure open the door to highly flexible and adaptive middleware for the IoT.

Decoupling the application logic from the embedded devices and moving it to the cloud will allow developers to provide applications for the heterogeneous devices that will compose the future IoT environment. It is possible to create a set of sensor services to be exploited in different applications for different users through the cloud. A Sensor-Cloud infrastructure provides the end user with service instances based on virtual sensors in an automatic way.

3. Actuate technologies: IoT enhances the passive objects around us with communication and processing capabilities to transform them into pervasive objects. However, this can only be realized with corresponding physical support. Cloud-Robotics abstracts robotic functionalities and provides a means for utilizing them. Various equipment and devices, like individual robots, sensors, and smartphone, that can measure the world or interact with people in both the physical and digital worlds are treated uniformly. These robots are logically gathered to form a cloud of robots by networking.

11.1.2 IoT Architecture

The Internet of Things connects a large number of "smart" objects, each of them possessing a unique address. This creates a huge amount of traffic and therefore the demand for large volumes of computational power and huge data storage capabilities. Additional challenges arise in the areas of scalability, interoperability, security and Quality of Service (QoS). Figure 11.1 shows the latered IoT architecture.

The envisaged architecture consists of:

1. The perception layer is the lowest layer in the IoT architecture and its purpose is to perceive the data from the environment and identify objects or things.

    The Perception layer consists of the physical objects and all the sensor devices. These devises can be RFID, barcodes, infrared sensors, embedded

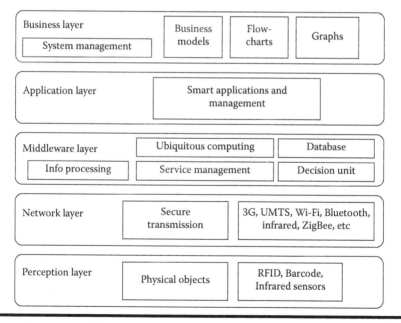

Figure 11.1   IoT architecture.

sensors as well as actuator nodes. In this layer the information is gathered and categorized. Firstly, the physical properties of each object (like location, orientation, temperature, motion, etc.) are perceived. However, in order to successfully perceive the desired properties, most objects need to have appropriate microchips installed in them that sense the desired information and perform preliminary processing to convert it into corresponding digital signals for their use by the next layer for network transmission

2. The network layer is like the Network and Transport layers of OSI model. It collects the data from the perception layer and sends it to the Internet. The network layer may only include a gateway, having one interface connected to the sensor network and another to the Internet. In some scenarios, it may include a network management center or information processing center.

   The main role of this layer is to securely transfer the information gathered by the sensor devices to the processing center of the system. The transmission is possible through all the common mediums, such as the wireless network, the cable network and even through LAN's (Local Area Networks). The different communication technologies and protocols enabling this transfer include 3G/4G cellular networks as well as Wi-Fi (Wireless Fidelity), Bluetooth, ZigBee, Infrared, etc. This layer also includes several protocols like IPv6 (Internet Protocol version 6), whose responsibility is the proper IP addressing of the objects

3. The middleware layer receives data from the network layer. Its purpose is service management, storing data, performing information processing and taking decisions based on the results automatically. It then passes the output to the next layer, the application layer.

   The Middleware layer or "Processing" layer and is considered as the core layer of the IoT system. Initially, all the information received from the Network layer is stored in the system's database. Furthermore, the information is analyzed and processed, and based on the results appropriate automated decisions are taken. This layer is also responsible for the service management of the devices. Since each IoT device implements specific types of services, this layer helps in the management of all the different services of the system, by deciding which devices should connect and communicate in order to provide the optimum requested service results.

4. The application layer performs the final presentation of data. The application layer receives information from the middleware layer and provides global management of the application presenting that information, based on the information processed by the middleware layer. According to the needs of the user, the application layer presents the data in the form of: smart city, smart home, smart transportation, vehicle tracking, smart farming, smart health and many other kinds of applications.

   The role of this layer is very important since it practically supports the applications envisaged by different industries. The applications implemented by the IoT cover a huge area of technology fields, varying from healthcare, intelligent transportation, smart home, smart cities, supply chains, and logistics management.

5. The business layer is all about making money from the service being provided. Data received at the application layer is molded into a meaningful service and then further services are created from those existing services. Based on the analysis of the results of the above, the users can determine their business strategies and future actions.

The Business layer is responsible for managing the higher level of the IoT system, mainly the applications and their services to the users. Unless IoT can provide efficient and effective business models to the users, their long-term use and development won't be feasible. Finally, another task of this layer is managing the issues related to the privacy and security of the users.

11.2 RFID (Radio Frequency Identification)

RFID, also known as radio frequency identification, is a form of Auto ID (automatic identification) that is the identification of an object with minimal human interaction. Barcodes identify items through the encoding of data in various sized bars using a variety of symbologies, or coding methodologies. The most familiar type of barcode is the UPC or universal product code, which provides manufacturer and product identification. While barcodes have proven to be very useful, and indeed have become an accepted part of product usage and identity, there are limitations with the technology. Barcode scanners must have line of sight in order to read barcode labels. Label information can be easily compromised by dirt, dust, or rips. Barcodes take up a considerable footprint on product labels. Even the newer barcode symbologies, such as 2D or two-dimensional, which can store a significant amount of data in a very small space, remain problematic.

Limitations of barcodes are overcome through the use of RFID labeling to identify objects. While using RFID, since the data is exchanged using radio waves, it is not necessary to have line of sight between a reader and a tag, such as is required with barcodes. This permits a great deal more flexibility in the use of the RFID. RFID was first used commercially in the 1960s by companies that developed security related devices called *electronic article surveillance* (EAS) equipment. Although EAS could only present the detection or absence of a tag, the tags were low cost and provided valuable deterrents to theft.

The mining industry was an early adopter of RFID technology. One use of RFID tags in mining was in validating the correct movement of haulage vehicles. These vehicles have read-only tags permanently attached to the vehicle's dump bed. As a vehicle approaches a dump area, a reader validates that it is approaching the correct dump bed. Information concerning the transaction, including the vehicle number, the weight of the vehicle before and after the dump, and the time, are recorded automatically. Using RFID obviates the need for human interaction between the scales operator and the vehicle driver

The radio frequency transmissions in RFID travel between the two primary components:

■ RFID reader can be mobile or stationary, consists of an antenna and a transceiver, is supplied with power, and generates and transmits a signal from its antenna to the tag and then reads the information reflected from the tag. The antenna is used to send and receive signals; the transceiver is used to control and interpret the signals sent and received.

■ RFID tag, a transponder, consists of three components: antenna, silicon chip, and substrate or encapsulation material. The antenna is used for receiving and transmitting radio frequency waves to and from the reader. The chip contains information pertaining to the item tagged, such as part number and manufacturer. Chips can be either read-only or read–write; the costs are higher for the read–write chips. There is a crucial difference between read-only chips and read–write chips. Read-only chips are essentially electronic barcodes. Once the data has been encoded onto the chip, it cannot be modified and, therefore, cannot transmit information about the product as it moves through a sequence of events. The tag is affixed to the object being identified, such as an automobile, a shipping pallet, or a tagged marine mammal.

The portion of the electromagnetic spectrum used by radio frequency identification includes LF (low frequency), HF (high frequency), and UHF (ultra-high frequency), which are all portions of the radio wave frequency bands, hence the term *radio frequency identification*. An advantage of radio waves over visible light is that radio waves can penetrate many substances that would block visible light. Radio waves range from 300 kHz to 3 GHz.

 Electromagnetic waves are comprised of a continuum of emanations, including visible light waves; invisible frequencies such as television and radio waves, which are lower frequency than light; and x-rays and gamma rays, which are higher frequency than light.

The range over which devices using radio waves can consistently communicate is affected by the following factors:

■ Power contained in the wave transmitted
■ Sensitivity of the receiving equipment
■ Environment through which the wave travels
■ Presence of interference

11.3 Sensor Networks

11.3.1 Wireless Networks

The main characteristics of wireless networks are as follows:

- Access for anybody, from anywhere, at any time—mobility
- On-line/real-time access
- Relative high communication speed
- Shared access to files, data/knowledge bases,
- Exchange of picture, voice—multimedia applications

Table 11.2 shows characteristics of several wireless networks

Wireless networks can be categorized into five groups based on their coverage range:

1. Satellite communication (SC):

    The handheld satellite telephones provide voice, fax, Internet access, short messaging, and remote location determination services (Global Positioning System [GPS]) in the covered area. All of this is provided through geosynchronous satellites, but when satellite coverage is not necessary, the handset can also access the GSM cellular network. Fax and digital data is transmitted at 9600 bps throughputs, but in case users need high-speed Internet access, in special cases, 2 Mbps data transmission rate can be achieved. A satellite phone can fulfill all the requirements regarding mobile communications in many application fields.

2. Wireless Wide Area Networks (WWAN):

    a. Mobile phone: Mobile phone was the device that offered a great number of people the possibility of making contact with others from anywhere, at any time, and for anybody.

       Different mobile systems/network protocols are:
       i. CDMA (Code Division Multiple Access—2G): CDMA networks incorporate spread-spectrum technology to gracefully allocate data over available cells.
       ii. CDPD (Cellular Digital Packet Data—2G): CDPD is a protocol built exclusively for sending wireless data over cellular networks. CDPD is built on TCP/IP standards.
       iii. GSM (Global System for Mobile Communications—2G): GSM networks, mainly popular in Europe.
       iv. GPRS (General Packet Radio Service—2.5 G): GPRS technology offers significant speed improvements over existing 2G technology.
       v. iMode (from DoCoMo—2.5G): iMode was developed by DoCoMo and is the standard wireless data service for Japan. iMode is known

Table 11.2   Characteristics of Several Wireless Networks

Wireless network type	Operation frequency	Data rate	Operation range	Characteristics
Satellite	2170–2200 MHz	Different (9.6 kbps–2 Mbps)	Satellite coverage	Relative high cost, availability
WWAN				
GSM (2–2.5 G)	824–1880 MHz	9.6–384 kbps (EDGE)	Cellular coverage	Reach, quality, low cost
3G/UMTS	1755–2200 MHz	2.4 Mbps	Cellular coverage	Speed, big attachments
iMode (3G/ FOMA)	800 MHz	64–384kpbs (W-CDMA)	Cellular coverage	Always-on, easy to use
FLASH-OFDM	450 MHZ	Max. 3 Mbps	Cellular coverage	High speed, respond time less than 50 milliseconds
WMAN				
IEEE 802.16	2–11 GHz	Max. 70 Mbps	3–10 (max. 45) km	Speed, high operation range
WWLAN				
IEEE 802.11 A	5 GHz	54 Mbps	30 m	Speed, limited range
IEEE 802.11b	2.4 GHz	11 Mbps	100 m	Medium data rate
IEEE 802.11g	2.4 GHz	54 Mbps	100–150 m	Speed, flexibility
WPAN				
BLUETOOTH	2.4 GHz	720 kbps	10 m	Cost, convenience
UVVB	1.5–4 GHz	50–100 Mbps	100–150 m	Low cost, low power
ZigBee	2.4 GHz, 915–868 Mhz	250 Kbps	1–75 m	Reliable, low power, cost-effective
Infrared	300 GHz	9.6 kbps–4 Mbps	0.2–2 m	Non-interfering, low cost
RFID	30–500 KHz 850–950 MHz 2.4–2.5 GHz	Linked to bandwidth, max. 2 Mbps	0.02–30 m	High reading speeds, responding in less than 100 milliseconds

for its custom markup language enabling multimedia applications to run on phones.

vi. 3G: 3G networks promise speeds rivaling wired connections. Both in Europe and North America, carriers have aggressively bid for a 3G spectrum, but no standard has yet emerged.

The introduction of WAP (Wireless Application Protocol) was a big step forward for mobile communication, as this protocol made it possible to connect mobile devices to the Internet. By enabling WAP applications, a full range of wireless devices, including mobile phones, smartphones, PDAs, and handheld PCs, gain a common method for accessing Internet information. The spread of WAP became even more intensive as the mobile phone industry actively supported WAP by installing it into the new devices. WAP applications exist today to view a variety of web content, manage e-mail from the handset, and gain better access to network operators' enhanced services. Beyond these information services, content providers have developed different mobile solutions, such as mobile e-commerce (mCommerce).

b. FLASH-OFDM: FLASH-OFDM (Fast, Low-latency Access with Seamless Handoff—Orthogonal Frequency Division Multiplexing) is a cellular, IP-based broadband technology for data services on the 450 MHz band. It has full cellular mobility, 3.2 Mbps peak data rates, 384 Kbps at the edge of the cell, and less than 20 ms of latency. The FLASH-OFDM system consists of an airlink, an integrated physical and media access control layer, and IP-based layers above the network layer (layer 3). The IP-based layers support applications using standard IP protocols.

FLASH-OFDM is a wide-area technology enabling full mobility up to speeds of up to 250 km/h (critical to vehicle and rail commuters). Its ability to support a large number of users over a large area and nationwide build outs (via wireless carriers) will do for data what the cellular networks did for voice. The IP interfaces In Flash-OFDM enable operators to offer their enterprise customers access to their LANs (Local Area Networks) and users the benefits of the mobile Internet. FLASH-OFDM support voice-packet switched voice (not circuit-switched voice), Radio routers, IP routers with radio adjuncts, would handle packet traffic, and serve as the equivalent of cellular base stations. Consumers would connect with Flash-OFDM networks via PC cards in their notebooks and via flash-memory cards in handheld devices.

3. Wireless Metropolitan Area Network (WMAN):

WiMAX is considered the next step beyond Wi-Fi because it is optimized for broadband operation, fixed and later mobile, in the wide area network. It already includes numerous advances that are slated for introduction into the 802.11 standard, such as quality of service, enhanced security, higher data rates, and mesh and smart antenna technology, allowing better utilization of the spectrum.

The term WiMAX (Worldwide Interoperability for Microwave Access) has become synonymous with the IEEE 802.16 Metropolitan Area Network (MAN) air interface standard. Metropolitan area networks or MANs are large computer networks usually spanning a campus or a city. They typically use optical fiber connections to link their sites. WiMAX is the new shorthand term for IEEE Standard 802.16, also known as "Air Interface" for Fixed Broadband Wireless Access Systems. In its original release (in early 2002), the 802.16 standard addressed applications in licensed bands in the 10–66 GHz frequency range and requires line-of-sight towers called fixed wireless. Here a backbone of base stations is connected to a public network, and each base station supports hundreds of fixed subscriber stations, which can be both public Wi-Fi "hot spots" and enterprise networks with firewall.

4. Wireless Local Area Networks (WLAN):

Local area wireless networking, generally called Wi-Fi or Wireless Fidelity, enabled computers to send and receive data anywhere within the range of a base station with a speed that is several times faster than the fastest cable modem connection. Wi-Fi connects the user to others and to the Internet without the restriction of wires, cables, or fixed connections. Wi-Fi gives the user freedom to change locations (mobility)—and to have full access to files, office, and network connections wherever she or he is. In addition, Wi-Fi will easily extend an established wired network.

Wi-Fi networks use radio technologies called IEEE 802.11b or 802.11a standards to provide secure, reliable, and fast wireless connectivity. A Wi-Fi network can be used to connect computers to each other, to the Internet, and to wired networks (that use IEEE 802.3 or Ethernet). Wi-Fi networks operate in the 2.4 (802.11b) and 5 GHz (802.11a) radio bands, with an 11 Mbps (802.11b) or 54 Mbps (802.11a) data rate or with products that contain both bands (dual band), so they can provide real-world performance similar to the basic 10BaseT wired Ethernet networks used in many offices. 802.11b has a range of approximately 100 m. Products based on the 802.11a standard were first introduced in late 2001.

Wi-Fi networks can work well both for home (connecting a family's computers together to share such hardware and software resources as printers and the Internet) and for small businesses (providing connectivity between mobile salespeople, floor staff, and "behind-the-scenes" departments). Because small businesses are dynamic, the built-in flexibility of a Wi-Fi network makes it easy and affordable for them to change and grow. Large companies and universities use enterprise-level Wi-Fi technology to extend standard wired Ethernet networks to public areas like meeting rooms, training classrooms, and large auditoriums, and also to connect buildings. Many corporations also provide wireless networks to their off-site and telecommuting workers to use at home or in remote offices.

5. Wireless Personal Area (or Pico) Network (WPAN)

WPAN represents wireless personal area network technologies such as Ultrawideband (UWB), ZigBee, Bluetooth, and RFID. Designed for data and voice transmission, low data rate standards include ZigBee and Bluetooth (IEEE 802.15.1) and enable wireless personal area networks to communicate over short distances, generating a new way of interacting with our personal and business environment.

a. Bluetooth: Bluetooth is a short-range radio device that replaces cables with low-power radio waves to connect electronic devices, whether they are portable or fixed. It is a WPAN specified in IEEE 802.15, Working Group for WPANs. Bluetooth, named after Harald Bluetooth, the tenth-century Viking king, is a consortium of companies (3Com, Ericsson, Intel, IBM, Lucent Technologies, Motorola, Nokia, and Toshiba) bonded together to form a wireless standard.

The Bluetooth device also uses frequency hopping to ensure a secure, quality link, and it uses ad hoc networks, meaning that it connects peer-to-peer. When devices are communicating with each other, they are known as piconets, and each device is designated as a master unit or slave unit, usually depending on who initiates the connection. However, both devices have the potential to be either a master or a slave. The Bluetooth user has the choice of point-to-point or point-to-multipoint links, whereby communication can be held between two devices or up to eight.

b. RFID: The main purpose of the RFID technology is the automated identification of objects with electromagnetic fields. An RFID system has three basic components: transponders (tags), readers (scanners), and application systems for further processing of the acquired data. There is a large variety of different RFID systems; they can use low, high, or ultra-high frequencies, and tags may emanate only a fixed identifier or they can have significant memory and processing capabilities. Transponders can contain effective security protocols or no security features at all. Most of the tags are passive powered by the radio field emitted by the reader, but there are also active tags with a separate power supply.

RFID systems can be distinguished according to their frequency ranges. Low-frequency (30–500 KHz) systems have short reading ranges and lower system costs. They are usually used in, for example, security access and animal identification applications. High-frequency (850–950 MHz and 2.4–2.5 GHz) systems, offering long read ranges (greater than 25 m) and high reading speeds, are used for such applications as railroad car tracking and automated toll collection. However, the higher performance of high-frequency RFID systems generates higher system costs.

11.3.2 Sensors

The objective of sensor is to measure a physical quantity from the environment and transform it into a signal (either analog or digital) that drives outputs/actuators or feeds a data analysis tool (see Figure 11.2). The choice of a sensor in a WSN is application dependent and strictly related to the physical phenomenon object of the monitoring action. The wide and heterogeneous range of possible physical phenomena to be monitored is well reflected by the complexity and the heterogeneity of the sensors that have been designed and developed to acquire data from them. Examples of possible applications, physical phenomena to be monitored, and the corresponding sensors of interest are summarized in Section 11.4, Tables 11.3 and 11.4.

Table 11.3 presents examples of possible applications, physical phenomena to be monitored, and the corresponding sensors; and Table 11.4 presents types of sensors for various measurement objectives.

The measurement of a physical quantity and the subsequent conversion into signals are performed by sensors through a *measurement chain* that is generally composed of three different stages:

- Transducer stage transforms one form of energy into another, here converting the monitored physical quantity into an electric signal.
- Conditioning circuit stage conditions the signal provided by the transducer to reduce the effect of noise, amplify the sensitivity of the sensor, and adapt the electrical properties of the signal to the needs of the next stage.
- Output formatting stage aims at transforming the conditioned signal into a signal ready to be used to drive outputs or actuators and to be processed by the data analysis tool.

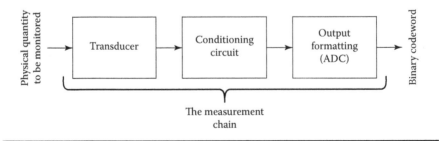

Figure 11.2 The measurement chain of sensors.

Table 11.3   Examples of Possible Applications, Physical Phenomena to be Monitored, and the Corresponding Sensors

Applications	Physical phenomenon	Sensors
Environmental monitoring	Temperature	Thermometers, thermocouples, thermistor
	Light	Photodiodes/phototransistor, CCD cameras
	Humidity	Humidity sensors
	Pressure	Switches, strain gauges
Visual and audio processing	Visual	CCD and other cameras
	Audio	Microphones
Motion/ acceleration analysis	Motion/ acceleration	Accelerometers, motion detectors, magnetic fields, angular sensors
Location	Indoor	Tags, badges
	Outdoor	GPS, GSM cells
Biological and chemical analysis	Biological	ECG, heart rate sensors, blood pressure sensors, pulse oximetry, skin resistance, DNA analyzer
	Chemical	Contaminant sensors, solid/ liquid/gas sensors, electrochemical cells

The measurement chain of sensors is characterized by

1. Functional attributes specifying the functional behavior. Functional attributes refer to specific functions or behaviors the sensor must exhibit. Examples of functional attributes are the measurement range (i.e., the range of measurements the sensor can acquire), the duty-cycle sampling rates (i.e., the range of sampling rates the sensor can support), and the condition stage parameters (e.g., the filter parameters).
2. Non-functional attributes specifying the requirements/properties of the sensor itself. Non-functional attributes refer to properties characterizing how the sensor is providing its functionalities. Examples of non-functional attributes are the size/weight of the sensor, the accuracy and the precision of the measurement chain, and the power consumption.

Table 11.4 Types of Sensors for Various Measurement Objectives

Sensor	Features
Linear/rotational sensor	
Liner/rotational variable differential transducer (LVDT/RVDT) Optical encoder	High resolution with wide range capability. Very stable in static and quasi-static applications Simple, reliable, and low-cost solution. Good for both absolute and incremental measurements.
Electrical tachometer Hall effect sensor capacitive transducer	Resolution depends on type such as generator or magnetic pickups. High accuracy over a small to medium range. Very high resolution with high sensitivity. Low power requirements.
Strain gauge elements	Very high accuracy in small ranges. Provides high resolution at low noise levels.
Interferometer	Laser systems provide extremely high resolution in large ranges. Very reliable and expensive. Output is sinusoidal.
Magnetic pickup Gyroscope Inductosyn	Very high resolution over small ranges.
Acceleration sensors	
Seismic and piezoelectric accelerometers	Good for measuring frequencies up to 40% of its natural frequency. High sensitivity, compact, and rugged. Very high natural frequency (100 kHz typical).
Force, torque, and pressure sensor Strain gauge, dynamometers/load cells, piezoelectric load cells, tactile sensor, and ultrasonic stress sensor	Good for both static and dynamic measurements. They are also available as micro- and nano-sensors. Good for high precision dynamic force measurements. Compact, has wide dynamic range. Good for small force measurements.
Proximity sensors	
Inductance, eddy current, hall effect, photoelectric, capacitance, etc.	Robust noncontact switching action. The digital outputs are often directly fed to the digital controller.

(Continued)

Table 11.4 (Continued)   Types of Sensors for Various Measurement Objectives

Sensor	Features
Light sensors	
Photo resistors, photodiodes, photo transistors, photo conductors, etc. Charge-coupled diode.	Measure light intensity with high sensitivity. Inexpensive, reliable, and noncontact sensor. Compares digital image of a field of vision.
Temperature sensors	
Thermocouples	This is the cheapest and the most versatile sensor. Applicable over wide temperature ranges (–200 to 1200°C typical).
Thermostats	Very high sensitivity in medium ranges (up to 100°C typical). Compact but nonlinear in nature.
Thermo diodes, and thermo transistors	Ideally suited for chip temperature measurements. Minimized self heating.
RTD-resistance temperature detector	More stable over a long period for time compared to thermocouple. Linear over a wide range.
Infrared type and Infrared thermograph	Noncontact point sensor with resolution limited by wavelength. Measures whole-field temperature distribution.
Flow sensors	
Pitot tube, orifice plate, flow nozzle, and venture tubes	Widely used as a flow rate sensor to determine speed in aircrafts. Least expensive with limited range. Accurate on wide range of flow. More complex and expensive.
Rotameter	Good for upstream flow measurements. Used in conjunction with variable inductance sensor.
Ultrasonic type	Good for very high flow rates. Can be used for upstream and downstream flow measurements.
Turbine flow meter	Not suited for fluids containing abrasive particles. Relationship between flow rate and angular velocity is linear.

(Continued)

Table 11.4 (Continued)   Types of Sensors for Various Measurement Objectives

Sensor	Features
Electromagnetic flow meter	Least intrusive as it is noncontact type. Can be used with fluids that are corrosive, contaminated, etc., the fluid has to be electrically conductive.
Smart material sensors	
Optical fiber as strain sensor, as level sensor, as force sensor, and as temperature sensor	Alternate to strain pages with very high accuracy and bandwidth. Sensitive to the reflecting surface's orientation and status. Reliable and accurate. High resolution in wide ranges. High resolution and range (up to 2000°C).
Piezoelectric as strain sensor, as force sensor, and as accelerometer	Distributed sensing with high resolution and bandwidth. Most suitable for dynamic applications. Least hysteresis and good set point accuracy.
Magnetostrictive as force sensors and as torque sensor	Compact force sensor with high resolution and bandwidth. Good for distributed and noncontact sensing applications. Accurate, high bandwidth, and noncontract sensor.
Micro- and nano-sensors	
Micro CCD image sensor, fiberscope micro-ultrasonic sensor, micro-tactile sensor	Small size, full field image sensor, Small (0.2 mm diameter) field vision scope using SMA coil actuators. Detects flaws in small pipes. Detects proximity between the end of catheter and blood vessels.

Sensor does not necessarily refer only to physical hardware devices but also to every source of data providing information of interest. Hence, in addition to physical hardware sensors (which are, however, the most frequently considered source of information in WSNs), virtual and logical sensors are often employed. Virtual sensors refer to non-physical sources of information; for example, the location of a person can be determined by means of tracking systems through GPS location (physical devices) as well as by looking at its electronic calendar or by analyzing travel bookings or e-mails (non-physical sources of information). Electronic calendars, travel bookings, or e-mails do not require a real measurement of the person's position and are referred as virtual sensors. Logical sensors rely on two or more sources of information to provide high-level data; for example, a logical sensor could aggregate data coming from both a physical sensor and a virtual sensor as well as information coming from a database system.

Regardless of the kind of sensor (physical, virtual, or logical) or the object of the sensing activities (places, people, or object), there are four essential characteristics of the sensing activity:

- *Identity* refers to the ability to univocally identify the entity that is the object of the sensing, for example, by assigning unique identifiers in the namespace used by the application.
- *Location* encompasses all the aspects related to the position of the sensed entity. It could include not only a position in the space but also orientation, elevation, and proximity to relevant locations.
- *Status* refers to the physical quantity (or the virtual/logical quantity) object of the sensing. In case of a temperature sensor, the status refers to the temperature value measured at a specific time instant.
- *Time* indicates temporal information associated with the sensed measurements. The temporal information often refers to a timestamp specifying the exact time instant at which the measurement has been acquired. A wide range of time coarseness could be considered (e.g., from a nanosecond to decades) depending on the application needs.

11.3.3 Wireless Sensor Networks

Wireless Sensor Networks (WSNs) have been widely considered as one of the most important technologies for the twenty-first century. Enabled by recent advances in microelectronic mechanical systems (MEMS) and wireless communication technologies, tiny, cheap, and smart sensors deployed in a physical area and networked through wireless links and the Internet provide unprecedented opportunities for a variety of applications like environmental monitoring and industry process control. In contrast with the traditional wireless communication networks like cellular systems and mobile ad hoc networks (MANET), There are many challenges in the development and application of WSNs because of many have unique characteristics like denser level of node deployment, higher unreliability of sensor nodes, and severe energy, computation, and storage constraints.

A sensor network consists of a large number of sensor nodes that are densely deployed in a sensing region and collaborate to accomplish a sensing task. It requires a suite of network protocols to implement various network control and management functions, for example, synchronization, self-configuration, medium access control, routing, data aggregation, node localization, and network security. However, existing network protocols for traditional wireless networks, for example, cellular systems and mobile *ad hoc* networks (MANETs), cannot be applied directly to sensor networks because they do not consider the energy, computation, and storage constraints in sensor nodes. On the other hand, most sensor networks are application specific and have different application requirements. For these reasons, a new suite of network protocols is required, which take into account not only the resource constraints in sensor nodes but also the requirements of different network applications. For this reason, it is important to define a protocol stack to facilitate the protocol design for WSNs.

As discussed in Subsection 11.1.1 earlier, the WSN hardware platforms are composed of various parts:

- The sensing module contains one or more sensors, each of which is devoted to measuring a physical quantity of interest and generating the associated codeword (i.e., the digital data).
- The processing module, which is generally equipped with a small memory/ storage unit, manages the unit and carries out the processing tasks according to the application needs.
- The transmission module provides the mechanisms to communicate with the other units of the WSN or with a remote-control room.

Hardware platforms for WSN are presented in Table 11.5.

Operating systems (OSs) represent the intermediate layer between the hardware of the WSN unit and WSN applications. They aim to control the hardware resources and provide services and functionalities to the application software (e.g., hardware abstraction, scheduling of tasks, memory management, and file system). Simplified versions of desktop/mainframe OSs could be considered only in high-performance hardware platforms (e.g., the StarGate platform is able to run a simplified version of Linux). The constraints on hardware and energy of WSN units (as pointed out in Table 11.5) led to the development of OSs specifically devoted to networked embedded systems. Examples of OSs for WSNs are TinyOS, Contiki, and MANTIS (see Table 11.6).

TinyOS is an open-source, flexible, and component-based OS for WSN units. It is characterized by a very small footprint (400 byte), which makes it particularly suitable for low-power hardware platforms (such as the MICAz). TinyOS relies on a monolithic architecture where software components (including those providing hardware abstraction) are connected together through interfaces. It supports a non-pre-emptive first-in-first-out scheduling activity (making it unsuitable for computational-intensive or real-time applications). TinyOS applications must be written

Table 11.5 Hardware Platforms for WSN

Platform	Processor					Radio		Sensors Types
	Type	Frequency	RAM (byte) int./ext.	Flash (byte) int./ext.	Power Consumption (mW) sleep/run	Type	TX Power (dB)	
MICAz	ATMegal 28	8 MHz	4K/n.a.	128K/n.a.	0.036/60	CC2420	Up to 0	n.a.
BTnode	ATMegal 28	7.38 MHz	4K/n.a.	128K/n.a.	0.036/60	CC1000	Up to +10	n.a.
Mulle	M16C/62P	Up to 24 MHz	20K/n.a.	128K/n.a.	0.015/75	Bluetooth	Up to +4	Temperature
Shimmer	MSP430	8 MHz	10K/n,a.	48K/µSD	0.006/4	CC2420	Up to 0	MEMS
TelosB	MSP430	8 MHz	10K/n.a.	48K/1 Mb	0.006/4	CC2420	Up to 0	Temperature, humidity, light
Imote2	PXA271	13–416 MHz	256K/32 Mb	32 Mb/n.a.	0.39/ up to 992	CC2420	Up to 0	n.a.
StarGate	PXA255	400 MHz	64K/64 Mb	32 Mb/ext.	15/1455	n.a.	n.a.	n.a.
NetBrick	STM32F103	8–72 MHz	64K/1 Mb	512 Kb/128 Mb	0.083/226	JN5148	Up to +20	Temperature, humidity, MEMS

n.a. not available, ext.external

Table 11.6 Operating Systems for WSN

	Architecture	Pre-emption	Multi-threading	Remote Reprogramming	Language
TinyOS	Monolithic	No	Partial	No	NesC
Contiki	Modular	Yes	Yes	Yes	C
MANTIS	Layered	Yes	Yes	Yes	C

in NesC (which is a dialect of the C language) and cannot be updated/modified at runtime (applications are compiled together with the OS kernel as a single image).

Contiki is an open-source OS for networked embedded systems. It is built around a modular architecture composed of an event-driven-based microkernel, OS libraries, a program loader, and application processes. Interestingly, Contiki supports pre-emptive multi-threading and remote reprogramming (through the program loader). The memory occupation is 2 KB of RAM and 4 KB of read-only memory (ROM). Both the OS and the applications are written in C.

MANTIS is a multithreaded OS for WSNs that is based on a traditional layered architecture. Each layer provides services to upper layers from the hardware to the application threads. MANTIS supports cross-platform design by preserving the programming interface across different platforms. The scheduling activity is based on a preemptive priority-based scheduler, while remote reprogramming is supported by the dynamic loading of threads. Even in this case, both the OS and the application threads are written in C.

11.3.3.1 WSN Characteristics

A WSN typically consists of a large number of low-cost, low-power, and multifunctional sensor nodes that are deployed in a region of interest. These sensor nodes are small in size but are equipped with sensors, embedded microprocessors, and radio transceivers, and therefore have not only sensing capability but also data processing and communicating capabilities. They communicate over a short distance via a wireless medium and collaborate to accomplish a common task.

1. Application specific: Sensor networks are application specific. A network is usually designed and deployed for a specific application. The design requirements of a network change with its application.
2. No global identification: Due to the large number of sensor nodes, it is usually not possible to build a global addressing scheme for a sensor network because it would introduce a high overhead for identification maintenance.
3. Dense node deployment: Sensor nodes are usually densely deployed in a field of interest. The number of sensor nodes in a sensor network can be several orders of magnitude higher than that in a MANET.

4. Frequent topology change: Network topology changes frequently due to node failure, damage, addition, energy depletion, or channel fading.

5. Many-to-one traffic pattern: In most sensor network applications, the data sensed by sensor nodes flows from multiple source sensor nodes to a particular sink, exhibiting a many-to-one traffic pattern.

6. Battery-powered sensor nodes: Sensor nodes are usually powered by battery. In most situations, they are deployed in a harsh or hostile environment, where it is very difficult or even impossible to change or recharge the batteries.

7. Severe energy, computation, and storage constraints: Sensor nodes are highly limited in energy, computation, and storage capacities.

8. Self-configurable: Sensor nodes are usually randomly deployed without careful planning and engineering. Once deployed, sensor nodes have to autonomously configure themselves into a communication network.

9. Unreliable sensor nodes: Sensor nodes are usually deployed in harsh or hostile environments and operate without attendance. They are prone to physical damage or failure.

10. Data redundancy: In most sensor network applications, sensor nodes are densely deployed in a region of interest and collaborate to accomplish a common sensing task. Thus, the data sensed by multiple sensor nodes typically has a certain level of correlation or redundancy.

11.3.3.2 WSN Design Challenges

The unique network characteristics present many challenges in the design of sensor networks, which involve the following main aspects:

1. Limited Energy Capacity. Sensor nodes are battery powered and thus have very limited energy capacity. This constraint presents many new challenges in the development of hardware and software and the design of network architectures and protocols for sensor networks.

 To prolong the operational lifetime of a sensor network, energy efficiency should be considered in every aspect of sensor network design, not only hardware and software but also network architectures and protocols.

2. Limited Hardware Resources. Sensor nodes have limited processing and storage capacities and thus can only perform limited computational functionalities. These hardware constraints present many challenges in network protocol design for sensor networks, which must consider not only the energy constraint in sensor nodes but also the processing and storage capacities of sensor nodes.

3. Massive and Random Deployment. Most sensor networks consist of hundreds to thousands of sensor nodes; node deployment can be either manual or random. In most applications, sensor nodes can be scattered randomly in an intended area or dropped massively over an inaccessible or hostile region. The sensor nodes must autonomously organize themselves into a communication network before they start to perform a sensing task.

4. Dynamic and Unreliable Environment. A sensor network usually operates in a dynamic and unreliable environment. On one hand, the topology of a sensor network may change frequently due to node failures, damages, additions, or energy depletion. On the other hand, sensor nodes are linked by a wireless medium, which is noisy, error prone, and time varying. The connectivity of the network may be frequently disrupted because of channel fading or signal attenuation.

5. Diverse Applications. Sensor networks have a wide range of diverse applications. The requirements for different applications may vary significantly. No network protocol can meet the requirements of all applications. The design of sensor networks is application specific.

11.3.3.3 WSN Design Objectives

Most sensors are impractical for implementing all the design objectives in a single network. Instead, only some parts of these networks are application specific and have different application requirements.

The main design objectives for sensor networks include the following:

1. Small node size: Reducing node size is one of the primary design objectives of sensor networks. Sensor nodes are usually deployed in a harsh or hostile environment in large numbers. Reducing node size can facilitate node deployment and can also reduce the cost and power consumption of sensor nodes.

2. Low node cost: Since sensor nodes are usually deployed in a harsh or hostile environment in large numbers and cannot be reused, it is important to reduce the cost of sensor nodes so that the cost of the whole network is reduced.

3. Low power consumption: Reducing power consumption is the most important objective in the design of a sensor network. Since sensor nodes are powered by battery and it is often very difficult or even impossible to change or recharge their batteries, it is crucial to reduce the power consumption of sensor nodes so that the lifetime of the sensor nodes, as well as of the whole network, is prolonged.

4. Self-configurability: In sensor networks, sensor nodes are usually deployed in a region of interest without careful planning and engineering. Once deployed, sensor nodes should be able to autonomously organize themselves

into a communication network and reconfigure their connectivity in the event of topology changes and node failures.

5. Scalability: In sensor networks, the number of sensor nodes may be on the order of tens, hundreds, or thousands. Thus, network protocols designed for sensor networks should be scalable to different network sizes.

6. Adaptability: In sensor networks, a node may fail, join, or move, which would result in changes in node density and network topology. Thus, network protocols designed for sensor networks should be adaptive to such density and topology changes.

7. Reliability: For many sensor network applications, it is required that data be reliably delivered over noisy, error-prone, and time-varying wireless channels. To meet this requirement, network protocols designed for sensor networks must provide error-control and correction mechanisms to ensure reliable data delivery.

8. Fault tolerance: Sensor nodes are prone to failures due to harsh deployment environments and unattended operations. Thus, sensor nodes should be fault tolerant and have the abilities of self-testing, self-calibrating, self-repairing, and self-recovering.

9. Security: In many military or security applications, sensor nodes are deployed in a hostile environment and thus are vulnerable to adversaries. In such situations, a sensor network should introduce effective security mechanisms to prevent the data information in the network or a sensor node from unauthorized access or malicious attacks.

10. Channel utilization: Sensor networks have limited bandwidth resources. Thus, communication protocols designed for sensor networks should efficiently make use of the bandwidth to improve channel utilization.

11. Quality-of-Service (QoS) support: In sensor networks, different applications may have different QoS requirements in terms of delivery latency and packet loss. For example, some applications, like fire monitoring, are delay sensitive and thus require timely data delivery. Some applications, for example, data collection for scientific exploration, are delay tolerant but cannot stand packet loss. Thus, network protocol design should consider the applicable or relevant QoS requirements of the specific applications.

11.3.3.4 WSN Architecture

A sensor network typically consists of a large number of sensor nodes densely deployed in a region of interest and one or more data sinks or base stations that are located close to or inside the sensing region, as shown in Figure 11.3a. The sink(s) sends queries or commands to the sensor nodes in the sensing region, while the sensor nodes collaborate to accomplish the sensing task and send the sensed data to the sink(s). Meanwhile, the sink(s) also serves as a gateway to outside networks, for

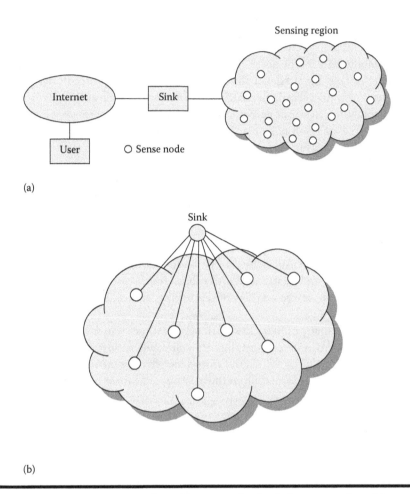

Figure 11.3   (a) Sensor Network Architecture, (b) Single-hop network architecture.

example, the Internet. It collects data from the sensor nodes, performs simple processing on the collected data, and then sends relevant information (or the processed data) via the Internet to the users who requested it or use the information.

To send data to the sink, each sensor node can use single-hop long-distance transmission, which leads to the single-hop network architecture, as shown in Figure 11.3b. However, long-distance transmission is costly in terms of energy consumption; in sensor networks, the energy consumed for communication is much higher than that for sensing and computation. Additionally, the energy consumed for transmission dominates the total energy consumed for communication, and the required transmission power grows exponentially with the increase in transmission distance. In order to reduce the amount of traffic and transmission distance and, consequently, increase energy savings and prolong network lifetime, multi-hop short-distance communication is highly preferred.

 Basic organization of the sensor network can be of two types:

1. Flat architecture: In a flat network, each node plays the same role in performing a sensing task, and all sensor nodes are peers. Due to the large number of sensor nodes, it is not feasible to assign a global identifier to each node in a sensor network. For this reason, data-gathering is usually accomplished by using data-centric routing, where the data sink transmits a query to all nodes in the sensing region via flooding, and only the sensor nodes that have the data matching the query will respond to the sink. Each sensor node communicates with the sink via a multi-hop path and uses its peer nodes as relays.

2. Hierarchical architecture: In a hierarchical network, sensor nodes are organized into clusters, where a node with lower energy can be used to perform the sensing task and send the sensed data to its cluster head at short distance, while a node with higher energy can be selected as a cluster head to process the data from its cluster members and transmit the processed data to the sink. This process can not only reduce the energy consumption for communication but can also balance traffic load and improve scalability when the network size grows. Since all sensor nodes have the same transmission capability, clustering must be periodically performed in order to balance the traffic load among all sensor nodes. Moreover, data aggregation can also be performed at cluster heads to reduce the amount of data transmitted to the sink and improve the energy efficiency of the network even further.

A sensor network can be organized into a single-hop clustering architecture or a multi-hop clustering architecture depending on the distance between the cluster members and their cluster heads. Similarly, a sensor network can be organized into a single-tier clustering architecture or a multi-tier clustering architecture depending on the number of tiers in the clustering hierarchy envisaged for the network. Figure 11.4a–c respectively show single-hop, multi-hop, and multi-tier clustering architecture.

11.3.3.4.1 Sensor Node Structure

A sensor node typically consists of four basic components: a sensing unit, a processing unit, a communication unit, and a power unit, shown in Figure 11.5.

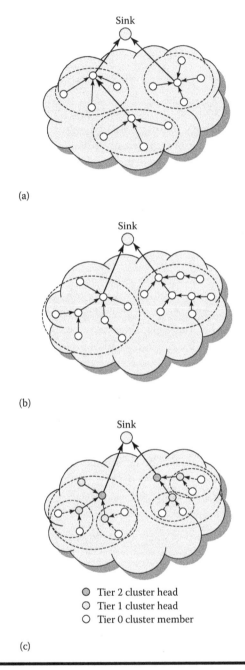

(a)

(b)

(c)

○ Tier 2 cluster head
○ Tier 1 cluster head
○ Tier 0 cluster member

Figure 11.4 (a) Single-hop multi-clustering architecture, (b) Multi-hop clustering architecture, and (c) Multi-tier clustering architecture.

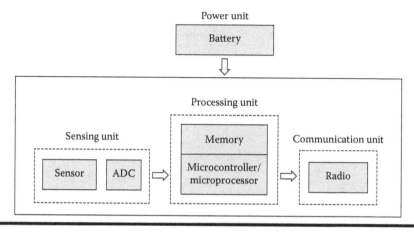

Figure 11.5 Sensor node structure.

1. Sensing unit usually consists of one or more sensors and analog-to-digital converters (ADCs).The sensors observe the physical phenomenon and generate analog signals based on the observed phenomenon. The ADCs convert the analog signals into digital signals, which are then fed to the processing unit.
2. Processing unit usually consists of a microcontroller or microprocessor with memory (e.g., Intel's StrongARM microprocessor and Atmel's AVR microprocessor), which provides intelligent control to the sensor node.
3. Communication unit consists of a short-range radio for performing data transmission and reception over a radio channel.
4. The power unit consists of a battery for supplying power to drive all other components in the system.

In addition, a sensor node can also be equipped with some other units, depending on specific applications. For example, a motor may be needed to move sensor nodes in some sensing tasks. A GPS may be needed in some applications that require location information for network operation. All these units should be built into a small module with low power consumption and low production cost.

11.3.3.4.2 WSN Protocol Stack

Figure 11.6 shows the generic WSN Protocol stack. The application layer contains a variety of application-layer protocols to generate various sensor network applications. The transport layer is responsible for the reliable data delivery required by the application layer. The network layer is responsible for routing the data from the transport layer. The data link layer is primarily responsible for data stream multiplexing, data frame transmission and reception, medium access, and error control.

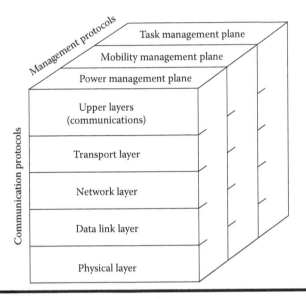

Figure 11.6   Generic WNS protocol stack.

The physical layer is responsible for signal transmission and reception over a physical communication medium, including frequency generation, signal modulation, transmission and reception, data encryption, and so on.

Table 11.7a,b presents possible protocol stack and possible lower layer protocols, respectively.

1. Application layer: The application layer includes a variety of application-layer protocols that perform various sensor network applications, such as query dissemination, node localization, time synchronization, and network security. For example, the sensor management protocol (SMP) is an application-layer management protocol that provides software operations to perform a variety of tasks, for example, exchanging location-related data, synchronizing sensor nodes, moving sensor nodes, scheduling sensor nodes, and querying the status of sensor nodes. The sensor query and data dissemination protocol (SQDDP) provides user applications with interfaces to issue queries, respond to queries, and collect responses .The sensor query and tasking language (SQTL) provides a sensor programming language used to implement middleware in WSNs. Although many sensor network applications have been proposed, their corresponding application-layer protocols still need to be developed.

2. Transport layer: The transport layer is responsible for reliable end-to-end data delivery between sensor nodes and the sink(s). Due to the energy,

Table 11.7 (a) Possible WSN Protocol Stack (b) Possible Lower-Layer WSN Protocols

(a)	
Upper layers	In-network applications, including application processing, data aggregation, external querying query processing, and external database
Layer 4	Transport, including data dissemination and accumulation, caching, and storage
Layer 3	Networking, including adaptive topology management and topological routing
Layer 2	Link layer (contention): channel sharing (MAC), timing, and locality
Layer 1	Physical medium: communication channel, sensing, actuation, and signal processing

(b)				
	GPRS/GSM lxRTT/CDMA	*IEEE 802.11b/g*	*IEEE 802.15.1*	*IEEE 802.15.4*
Market name for standard	2.5G/3G	Wi-Fi	Bluetooth	ZigBee
Network target	WAN/MAN	WLAN and hotspot	PAN and DAN (desk area network)	WSN
Application focus	Wide area voice and data	Enterprise applications (data and VoIP)	Cable replacement	Monitoring and control
Bandwidth (Mbps)	0.064–0.128+	11–54	0.7	0.020–0.25
Transmission range (ft)	3000+	1–300+	1–30+	1–300+
Design factors	Reach and transmission quality	Enterprise support, scalability, and cost	Cost, ease of use	Reliability, power, and cost

computation, and storage constraints of sensor nodes, traditional transport protocols like the conventional end-to-end retransmission-based error control and the window-based congestion control mechanisms used in the transport control protocol (TCP) cannot be applied directly to sensor networks without modification.

3. Network layer: The network layer is responsible for routing the data sensed by source sensor nodes to the data sink(s). In a sensor network, sensor nodes are deployed in a sensing region to observe a phenomenon of interest; the observed phenomenon or data need to be transmitted to the data sink. Sensor nodes are densely deployed and neighboring nodes are close to each other, which makes it feasible to use short-distance communication. In multi-hop communication, a sensor node transmits its sensed data toward the sink via one or more intermediate nodes, which can not only reduce the energy consumption for communication but also effectively reduce the signal prop-agation and channel fading effects inherent in long-range wireless communi-cation, and is therefore preferred.

   However, routing protocols for traditional wireless networks are not suit-able for sensor networks because they do not consider energy efficiency as the primary concern. Also, data from the sensing region toward the sink exhibits a unique many-to-one traffic pattern in sensor networks. The combination of multi-hop and many-to-one communications results in a significant increase in transit traffic intensity and thus packet congestion, collision, loss, delay, and energy consumption as data moves closer toward the sink. Therefore, it is important to take into account the energy constraint of sensor nodes as well as the unique traffic pattern in the design of the network layer and routing protocols.

4. Data link layer: The data link layer is responsible for data stream multiplex-ing, data frame creation and detection, medium access, and error control in order to provide reliable point-to-point and point-to-multipoint trans-missions. One of the most important functions of the data link layer is medium access control (MAC), the primary objective of which is to fairly and efficiently share the shared communication resources or medium among multiple sensor nodes in order to achieve good network performance in terms of energy consumption, network throughput, and delivery latency. However, MAC protocols for traditional wireless networks cannot be applied directly to sensor networks without modifications because they do not take into account the unique characteristics of sensor networks, in particular, the energy constraint. For example, the primary concern in a cellular system is to provide QoS to users. Energy efficiency is only of secondary importance because there is no power limit with the base stations and the mobile users can replenish the batteries in their handsets. In MANETs, mobile nodes are equipped with portable devices powered by battery, which is also replaceable.

In contrast, the primary concern in sensor networks is energy conservation for prolonging network lifetime, which makes traditional MAC protocols unsuitable for sensor networks.

In many applications, a sensor network is deployed in a harsh environment where wireless communication is error prone. In this case, error control becomes indispensable and critical for achieving link reliability or reliable data transmission. In general, there are two main error control mechanisms: Forward Error Correction (FEC) and Automatic Repeat reQuest (ARQ). ARQ achieves reliable data transmission by retransmitting lost data packets or frames. Obviously, this incurs significant retransmission overheads and additional energy consumption and therefore is not suitable for sensor networks. FEC achieves link reliability by using error-control codes in data transmission, which introduces additional encoding and decoding complexities that require additional processing resources in sensor nodes. Therefore, a trade-off should be optimized between the additional processing power and the corresponding coding gain in order to have a powerful, energy-efficient, and low-complexity FEC mechanism.

5. Physical layer: The physical layer is responsible for converting bit streams from the data link layer to signals that are suitable for transmission over the communication medium. It must deal with various related issues like
   a. Transmission medium and frequency selection, carrier frequency generation, signal modulation and detection, and data encryption
   b. Design of the underlying hardware
   c. Electrical and mechanical interfaces

Medium and frequency selection is an important problem for communication between sensor nodes. One option is to use radio and the industrial, scientific and medical (ISM) bands that are license-free in most countries. The main advantages of using the ISM bands include free use, large spectrum, and global availability. However, the ISM bands already have been used for some communication systems, such as cordless phone systems and WLANs. On the other hand, sensor networks require a tiny, low-cost, and ultra-low power transceiver. For these reasons, the 433-MHz ISM band and the 917-MHz ISM band have been recommended for use in Europe and North America, respectively.

Across each layer, the protocol stack can be divided into a group of management planes:

1. *Power management plane* is responsible for managing the power level of a sensor node for sensing, processing, and transmission and reception, which can be implemented by employing efficient power-management mechanisms at different protocol layers. For example, at the MAC layer, a sensor node can turn off its transceiver when there is no data to transmit and receive. At

the network layer, a sensor node may select a neighbor node with the most residual energy as its next hop to the sink.

2. *Connection management plane* is responsible for the configuration and reconfiguration of sensor nodes to establish and maintain the connectivity of a network in the case of node deployment and topology change due to node addition, node failure, node movement, and so on.

3. *Task management plane* is responsible for task distribution among sensor nodes in a sensing region in order to improve energy efficiency and prolong network lifetime. Since sensor nodes are usually densely deployed in a sensing region and are redundant for performing a sensing task, not all sensor nodes in the sensing region are required to perform the same sensing task. Therefore, a task-management mechanism can be used to perform task distribution among multiple sensors.

11.4 Sensor Data Processing

11.4.1 Sensor Data-Gathering and Data-Dissemination Mechanisms

Two major factors that determine the system architecture and design methodology are

1. The number of sources and sinks within the sensor network: Sensor network applications can be classified into three categories:
   a. One-sink–multiple-sources
   b. One-source–multiple-sinks
   c. Multiple-sinks–multiple-sources

   An application wherein the interaction between the sensor network and the subscribers is typically through a single gateway (sink) node falls in the multiple-sources–one-sink category. On the other hand, a traffic-reporting system that disseminates the traffic conditions (e.g., an accident) at a certain location to many drivers (sinks) falls in the one-source–multiple-sinks category.

2. The trade-offs between energy, bandwidth, latency, and information accuracy: An approach cannot usually optimize its performance in all aspects. Instead, based on the relative importance of its requirements, an application usually trades less important criteria for optimizing the performance with respect to the most important attribute. For instance, for mission-critical applications, the end-to-end latency is perhaps the most important attribute and needs to be kept below a certain threshold, even at the expense of additional energy consumption.

Data-gathering and dissemination mechanisms are based on the following three factors:

- Storage location
- Direction of diffusion
- Structure of devices

11.5 Sensor Database

The main purpose of a sensor database system is to facilitate the data-collection process. Users specify their interests via simple, declarative structured query language–like (SQL) queries. Upon receipt of a request, the sensor database system efficiently collects and processes data within the sensor network and disseminates the result to users. A query-processing layer between the application layer and the network layer provides an interface for users to interact with the sensor network. The layer should also be responsible for managing the resources (especially the available power).

Sensor networks can be envisioned as a distributed database for users to query the physical world. In most sensor-network applications, sensors extract useful information from the environment and either respond to queries made by users or take an active role to disseminate the information to one or more sinks. The information is then exploited by subscribers and/or users for their decision making.

Consider an environment monitoring and alert system that uses several types of sensors, including rainfall sensors, water-level sensors, weather sensors, and chemical sensors, to record the precipitation and water level regularly, to report the current weather conditions, and to issue flood or chemical pollution warnings.

A complete hierarchical architecture (four-tier) of sensor database systems for such a monitoring application is shown in Figure 11.7a. The lowest level is a group of sensor nodes that perform sensing, computing, and in-network processing in a field. The data collected within the sensor network are first propagated to its gateway node (second level). Next, the gateway node relays the data through a transit network to a remote base station (third level). Finally, the base station connects to a database replica across the Internet. Among the four tiers, the resource within the sensor networks is the most constrained. In most of the applications, the sensor network is composed of sensors and a gateway node (sink), as shown in Figure 11.7b, although the number of sinks or sources might vary from application to application.

TinyDB evolved from tiny aggregation (TAG), and is built on top of the TinyOS operating system. The sink and sensors are connected in a routing tree, shown in Figure 11.7b. A sensor chooses its parent node, which is one hop closer to the root (sink). The sink accepts queries from users outside the sensor network. Query processing can be performed in four steps:

1. Query optimization
2. Query dissemination

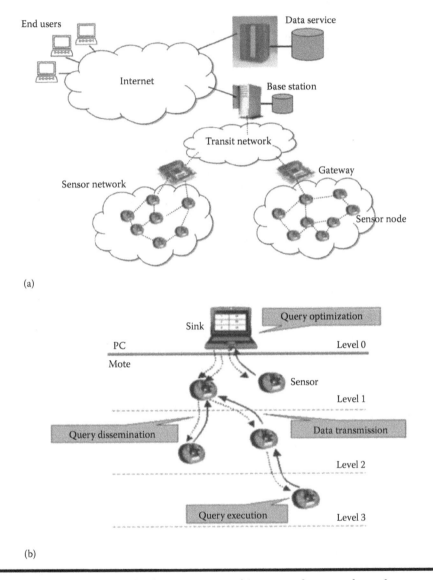

(a)

(b)

Figure 11.7 (a) Sensor database system architecture, (b) procedures for query and data extraction in TinyDB.

3. Query execution
4. Data dissemination

For the monitoring application under consideration, there are five types of queries that users typically make:

1. Historical queries. These queries are concerned with aggregate, historical information gathered over time and stored in a database system, for example, "What was the average level of rainfall of Thane District in May 2010?"
2. Snapshot queries. These queries are concerned with the information gathered from the network at a specific (current or future) time point, for example, "Retrieve the current readings of temperature sensors in Thane District."
3. Long-running queries. These queries ask for information over a period of time, for example, "Retrieve every 30 min the highest temperature sensor reading in Thane District from 6 P.M. to 10 P.M. tonight."
4. Event-triggered queries. These queries pre-specify the conditions that trigger queries, for example, "If the water level exceeds 10 meters in Thane District, query the rain-fall sensors about the amount of precipitation during the past hour. If the amount of precipitation exceeds 100 mm, send an emergency message to the base station to issue a flood warning."
5. Multi-dimensional range queries. These queries involve more than one attribute of sensor data and specify the desired search range as well, for example, "In Thane District, list the positions of all sensors that detect water level between 5 and 8 m and have temperatures between 50°F and 60°F."

TinyDB provide a declarative SQL-like query interface for users to specify the data to be extracted. Similar to SQL, the acquisitional query language used in TinyDB, TinySQL, consists of a select-from-where clause that supports selection, join, projection, and aggregation. The data within sensor networks can be considered as virtually a table, each column of which corresponds to an attribute and each row of which corresponds to a sample measured at a specific location and time. The query language in the sensor database differs from SQL mainly in that its queries are continuous and periodic.

Upon reception of a query, the sink performs query optimization to reduce the energy incurred in the pending query process:

■ Ordering of sampling operations: Since the energy incurred in retrieving readings from different types of sensors is different, the sampling operations should be reduced for sensors that consume high energy.
■ Query aggregation: By combining multiple queries for the same event into a single query, only one query needs to be sent.

 One distinct characteristic of query execution in TinyDB is that sensors sleep during every epoch and are synchronized to wake up, receive, transmit, and process the data in the same time period.

After a query is optimized at the sink, it is broadcast by the sink and disseminated to the sensor network. When a sensor receives a query, it has to decide whether to process the query locally and/or rebroadcasts it to its children. A sensor only needs to forward the query to those child nodes that may have the matched result. To this end, a sensor has to maintain information on its children's attribute values. In TinyDB, a semantic routing tree (SRT) containing the range of the attributes of its children is constructed at each sensor. The attributes can be static information (e.g., location) or dynamic information (e.g., light readings). For attributes that are highly correlated among neighbors in the tree, SRT can reduce the number of disseminated queries.

11.6 Summary

This chapter began with an introduction to the Internet of Things (IoT) enabled by primarily by the availability of cloud and Big Data technologies. It then described the radio frequency identification (RFID), a wireless automatic identification technology whereby an object with an attached RFID tag is identified by an RFID reader. Following this was introduced the principal concept of wireless sensor network technology enabled by the availability of smaller, cheaper and intelligent sensors, which has important applications like remote environmental monitoring. The last part of the chapter discussed processing and storage of the sensor data.

Appendix A: Internet as Extended Brain

With the advent of the Internet, one may be hard pressed to explain the plethora of technologies like social media, mobile computing, and Internet of Things (IoT) technologies, which seem to have suddenly sprung up out from nowhere. This appendix suggests that Internet functions are quite similar to the human brain and that the Internet-based technologies listed earlier are not unlike the sensing mechanisms of the human body, which are, in some ways, extensions of human intelligence.

Of all the ideas that led to the advent of the Internet, the most ancient one was the desire to make readily available the world's store of knowledge. It was this idea, for example, that drove the French philosopher Denis Diderot to create the first great encyclopedia in the eighteenth century. The multi-volume *Encyclopédie* was one of the central projects of the Age of Enlightenment, which tried to bring about radical and revolutionary reform by giving knowledge and therefore power to the people. The first English-language encyclopedia, the *Encyclopedia Britannica*, appeared in 1768 and was modeled directly on the *Encyclopédie*. Neither the *Encyclopédie* nor the *Encyclopedia Britannica* contained all of the world's knowledge, but what was significant was that they brought order to the universe of knowledge, giving people a sense of what there was to know.

During the 1930s, British socialist, novelist, and science writer H. G. Wells, best known in the United States as the author of *The War of the Worlds* and *The Time Machine*, wrote pamphlets and articles and gave speeches about his project for a World Encyclopedia that would do for the twentieth century what Diderot had done for the eighteenth. Wells failed to interest publishers owing to the enormous cost of such a project and, in the fall of 1937, he embarked on a US lecture tour, hoping to raise funds. He covered five cities, and the lecture he gave in his last venue, in New York, was also broadcast on the radio. In his talk, titled "The Brain Organization of the Modern World," Wells explained that his World Encyclopedia would not be an encyclopedia in the ordinary sense:

A World Encyclopedia no longer presents itself to a modern imagination as a row of volumes printed and published once for all, but as a sort of mental clearing house for the mind, a depot where knowledge and ideas are received, sorted, summarized, digested, clarified and compared…This Encyclopedic organization need not be concentrated now in one place; it might have the form of a network [that] would constitute the material beginning of a real World Brain.

In the postwar period, the idea was given new vigor by Vannevar Bush, the scientist and inventor who had developed analog computers and had risen to become chief scientific advisor to the president and head of the Office of Scientific Research and Development, where he directed much of the United States' scientific war effort. In July 1945, he set his ideas down in a popular article, "As We May Think," for the *Atlantic Monthly*. This article established a dream that had been pursued by information scientists for decades—and ultimately led to the Internet and World Wide Web (WWW).

The appendix starts with an overview of artificial intelligence, the Turing machine, and the Turing test, which is directed at the assessment of computer intelligence from the reference of human intelligence. Failure to realize artificial intelligence (AI), instead of being an impediment, is interpreted as motivation for the main theme of this appendix, namely, to explore the power and potential of the Internet as Extended Brain.

Although we make a quick acquaintance with the Turing test and its implications, we do not wade too deeply in the philosophical waters of whether or not machines can ever be "truly intelligent"; whether consciousness, thought, self, or even "soul" have reductionist roots or not. We shall neither speculate much on these matters nor attempt to describe the diverse philosophical debates and arguments on this subject. These are rather involved matters and out of scope for this book, which is reverse-focused on Internet intelligence and the degree to which it can augment particular aspects of human intelligence, or in other words, Internet as Extended Brain.

We start the journey by taking an overview of human intelligence, its gap from other animals, followed by the architecture of the brain that endows it with the characteristics of memory, thinking, and thoughts. Then it traces the concept of networks, neural networks, artificial neural networks (ANN) on one hand; and computer networks, the Internet, and the WWW on the other. Then we visit various areas of brain-augmentation enabled by the Internet, namely, social networks, Internet of Things (IoT), Semantic Web, context-aware applications, and collaboration applications.

The stance of Internet as Extended Brain enables highlighting the final significance or the purpose of continued advancements in technologies like the Internet and its latest or future avatars—they enhance human ability to contain and control the deleterious effects of disruptive technologies for ensuring the continual well-being, progress, and prosperity of humans and human society (see Section A.9.1, "Human Brain versus Internet Brain").

A.1 Artificial Intelligence

Machines are considered smart in comparison with humans, performing the same kinds of mental tasks that humans do—only faster and more accurately. Early humans first created mechanical computers (like Stonehenge) to keep track of the time, the seasons, the positions of heavenly bodies, and the rise and fall of the tides. These machines served as a kind of memory aid that followed the cycles of nature and helped the first farmers make decisions about planting and sailors to navigate the seas. After the invention of currency, mechanical calculators like the abacus made arithmetic and trade easier and faster. A third human function that machines help us with is making decisions. We continue to develop machines that serve these three as well as more advanced human abilities like sensors that interact with their surroundings, speech, vision, language, and locomotion—even the ability to learn from their experience to better achieve their goals and objectives (see Sections A.11 and A.13).

A.1.1 Turing Machine

In the 1940s, people like British mathematician Alan Turing and John von Neumann conceived the idea of a universal computer. Their idea was to build a general-purpose computer that manipulates symbols according to a sequence of instructions called a program, which could be changed to perform different tasks. In other words, you don't have to build an entirely new machine to perform each desired function. You merely change the program to a new set of instructions appropriate to the function you want it to perform. Since the real intelligence would lie in its program, the hardware required to create Turing's universal computer could be very simple but flexible. He imagined a simple realization that worked by writing and changing binary digits (e.g., zeros and ones) on some storage medium, such as a moving paper tape, and manipulating the arrangement of the binary digits on the tape according to programmed rules. He also imagined that the program itself could be encoded as binary digits on the same storage medium.

Turing proved mathematically that such a programmable machine could, with sufficient storage capacity and speed, fully emulate the function of any other machine, including, he thought, the human brain. If Turing was right (and no one has yet proven otherwise), then only engineering limitations on its speed and capacity prevent a universal computing machine from accomplishing any physically possible task!

Most computers in use today are the direct descendants of Turing's concept of a universal computer. When you dig down inside a modern digital computer to the level at which information is being processed, you find an electronic version of Turing's paper-tape machine. All the computer functions that we take for granted today—word processing, e-mail, the WWW—are performed by programs that simulate these functions on general-purpose digital computers. The computer manipulates strings of zeros and ones, or more precisely, it switches electrical voltages between two states representing zeros and ones—they are just electrical circuits for manipulating arrays of binary digits, or bits. Anything a digital computer does can be reduced to a huge number of simple operations on these binary off–on voltages.

A brain performs its basic switching functions at the level of a neuron; a digital computer carries out its elemental switching at the level of a transistor. In the future, instructions may be carried out more efficiently by switching beams of light or quantum states, but the nature of the machine that carries out the steps is unimportant. The key to performing a complex job lies in breaking it down into many simpler steps, or *instructions*. Opening and closing a switch is one of the simplest steps imaginable. Information-theory pioneer Claude Shannon showed that you can perform any logical task, no matter how complex, using an arrangement of off–on switches.

Advances in storage capacity and processing speed will simply keep up with the demands of more complex tasks. What makes machines so smart is that they organize and manipulate information that is represented symbolically by complex switching networks. Thus, any computer, no matter how simple or complex, is no more and no less than a switching network that takes one set of symbols and transforms them into another set of symbols.

AI is based on the premise that any task whose details we can describe precisely can be done by a machine. Some AI researchers believe that all that is required to reproduce any behavior on machines is to precisely describe its logical structure.

A.1.1.1 Behavior Simulation

Purposeful behavior, no matter how intricate, subtle, or complex, must be understood as a large collection, or web, of relatively simple operations acting together. Acting together means that the steps must be organized and coordinated so that they work in concert, like the instruments of an orchestra, to produce the desired result. Complicated tasks may require many sub-tasks to be completed in parallel and their results integrated. Many jobs require complex branching or recursion (taking the results of sub-tasks and feeding them back to the beginning again and again). But monitoring, coordinating, and integrating large numbers of sub-tasks is the job of an executive that takes a holistic view and checks to be sure that the result is the desired one. The top executive, who may be a human or another program, is said to be smart enough to know what the overall problem is and to organize the steps required to solve it. This purposeful organization of tasks and sub-tasks is what makes computers so smart—and is indistinguishable from what we call *thinking*.

Thus, it would seem, then, that there should be no limit to the number of tasks, each with its own executive, that can be organized into hierarchies, like human corporations, and combined to perform ever more complex tasks, including tasks that we would call *purposeful* or *intelligent*.

There are two ways that such purposeful organizations can come about. One is the traditional top-down method of design, in which a functional requirement is first defined and then the necessary systems and sub-systems are created and integrated to produce the desired outcome. This is how human beings are used to thinking about and solving problems. A second way to create complex organizations is called the *bottom-up* approach. It begins with simple pieces that self-assemble in a random, trial-and-error fashion. Some combinations persist that are able to make copies of themselves or to further assemble into more complex combinations. Environmental forces determine which combinations survive or die. This is the mechanism we call *natural selection*, a much more time-consuming process whose results are highly optimized but essentially unpredictable.

But once you are confronted with intelligence, how will you assess or measure it? That is where we turn to understand the Turing test in the next section.

 Lamarckian Evolution for Machines

Machines are just beginning to learn how to modify their own programs, even to reproduce and improve their own kind, but in a way far superior to the way biological organisms do. Machines can pass along everything they have learned to succeeding generations. This ability gives machines a tremendous evolutionary advantage over humans, who do this in a crude way by recording knowledge and experiences outside their brains in external media, like books or the Internet. Only fragments of this knowledge and experience are actually absorbed by succeeding generations. To discuss the profound implications of Lamarckian evolution for machines would need a whole book in itself.

A.1.2 Turing Test

Many of us refuse to label any machine, no matter what it does, as truly intelligent. Others glibly use the term to describe any apparently purposeful behavior, be it machine, human, or other animal. Are there any truly objective indicators of intelligent behavior? The Turing test is a test meant to ascertain behavior that can be termed as *intelligent*.

The Turing test is an adaptation of an "imitation game" suggested by Alan Turing in 1950. The idea of this thought experiment is that a blind interview would be set up, in which a human interviewer would converse, by typing on a terminal, with an unseen something or someone in the next room. Any subject matter is allowed in the conversation. Various humans and machines are given a turn conversing with the interviewer, whose job is to guess, in each case, whether he or she is communicating with another human or a machine. Any subject that succeeds in fooling the interviewer after some suitable time is said to be intelligent.

 Perhaps the modern equivalent of a blind interview would be trying to determine whether your e-mail pen pal is a machine or a person.

In the coming decades, we will build machines and networks of machines that excel (i.e., are "smarter") in some significant, but not all, aspects of human intelligence. It is highly unlikely, however, that there will be machines indistinguishable in all respects from humans any time soon, if ever. (There would simply be no point in doing so.) So rather than measuring a machine's overall intelligence against a human's, we will find it more useful to compare the speed, cost, efficiency, and accuracy of a given task when performed by a human with the results of assigning a machine to perform the same task. Thus, intelligence is multi-dimensional—like linguistic, mathematical, logical, musical, kinesthetic, spatial, physical, interpersonal, emotional, and social intelligence—and superlative performance in some tasks (compared to humans) will span across more than one dimension of intelligence.

But make no mistake; sooner than later, we will find that intelligent machines are capable of far more than just doing things better than humans do. Machines that are able to learn and innovate and modify themselves will begin to exhibit new forms of intelligence that we will barely comprehend. If we meekly conform to a world shaped by the needs of machines instead of the needs of humans, then the days to our extinction are surely numbered. If, on the other hand, we actively demand that our machines enrich our lives, and if we take part in the process, then it is more likely to turn out that way.

Machines will easily displace us only if we allow our overall intelligence to languish. However, nothing stops us from compensating for the widening chasm from the burgeoning machines by employing the machines themselves. That is what this appendix is about—how we can augment human intelligence and, hence, the human brain with the intelligence of the Internet; in other words, Internet as Extended Brain.

A.2 Human Intelligence

Intelligence is certain kinds of behavior, regardless of the package it comes in— be it human, animal, extra-terrestrial, or machine. We recognize that intelligent behavior is multi-dimensional, that is, not measurable along a single (e.g., IQ) scale. We can distinguish between linguistic, mathematical, logical, musical, kinesthetic, spatial, physical, interpersonal, emotional, and social intelligence, to name a few, and we recognize that each is present to different degrees in each creature.

Here is a list of some behaviors that most people will agree indicate intelligent behavior when present to any recognizable degree:

1. Stores and retrieves knowledge
2. Learns from experiences and adapts to novel situations
3. Discriminates between what is important and what is irrelevant to the situation at hand
4. Recognizes patterns, similarities, and differences in complex environments
5. Creates new ideas by combining old ideas in new ways
6. Plans and manages strategies for solving complex problems
7. Sets and pursues goals
8. Recognizes its own intelligence and its place in the world

Just as IQ tests have well-known cultural and gender biases, our present thinking about intelligence surely has species biases as well. If we define intelligence to be human intelligence, then no non-human can be intelligent, by definition. These eight qualities say nothing about the package in which they come, yet they are abstractions drawn entirely from our human experience. Limiting our definition of intelligence to the human kind is not only unduly restrictive; it also severely hampers our quest to understand the nature of intelligent thought in a scientific fashion by reducing it to its bare essentials. It may even be impossible to uncover the basic computational nature of thought by starting with such a specific and complex example as the human mind.

We are learning about intelligence by isolating particular aspects of thought—memory, learning, recognizing patterns, language, emotions, and consciousness—one at a time, starting with simple artificial models. By trying to build intelligent machines, we learn not only about intelligence in general but about our own as well. The challenge is not to build things that act like humans (we already know how to do that) but to imagine completely different kinds of intelligence, to open up opportunities that are not limited by our genetic heritage.

Intelligence is less about anything objective or measurable and more a semantic question about what entities our egos allow to have that label. Before the electronic age, the term *computer* used to mean people who did arithmetic for a living. Computation was regarded as an activity requiring intelligence. Nowadays, the term almost always refers to a machine, and mere computation, no matter how fast or accurate, is rarely called *intelligent*. Playing a creditable game of chess or composing music was once thought to require intelligence. Now, we're not so sure. We can avoid this kind of species chauvinism by having definitions of intelligence that are independent of who or what exhibits it.

Kinds of intelligence that are uniquely human are as follows:

- Common Sense
- Understanding
  - Understanding is not Predictability
- Chunking
- Vision and Pattern Recognition
- Imagination and Creativity

A.3 Gap from Other Animals

Humans tend to think of themselves as better than, or at least separate from, all other species on this planet. But every species is unique, and in that sense, humans are no different. In the tree of life, each species is a distinct branch with characteristics that set it apart from others. Humans differ from chimpanzees and other primates in some notable respects. We can lock our knees straight, have longer legs than arms, and habitually walk upright, freeing our hands to do things other than carry our weight. These are not exactly ground-breaking traits, compared to, say, the emergence of wings in birds, which predictably catapulted their bearers into a new sphere of possibility. Yet despite the paltry list of distinct physical attributes, we have managed to seize control of much of the planet. That is because our extraordinary powers do not derive from our muscles and bones but from our minds.

It is our mental capacities that have allowed us to tame fire and invent the wheel. They enable us to construct tools that make us stronger, fiercer, faster, and more precise, resilient, and versatile than any beast. We build machines that speed us from one place to the other, even to outer space. We investigate nature and rapidly accumulate and share knowledge. We create complex artificial worlds in which we wield unheralded power— power to shape the future and power to destroy and annihilate. We reflect on and argue about our present situation, our history, and our destiny. Our minds have spawned civilizations and technologies that have changed the face of the Earth, while our closest living animal relatives sit unobtrusively in their remaining forests. There appears to be a tremendous gap between human and animal minds, the nature and origin of which is the topic of this sub-section.

On the contrary, the evidence for continuity between human and animal bodies is overwhelming. The similarities in anatomy and bodily functions between humans and other primates are quite plain. We are made of the same flesh and blood; we go through the same basic life stages. In fact, many reminders of our shared inheritance with other animals have become the subject of cultural taboos: sex, menstruation, pregnancy, birth, feeding, defecation, urination, bleeding, illness, and dying.

Modern neuroscience is beginning to identify finer differences. The first documented microscopic distinction between ape and human brains has been a unique cell organization in a layer of humans' primary visual cortex—not an area typically associated with higher cognitive functions. There is also some suggestion that humans differ in the neural connections in the prefrontal cortex, an area very much associated with higher cognitive functions. While neurons in the back of the brain have relatively few connections, and human brains differ little from other primates in this respect, there are many connections in the prefrontal cortex. Their density is much higher in humans than in other primates that have been examined thus far.

> Behaviorally, two major features set us apart: our open-ended nested (or recursive) ability to imagine and reflect on different situations, that is, scenario building or predicting; and our deep-seated drive to link our scenario-building minds together. It seems to be primarily these two attributes that carried our ancestors across the gap, turning animal communication into open-ended human language, memory into mental time travel, social cognition into theory of mind, problem solving into abstract reasoning, social traditions into cumulative culture, and empathy into morality. Nested scenario building refers not to a single ability but to a complex faculty, itself built on a variety of sophisticated components that allow us to simulate and to reflect. We exchange our ideas and give feedback. We are wired to connect with others around us—we are wired to connect individual scenario-building capabilities into larger systems of scenario builders. We make and pursue shared goals. Our urge to connect was essential for the creation of cumulative cultures that shape our minds and endow us with our awesome powers. Our drive ultimately led to today's networks of mobile phones and social media that let us exchange our minds across the globe.

Even within each area of expertise, we differ vastly from each other. Each of us is unique. Our extensive cooperation and division of labor means that groups, and the individuals within them, benefit less from everyone being good at the same thing than from being good at a host of complementary skills. Groups composed of individuals with high multi-skills may have had a particular advantage. Perhaps we have evolved to be so individually different because our species is extraordinarily social and cooperative.

A.4 Human Brain

Neurons are cells, like other cells in the body: skin cells, liver cells, and so on. The difference is that neurons are specialized to send messages; they receive electrical inputs and send electrical outputs. They can be thought of a bit like simple little calculators that add up their inputs and send an electrical message as an output. The "messages" they send are just electrical pulses, and those brief transmissions contain no information other than their presence or absence; at any given moment, they are either on or off. A neuron receiving these messages or inputs reacts by setting up an electrical signal; from that point on, all further signals are sent from neuron to neuron via electricity. And at the "output" side, they send an electrical signal to a muscle, which extends or contracts, moving part of your body.

Neurons receive and send messages via electrical pulses, through wires that form their inputs and outputs. The input wires to a neuron are called *dendrites* and the outputs are *axons*. Axons from many neurons tend to become bundled together, traveling like an underground cable from one region of the brain to another. Nerves are just thick bundles of axons coming from large groups of neurons. Each input structure—olfaction, vision, touch—has neurons that send their nerves or axon bundles to specialized structures in the brain.

In the brain, the locations of target regions line up with the corresponding position of sensory systems on the body: chemical smell sensors at the front of the animal activate frontal divisions of the brain (forebrain); the eyes, somewhat further back, send their axons to the next brain divisions in the sequence; the rest of the animal's body projects itself into the hindbrain and spinal cord. In general, each of our senses is a segregated operation with its own dedicated structures, with no central processor unifying them.

There is a continued correspondence within each of these areas. For instance, within the vision area, there is a point-to-point map, akin to that in a film camera; inputs from the left part of the visual field activate neurons that, in turn, send their axons to a corresponding part of the diencephalon, whereas the right part of the visual field projects to a segregated region dedicated to the right-hand side, and so on for inputs that are in high versus low parts of the visual field. The result is much like a map drawn inside the brain, corresponding to locations on the skin, or in the image sensed by your eye, as seen in the figure. The resulting map in the brain is a direct point-to-point analog representation of the locations out in the world. These maps form naturally in the brain as an embryo grows to adulthood.

On the output side, the hindbrain and spinal cord form a kind of motor column aligned with the map of body muscles. So neurons located at the very top edge of the spinal cord send axons to the face: to the nose, mouth, and eye muscles. Next in line, neurons near the front of the spinal cord project to the muscles of the upper body, just below the face. The pattern continues all the way down to the bottom of the spinal cord, which provides input to tail muscles. In addition to the engines of locomotion in the hindbrain, there is a set of forebrain structures that is also critically involved in movement. This system, called the *striatum* or the *striatal complex*, acts like an organizer, globally coordinating the small movements of the hindbrain together into integrated actions.

The visual areas of the midbrain, the neighboring auditory zones, the cerebellum, and the tactile areas all project into collections of neurons in the mid- and hindbrain that act as relays (with an elaborate structure) to the hindbrain–spinal cord motor column. The relays operated by the visual areas project to outputs aimed at the head, so as to orient the animal in the direction of a sensed cue. Analogously, touch areas connect to motor outputs that trigger muscle responses appropriate to the location of the stimulus on the body.

However, the olfactory system is an exception in that it has no hint of the point-to-point organization of the other systems.

As stated earlier, all communication is accomplished through connections between neurons. The actual contacts between a transmitting neuron's axons, and a receiving neuron's dendrites, are *synapses*. The electrical pulse traveling down the axon causes the synapse to release a chemical neurotransmitter called glutamate, which then crosses a very thin space to reach the dendritic spine of the other neuron. A glutamate neurotransmitter molecule binds to the synapse at a "docking" site called a *receptor*. The binding of the transmitter causes a new electrical signal to be induced in the target neuron.

The olfactory (smell) system is constituted of cells in the nose connecting to the olfactory bulb, which in turn connects to the olfactory cortex. The axons from the nose to the bulb are organized as point-to-point connections, so that any pattern of activity activated by a particular odor in the nose is faithfully replicated in the olfactory bulb. But the connections from the bulb to the cortex are random-access circuits.

Synapses are notoriously unreliable. Any given input message will release the glutamate neurotransmitter only about half the time, and reliable thoughts and actions arise only from the co-occurrence of thousands of such chancy events. One of the great mysteries that has been unraveled is how the mediocre components in a brain can perform together to generate systems that perform so well. If there are different parts to a visual input pattern, for example, the lower trunk and upper branches in the shape of a tree, there will be corresponding parts to the output pattern. But in random-access circuits, those same parts of an input, the visual images of a trunk and boughs, may select a single target output that denotes the simultaneous occurrence of all the parts of the tree pattern rather than its separate parts in isolation; thus, the responding neurons denote the whole tree rather than just its parts. That is, a target neuron that responds to all parts of the tree input, converging from various parts of the trunk and branches, is acting as a recognizer, a detector, of the overall tree pattern. Random-access networks enable unified perceptions of disparate ingredients.

The great advantage of random-access circuits is that there will be some scattered population of cells in random-access cortex that respond to any possible combination of tree variants, including combinations that are entirely unexpected and that may never have occurred before. Random-access circuits solve the problem of how to assemble a diverse and unpredictable collection of inputs into a unitary and unique output. The target neurons in a random-access circuit have the ability to detect these gestalt-like patterns—patterns of the whole, not just the parts. Each neuron in a point-to-point network can only respond to its assigned isolated parts of the input, but each neuron in a random-access circuit may, all by itself, respond to aspects of the entire input pattern. Different cells in a random-access circuit lie in wait for their particular combinatorial pattern—an input arrangement from any parts of the scene to which they happen to be very well connected.

A.4.1 Learning

The single most crucial feature of random-access circuits is this: they can be modified by experience. The more a particular set of connections are activated, the more they are strengthened, becoming increasingly reliable responders. The ability to strengthen synaptic connections is a simple form of learning. Strengthening a connection simply locks in a particular pattern in the brain, and that responding pattern becomes the brain's internal "code" for whatever is being sensed.

The initial sensory cortical expansion was based on point-to-point organization, sending faithful representations of images and sounds forward into a neocortex that was set up with the random-access network designs representative of the olfactory cortex. Thus, the point-to-point world of the visual system becomes abandoned after just the first few connections of processing in the rest of the visual cortex. We have already seen that the same thing occurs in the olfactory system, where neat spatial organizations in the nose and in the olfactory bulb are replaced with scattered random-access representations in the olfactory cortex.

Once the cortex developed from the olfactory precursor circuits [#] became independent; the cortex no longer had to operate solely on olfaction, its original mode. In mammals, it became the engine that analyses olfactory odors, and visual images, and auditory sounds, and the sensation of touch, and a great deal more. How the nearly uniform structures of the cortex can end up doing the very different jobs of the different senses is another of the major mysteries of the brain.

Once all the different sensory inputs—vision, hearing, touch—became encoded in the same random-access manner, then there were no further barriers to cross-modal representations. That is, the switch from specialized midbrain apparatus to cortical modes of processing allows the brain to build multi-sensory unified representations of the external world. Images and sounds are converted into internal random-access codes much like olfactory codes. As these codes are created, they can be readily transmitted downstream to any other brain area, all of which now use the same internal coding scheme. Using the shared cortical design, every sense acquires the same capability. For instance, the sound of a song can remind you of the band that plays it, the cover art on their CD, the concert where you saw them play, and whom you were with. All these senses participate in perceiving the event, creating memories of the event, and retrieving those memories.

The result underlies the difference between the reptiles, largely lacking cross-modal representations; and the mammals, possessing them. Even the lowliest mammals appear in many ways cleverer, more intelligent, and more flexible than most reptiles; it is the new mammalian brain organization, centered around the neocortex, that is responsible for mammals' more adaptive behavior.

The exquisite and specialized machinery found in the visual, auditory, and tactile regions of neocortex of modern mammals arose as secondary adaptations that sharpened the acuity of perception. There is a great deal more visual information than olfactory information to be processed by the brain, more than the retina and the first levels of visual processing can extract. It seems that the visual and auditory areas of cortex are upper-stage sensory processors that supplement the information extraction of the initial brain stages.

A traditional view is that the point-to-point structures in our brains arose first, and the random-access "association" areas arose later in evolution.

A.4.2 Memory

Memory systems permit flexible adaptation. Modern theories of memory recognize different levels of memory that themselves vary in flexibility. Figure A.1 shows the now classic distinction between declarative and non-declarative memory (sometimes known as implicit and explicit memory, respectively), and, within declarative memory, the distinction between semantic and episodic memory. *Non-declarative* memory refers to the stimulus-driven, unconscious memory systems that drive such phenomena as procedural skills and habits, priming and perceptual learning, and simple classical conditioning. Declarative memory provides more flexible adaptation to the world than does simple learning or non-declarative memory.

Declarative memory is so named because it can be declared. It is conscious and corresponds to what we normally think of as "memory" in everyday language and provides the basis for language itself. It provides an explicit and often detailed model of the world in which we live. We know precisely where we live, the neighborhoods,

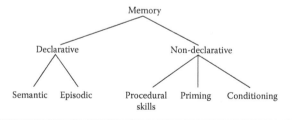

Figure A.1   Taxonomy of memory systems.

the geographical areas in which we work, play, and travel. As humans, we have a huge array of facts at our disposal that enable us to make precise plans for the future and meet different obligations and contingencies. Declarative memories can be voluntarily triggered top-down from the frontal lobes, rather than bottom-up through perception. They can therefore be brought into consciousness "off-line" for flexible planning and decision making. We can contrast and compare different pieces of knowledge and choose knowledge relevant to a particular activity, such as planning a career or a vacation.

Within declarative memory, *semantic* memory is the memory for facts, and *episodic* memory is the memory for events. Roughly, semantic memory can be likened to a combined dictionary and encyclopedia, while episodic memory can be likened to a personal diary. The distinction between semantic and episodic memory has also been characterized as that between knowing and remembering, respectively. Episodic memory is perhaps the ultimate in flexibility, since it records the particularities of one's life and allows the fine-tuning of personal events in the future.

A.4.3 Remembrance and Thinking

Cortical circuits do not operate in isolation; they are tightly connected to a set of four crucial brain structures just beneath the cortex:

- *Striatum* sends its outputs to ancient hindbrain and brainstem areas connected to muscles and the spinal cord. It is clearly involved in getting the body to move.
- *Amygdala* sends massive connections to a small region called the *hypothalamus*, a set of regulatory structures that virtually runs the autonomic systems of your body. The hypothalamus operates your endocrine glands (testosterone, estrogen, growth hormones, adrenaline, thyroid hormone, and many others) and generates simple primitive behaviors that are appropriate to these hormones. Amygdala can not only evoke primitive hard-wired behaviors via the hypothalamus but also the emotions that correspond to those behaviors.
- *Hippocampus* is central to the encoding of memory. Since memories from before hippocampal damage are intact but new memories can't be created, it has often been hypothesized that the hippocampus is a temporary repository of memories, which subsequently move onward to final, permanent, cortical storage sites.
- *Thalamus.*

These structures work with the cortex to control not just our behaviors and reactions but also our thoughts, our decisions, and our memories. All the parts participate in a unified architecture; in particular, both the hippocampus and amygdala send their messages to the striatum, and the striatum in turn is linked back to other cortical and thalamo-cortical circuits. These interactions themselves give a glimmer of coordinated intelligent behavior.

Cues are recognized by a primary cortex, which then, in parallel, distributes signals to regions that initiate movement (striatum), intensify or weaken the movements (amygdala), detect anomalies during the search (hippocampus), associate the cue with objects (hippocampus again), and organize actions in appropriate behavioral sequences (frontal striatal-thalamo-cortical loops). The other sensory systems—vision, audition, and touch—follow the same basic pathways in connecting the outside world to useful responses. Rather than the sensory areas, association areas connect heavily with the large sub-cortical areas, namely, striatum, amygdala, and hippocampus; and the frontal thalamo-cortical systems. This allows the associational cortex to generate movements, trigger emotional responses, and engage the planning system.

The frontal cortex has three primary output paths.

- The first goes to the motor cortex, which contains a point-to-point map of the body's muscles.
- The second pathway from frontal cortex connects to the striatum, which in turn projects right back to thalamo-cortical circuits.
- The third and final pathways are two-way connections from the frontal cortex to the sensory association cortical areas and back again. Taken together, these connection pathways explain three primary roles of the frontal cortex: planning movements, timing them, and coordinating internal thought patterns. Unified information about our sensory perceptions allow us to walk smoothly, to learn to pronounce words to sound the way we want them to, and to parallel park our cars.

The system does more than just organize actions, though; it also enables the organization of thoughts. Since the frontal cortex can assemble long temporal sequences, we can construct and reconstruct memories of past episodes. The system lends itself to creative use: the frontal cortex essentially has its pick of all the vast amounts of sensory material stored throughout association cortical regions.

Cortical circuits generate projections in both directions, implying that the initial processing of an input—a sight or a sound—becomes altered by the downstream conception of what that sight or sound may be. Thus, perception is not pure and direct; it is affected by our learned "expectations." So our prior experience with birds—what they look and sound like, where they occur, when we've seen them before—all can quite literally affect the way we perceive the bird today. One effect of these projections is the re-creation of sensation. The random-access abstract representations in sensory association areas are capable of reactivating the point-to-point maps in sensory cortical areas, re-creating more realistic images of the environment.

Studies have confirmed that this may indeed be going on in your brain: no matter what you see, you first recognize only its category and only later recognize it as an individual. The implication is that recognition is not as we thought: recognition occurs only as a special case of categorization and sub-categorization. It is not a separate, or separable, brain operation, but an integral part of the process of category recognition.

A.4.3.1 Thoughts

There are perhaps 100 billion neurons in your brain, each of which may, at any moment, send a signal via a brief, tiny pulse of electricity to other neurons, via roughly 100 trillion connections or synapses. Each neuron can, in turn, re-route the message to still other target neurons. The spreading activity, coursing through the pathways of the brain, constitutes the message—this activity is the substance of thought.

Regarding cortical circuits, contrary to common sense, there is demonstrable value in eliminating finer distinctions. Eight slightly different views of a bird are still that bird. If every different view triggered a different pattern of cortical cell activity, each view would correspond to a different mental object. Indeed, if every separate view was registered as an entirely different percept, we'd be overwhelmed by the details of the sensory world, unable to recognize the patterns of similarity that recur. Clustering gives rise to internal organization of our percepts; it enables generalization from individual birds to the category of all birds.

The association cortices proceed hierarchically, building ever more complex representations condensed into further and further downstream cortical regions. Connection paths through the brain take a range of directions, branching from initial generic features, to certain objects, to sub-groups of objects. As we progress inward, further along the process, following various brain paths, we reach regions that are increasingly "specialized" for the particular assemblages of inputs that they happen to receive. All these brain paths are traversed in parallel with each other; the ones that respond to a given sight or sound are the ones that we perceive as registering recognition of a memory. Memories are not stored in their entirety, as books on a shelf. Rather, during traversal of a brain connectivity path, stages along the path add to the reconstruction of the memory: *the memory becomes "assembled" incrementally along the path.*

The memory structures being built inside these systems have a recognizable organization. At each processing stage along a path, sequences of categories are constructed. These are nested hierarchically, such that a single category at one stage may itself be part of another entire sequence of categories. The brain constructs these hierarchical sequences of categories throughout. Starting from purely perceptual information, such as visual and auditory data, they build up hierarchically to representations in the brain of complex entities such as faces, places, and houses. And proceeding further, as more and more association areas are added, they continue to build ever more abstract relations among memories; relations such as movement, or containment, or ownership. Proceeding far enough downstream, we arrive at almost arbitrary and abstract combinations of thoughts. Starting with just these internal entities, hierarchical sequences of categories can represent the entire range of our experience with the world.

A.5 Augmentation

The brain of homo sapiens ("wise man" in Latin) is just about 100,000 years old. This newly evolved organ endows us with unique creative capabilities that no other living creature has. Humans—having become conscious of the fact that they have a brain and that their very survival and success in life depends on utilizing its power—have begun to race to reverse-engineer it, understand it, and augment it.

The human brain is probably the most plastic and adaptive device in the universe, constantly changing its network connectivity to enable new capabilities each time it is called upon to face challenging situations. Using hundreds of billions of neurons—as many as there are stars in our milky way galaxy—and 1000 trillion synapses to send billions of messages every second through its intense network, the human brain has remained largely unexploited for 100,000 years.

Lately, there has been increasing focus on the development of scientifically based rigorous genetic, pharmacological, electrical, and optical devices, combined with brain–computer interfaces (BCI), for restoring and augmenting cognition (e.g., cochlear implants for restoring hearing or using deep-brain stimulations in Parkinson's disease).

A.6 Networks

This appendix highlights the rapid ascendancy of networks as the paradigmatic theme (or what the famous philosopher Thomas Kuhn came to term as exemplar or artifact) of computational sciences on par with the traditional concepts of algorithms (and data structures). Networks have become the basic conceptual building blocks of the computational sciences, especially triggered by the burgeoning growth of the Internet and fueled by the rising significance of cloud computing, Big Data, mobile computing, and social networking solutions and applications.

This appendix presents a quick overview of the concept of networks and enterprises based on characteristics of networks, namely, network enterprises (Kale 2017) that are likely to swamp the business environment in the future.

A.6.1 Concept of Networks

At its most basic level, a network is any system or structure of interconnected elements that can be represented by a graph of nodes (the elements) connected by some kind of links (whatever ties them together). The nodes of a network may be anything from land masses to cells in a body, political institutions, or people. The links between the nodes might be physical connections, biochemical interactions, relationships of power and authority, or reciprocal social ties such as friendship.

The concept of a network first arose in a field of mathematics known as *graph theory*, pioneered by Swiss-born mathematician Leonhard Euler in 1736. In a seminal paper, Euler solved a long-standing puzzle of geography known as the Konigsberg Bridge problem: Could someone cross each of the seven bridges of that Baltic seaport without repeating once? Euler found the solution (which was in the negative) by treating the city's islands and river banks as featureless nodes and Konigsberg's bridges as links connecting them. By reducing urban geography to a simple mathematical graph, the puzzle was easily solved, and the mathematics of networks was born.

In the mid-twentieth century, Hungarian mathematicians Paul Erdos and Alfred Renyi greatly expanded the theory of nodes and links in eight papers exploring the topology and behavior of randomly generated networks. In the late twentieth century, the mathematics of graph theory gave birth to a new inter-disciplinary science of networks, devoted to examining the common principles of network graphs that are found across domains ranging from engineering to information science to biology to sociology.

Decades before the arrival of websites like Facebook, sociologists attempted to map the social ties within groups via the field of social network analysis. Different typologies of networks were seen to represent varying organizational structures, from the hierarchical models of companies and traditional militaries to the more distributed, centerless topologies of voluntary organizations whose numerous cells are only loosely connected to one another. Similarly, social network analysis has often focused on how and why certain innovations spread rapidly, be they new technologies (use of smartphones), new language (Twitter), or new ideas (video call). In all these cases, a network model has allowed for new insights to be gained into the behavior and properties of extremely complex systems—insights that may not be visible by simply observing the actions of the individual constituent parts.

In the field of communications, networks were used to map telephone systems, with their wires (links) connecting phone lines and exchanges (the nodes). Later, these same phone networks began to link computers into the Internet. In terms of communications content (rather than communications hardware), the WWW has been mapped as a network of interconnected Web pages linked together by hyperlinks. Transportation systems have been mapped as networks, starting with Euler's bridges of Konigsberg, and continuing later as train networks, with stations (the nodes) linked by lines of track; road networks, with cities connected by interstate highways; and air-traffic networks, with airports linked by the airline routes that crisscross our globe. In biology, network science has been used to map out the relationships of nerve cells connected by the dendrites and axons that transmit and receive their messages. Networks are used to map molecules in an organism by how they are linked through biochemical reactions. Network maps have also been applied to tracking the spread of infectious diseases, with patients representing the nodes and vectors of disease transmission being the links between them.

A.6.2 Principles of Networks

A.6.2.1 Metcalfe's Law

Robert Metcalfe, the inventor of the Ethernet and founder of 3Com, evaluated that the value of a network increases as the square of the number of users; consequently, additional users are attracted to connect to the network resulting in a virtuous cycle of positive feedback. Considering that the original observation was inspired by telephonic systems that are typically bilateral, the value associated with computer networks that admit multi-lateralism is manyfold. Thus, for computer networks with n number of nodes allowing conversations of m users simultaneously, the value of the computer network may increase as n^m! This phenomenon has important implications for corporations competing in network markets.

While in the traditional economy, value is derived from scarcity, in the network economy, critical mass supersedes scarcity as a source of value. Positive feedback works to the advantage of big networks and to the detriment of smaller networks. Consequently, the bigger networks continue to grow bigger, while the smaller networks are sucked into a vortex of negative feedback and shrink to insignificance. The classic examples of this phenomenon are the rapid ascendancy of Microsoft Windows to market domination against other alternatives like Apple or UNIX operating systems or the VHS-versus-Betamax standard battle.

A.6.2.2 Power Law

Many natural phenomena, such as the height of a species, follow the random distribution known as a *bell curve*: most animals grow to be quite close to the average height of their species, and those that deviate will be only slightly taller or shorter. But among phenomena that follow a power law curve, there is no clustering around the average; instead, there are a few extremely high values and then many, many more increasingly small values. Power law distributions are seen in the distribution of wealth, as famously observed by Vilfredo Pareto's principle (also termed *the 80–20 rule*) that 80% of the wealth is held by 20% of the population. Network enterprises (network customers) follow this kind of power law distribution as well: some enterprises (customers) are much more or less connected or active within a network than the average enterprise (customer) (Kale 2017).

A.6.2.3 Small Worlds Networks (SWNs)

The phenomenon of networks is pervasive, and they deeply affect all aspects of human life and relationships. Networks matter because local actions have global consequences, and the relationship between local and global dynamics depends on the network structure. The idea of small worlds is applicable to diverse problems—community of prospects or customers, organizations, national markets, global economy, flying routes, postal services, food chains, electrical power grids, disease propagation, ecosystems, language, or firing of neurons. In 1998, Cornell mathematician Duncan Watts, with his advisor, Steve Strogatz, recognized the structural similarity between graph problems describing any collection of dots connected by lines and

- The coordinated lightning of fireflies
- The 1967 idea of sociologist Stanley Milgram that the world's six billion people are all connected by *six degrees of separation*, that is, the average number of steps needed to get from one selected person to another is six

They showed that when networks of connected dots have a degree of order to their clustering, the degree of separation is correspondingly high, but adding random links shrinks the degree of separation rapidly. Real-world networks are far from being a bunch of nodes randomly linked to each other; instead, a few well-connected hubs keep most of the networks together. They showed that networks operate on the power law—the notion that a few large interactions carry the most action, or the rich get richer! This explains why the Internet is dominated by a few highly connected nodes or large hubs such as Yahoo!, Google, or Amazon.com, and also the dominance of Microsoft Windows on desktops. Similarly, in a separate context, a few individuals with an extraordinary ability to make friendships keep the society together.

Thus, networks combine order and randomness to reveal two defining characteristics of the small worlds networks: local robustness and global accessibility. Local robustness results from the fact that, excepting the hubs, malfunctioning at other smaller nodes does not disrupt or paralyze the network; it continues to function normally. However, paradoxically, the elegance and efficiency of these structures also make them vulnerable to infiltration, failures, sabotage, and, in case of the Internet, virus attacks.

A.7 Neural Networks

In the human brain, a typical neuron receives incoming information from approximately 10,000 other neurons. Each bit of information either stimulates (positive input) or inhibits (negative input) cell firing. The neuron acts like a small calculator. If the sum of the inputs reaches a critical threshold level, an electrical charge travels down the nerve fiber (axon) to the region where neurotransmitters are stored. The transmitters are released into the synaptic cleft—a tiny gap between adjacent neurons. If a neurotransmitter finds a docking site (receptor) on the adjacent neuron, the process will be repeated on this adjacent neuron.

Every step in the process of neuronal activity—from the most distant dendrite to the farthest axon terminal—is fine-tuned by a slew of control mechanisms. There are estimated to be at least 30 separate neurotransmitters, with enzymatic steps in the creation and destruction of each transmitter affected by everything from genetics to disease. Feedback loops alter the availability and receptivity of post-synaptic receptor sites and even how cells signal and adhere to one another.

Despite a veritable symphony of interacting mechanisms, the neuron ultimately only has two options—it either fires or it doesn't. At this most basic level, the brain might appear like a massive compilation of on and off switches. But the connections between neurons are not fixed entities. Rather, they are in constant flux—being strengthened or diminished by ongoing stimuli. Connections are enhanced with use and weakened with neglect and are themselves affected by other connections to the same neurons. Once we leave the individual synapse between two neurons, the complexity skyrockets—from individual neurons to a hundred billion brain cells each with thousands of connections. Although unraveling how individual neurons collectively create thought remains the Holy Grail of neuroscience, the artificial intelligence (AI) community has given us some intriguing clues as to how this might occur.

A.7.1 Artificial Neural Networks

Using the biological neuron and its connections as the model, AI scientists have been able to build artificial neural networks (ANN) that can play chess and poker, read faces, recognize speech, and recommend books on Amazon.com. While standard computer programs work line by line, yes or no, with all eventualities programmed in advance, the ANN takes an entirely different approach. The ANN is based upon mathematical programs that are initially devoid of any specific values. The programmers only provide the equations; incoming information determines how connections are formed and how strong each connection will be in relationship to all the other connections (or *weightings*). There is no predictable solution to a problem—rather, as one connection changes, so do all the others. These shifting inter-relationships are the basis for "learning."

The virtual space where the weightings take place is treated as the hidden layer. With an ANN, the hidden layer is conceptually located within the complex inter-relationships between all acquired (incoming) information and the mathematical code used to process this information. In the human brain, the hidden layer doesn't exist as a discrete interface or specific anatomic structure; rather, it resides within the connections between all neurons involved in any neural network. A network can be relatively localized (as in a specialized visual module confined to a small area of occipital cortex), or it can be widely distributed throughout the brain.

The *hidden layer*, a term normally considered AI jargon, offers a powerful metaphor for the brain's processing of information. It is in the hidden layer that all elements of biology (from genetic predispositions to neurotransmitter variations and fluctuations) and all past experience, whether remembered or long forgotten, affect the processing of incoming information. It is the interface between incoming sensory data and a final perception, the anatomic crossroad where nature and nurture intersect. Similarly, all thought that manipulates ideas and information by shifting associations (relative valuations) among myriad neural networks must also arise from these hidden layers.

The schema of the hidden layer provides a conceptual model of a massive web of neuronal connections microscopically interwoven throughout the brain. Such neural networks are the brain's real power brokers, the influence peddlers and decision makers hard at work behind the closed doors of darkened white matter. How consciousness occurs remains an utter mystery, but conceptually, it must arise out of these hidden layers.

It has recently been suggested that a combination of micro-neurosurgical techniques, implanted computer processors, and evolving molecular biological strategies might be able to replace entire neural networks that become affected by psychiatric and other neurological diseases.

A.8 Computer Networks

Two computers are said to be networked if they are able to exchange information. The connection need not be via a copper wire; fiber optics, microwaves, infrared light, and communication satellites can also be used. Networks come in many sizes, shapes, and forms, as we will see later. They are usually connected together to make larger networks, with the Internet being the most well-known example of a network of networks.

Computer Network and a Distributed System: The key distinction between them is that in a distributed system, a collection of independent computers appears to its users as a single coherent system. Usually, it has a single model or paradigm that it presents to the users. Often, a layer of software on top of the operating system, called *middleware*, is responsible for implementing this model. A well-known example of a distributed system is the WWW. It runs on top of the Internet and presents a model in which everything looks like a document (Web page). On the other hand, in a computer network, coherence, model, and software are absent. Users are exposed to the actual machines, without any attempt by the system to make the machines look and act in a coherent way. If the machines have different hardware and different operating systems, that is fully visible to the users. If a user wants to run a program on a remote machine, it entails logging onto that machine and running it there. In effect, a distributed system is a software system built on top of a network. The software gives it a high degree of cohesiveness and transparency.

Thus, the distinction between a network and a distributed system lies with the software (especially the operating system), rather than with the hardware. Nevertheless, there is considerable overlap between the two subjects. For example, both distributed systems and computer networks need to move files around. The difference lies in who invokes the movement, the system or the user.

A.8.1 Internet

The origins of the Internet can be traced to the US government support of the ARPANET project. Computers in several US universities were linked via packet switching, and this allowed messages to be sent between the universities that were part of the network. The use of ARPANET was limited initially to academia and to the US military, and in the early years, there was little interest from industrial companies.

However, by the mid-1980s, there were over 2000 hosts on the TCP/IP-enabled network, and the ARPANET was becoming more heavily used and congested. It was decided to shut down the network by the late 1980s, and the National Science Foundation in the United States commenced work on the NSFNET. This work commenced in the mid-1980s, and the network consisted of multiple regional networks connected to a major backbone. The original links in NSFNET were 56 Kbps, but these were later updated to the faster T1 (1.544 Mbps) links. The NSFNET T1 backbone initially connected 13 sites, but this increased due to a growing interest from academic and industrial sites in the United States and from around the world. The NSF began to realize from the mid-1980s onward that the Internet had significant commercial potential.

A.8.2 World Wide Web (WWW)

The WWW was invented by Tim Berners-Lee in 1990 at CERN in Geneva, Switzerland. One of the problems that scientists at CERN faced was that of keeping track of people, computers, documents, databases, and so on. This problem was more acute due to the international nature of CERN, as the center had many visiting scientists from overseas who spent several months there. Berners-Lee essentially created a system to give every page on a computer a standard address. This standard address is called the *universal resource locator* and is better known by its acronym URL. Each page is accessible via the hypertext transfer protocol (HTTP), and the page is formatted with the hypertext markup language (HTML). Each page is visible using a web browser.

Inventors tend to be influenced by existing inventions and especially inventions that are relevant to their areas of expertise. The internet was a key existing invention, and it allowed worldwide communication via electronic e-mail, the transfer of files electronically via FTP, and newsgroups that allowed users to make postings on various topics. Another key invention that was relevant to Berners-Lee was that of hypertext. This was invented by Ted Nelson in the 1960s, and it allows links to be present in text. For example, a document such as a book contains a table of contents, an index, and a bibliography. These are all links to material that is either within the book itself or external to the book. The reader of a book is able to follow the link to obtain the internal or external information. The other key invention that was relevant to Berners-Lee was that of the mouse. This was invented by Doug Engelbart in the 1960s, and it allowed the cursor to be steered around the screen. The major leap that Berners-Lee made was essentially a marriage of the Internet, hypertext, and the mouse into what has become the WorldWideWeb.

The invention of the WWW by Berners-Lee was a revolution in the use of the Internet. Users could now surf the web, that is, hyperlink among the millions of computers in the world and obtain information easily. The WWW creates a space in which users can access information easily in any part of the world. This is done using only a Web browser and simple Web addresses. Browsers are used to connect to remote computers over the Internet and to request, retrieve, and display the Web pages on the local machine. The user can then click on hyperlinks on Web pages to access further relevant information that may be on an entirely different continent. Berners-Lee developed the first Web browser, called the *World-Wide Web browser*. He also wrote the first browser program, and this allowed users to access Web pages throughout the world. The invention of the WWW was announced in August 1991, and the growth of the Web has been phenomenal since then.

The WWW is revolutionary in that

- No single organization is controlling the Web
- No single computer is controlling the Web
- Millions of computers are interconnected
- It is an enormous market place of millions (billions) of users
- The Web is not located in one physical location
- The Web is a space and not a physical thing

The WWW has been applied to many areas including

- Travel industry (booking flights, train tickets, and hotels)
- E-marketing
- Portal sites (such as Yahoo! and Hotmail)
- Ordering books and CDs over the Web (such as www.amazon.com)
- Recruitment services (such as www.jobserve.com)
- Internet banking
- Online casinos (for gambling)
- Newspapers and news channels
- Online shopping and shopping malls

A.9 Internet as Extended Brain

For the first time in history, we have available to us both the computing power as well as the raw data that matches, and shall very soon far exceed, that available to the average human. Since impressions are the basic currency of the Internet-based economy, the machines in the Web have to correctly assess the potential custom value of any agent visiting the Web—to undertake precision targeting of advertisements for the best return on investment (RoI) on the e-marketing effort. The software required for accomplishing this mimics many of the capabilities required for intelligent thought. However, the manner in which these seemingly intelligent capabilities are computationally realized in the Web does not, for the most part, even attempt to mirror the mechanisms nature has evolved to bring intelligence to life in real brains.

Achieving this entails combing through the vast trails of data left in the wake of visits to the Web, which needs expertise from different fields of AI, be they language processing, learning, reasoning, or vision, to come together and connect the dots. The very synthesis of techniques that the Web-intelligence programs need in order to connect the dots in their practical enterprise of online advertising appears, in many respects, similar to how we ourselves integrate our different perceptual and cognitive abilities. We consciously scan around us to gather information about our environment as well as listen to the ambient sea of information continuously bombarding us all. Miraculously, we learn from our experiences and reason in order to connect the dots and make sense of the world—all this so as to predict likely scenarios, be it in the next instant or eventually in the course of our lives. Finally, we correct our actions so as to achieve our goals and objectives more effectively.

The cumulative use of AI techniques at Web scale, on hundreds of thousands or even millions of computers, can result in behavior that exhibits the very basic features of human intelligence. Applying Web-scale computing power on the vast volume of Big Data now available because of the Internet offers the potential to create far more intelligent systems in some of the identified areas of computation than ever before.

A.9.1 Human Brain versus Internet Brain

Even though the two contexts and purposes are very different, there are surprising parallels between the human brain and the Internet brain. It is these connections that offer the potential for possibly deeper understanding and appreciation of our own remarkable abilities as well as the increasingly capable Web or Internet-intelligence systems of the future.

We dissect below the ability to connect the dots, be it in the context of our own ability to understand and make sense of the world or of Web-intelligence programs trying to understand us as customers:

- ◼ The ability to scan and experience the world around us: a Web-intelligence program looks at the data stored in or streaming across the Internet. In either case, information needs to be stored as well as retrieved, be it in the form of memories and their recollection in the former, or our daily experience of Web search in the latter.

■ The ability to sense, to focus on the important and discard the irrelevant: to recognize the familiar, discern between alternatives, or identify similar things. "Sensing" is also about a momentary experience, be it a personal feeling, an individual decision, or the collective sentiment expressed by the online masses.

■ The ability to learn about the structure of the world in terms of facts, rules, and relationships, just as we learn common-sense knowledge about the world around us. Whether derived from our personal experiences while growing up, or via the vast data trails left by our collective online activities, the essential underlying processes appear quite similar: detecting the regularities and patterns that emerge from large volumes of data. Internet-intelligence systems learn about our preferences and behavior.

■ The ability to collate different facts and derive new conclusions giving rise to reasoning, logic, and the ability to deal with uncertainty. Reasoning is what we normally regard as unique to our species, distinguishing us from animals.

■ The ability to make predictions about the future, albeit weighted with different degrees of confidence. Just as we predict and speculate on the course of our lives, both immediate and long term, machines are able to predict as well—be it the supply and demand for products or the possibility of crime in particular neighborhoods.

■ The ability to control and correct actions or decisions, be they human decisions in marketing or law enforcement, as well as controlling complex, autonomous Internet-intelligence systems such as car-navigating systems.

This points to a future where the Internet (and the Web) will not only provide us with information and serve as a communication platform but where the computers that power the Internet could also help us to control our world through complex Internet (and/or) intelligence systems.

In the following sections, we acquaint ourselves with the latest advances on the Internet that are efficiency and effectiveness enhancing, and the productivity-multiplying features of the Internet (and Web) brain (or intelligent systems), like social networks, Internet of Things (IoT), semantic web, context-aware applications, and collaboration applications.

A.10 Social Networks

Starting as early as 1995, online social network (OSN) pioneers Classmates. com, SixDegrees.com, and Friendster introduced the notion of profile pages and friend connections. These sites paved the way for today's popular sites, including Facebook, MySpace, LinkedIn, Orkut, Hi5, and CyWorld, each of which boasts tens or hundreds of millions of active members around the world. Facebook, Twitter, MySpace, and an increasing number of other social networks now offer Web services application programming interfaces (APIs), which make it possible for other websites and Web applications to tap into profile and social data. These advances are extending the reach and impact of the OSN beyond specific social networking sites to potentially every Web experience.

1. Discovery sites: The OSN can be manually built up over time by individuals on sites like Facebook or approximated with algorithms. Discovery sites like ZoomInfo and business/professional services like LexisNexis construct a person database by trawling the Web for publicly available information and making associations. They are able to approximate user profiles and social networks without any user participation. Because there is not enough public data available or accessible about people and connections, automated discovery sites are error prone, carrying data that is incorrect, incomplete, redundant, or out of date.

2. Affinity networks: Many clubs and organizations, such as university alumni associations, have added online networking capabilities to their websites to reach and better engage their membership. Other affinity networks are entirely virtual. For instance, on LinkedIn, the MIT Sloan CIO Network is an exclusive online community of senior IT executives from around the world who are given gated access to one another, in addition to specialized content, discussion boards, and polls. CIOs sign up to network with their peers and access news across the IT community.

A.10.1 Social Network Platforms

Initially, social networking sites were simple communication utilities that let people send messages to one another and share photos and event information. But OSN wanted their members to spend more time on their sites to maximize ad impressions and clicks so that they could make money. For this reason, just about every major social network has unveiled a platform to enable new applications. Social networking platforms expose data, tools, and placement on social networking sites to third-party developers, allowing them to create new functionality that sits on top of the social network. The platform ecosystem is a win–win–win for everyone: Users have access to more functionality, software developers have access to data and users, and the social network becomes more interesting, valuable, sticky, and engaging.

Internet users want applications that are "socially aware" of their identity and relationships; most users do not want to re-enter profile information and re-establish friend connections on every new site they visit. Social networking platforms allow developers and businesses to tap the existing social graph for their applications and websites instead of having to reinvent the wheel. Similarly, social network

APIs such as the MySpace API, Facebook Connect, and Google Friend Connect take the online social network beyond the native social networking sites to external websites and applications. Thus, social network is enabling a new Web experience that allows us to bring our online identities and friends with us to whatever site or application we choose to visit on the Internet.

> Facebook and LinkedIn established a clear friend-request protocol and culture of trust for their networks. Facebook did so through e-mail–based identity confirmation and modeling their online networks off real offline networks. For example, when you join Facebook, one of the first things you must do is choose one or more networks with which to be associated. Your options include schools, employers, cities, and other real offline networks that have real offline trust. LinkedIn took a different approach to establishing protocol. By accepting a LinkedIn connection request, you implicitly agree to share your network and to professionally vouch for this person. Most people are not willing to vouch for strangers, so they are more careful about accepting LinkedIn connection requests from strangers.

An important precursor to social platforms was the ability to embed YouTube videos on MySpace pages. Prior to MySpace, YouTube struggled to hit a tipping point and really take off. It had a small and scattered community of fans that used its video-sharing service as one-offs. Joining forces with MySpace changed everything overnight—YouTube found itself with a large global audience and infrastructure for word-of-mouth distribution. MySpace saw its pages come to life with rich, multimedia video, and its Web traffic shot up impressively. Naturally, a host of similar successes leads to a high degree of heterogeneity in terms of social network platforms. This quickly led to the demand for interfacing standards. In 2007, product managers at Google led an effort, called OpenSocial, to define a set of open-source social APIs that could work across any social networking site or other website. Having a standard set of APIs would theoretically enable developers to write an application once and have it work on any OpenSocial site. OpenSocial has since spun off from Google as its own independent non-profit organization and is supported by an industry consortium of social networking sites.

A.10.2 Social Intelligence

Traditional CRM is effectively a networking tool that lets sales reps view "profiles" of their accounts, capture deal information, track performance, communicate with contacts, and share information internally with sales managers and other members of their account team. However, the social networking sites differ from traditional CRM in one critical dimension—they are conduits for bidirectional visibility and interaction. By making the customer an active participant in CRM, not only will companies benefit from more accurate data and better engagement, but they will also finally achieve a true 360-degree view of their customers across every touch point—whether it is online, on the phone, pre-sales, mid-deal, post-sales, or beyond.

The defining characteristics of social CRM are

- Social experience
- Mobile engagement
- Co-creation
- Gamification

A.11 Internet of Things

The Internet as we know it is transforming radically, from an academic network in the 1980s and early 1990s to a mass-market, consumer-oriented network. Now, it is set to become fully pervasive, connected, interactive, and intelligent. Real-time communication is possible, not only by humans but also by things at any time and from anywhere.

It is quite likely that, sooner or later, the majority of items connected to the Internet will not be humans but things. Internet of Things (IoT) will primarily expand communication from the 7 billion people around the world to the estimated 50–70 billion machines. This would result in a world where everything is connected and can be accessed from anywhere—this has a potential to connect 100 trillion things that are deemed to exist on Earth. With the advent of IoT, the physical world itself will become a connected information system. In the world of the IoT, sensors and actuators embedded in physical objects are linked through wired and wireless networks that connect the Internet. These information systems churn out huge volumes of data that flows to computers for analysis. When objects can both sense the environment and communicate, they become tools for understanding the complexity of the real world and responding to it swiftly.

 This would also mean significant opportunities for the telecom industry to develop new IoT subscribers that would easily overtake the number of current subscribers based on population.

IoT can be defined as the network formed by things or objects having identities and virtual personalities, which interact using intelligent interfaces to connect and communicate with the users and social and environmental contexts. IoT is also referred to as pervasive or ubiquitous computing systems.

The goal of IoT is to achieve pervasive IoT connectivity and grand integration and to provide secure, fast, and personalized functionalities and services such as monitoring, sensing, tracking, locating, alerting, scheduling, controlling, protecting, logging, auditing, planning, maintenance, upgrading, data mining, trending, reporting, decision support, dashboard, back-office applications, and so on.

In terms of the type of technological artifacts involved, the IoT applications can be subdivided into four categories:

1. The Internet of Devices: Machine-to-Machine (M2M): M2M refers to technologies that allow both wireless and wired devices to communicate with each other or, in most cases, a centralized server. An M2M system uses devices (such as sensors or meters) to capture events (such as temperature or inventory level), which are relayed through a network (wireless, wired, or hybrid) to an application (software program) that translates the captured events into meaningful information. M2M communication is a relatively new business concept, born from the original telemetry technology, utilizing similar technologies but modern versions of them.
2. The Internet of Objects: Radio-frequency Identification (RFID): RFID uses radio waves to transfer data from an electronic tag attached to an object to a central system through a reader for the purpose of identifying and tracking the object.
3. The Internet of Transducers: Wireless Sensor Networks (SNS): SNS consists of spatially distributed autonomous sensors to monitor physical or environmental conditions, such as temperature, sound, vibration, pressure, motion, or pollutants, and to cooperatively pass their data through the network to a main location. The more modern networks are bidirectional, becoming wireless sensor and actuator networks (WSANs) enabling the control of sensor activities.
4. The Internet of Controllers: Supervisory Control and Data Acquisition (SCADA)SCADA is an autonomous system based on closed-loop control theory or a smart system or a cyber physical system (CPS) that connects, monitors, and controls equipment via the network (mostly wired short-range networks, sometimes wireless or hybrid) in a facility such as a plant or a building.

A.11.1 Physical Intelligence

IoT would be closely associated with environmental, societal, and economic issues such as climate change, environment protection, energy saving, and globalization. For these reasons, the IoT would be increasingly used in a large number of sectors like healthcare, energy and environment, safety and security, transportation, logistics, and manufacturing.

Major IoT applications in various sectors are as indicated below:

- Energy and power: Supply/Alternatives/Demand. Turbines, generators, meters, substations, switches
- Healthcare: Care/Personal/Research. Medical devices, imaging, diagnostics, monitoring, surgical equipment
- Buildings: Institutional/Commercial/Industrial/Home. HVAC, fire and safety, security, elevators, access control systems, lighting
- Industrial: Process Industries/Forming/Converting/Discrete Assembly/ Distribution
- Supply chain: Pumps, valves, vessels, tanks, automation and control equipment, capital equipment, pipelines
- Retail: Stores/Hospitality/Services. Point-of-sale terminals, vending machines, RFID tags, scanners and registers, lighting and refrigeration systems
- Security and infrastructure: Homeland Security/Emergency Services/National and Regional Defense. GPS systems, radar systems, environmental sensors, vehicles, weaponry, fencing
- Transportation: On-Road Vehicles/Off-Road Vehicles/Non-vehicular/ Transport Infrastructure. Commercial vehicles, airplanes, trains, ships, signage, tolls, RF tags, parking meters, surveillance cameras, tracking systems
- Information technology and network infrastructure: Enterprise/Data Centers. Switches, servers, storage
- Resources: Agriculture/Mining/ Oil/ Gas/ Water. Mining equipment, drilling equipment, pipelines, agricultural equipment
- Consumer/Professional: Appliances/White Goods/Office Equipment/Home Electronics. M2M devices, gadgets, smartphones, tablet PCs, home gateways

A.12 Semantic Web

While the Web keeps growing at an astounding pace, most Web pages are still designed for human consumption and cannot be processed by machines. Similarly, while the Web search engines help retrieve Web pages, they do not offer support to interpret the results—for that, human intervention is still required. As the size of search results is often just too big for humans to interpret, finding relevant information on the Web is not as easy as we would desire. The existing Web has evolved as a medium for information exchange among people rather than machines. As a consequence, the semantic content, that is, the meaning of the information in a Web page, is coded in a way that is accessible to human beings alone. Today's Web may be defined as the Syntactic Web, where information presentation is carried out by computers, and the interpretation and identification of relevant information is delegated to human beings. With the volume of available digital data growing at an exponential rate, it is becoming virtually impossible for human beings to manage the complexity and volume of the available information. This phenomenon, often referred to as *information overload*, poses a serious threat to the continued usefulness of today's Web.

As the volume of Web resources grows exponentially, researchers from industry, government, and academia are now exploring the possibility of creating a Semantic Web in which meaning is made explicit, allowing machines to process and integrate Web resources intelligently. Biologists use a well-defined taxonomy, the Linnaean taxonomy, adopted and shared by most of the scientific community worldwide. Likewise, computer scientists are looking for a similar model to help structure Web content. In 2001, T. Berners-Lee, J. Hendler, and O. Lassila published a revolutionary article in the magazine *Scientific American*, titled "The Semantic Web: A New Form of Web Content That Is Meaningful to Computers Will Unleash a Revolution of New Possibilities."

A.13 Context-Aware Applications

Most mobile applications are location-aware systems. Specifically, tourist guides are based on users' location in order to supply more information on the city attraction closer to them or the museum exhibit they are seeing. Nevertheless, recent years have seen many mobile applications trying to exploit information that characterizes the current situation of users, places and objects in order to improve the services provided.

The principle of context-aware applications (CAA) can be explained using the metaphor of the Global Positioning System (GPS). In aircraft navigation, for example, a GPS receiver derives the speed and direction of an aircraft by recording over time the coordinates of longitude, latitude, and altitude. This contextual data is then used to derive the distance to the destination, communicate progress to date, and calculate the optimum flight path.

For a GPS-based application to be used successfully, the following activities are a pre-requisite:

1. The region in focus must have been GPS-mapped accurately.
2. The GPS map must be superimposed with the relevant information regarding existing landmarks, points of civic and official significance, and facilities and service points of interest in the past to the people—this is the context in this metaphor.
3. There must be a system available to ascertain the latest position per the GPS system.
4. The latest reported position must be mapped and transcribed onto the GPS-based map of the region.
5. This latest position relative to the context (described in b above) is used as the point of reference for future recommendation(s) and action(s).

It should be noted that the initial baseline of the context (described in 2 above) is compiled and collated separately and then uploaded into the system to be accessible by the CAA. However, with passage of time, this baseline gets added further with the details of each subsequent transaction.

Most of the current context-aware systems have been built in an *ad-hoc* approach and are deeply influenced by the underlying technology infrastructure utilized to capture the context. To ease the development of context-aware ubicomp (ubiquitous computing) and mobile applications, it is necessary to provide universal models and mechanisms to manage context. Even though significant efforts have been devoted to research methods and models for capturing, representing, interpreting, and exploiting context information, we are still not close to enabling an implicit and intuitive awareness of context, nor efficient adaptation to behavior at the standards of human communication practice.

Context information can be a decisive factor in mobile applications in terms of selecting the appropriate interaction technique. Designing interactions among users and devices, as well as among devices themselves, is critical in mobile applications. Multiplicity of devices and services calls for systems that can provide various interaction techniques and the ability to switch to the most suitable one according to the user's needs and desires. Current mobile systems are not efficiently adaptable to the user's needs. The majority of ubicomp and mobile applications try to incorporate the users' profile and desires into the system's infrastructure either manually or automatically, observing their habits and history. According to our perspective, the key point is to give them the ability to create their own mobile applications instead of just customizing the ones provided.

Thus, mobile applications can be used not only for locating users and providing them with suitable information, but also for

- Providing them with a tool necessary for composing and creating their own mobile applications
- Supporting the system's selection of appropriate interaction techniques
- Making a selection of recommendation(s) and consequent action(s) conforming with the situational constraints judged via the business logic and other constraints sensed via the context.
- Enabling successful closure of the interaction (answering a query, qualifying an objection, closing an order, etc.)

A.13.1 Concept of Patterns

The concept of patterns used in this book originated from the area of real architecture. C. Alexander gathered architectural knowledge and best practices regarding building structures in a pattern format. This knowledge was obtained from years of practical experience. A pattern, according to Alexander, is structured text that follows a well-defined format and captures nuggets of advice on how to deal with recurring problems in a specific domain. It advises the architect on how to create building architectures, defines the important design decisions, and covers limitations to consider. Patterns can be very generic documents, but may also include concrete measurements and plans. Their application to a certain problem is, however, always a manual task that is performed by the architect. Therefore, each application of a pattern will result in a different-looking building, but all applications of the pattern will share a common set of desired properties. For instance, there are patterns describing how eating tables should be sized so that people can move around the table freely, get seated comfortably, and find enough room for plates and food, while still being able to communicate and talk during meals without feeling too distant from people seated across the table. While the properties of the table are easy to enforce once concrete distances and sizes are specified, they are extremely hard to determine theoretically or by pure computation using a building's blueprint.

In building architecture, pattern-based descriptions of best practices and design decisions proved especially useful, because many desirable properties of houses, public environments, cities, streets, and so on are not formally measurable. They are perceived by humans and, thus, cannot be computed or predicted in a formal way. Therefore, best practices and well-perceived architectural styles capture a lot of implicit knowledge about how people using and living in buildings perceive their structure, functionality, and general feel. Especially, the different emotions that buildings trigger, such as awe, comfort, coziness, power, cleanness, and so on, are hard to measure or explain and are also referred to as the *quality without a name* or the *inner beauty* of a building. How certain objectives can be realized in architecture is, thus, found only through practical experience, which is then captured by patterns. For example, there are patterns describing how lighting in a room should be realized so that people feel comfortable and positive. Architects capture their knowledge gathered from existing buildings and feedback they received from users in patterns describing well-perceived building design. In this scope, each pattern describes one architectural solution for an architectural problem. It does so in an abstract format that allows implementation in various ways. Architectural patterns, thus, capture the essential properties required for the successful design of a certain building area or function while leaving large degrees of freedom to architects.

Multiple patterns are connected and inter-related, resulting in a pattern language. This concept of links between patterns is used to point to related patterns. For example, an architect reviewing patterns describing different roof types can be pointed to patterns describing different solutions for windows in these roofs and may be advised that some window solutions, thus, the patterns describing them cannot be combined with a certain roof pattern. For example, a flat roof top cannot be combined with windows that have to be mounted vertically. Also, a pattern language uses these links to guide an architect through the design of buildings, streets, cities, and so on by describing the order in which patterns have to be considered. For example, the size of the ground on which a building is created may limit the general architecture patterns that should be selected first. After this, the number of floors can be considered, the above-mentioned roofing style, and so on.

A.13.2 Contextual Intelligence

This subsection discusses location-based services applications as a particular example of context-aware applications. But context-aware applications can significantly enhance the efficiency and effectiveness of even routinely occurring transactions. This is because most end-user application's effectiveness and performance can be enhanced by transforming it from a bare transaction to a transaction clothed by a surround of a context formed as an aggregate of all relevant decision patterns utilized in the past.

The decision patterns contributing to a transaction's context include the following:

- Characteristic and sundry details associated with the transaction under consideration
- Profiles of similar or proximate transactions in the immediately prior week or month or 6 months or last year or last season
- Profiles of similar or proximate transactions in same or adjacent or other geographical regions
- Profiles of similar or proximate transactions in same or adjacent or other product groups or customer groups

To generate the context, the relevant decision patterns can either be discerned or discovered by mining the relevant pools or streams of primarily the transaction data. Or they could be augmented or substituted by conjecturing or formulating decision patterns that explain the existence of these characteristic pattern(s) (in the pools or streams of primarily the transaction data).

A.14 Collaboration Applications

The business environment has been witnessing tremendous and rapid changes since the 1990s. There is an increasing emphasis on being customer focused and on leveraging and strengthening the company's core competencies. This has forced enterprises to learn and develop abilities to change and respond rapidly to the competitive dynamics of the global market.

Companies have learned to effectively reengineer themselves into flatter organizations, with closer integration across the traditional functional boundaries of the organization. There is increasing focus on employee empowerment and cross-functional teams. In this book, we are proposing that what we are witnessing is a fundamental transformation in the manner that businesses have been operating for the last century.

This change, which is primarily driven by the information revolution of the past few decades, is characterized by the dominant tendency to integrate across transaction boundaries, both internally and externally. The dominant theme of this new system of management with significant implications on organizational development is collaboration. We will refer to this emerging and maturing constellation of concepts and practices as management by collaboration (MBC). CRM packages such as SAP CRM are major instruments for realizing MBC-driven organizations.

MBC is an approach to management primarily focused on relationships; relationships, by their very nature, are not static and are constantly in evolution. As organizational and environmental conditions become more complex, globalized, and therefore competitive, MBC provides a framework for dealing effectively with the issues of performance improvement, capability development, and adaptation to the changing environment. MBC, as embodied by CRM packages such as SAP CRM, has had a major impact on the strategy, structure, and culture of the customer-centric organization.

The beauty and essence of MBC are that it incorporates in its very fabric the basic urge of humans for a purpose in life, for mutually beneficial relationships, for mutual commitment, and for being helpful to other beings, that is, for collaborating. These relationships could be at the level of individual, division, enterprise, or even between enterprises. Every relationship has a purpose and manifests itself through various processes as embodied mainly in the form of teams; thus, the relationships are geared toward attainment of these purposes through the concerned processes optimally.

Because of the enhanced role played by the individual members of an enterprise in any relationship or process, MBC not only promotes their motivation and competence but also develops the competitiveness and capability of the organizations as a whole. MBC emphasizes the roles of both the top management and the individual member. Thus, the MBC approach covers the whole organization through the means of basic binding concepts such as relationships, processes, and teams. MBC addresses readily all issues of management, including organization development. The issues range from organizational design and structure, role definition and job design, output quality and productivity, interaction and communication channels, and company culture to employee issues such as attitudes, perception, values, and motivation.

The basic idea of collaboration has been gaining tremendous ground with the increasing importance of business processes and dynamically constituted teams in the operations of companies. The traditional bureaucratic structures, which are highly formalized, centralized, and functionally specialized, have proven too slow, too expensive, and too unresponsive to be competitive. These structures are based on the basic assumption that all the individual activities and task elements in a job are independent and separable. Organizations were structured hierarchically in a command-and-control structure, and it was taken as an accepted fact that the output of the organization as a whole could be maximized by maximizing the output of each constituent organizational unit.

On the other hand, by their very nature, teams are flexible, adaptable, dynamic, and collaborative. They encourage flexibility, innovation, entrepreneurship, and responsiveness. For the last few decades, even in traditionally bureaucratic-oriented manufacturing companies, teams have manifested themselves and flourished successfully in various forms such as superteams, self-directed work teams (SDWT), and quality circles. The dynamic changes in the market and global competition being confronted by companies necessarily lead to flatter and more flexible organizations with a dominance of more dynamic structures like teams.

People in teams, representing different functional units, are motivated to work within constraints of time and resources to achieve a defined goal. The goals might range from incremental improvements in responsiveness, efficiency, quality, and productivity to quantum leaps in new product development. Even in traditional businesses, the number and variety of teams instituted for various functions, projects, tasks, and activities has been on the increase. Increasingly, companies are populated with worker teams that have special skills, operate semi-autonomously, and are answerable directly to peers and to the end customers. Members not only must have a higher level of skills than before but must also be more flexible and capable of doing more jobs. The empowered workforce, with considerably enhanced managerial responsibilities (pertaining to information, resources, authority, and accountability), has resulted in an increase in worker commitment and flexibility. Whereas workers have witnessed gains in the quality of their work life, corporations have obtained returns in terms of increased interactivity, responsiveness, quality, productivity, and cost improvements.

Consequently, in the past few years, a new type of non-hierarchical network organization with distributed intelligence and decentralized decision-making powers has been evolving. This entails a demand for constant and frequent communication and feedback among the various teams or functional groups. A CRM package such as SAP CRM essentially provides such an enabling environment through modules like WebFlow, SAP Business Intelligence, and SAP Product Lifecycle Management (PLM).

A.14.1 Collaborative Intelligence

Collaboration enables intelligent enterprises in terms of realizing

- The Relationship-Based Enterprise (RBE)
- The Information-Driven Enterprise
- The Process-Oriented Enterprise

- The Value-Add-Driven Enterprise
- Enterprise Change Management
- The Learning Enterprise
- The Virtual Enterprise
- The Agile Enterprise

The era of big data is the basis for innovative cognitive solutions that cannot rely only on traditional systems. While traditional computers must be programmed by humans to perform specific tasks, cognitive systems will learn from their interactions with data and humans. Cognitive Computing is the use of computational learning systems to augment cognitive capabilities in solving real world problems. Cognitive systems are designed to draw inferences from data and pursue the objectives they were given. Cognitive System can deal with this massive amount of data amplifying human intelligence, which is not scalable in the way that data is growing.

However, cognitive computing is not trying to replicate what the human brain does. Cognition is the mental action or process of acquiring knowledge and understanding through thought, experience, and the senses. Cognitive computing solutions build on established concepts from artificial intelligence, natural language processing, ontologies, and leverage advances in big data management and analytics.

Traditional computers must be programmed by humans to perform specific tasks and they are designed to calculate rapidly and have only rudimentary sensing capabilities, such as license-plate-reading systems on toll roads. Cognitive systems will be designed to draw inferences from data and pursue the objectives they were given and

References

Ballard, D.H., *Brain Computation as Hierarchical Abstraction* (The MIT Press, 2015).

Bellavista, P. and Corradi, A., *The Handbook of Mobile Middleware* (CRC Press, 2006).

Bessis, N. and C. Dobre, *Big Data and Internet of Things: A Roadmap for Smart Environments* (Springer, 2014).

Chin, A. and D. Zhang (Eds.), *Mobile Social Networking: An Innovative Approach* (Springer, 2014).

Coulouris, G., J. Dollimore, T. Kindberg, and G. Blair, *Distributed Systems: Concept and Design* (Boston, MA: Addison-Wesley, 2011).

Dey, A. K., Understanding and using context. *Personal and Ubiquitous Computing Journal*, 1, 4–7, 2001.

Dinsmore, T. W., *Disruptive Analytics: Charting Your Strategy for Next-Generation Business Analytics* (Apress, 2016).

Domingue, J., D. Fensel, and J. A. Hendler (Eds.), *Handbook of Semantic Web Technologies* (Springer, 2011).

Epstein, R., Roberts, G., and Beber, G. (Eds.), *Parsing the Turing Test: Philosophical and Methodological Issues in the Quest for the Thinking Computer* (Springer, 2009).

Evans, J. R., *Business Analytics: Methods, Models and Decisions* (Pearson, 2nd Ed. 2017).

Friedenberg, J. and Silverman, G., *Cognitive Science: An Introduction to the Study of Mind* (Sage Publications, 3rd Ed. 2015).

Helal, S., Li, W., and Bose, R., *Mobile Platforms and Development Environment* (Morgan & Claypool Publishers, 2012).

Henderson, J. C. and Venkatraman, N. (1993). Strategic alignment: Leveraging information technology for transfering organizations. *IBM Systems Journal*, 32(1), 4–16.

Hwang, K. et al., *Distributed and Cloud Computing: From Parallel Processing to the Internet of Things* (Morgan Kaufmann, 2011).

Jannach, D., Zanker, M., Felfernig, A., and Friedrich, G., *Recommender Systems: An Introduction* (Cambridge University Press, 2011).

Kale, V., *Guide to Cloud Computing for Business and Technology Managers: From Distributed Computing to Cloudware Applications* (London, U.K.: Auerbach Publications, 2015)

Kale, V., *Big Data Computing: A Guide for Business and Technology Managers* (CRC Press, 2017).

Konar, A., *Artificial Intelligence and Soft Computing: Behavioral and Cognitive Modeling of the Brain* (CRC Press, 2000).

Loke, S., *Context-Aware Pervasive Systems: Architectures for a New Breed of Applications* (Boca Raton, FL: Auerbach Publications, 2006).

Liu, B., *Sentiment Analysis: Mining Opinions, Sentiments, and Emotions* (Cambridge University Press, 2015).

Marinescu, D., *Cloud Computing: Theory and Practice* (Boston, MA: Morgan Kaufmann, 2013).

McGovern, J., O. Sims, A. Jain, and M. Little, *Enterprise Service Oriented Architectures: Concepts, Challenges, Recommendations* (Dordrecht, the Netherlands: Springer, 2006).

Pacheco, P., *An Introduction to Parallel Programming* (Amsterdam, the Netherlands: Morgan Kaufmann, 2011).

Palfrey, J. and U. Gasser, *Interop: The Promise and Perils of Highly Interconnected Systems* (Basic Books, 2012).

Papazoglou, M. P. and Ribbers, P. M. A., *e-Business: Organizational and Technical Foundations* (John Wiley & Sons, 2006).

Pastor-Satorras, R. and Vespignani , A., *Evolution and Structure of the Internet: A Statistical Physics Approach* (Cambridge University Press, 2004).

Scoble, R. and S. Israel, *Age of Context: Mobile, Sensors, Data and the Future of Privacy* (Patrick Brewster Press, 2014).

Sporns, O., *Networks of the Brain* (The MIT Press, 2011).

Tang, Z. and Walters, B., The interplay of strategic management and information technology, in A. W. K. Tan and P. Theodorou (eds.), *Strategic Information Technology and Portfolio Management* (IGI Global, 2009).

Weisberg, R. W. and Reeves, L. M., *Cognition: From Memory to Creativity* (Wiley, 2013).

Wong, D., Abdelzaher and Kaplan, L., *Social Sensing: Build Reliable Systems on Unreliable Data* (Elsevier, 2015).

Yang, L., A. Waluyo, J. Ma, L. Tan, and B. Srinivasan, *Mobile Intelligence* (Hoboken, NJ: Wiley, 2010).

Yin, H. and Cui, B. *Spatio-Temporal Recommendation in Social Media* (Springer, 2016).

Zomaya, Albert Y. and Sakr, S., (Eds.) *Handbook of Big Data Technologies* (Springer, 2017).

Index